Irreconcilable Politics

★

OUR RIGHTS UNDER A JUST GOVERNMENT

Michael T. Hutchins

DEERBRIDGE
PRESS

Published by Deerbridge Press, Ridgewood, NJ

 Edited and Designed by Girl Friday Productions
www.girlfridayproductions.com

Editorial: Scott Calamar
Interior Design: Paul Barrett
Cover Design: Emily Weigel
Cover Image Credits: © Shutterstock/silvae; © Shutterstock/Fedorov Oleksiy

ISBN (Hardcover): 978-0-9996725-0-1
ISBN (Paperback): 978-0-9996725-1-8
e-ISBN: 978-0-9996725-2-5

First Edition
Printed in the United States of America

CONTENTS

To Teresa, Emily, Sydney, Phoebe, Jacob, and Sandra

Thank you

ACKNOWLEDGMENTS

It is difficult to pinpoint exactly when I began to work on this book; it seems that I may have started it during graduate school. I was amazed then and continue to be astonished by the breadth and depth of disagreement over the solutions to social problems. Initially, like many people, I thought those who disagreed with me were just plain wrong. I believed their views were due to either faulty reasoning or poor assumptions about social interaction. Only later did it occur to me that their opinions were sound from their perspectives, and that most political views, including mine, are in fact opinions and not based on provable facts. As such, this work is as much due to those who have historically disagreed with my views as to those whose ideologies are similar to mine.

When writing this book, I attempted to present a balanced discussion of opposing views, and I imagined that I was communicating with those whose underlying political philosophy is different from my own. In particular, I imagined that I was writing to a good friend, who shall remain anonymous, and whose heartfelt politics are, in my opinion, incorrect.

There were many *aha* moments along the way, especially as I thought through the full implications of differing ideologies. An important realization was that, in a democracy, everyone must absorb the psychic costs incurred by accepting laws that they fundamentally disagree with. And that people will do so because of the benefits of being a citizen, even if they do not receive incremental rewards from compromising. Another epiphany occurred while reexamining *Games and Decisions: Introduction and Critical Survey* by R. Duncan Luce and Howard Raiffa (John Wiley & Sons Inc., 1957). Their analysis and discussion provided the inspiration for how to model people's differing political views within a structure where they could reach agreements. This led to a two-stage approach. First, a procedure is used to incorporate a formal method for people to reach a compromise—not fundamental agreement, but a bargain where the participants retain their differing political views. This procedure is designed so that it is objective from almost every person's perspective. Next, a subjective question is posed as to whether this objective process is fair and just. People with vastly different political opinions, including those with modern liberal views and those who favor libertarian policies, can answer yes to this question. In so doing, they have reached an agreement on a just form of government.

Luce and Raiffa's book was clearly not the only research that had an impact on this manuscript; it is very much dependent on the scholarship of the many philosophers, economists, lawyers, and academics whose works preceded mine. The endnotes list some, but obviously not all, of the intellectual pioneers whose endeavors have made this work possible. Of course, any errors or omissions in this work are solely my responsibility.

I also owe an intellectual debt to the Supreme Court justices whose differing written opinions elucidate in a way that I cannot the political divide that has always existed within the United States. Their sincere debate about society and the meaning embedded in the astonishing document that we call the Constitution is a critical part of the public exchange of ideas. Even more importantly, their historical views and majority opinions determine the basic rights for those residing in the United States.

In addition, I would like to recognize and thank the many people over the last few years who spent time reading and discussing the manuscript. This especially includes my wife, Teresa Hutchins, and my children and their significant others. Finally, the efforts of the editors at

Girl Friday Productions should also be acknowledged for significantly improving the original manuscript.

PART ONE

DIFFERING WORLDVIEWS

I

★

INTRODUCTION

People disagree on governmental rules and laws. That is obvious. But *why* do they disagree? Is it only because people have different personal interests that they selfishly want to pursue? Numerous political philosophers have proposed solutions to address this. However, what if these disagreements are due to factors besides self-interest? What if social interaction is so interconnected that no one can accurately discern all the implications of potential governmental policies? What if the world is so complex that people cannot convince others that their views are wrong? Under these conditions, what policies *should* a government pursue? Even more fundamentally, how *should* such policies and laws be determined when we have different political philosophies that cannot be reconciled through public reasoning? These are the questions that will be answered in the forthcoming pages. This book is a work in political economy that is concerned with the structure of government for people who have irreconcilable disagreements about their preferred laws and governmental policies.

OPINIONS AND BELIEFS

I did not set out to answer these questions. This book is the result of a personal quest that began with quite a few disordered questions concerning government, society, justice, fairness, social obligations, personal rights, equality, and efficiency. These questions led to an examination and reexamination of the answers that have been provided by many people over time. What the answers reveal are vast differences of opinions and views on almost every aspect of government. People do not agree on the objectives or goals of government, much less the methods or procedures that should be pursued to accomplish these various goals. The differences in opinion run the gamut from government as a force of good that can improve people's lives to government as an unnecessary entity that reduces people's innate rights.

Political disagreement is part of the human condition. It is not limited to those who study politics, philosophy, or economics. These political opinions are not simply personal preferences, such as an individual's demand for a specific style of clothing or color of car. They are not facts either. Opinions are based on a variety of behaviors, including rules of thumb, biases, prejudices, values, morals, ethics, beliefs, discussion, reflection, and reasoning. People can prefer certain laws to other laws for what they consider logical reasons. Others can disagree with these laws for what they consider equally valid and logical reasons.

Even though we reason, learn, and communicate, these processes are rarely capable of ensuring that people develop the same views of the world. The truth about society can rarely be discerned, given the complicated interconnectivity of human interaction. This complexity prevents everyone from accurately judging the cause and effect of social interactions. When making social decisions, people develop "models" of the world as a reference or guide. These models are representations of reality and differ from person to person. As we will discuss in chapter 3, the economist and Nobel laureate Douglass North labeled a person's model of the world as their "ideology," and we will term it as their "worldview."

I will repeatedly argue throughout the book that people cannot identify and agree on one "true" model of cause and effect. They cannot discern all the ramifications of every potential action. At best, their worldviews are approximations of the "true" worldview, if such a thing is conceivable. And approximations will vary. People will not be able to convince others that their views are right and everyone else's are wrong. Their individual worldviews will not converge into one agreed-upon model of reality. Therefore, their opinions will lead to different preferred actions by government. Many people want government to address and reduce perceived injustices and improve the lives of others. The problem with these "good" intentions is that people have different views as to the appropriate goals of coercive collective action. They also have varying opinions on the best means of achieving common goals.

DIFFERENCES OF OPINION

There are a vast number of social decisions that need to be made by a government. They include pressing issues that are currently the source of political controversy, including taxation, inequality, health insurance, regulations, immigration, policies on imports and exports, environmental policies, marital rules, gun control, police tactics, foreign policy, nuclear arms, privacy, and abortion. Many of these are considered in part three. Each of these is controversial. Some because of people's self-interest. All because people have different worldviews. To illustrate the depths of the differences, we will examine two controversial issues in more detail.

There are differing perspectives on the burkini, the swimsuit worn by some Muslim women that was banned by local communities in France. Some view the ban as warranted, both because they view communities as having the right to some self-governance, and because they think that wearing the swimsuit is objectionable.[1] The French prime minister, Manuel Valls, supported the restrictions. Valls seemed to view the burkini as a political statement, as a symbol of oppression. He found the swimsuit objectionable because it violates the "values" held

by the country.[2] Of course, there were those, including the women who
wanted to wear them, who thought that they should have the right to
wear a burkini. They likely viewed it as increasing their personal freedom. The swimsuit allowed them to be on a public beach with both
women and men, while adhering to their religious and cultural beliefs.

Why shouldn't a woman, any woman, have the right to wear clothing that she chooses, irrespective of its religious significance? On the
other hand, shouldn't people be able to go to the beach without feel-
ing threatened or unsafe? Who is right and who is wrong? There is a
fundamental conflict between Muslim women who want to wear the
swimsuit and some non-Muslim residents who do not want burkini
wearers on their beaches. Both groups need to somehow reconcile
their actions. One method of reconciliation is that their views somehow converge so they no longer disagree. While this is possible, it is
unlikely that every person on both sides of the issue will change his
or her view after discussion and further reflection. Another method is
violence between the antagonists, with the victor making the decision.

Of course, the residents of the French community do not need to
resort to violence; they can pass laws and use police to force Muslim
women not to dress in their illicit clothing. But is it fair for the majority
of people to pass a law that forces the minority to follow their views? In
this instance, France's highest court did not think the majority had that
right, viewing the ban as potentially unconstitutional and violating the
"equality of citizens."[3] But, is that fair to the people who feel threatened
by the sight of someone wearing a burkini or who think that the burkini subjugates women?

Before addressing these questions, let's touch on another controversial issue: global warming. Many are convinced that human activity is causing the world to become warmer. They want to significantly
curtail the release of carbon dioxide into the atmosphere. Failure to
do so, from their perspective, will be catastrophic for the earth and
humankind. Others think these concerns are overblown. Those who
fear global warming often try to use the existing political structures
to curtail the issuance of greenhouse gases. This involves policies and
laws at all levels of government to increase the cost of activities that
produce these gases as well as regulations and procedures to subsidize

actions that reduce mankind's carbon footprint. People who do not think global warming is a serious issue believe that these types of actions are unwarranted and will lead to an unnecessary reduction in global income, thus causing people to, on average, lead poorer lives. As such, they resist rules and laws that "artificially" increase the cost of human production.

Given these differing perspectives, what regulations, rules, and laws concerning global warming should exist? How should we and government make the trade-offs between decreases in certain economic activities and protecting the environment? How should people's differing views be weighed? How should society make decisions that improve or worsen some people's welfare at the expense of other people's perceived well-being? What rights should we have when we think we are being harmed by the actions of others in our own society or by the actions of those in another society? Governments answer these questions nearly every day, and their choices alter lives. But how should government make decisions and weigh the various trade-offs? Is there an optimal or best structure for deciding on these controversial political actions?

OPTIMAL GOVERNMENT

Some argue that government is not necessary and that an anarchistic community will produce an environment that will be peaceful and stable. The individuals who hold this view are convinced that each person is the best judge of his or her own life, and that the coercive nature of government impinges on the "natural" rights of each person. Anarchists recognize that there is conflict between people, but typically believe that nongovernmental processes will develop over time to prevent or at least ameliorate antisocial behavior. Other people view anarchy as seventeenth-century political philosopher Thomas Hobbes did—a social environment where life is "short and brutish." A popular conception of anarchy is not a peaceful pre-governmental societal organization, but a breakdown in government. Many imagine that anarchy is a place like Somalia in the 1990s, a country faced with nearly endless violent conflict. Government, almost any type of it, is preferred to the chaos viewed as ensuing from various factions trying to fill the power vacuum caused by the absence of a formal political structure.

While anti-anarchists believe that coercively enforced rules are necessary for the long-term stability of society, they have widely varied opinions on the best design and goals of government. It is nearly impossible to find a place on earth not currently claimed by a political institution that coercively enforces its rules. Is this because, as an institution, it is preferred by almost everyone? Or is it because, historically, various governments have forcibly annexed those areas not controlled by other regimes? Or both? If there is a better alternative to government, why haven't groups seceded from some country and formed a stable community that did not have coercively enforced rules? We review the philosophical thinking on this in chapter 5.

Is there some similarity among people that leads government to occur naturally as a solution to certain coordination issues, like Adam Smith's invisible hand? Given the ubiquity of government, it does appear to be a naturally occurring institutional arrangement. While this may seem obvious, the proposition that it occurs systematically implies that it is susceptible to rigorous analysis, if true. If government exists because there are perceived gains from association, then conceptually, government formation can be modeled. The question of the role of government and the relationship between it and its citizens is obviously an important one. Scottish philosopher David Hume, for one, thought it was perhaps the most important question. He stated:

> As one form of government must be allowed more perfect than another, independent of the manners and humours of particular men; why may we not enquire what is the most perfect of all, though the common botched and inaccurate governments seem to serve the purposes of society, and though it be not so easy to establish a new system of government, as to build a vessel upon a new construction? The subject is surely the most worthy curiosity of any the wit of man can possibly devise.[4]

Answering this question is at the core of the discussion in parts three through five.

To discern the optimal structure of voluntary government, as distinct from the analysis of historical institutional structures, a model of government formation is required. Even though the reality is that government has been imposed on people, and that there has never been a truly voluntary government, the characteristics of a voluntary government need to be derived. Is such an entity even theoretically possible?[5] Would people, as we know them, voluntarily subject themselves to the coercive action of others to achieve some perceived benefit? We discuss two nongovernmental situations in chapter 6, where people place themselves in this position.

In the context of voluntary government, various theorists have proposed hypothetical logical situations designed to answer questions about collective decision-making. They include works by the philosopher John Rawls and the economist John Harsanyi, which are reviewed in the next chapter. Ronald Dworkin, an eminent legal philosopher, also considered such a situation.[6] He posited a state of affairs in which people were shipwrecked on a deserted island with little chance of rescue. He imagined the island as having abundant natural resources, and that people could easily bargain and negotiate with one another. He hypothesized that the shipwrecked people would unanimously agree to equally divide all the resources so that there would be an allocation that is "envy free."[7] He also argued that they would unanimously agree to an insurance scheme whereby people who did not equally benefit from their allocation could receive some form of additional compensation from the group. While these agreements completely conform to Dworkin's worldview, it is doubtful that every shipwrecked person, out of a population of people with diverse worldviews, would agree with this governmental structure and allocative scheme. But what will they agree to?

Let's expand his thought experiment and consider an extremely large deserted island where hundreds of millions of people have been instantaneously transported from other parts of the world, without any possessions. Each of these people has a different skill set, different perceived knowledge, different values, and different views on the various implications of social interaction. In addition, the castaways have no prospect of ever leaving the island or contacting people off the island. What type of society will develop from this initially anarchical position?

Most people in this situation are likely to conclude that there is value in collaborating with others, for the benefits of increased safety, productivity, and companionship. This collaboration requires some type of coordination. Some will view this as occurring naturally, with island residents voluntarily providing services to others in exchange for others providing something that they value. Some may think coordination can be enhanced through some type of central planning. In either case, people will be concerned with inevitable conflicts that will arise and will want rules designed to curtail antisocial behavior such as theft, violence, murder, and fraud. However, given the varying worldviews, the island dwellers will have significant differences of opinion as to the best approach to address these personal conflicts and about the definitions of these negative behaviors. They will disagree on the penalties for these acts, the best methods for determining people's guilt, and the optimal regulations for preventing theft and fraud. They will also have differing views on "acceptable" behavior, including the appropriateness of certain types of clothing, infidelity, marriage, homosexuality, abortion, noise, and pollution. Some of the transported people may want to use extreme measures—like death penalties and lengthy incarceration—to enforce their views. Still others may be religious and, on one end of the spectrum, not tolerant of divergent beliefs, like members of the Islamic State of Iraq and al-Sham (ISIS), or, on the other end, forgiving of all perceived transgressions.

There are great gains from people working together to achieve common goals, such as collective defense and public safety. Many people who are interested in political philosophy, like Dworkin, are concerned with what they perceive to be the main conflict between people as they pursue collective effort: how to fairly divide these gains. But there are other conflicts that must be addressed in the formation of a collective organization. People will differ in their views on the appropriate collective goals, methods of achieving these goals, and personal sacrifices required to be a member of the collective. Their differing worldviews may cause many of these conflicts and exacerbate the others. Differing values and opinions can lead to social dissonance or decision congestion. People need to make joint decisions on rules and laws. Yet they disagree. They need to somehow agree or at least accept the rules governing behavior of those in their society if they want to form a voluntary government. They must find some method of compromising with other people on these common rules. Compromise—accepting rules that you do not prefer—can be viewed as a psychic cost. These costs reduce the net value of working with other people. If the cost is too high, as with compromising with extremist members of the group, there will be negative net value from being in the same society and following common rules. People will not voluntarily subject themselves to this negative value. Stated somewhat differently, there is a limit to the diversity of worldviews that can exist in a voluntary society. This implies that there is also a limit to the amount of compromise that people will make to participate in a common government.

The gains from collective effort and the differing values and opinions of those participating in this effort are opposing social forces that will lead the people on the island to bargain over the formation of government. In part three, using a simplified version of the island situation, we will use a bargaining *process* and determine that people with differing worldviews will form various independent national governments. They will also form a unique equilibrium structure for these national governments, at least for the subset of people who will not use violence to force their worldview onto others. The willingness of these people to make trade-offs and reach agreements with other people for mutual gain will lead them to compromise on a unique federalist structure of government, which will be labeled as "collectivity" in chapter 18.

The most critical aspect of collectivity is not its structure, although that is important; its critical characteristic is the process of deriving it. Not everyone will a priori accept it as the optimal structure of government. No one has historically proposed it, and no government, either current or historical, possesses all the elements of collectivity. However, as will be argued in part four, it is derived by a process that many people will accept. The process is one that satisfies Rawls's concept of "procedural justice." It is also in accord with the philosopher

Robert Nozick's idea of being "ethically objective." People can accept a result produced by a "fair" process even though they do not prefer the result. For example, a person can disagree with a controversial jury decision, but accept it because of the process that derived the result. If they view the jury and court process as fair, or objective, or just, then they can view the results of the process as fair, objective, and just, even when they disagree with the resulting decision. Part six argues that the bargaining process that derives collectivity is a "just" process.

Most of the book is not concerned with exploring the decisions that "just" people will make. Instead, it is an investigation into the type of government that people in an anarchical situation, with differing worldviews, will agree to form when they selfishly want to live under laws that most conform to their worldview. This part of the overall analysis is objective. It reasons through the type of government that pluralistic people "will" form, not "should" form. The normative question of "should" arises from asking whether we "should" design a government from the blueprint derived from logically reasoning through the type of government that a diverse group of people will choose for themselves. This leads to the proposition that the only "just" government, the only government that we "should" accept as having power over us, and where we accept we are in a bargain with people we did not actually bargain with, is a government that diverse people will select if they have the choice.

Collectivity is different than the governmental structure envisioned by Dworkin or supported by social philosophers who have examined two-person bargaining situations. A large group of people, with differing worldviews, have a myriad of potential bargaining options to accomplish their objectives. However, as will be discussed in parts three through five, their ability to enter alliances with many people, even people with significantly different values and opinions, incent them to form a democratic government. Not just any democratic government, but a specific type of federalist structure of government. This holds irrespective of people's values, opinions, political leanings, and biases (as long as they will not sanction violence to enforce their worldview).

While this type of government has elements of existing federalist structures, it is fundamentally different from any historical political organization. It is characterized by a large central government whose primary responsibility is external defense, yet with few domestic powers. This umbrella organization will also consist of various domestic governments, completely independent from the central government. Some of these political entities will be large with nearly unlimited domestic scope and power. Imagine existing US states or combinations of some of these states, checked by their own constitutions, but unconstrained by a federal constitution. Some of these internally oriented political entities could completely conform to the vision of government endorsed by Dworkin. These governments will exist side by side with other domestic governments that have constitutions that significantly curtail their potential scope and actions. Some of these could resemble the type of state envisioned by libertarians, who prefer narrower and less intrusive authorities.

The governments that exist under collectivity also have incentives to reach agreements with each other to address their conflicts, spillovers, and lack of scale. These arrangements allow them to achieve some of the benefits of being part of a larger entity without completely subjecting every decision to the views and values of the combined population. Agreements will still affect the policies of the subscribing parties and will produce psychic losses for both sides from the compromises that they make. However, these losses are likely to be smaller for people with differing views than the alternative of permanently combining into a single government. Compacts between domestic governments will not be all encompassing; they will have limited scope and typically have a limited duration. They will focus on specific points of collaboration or conflicts and will encourage cooperation without the requirement that every domestic coercive decision be uniform or meet some minimum standard. As with the national or central governments, repeated interaction between citizens of different domestic governments and between the various domestic governments will incent these governments to reach an understanding and to abide by the agreements. Unlike national governments, the domestic governments can agree to use a third-party mediator or enforcer such as a neutral independent party or the central government.

A pluralistic group of people will suffer the compromises required to form a central government to defend them against external threats, given the large gains from a stable governance structure. Yet, they will search for methods of reducing the amount of required compromise over domestic issues. In a world where constitutions are complete and fully specified, this can theoretically be achieved by having different and nonuniform domestic rules and laws. However, in the more realistic scenario where constitutions are incomplete and do not fully specify every possible collective decision in every possible scenario, the only method of reducing required compromise is by forming independent, but related, domestic governments. Collectivity is essentially a federalist structure of government with an externally focused central government and "polycentric" domestic governments.

As will be discussed in chapter 16, voting is a partial solution to joint decision-making when collective actions cannot be prespecified. Voting procedures have material effects on the laws, rules, and processes chosen by each government. As such, they are critical elements in allowing people to have the highest chance of living the life that means the most to them. People will use the authorized voting procedures to influence governmental policy to conform to their worldview. This implies that diverse people who voluntarily form a common government will not structure it either as a unitary government or as a traditional federalist government. If the central government has the authority to control or even influence the policies of the domestic governments, those with differing worldviews will naturally use their influence over the central government to affect the policies of the various domestic governments. Therefore, diverse citizens will not voluntarily compromise on any structure of government other than collectivity. People will choose collectivity, even though some would rather have a more powerful and expansive central government.

Among the key topics of chapter 16 are some of the inefficiencies that are endemic to voting. Voting does not directly incorporate people's intensities for their preferences. It does not reveal how much citizens care about issues. Thus, collective decisions that are made by some type of voting will likely diverge from collective decisions that minimize people's aggregate psychic losses from compromise. In part three, we will show that when governmental decisions can be completely prespecified, people with diverse worldviews will make compromise decisions to minimize their aggregate psychic losses.

However, the inability to prespecify all collective decisions will lead to the need for some type of voting, either directly or indirectly, as a method to determine laws and rules. Interestingly, in chapter 16, we will also demonstrate that the constitutional process of forming the various governments, and periodic negotiations of agreements between these governments (including domestic governments), address some of this voting inefficiency. The negotiating process reveals, at least partially, the negotiators' intensities for their preferences. Both their preferences and their intensity for these preferences will affect the result of the negotiations. Different contract terms and provisions are not equally important to each person or each bargainer. The negotiation process and the equilibrium compromises over specific contract terms include the intensity of people's views. As such, periodic contracts between domestic governments serve as an additional institutional arrangement that improves the overall efficiency of coercive social decision-making. Intergovernmental contracting and a choice in domestic governments allow citizens to improve their lives even in the presence of incomplete constitutions.

NONUNIFORM DOMESTIC LAWS

Laws are designed to modify potential behavior. They affect the allocation of resources and people's well-being. They matter greatly in allowing people to live the lives that provide them the highest value. And they do not occur randomly. All laws are the products of some political process. Different political processes and different demographics are just two variables that lead to different laws. In a democracy like the United States, they are the result of a combination of numerous factors. These include the federal constitution; state constitutions; periodic voting by citizens at the federal, state, and local level; periodic voting by federal, state, and local representatives; decisions of presidents, governors, county executives, and mayors; periodic decisions by various bureaucrats; periodic decisions by various judges, including Supreme Court justices; public and private discussion; and lobbying. This complex process does not determine the truth. Nor does it produce laws that conform to facts. Laws in a democracy are not the laws that would be determined by some type of all-knowing power. They are produced by a process that is a result of history and circumstance and based on people's differing opinions and views. These opinions cannot be definitively proven or disproven to everyone's satisfaction, and yet they affect the laws that are coercively enforced.

If laws are not produced by a process that is the product of truth, if they are merely culturally derived and they conflict with your worldview—the worldview you sincerely believe is the most accurate representation of how the world actually works, are there logical reasons to obey these laws, other than the risk of incarceration, fines, and potential embarrassment? People with imperfect worldviews make laws that are legally valid. Why should these people be able to negatively affect our future? Are there reasons other than the accident of history and "the nature of things" as justifications for obeying rules that seem to favor one part of society over another as well as obeying laws that we view as inefficient and irrational?

In the beginning of this inquiry, I thought there were many possible answers, including the most likely one that the world is so complex and idiosyncratic that there is no determinable universal truth about government. To my surprise, the inquiry led to the conclusion that there are many reasons why it is in our interest to obey laws made by imperfect people with imperfect models of the world, besides moral suasion or the use of force. However, it also led to a realization that not all laws are justifiable. A rule or law is not just simply because a constitutionally authorized person or group determines that it should be obeyed. This is true even in a government that uses various types of voting to make collective decisions. People who have different worldviews will also have differing views of which laws are just. The relevant question then becomes how to produce laws that every citizen thinks are "fair" and "just" when people have differing views of justness.

Just laws can arise in two ways. First, people can view the law as inherently just. This will occur when the law conforms to their worldview. Alternatively, just laws may not be inherently just, but may be just because they are produced by a process that people view as just. When people have differing worldviews, there is a much higher likelihood that they will agree on just procedures rather than on just outcomes. The only way for people with differing worldviews to make just laws is to use a just procedure. Since laws are the product of government, the only way for pluralistic people to produce just laws is through a just government. But what is a just structure of government? As discussed above, it is collectivity. In fact, as we will argue in part four, collectivity is the only just form of government for pluralistic people who will not sanction violence in an attempt to force their worldview onto others. Collectivity can still produce laws that seem inane and biased. But obeying rules you do not agree with is part of the grand bargain involved in being a citizen of a just government.

But some may still ask: How can this type of government be just? What about people who are born and live in one part of a country that has laws and governmental regulations that they find appalling, inefficient, or unfair? Will they have to leave their home, disrupt their lives, abandon their friends and family, and incur other moving costs to relocate to a part of the country whose laws they find less objectionable? How can this structure of government be fair to those who move to a city or state for work and yet are prohibited by rules of these jurisdictions from smoking marijuana, having an abortion, or having access to free health care? Shouldn't just governmental rules and laws be uniform so that people can live where they want without being subject to laws that constrain their basic rights? The answers to these questions all revolve around the fundamental fact that people have different worldviews; social interaction is too complex for people to agree on the costs and benefits of different governmental policies. There are some laws and rights that a "broadly liberal" people—those whose political views are such that they do not feel justified in using violence to enforce their views onto people with differing beliefs—will agree are inherently just, but these are few and far between.

The choice is stark—uniform laws or laws that vary across parts of the country. "Just" uniformity in intranational rules, rights, obligations, procedures, policies, and laws requires convergence in people's views. This convergence, even if it occurs, is unlikely to center on the "true" worldview. The discovery of truth or facts related to human action and interaction is rare.

As we will discuss in chapter 3, information and public discussion will not resolve people's differences, as some advocate. Communication has increased enormously over the centuries. But did the creation of print, of newspapers, and of books cause people's values and opinions to converge? Did the invention of radio or television cause people's differences in views to disappear? The Internet has led to a vast increase in the volume and speed of communication, but it has not led to a convergence of views between everyone in the United States, in Britain, or in other countries. Instead, many people think the world is more polarized now than it has been in the past.

These continuing differences in views and opinions have led to various countries enacting diverse laws and regulations. People, for the most part, accept these differences, not because they agree with them, but because they know they cannot change them. Yet, when it comes to countries themselves, many people prefer and demand uniform rights and obligations. However, differences of values and opinions exist both between countries and within countries. Uniformity in domestic laws implies that many more people within a country will be coerced to obey laws that they find objectionable than if they had the right to live in a part of the country that had laws closer to the ones they prefer. Broad uniformity in laws will lead to unnecessary societal dissonance. As stated above, this does not imply that there are not some rights and laws that people will agree should apply to everyone; nonetheless, the number of these rights and laws is far less extensive than currently exists in any country.

This, of course, implies that people in the same country will be subject to different laws, and that if a person moves between domestic jurisdictions, they will become subject to different regulations and procedures. This happens between countries; given people's differing worldviews, why shouldn't it happen for moves within a country? As will be discussed in chapter 13, diverse people will choose a structure of government that allows for nonuniform domestic laws because it permits them to achieve the large gains from joint national defense with a great number of people they do not necessarily agree with, without simultaneously requiring them to compromise on most domestic rules. But what about the people who favor uniform laws? Don't their views count? Of course, in a just government, their views must be considered. However, a process that is unbiased and just will determine that the only just government for a broadly liberal group of diverse people is one where there are few uniform domestic laws. In chapter 20, this type of social justice will be called "justice as choice." It will determine that people have a right to live under different domestic laws that trump some of the population's desire to live in a country with completely uniform domestic laws.

RIGHTS

People's views on rights depend on their worldviews. All rights, in some way, involve government. Some people think that government should guarantee people's "natural" rights, the ability to make certain personal decisions free from interference from either the government or other people. Many believe that every citizen should have certain political rights, such as the right to vote or protest a government official's speech. Some have the view that everyone should have certain economic rights. For example, they may think that each person should be guaranteed a minimum level of income or be able to sell their services with minimal governmental oversight. Others have the opinion that everyone should have various social rights like nondiscrimination or free college education. These views on rights will rarely converge into one unified worldview, given the complexity of society. In fact, some phenomena such as income inequality, the pace of technological change, economic volatility, and climate change are so complex that opinions differ on whether they are legitimate issues for government to address.

Under these circumstances, what rights "should" people have? Should rights be dependent on the majority view? Should people's rights be based on interpretations of the founding constitution? The bargaining situation discussed above in the section on Optimal Government, which led to collectivity as the equilibrium structure of government, can be used to logically deduce the rights that pluralistic and broadly liberal people agree that everyone should legally have.

In chapter 11, the bargaining situation will reveal that very large central governments, composed of citizens whose worldviews are broadly liberal, will have constitutions that entitle every citizen to receive the same allocation of the benefits from collective defense. These overall benefits are the difference between the aggregate costs of each person independently defending themselves and the costs of collective defense. The bargaining process will also show that people are not required to compromise equally. This will lead to different perceptions by citizens of these equal benefits. Those who compromise the most will place a lower value on these gains because of their larger psychic losses from compromising. As such, they will be less politically satisfied than those who were not required to compromise as much.

Furthermore, equality in benefits from collective defense does not imply equality in wealth or in incomes, since people's incomes and wealth can differ from the efficiency gains from collective defense. The equal allocation of the benefits from collective defense is independent of people's worldviews and is a *universal* right for people with diverse worldviews. However, the allocation of the gains from the formation of domestic governments depends on the worldviews of their founding and subsequent citizens. If a sufficient number of people value income equality, then they can form a domestic government with this objective or with this right. Under collectivity, the policies concerning income equality can and will differ among the various domestic governments.

Broadly liberal people will reach a compromise to severely limit the central government's domestic authorities and provide for the existence of different types of independent domestic governments. As discussed above, these include "general governments" with unlimited domestic scope and "limited governments" with narrow and restricted authorities. These various domestic governments will not all have the same laws. People will compromise and restrict the scope of the central government, even though many may think that the laws, rights, and social obligations in at least some of the domestic governments are wrong, and that extensive decentralization is inefficient. The bargaining analysis in subsequent chapters will also reveal that people's rights to participate in the decision-making for the central government of their choice are not sufficient to maximize their net gains and achieve the most they can from compromising with those who hold different views. They will negotiate for the additional right to form and join a wide variety of independent domestic governments that are not controlled or influenced by the policies and laws of the central government.

This right to have independent domestic governments will be labeled as the "right to be wrong" in chapter 21, since people will think that at least some of the policies of the domestic governments in which they are not citizens are wrong. This right along with the right of universal suffrage, can be viewed as "fundamental" rights, since they effectively determine the process the state will use to make decisions and grant people additional rights and obligations. While many people may view majority voting as an important control right, especially for its psychological benefit, it is a weak right with respect to resolving the conflict between people with differing worldviews who are members of the same central government. The right of existence of independent domestic governments significantly expands people's ability to reduce the conflicts associated with differing points of view. Like other rights, it is controversial. But unlike most other rights, it is independent of people's worldviews, at least for those people whose worldviews are broadly liberal. The right to be wrong is essentially the right to have a differing worldview and the right to live under domestic rules with people who have a relatively similar view. Like other rights, it also is an obligation—an obligation to allow other people to attempt to live the lives they value by living under coercive domestic laws that can vary from the majority view. It is an obligation by citizens of a common central government to respect the worldviews embedded in the decisions of domestic governments in which they are not citizens. It is an obligation on the part of each person to acknowledge the fact that his or her worldview may not be right or accurate—that the worldviews of others may be less wrong than their own worldview. The right to be wrong is an obligation to allow people in differing domestic governments to act on what others may think are wrong opinions and beliefs.

NEXT STEPS

The next chapter will review the writings and opinions of five world-renowned economists and philosophers who fundamentally disagree with one another. Throughout the book, the political philosophies of these five thought leaders will be applied to the issues under consideration. Chapter 3 will discuss reasons why they disagree and the historical difficulty of amalgamating their views in a rational and just fashion. Chapter 4 begins part two, which sets the stage for the bargaining process that will be used to derive the just structure of government for people with differing worldviews. That chapter reviews some of the previous studies that have used bargaining in the context of political philosophy, as well as some of the philosophical issues of using individual decision-making in this context. Bargaining must begin somewhere, at some status-quo point. For the bargainers determining the type of government they can agree to, this point is anarchy or a common position before the formation of government. Chapter 5 is concerned with the many different philosophical views on anarchy and the difficulties of collective action without government. Chapter 6 is the last chapter in this part. It uses two examples to illustrate the conflicts that are endemic to any organization, including government.

Chapter 7 begins the formal part of the analysis of government formation out of an anarchical situation by people with differing worldviews. This chapter provides an introduction for the bargaining protocol that people in anarchy will use to negotiate over coercive collective rules. "Collective defense" is a key goal that everyone who views government as important can agree to. Chapter 8 provides an analysis of this type of defense, comparing it to anarchical defense. The focus is on the relative efficiency benefits of collective defense. However, these benefits come with a cost when people have differing worldviews. As a group, they must somehow choose from among a wide variety of equally logical collective defense actions.

Chapter 9 continues this analysis by examining a simple two-person environment. In particular, it derives the bargain that will be reached over collective defense when people possess differing worldviews. Chapter 10 analyzes this same situation when another person is added into the bargain. Chapter 11 investigates the characteristics of the "democratic defense collective," which is the bargaining solution involving large numbers of people. The analysis of bargaining to this point has only been concerned with one collective decision: defense. Chapter 12 considers the other potential social goals and discusses the controversies involved when people have differing worldviews. Chapter 13 ends part three by discussing the bargaining solution among a large number of people, given their differing political philosophies on both external defense and domestic rules.

Chapter 14 begins part four, which explores more deeply the bargain that people will reach as they exit anarchy. It analyzes the implications from relaxing many of the assumptions that simplified the analysis in the prior chapters. It discusses the complex web of different types of governments that people will agree to form. The analysis to this point has not addressed the provision of goods and services. Chapter 15 remedies this by exploring the types of private entities that people will form as they exit anarchy, and the relationship between these organizations and government. Chapter 16 provides a discussion of the issues involving voting and the institutional remedies to these issues that people reaching a bargaining equilibrium will utilize. Chapter 17 shows the impact that time can have on the decisions that people will make as they exit anarchy.

Chapter 18 begins part five, which is concerned with the specific constitutional terms that people will reach as they exit anarchy. This chapter examines why people exiting anarchy will not choose a traditional federalist form of government, where the central government can influence or control many nondefense-related domestic decisions. In chapter 19, collectivity will be compared to other federalist concepts, including fiscal federalism, American Federalism, and competitive federalism.

Chapters 20 and 21 are the final chapters and compose part six. They formally discuss the reasons why collectivity is a just form of government. Collectivity is designed by diverse people in a "just" bargain to improve their lives when they cannot agree on optimal laws to help coordinate their activities. It is the answer to the question of how government *should* make decisions when its citizens have irreconcilable politics.

2

COMPETING POLITICAL PHILOSOPHIES

Achieving unanimity as to the best governmental policies is uncommon if not impossible. People's views differ on which laws and rules are most appropriate. Some of these views are due to differing morals, others because people are selfish and prefer policies that improve their welfare at the expense of others. Many others favor different social policies and laws even though they have similar morals and do not let their self-interest influence their views. These are the people who are of particular interest. Very often, their incompatible opinions persist even after these people have communicated their differences and have done their utmost to persuade others that they may be in error. How can this be possible? How can people have fundamental differences of opinion that cannot be reconciled by logic, scientific examination, and/or communication? Why doesn't open and sincere communication resolve these significant differences? How can honest and diligent people ignore the truth that is perceived by others? In this situation, who is right and who is wrong? Most importantly, what social policies "should" we pursue in the face of this controversy?

It will prove helpful in addressing these questions to first review the political philosophies of five eminent scholars: John Rawls, Amartya Sen, John Harsanyi, Friedrich Hayek, and Robert Nozick. By design, the discussion of their writings and views will not be thorough or all-inclusive. Furthermore, it is based on my interpretation of their writings and may not represent their actual views. These five were chosen for many reasons. First, each of their views can be classified as "broadly liberal." Even though they appear to strongly believe that their preferred social policies are the most appropriate and should be broadly applied, they do not favor using physical force or coercion to enforce their views. Second, they each represent a body of thought that many other people accept and believe is an accurate guide to determining governmental rules and laws. Third, they are widely considered to be experts in their fields. Finally, they were contemporaries and therefore had the opportunity to read each other's works. This sometimes led them to provide critical analyses of each other's positions. Maybe somewhat surprisingly, however, none of them seemed to change their fundamental view after reviewing each other's books and papers. While they agreed on a few elements concerning the proper role of government, there are substantially more differences than similarities in their recommendations and conclusions.

JOHN RAWLS

John Rawls (1921–2002) was an American who is widely viewed as one of the most important political philosophers of the twentieth century.[8] His most influential book was *A Theory of Justice*.

Rawls was convinced that an unbiased, reasonable, and rational person can discern the proper role of government, and that all such individuals will agree with this identified role. In his works, Rawls contends that government is a theoretical compact between all members of a particular society viewed from the perspective of the citizens' roles in that society. He viewed society as a naturally occurring cooperative phenomenon in which people gather together because it provides value to each of them. While social cooperation produces an improved life for all its participants, it also results in conflict between people. The conflict that he focused on is the division of the gains from collective action.

In his attempt to resolve this conflict, he placed people in a pre-governmental "original position." This is a status-quo point from which they will decide on how they will divide the gains arising from government. This type of initial situation, prior to the formation of any type of government, is an important concept for Rawls and will prove essential to our analysis in the forthcoming chapters. The original position can be viewed as a theoretical way station before a government is formed and more particularly before people begin bargaining over their desired government. Rawls viewed people in the original position to actually be engaged in a "bargaining problem," but given its complexity, he did not see a direct way to solve that problem.[9] Instead, he attempted to derive a unanimous decision on how to divide the gains from collective action by restricting the potential biases of people in the original position. In his initial formulation, he placed them behind a "veil of ignorance" where certain things are hidden from them such as their identity, social status, and wealth. In a later work, he strengthened the veil by also obscuring their "philosophical" views.[10]

Behind the veil, these people determine the political tenets that they want to apply in their society. They decide on people's rights and obligations as well as on the coercive institutional structure to enforce them. In Rawls's view, behind the original veil, they will unanimously agree that the primary objective of government is to assist the least-well-off group in society. This is often labeled as a maxi-min principle. He viewed this as a "fair" bargain between people of differing economic and social status.[11]

Objectively determining the least-well-off people and redistributing resources to them obviously requires interpersonal comparisons of value. Rawls argued that people within a society are sufficiently similar so that each person has certain "primary goods" that have the most value to them. These primary goods include income, wealth, job opportunities, political liberties, and self-respect. He thought that the people behind the veil would determine that everyone should have an equal share of these. Inequality between people, according to Rawls's political philosophy, is just only when it provides value to the least-well-off group of people within a closed existing society. The ideal, determined by the people behind the veil, is a guide to real-world institutions that are necessary for determining the rules that a just government will enforce. For Rawls, the original position in conjunction with the veil is an example of "pure procedural justice" that determines the rules that will be administered by a just government, as compared to people's preferred social rules arising from their underlying philosophical views. He called this derived political conception of justice "justice as fairness."

While he was not sure what type of government the reasonable individuals behind the veil would choose, he presumed that the most likely structure would be a constitutional democracy. He conceptually viewed government as consisting of four branches. The first two have the responsibility for regulating economic activity, increasing employment, and decreasing monopolies. The other two are tasked with administering his conception of social justice. Rawls viewed government as using its agreed-upon coercive powers to protect its citizens, regulate commerce, provide public goods, and redistribute things that people value to those who are less well off.

He recognized that political power is coercive, but his political philosophy is a peaceful one. His writings were designed to influence how existing societies order their priorities, since he was convinced that in the institutional structure of today's society there is a near-permanent inequality between different "classes" of people. Rawls argued that a society that follows justice as fairness will not be meritocratic nor will it be the most efficient, but it will be liberal, "just," and "fair."

For Rawls, the concept of justice as fairness only applied to a closed society concerned with domestic issues. He later developed a concept he called the "law of peoples" for relationships between the various domestic governments.[12] He did not think that the original position and the veil could be directly applied to international or interdomestic governments given the diversity of philosophical views and the variety of governmental institutions. As such, he did not argue that governments should force or even encourage justice as fairness on other governments. He also agreed with the eighteenth-century German philosopher Immanuel Kant that a global government will result in one controlled by a despot or one where groups are continually fighting for political independence.[13] In his law of peoples, Rawls thought that liberal governments, such as those organized along the lines of justice as fairness, should be "tolerant" of nonliberal governments that he views as "decent." However, he did believe that war between societies is justified, when a government is violating certain rights of those under its coercive control such as practicing "genocide" or condoning "slavery."[14]

Rawls also thought that governments can reach cooperative agreements with each other and be members of various types of organizations, including free-trade groups, cooperative banks, and confederations. As will be seen in the forthcoming chapters, the ability of domestic governments to cooperate peacefully and enter into agreements with other domestic governments is an important element in coming to the solution for irreconcilable politics.

Rawls's arguments about the role of government and how the gains from government should be divided are critical elements in distinguishing his political philosophy from the views of the other four scholars. This leads to the central question of how to amalgamate his views with those who disagree with him, when they cannot definitively prove that he is wrong. And importantly, when he cannot definitively prove, to their satisfaction, that his views are the most accurate representation of reality.

AMARTYA SEN

The second view on the proper role of government is one espoused by Amartya Sen. His overall view of government appears not to be about the ideal governmental structure but about appropriate governmental policies to help people escape injustice and have the opportunities to enjoy their lives.[15] Sen is an Indian economist and a professor at Harvard University. He received the Nobel Prize in economics in 1998 for his work in welfare economics and social choice theory.

Sen is one of the principal architects of social choice theory, and as such, understands the difficulties involved in group decision-making. He seems to think that "just" political decisions are relative and not absolute. In his book *The Idea of Justice*, he focuses on the importance of public debate in performing this comparative analysis of possible governmental policies. He reintroduces Adam Smith's concept of the "impartial spectator" as a procedural device designed to reduce bias and thereby help to determine relative social justice.[16] Public reasoning that is sincere and adheres to the concept of objectivity, exemplified by the impartial spectator, appears to, in Sen's view, lead to the best (most just) social policies.

While Sen seems to agree with Rawls that an active government is a force of good in society, he does not seem to think that anyone can derive an "idealized state" through analytical reasoning. He maintains that reasonable people's views can logically differ even if they are behind the veil and therefore impartial. Instead of determining rights and obligations based on the original position, he advocates for an agreement among people founded on public reasoning.[17] However, given the complexity embedded in cooperation and the intricacies of the interrelationships between people, he allows for the possibility of partial resolutions to issues. Furthermore, he suggests that there can be various views on justice that cannot be combined into a unifying framework.

Sen appears to be a realist. He seems to be concerned with achievable policies that can make a practical difference in people's lives. He realizes that poorly constructed governmental policies can be gamed and prove ineffective if they do not adequately consider people's motivations and incentives. For him, this should lead to public deliberation and honest debate about social values and governmental policies, with the goal of living in a world that is more just and free.

He essentially argues that freedom is a complex concept involving both "process" and "opportunities."[18] For Sen, it includes economic opportunities, political freedoms, and protection. He does not appear to think that people are free if they are illiterate, unemployed, undernourished, or in poor health. Given his advocacy of increasing people's liberty, he seems supportive of government-enforced social and economic rights such as health care and education. He is also an advocate of what he calls "sustainable freedom," which is concerned with increasing people's freedom while ensuring that this does not reduce the freedoms of our descendants.[19]

Sen seems to believe that traditional approaches to governmental policy concerned with single aggregates such as "primary goods" or national income will not be as effective as tactics that use more information about people. He appears to think that focusing on people's capabilities to turn their means into their desired ends is crucial for governmental policy formation. For example, a person with a severe illness or disability may have a more difficult time converting income into his or her desired goal than would a relatively healthy individual. However, Sen does not seem to think that government should necessarily attempt to equalize everyone's capabilities.

Sen argues that the market mechanism is a positive force in people's lives, since it allows them to engage in mutually advantageous exchange. However, he also argues markets require government intervention to work better. He acknowledges the positive role that exchange and trade have on society. But he is also concerned with the inefficiencies and potential unfairness of unregulated private enterprise. He seems to view the complicated nature of proper government regulation of the market as requiring public discussion and analysis. Sen appears to also argue that governmental policy is required for certain goods that he does not think the market can produce, such as public goods like defense, public health, and environmental protection.

Sen is an advocate of democracy, but seems to view it as having potential flaws. Given his professional focus on social choice and its recognition of the information handicap of traditional voting procedures, he is more concerned with the public-discussion nature of democracy than the structure of the voting process. For him, one of the weaknesses of democracy appears to be its inability to ensure that all governmental decisions are made through "public reasoning."[20]

While many people will agree with Sen's political philosophy, his views will not be held by everyone, and they obviously differ from Rawls's. This again leads to the question of reconciling people's differing philosophies on government. Sen seems to be strongly of the opinion that public discussion and the impartial spectator are the best methods of addressing this type of disagreement. The problem, of course, is what to do when the impartial spectators fundamentally disagree.

JOHN HARSANYI

John Harsanyi (1920–2000) believed in freedom, rationality, and ethics from an individualistic perspective. His views on justice and the role of government were in the utilitarian tradition that was established by Jeremy Bentham, John Stuart Mill, Henry Sidgwick, and Francis Edgeworth.[21] Harsanyi was an economics professor at the University of California, Berkeley, and received the Nobel Prize in economics in 1994 for his work in game theory and utilitarian ethics.

In his works, Harsanyi thinks of public policy as determining rules that best address people's preferences and conflicts in an unbiased manner. Unlike the early utilitarians, he did not think social welfare is determined by summing each person's value that they place on actions, goods, or services. Instead, he viewed each person as having an individual model of social welfare that can be expressed as a mathematical function they use to determine their preferences and judgments concerning public policy. For him, each of these individual models is based on each person's value judgments, but independent of their self-interest. In addition, they all have the same general form. They are the sum of a person's values of potential actions as they perceive them from an unbiased perspective.

He thought that every person, in imagining how others would value a particular situation, would assume that these people have full information and do not possess unsocial values such as jealously. He argued that these values should be excluded because they violate the ethical principles of utilitarianism, which is built on "human sympathy."[22] By limiting people's social preferences, he was effectively acknowledging that certain morals are universal and not dependent on a person's individual perspective. However, in general, he did not think that utilitarianism should be imposed on people with different views of morality.

Harsanyi's modern version of utilitarianism is typically called "rule preference utilitarianism" because it recommends social rules based on the sum of people's assumed preferences. His view of judgments concerning governmental policy requires each person to make interpersonal comparisons of people's preferences and values. While he acknowledged that no one can know other people's values, he argued that everyone in their everyday decision-making compares interpersonal values by considering other people's perspectives. He postulated that this can be achieved by each person assuming it is equally likely that they can be anyone else in society. He demonstrated that this "equiprobability" perspective leads to the decision theory of expected utility maximization, where each person's preferred social decision rule is the arithmetic mean of their unbiased view of everyone else's restricted preferences.[23]

For Harsanyi, the equiprobability assumption is equivalent to Smith's sympathetic impartial observer. It is also similar to Rawls's veil of ignorance. However, he argued that his type of utilitarianism could produce radically different policy decisions than those produced by Rawls's maxi-min decision rule. He suggested that the maxi-min rule could lead to illogical moral choices, since it overemphasizes unlikely possibilities. He used the example of allocating scarce medical resources between terminally ill patients and those who would have a longer life span if given the scarce care. Harsanyi would allocate the resources to those expected to recover instead of the worst-off patients.

Harsanyi's views on inequality also differ from both Rawls's and Sen's. He acknowledged that people's social and economic situations vary and that these differences are not necessarily morally justifiable. However, he contended that governmental policies that attempt to correct these inequalities have their own ethical issues. For example, he would only support redistribution if it improves average utility. He thought that everyone has a similar individual utility function and has diminishing marginal utility from income. This implies that reducing the income of the relatively well off and redistributing it to those who are relatively poorer will improve overall average social utility. As such, he supported a highly progressive tax system. However, he was not in favor of equalizing incomes because of the disincentives from high marginal taxes on those with high incomes and negative income taxes on the poor. His focus on motivations also led him to favor some form of inheritance, since he viewed it as having a positive impact on society given the likely higher levels of altruism and interest in social causes and cultural activities—although he acknowledged the negative effects from the reduced incentive to work. He contends that any social policy that recommends less inequality than that suggested by utilitarianism is biased.

Harsanyi viewed everyone in a particular society to be in some type of interpersonal conflict that requires public policy decisions to resolve. He believed that even people with the same moral philosophy will disagree on the appropriate public policies given the complexity of societal problems. However, he thought that each social decision maker in each society, including voters, should follow an ethical rule, which establishes logical rules to address interpersonal conflicts. Not surprisingly, the moral rule he advocates is "rule preference utilitarianism."

As previously stated, this rule leads to different laws than those preferred by both Sen and Rawls. Not surprisingly, Sen and Rawls strongly criticized utilitarianism. These critiques did not alter Harsanyi's opinions. This leads to the important question of how people *should* make laws when they have fundamental disagreements and neither reasoning nor public discussion is able to cause agreement.

FRIEDRICH HAYEK

Friedrich Hayek (1899–1992) thought that governmental policies and the overall structure of government should be designed to enable all randomly chosen people, now or in the future, to have the highest opportunity of accomplishing their desired aims. He was an Austrian-born British economist who was awarded the Nobel Prize in economics in 1974.

In his writings, the formation of knowledge and its dissemination and utilization are fundamental to his conclusions on the proper role, function, and decision-making structure of government.[24] He argued that any sympathetic person who has an accurate view of people and their interaction will agree with his conclusions.

To Hayek, government has three functions: (i) external defense and response to disasters such as floods and epidemics, (ii) providing domestic services that are not being offered by the market, and (iii) determining rules to improve overall order that are within the control of the government. Hayek viewed these rules as being conditioned on the necessity of competition in society. He followed the ancient Stoics in viewing life as a game of survival. A key component of success in this game is discovering rules governing interpersonal behavior that improve the random person's chance of success in life. For Hayek, these discovered rules include traditions, morals, and ethics. He thought that an important function of government is to build on past societal practices and ascertain better rules to live by and coercively enforce these rules. Hayek also thought these rules must allow people a "private sphere" of freedom of personal action as well as engender competition between people.[25] He believed that competition is the most effective way that knowledge is acquired and transmitted, even though this process will likely cause temporary monopolies and excess profits.

Hayek had a complex understanding of the world that fundamentally shaped his vision about the functions and limitations of government. To him, the two fundamental economic forces of Smith's division of labor and David Ricardo's comparative advantage logically lead to the spreading of information, conflicting views of the accuracy of the information, and doubt as to whether acquired information is in fact knowledge.[26] People learn from accomplishing tasks, experimenting, and seeing others succeed and fail. For Hayek, central direction and any limitation on individual ingenuity will lead to a lower path of growth for people on average and, in the extreme, to the reduction in the sustainable population. Hayek's opinions on the importance of individual freedom and personal liberty were due to his beliefs that they are necessary for society to advance and have the highest chance of solving today's and tomorrow's perceived problems.

Even though Hayek thought that the delineation of individual freedom is the most critical element of government design, he recognized that people can intentionally harm one another, coerce others, and commit fraud. He viewed government as having a declared "monopoly" over coercion within its domain and thought that it should make coercion predictable and applicable to all. To Hayek, government could improve people's chances of achieving their aims by reducing the chance of unpredictable individual violence and fraud. As stated above, he believed that just governmental rules concerning coercive activities should be guided by broadly applicable governing principles, and that individual freedom is the fundamental guiding principle. Hayek's justification for the focus on liberty is not because it is a just cause in and of itself, but because he viewed it as essential to enable the majority of people to accomplish their desired aims.

Hayek thought that another legitimate function of government is to provide programs for the poor that are indexed to the wealth of society. That said, Hayek was strongly of the opinion that governmental programs aimed at reducing inequality of people's income and wealth in society are incompatible with individual liberty and will lead to a higher chance that the random person will not achieve his or her goals. This occurs because the government, in trying to equalize people's incomes, will interfere with the transmission and discovery of information. He recognized that these types of governmental policies can be effective in the short run, but he viewed them as being destructive over the medium and long term. He regarded people as constituting part of a vast network of continuous path-dependent relationships. If government attempts to artificially improve or protect people's positions, it will cause the future paths of most people to turn out worse than they otherwise would have been.

To Hayek, individual responsibility and freedom of action are intertwined and inseparable. He was convinced that the overall success of the majority of people is dependent on people benefiting and potentially suffering from their actions irrespective of their best intentions. While not everyone is motivated by material goods, many are, and to induce them to discover what they should do with their time and effort, they need to have as high a chance as possible to be compensated for their success. However, luck and skill are difficult to distinguish, which implies that people may receive compensation by chance instead of "merit."[27] Hayek's view of liberty was that people need to be free to discover new information not only by thinking and writing but also by doing; this inevitably will produce winners and losers, leading to natural inequality.

As previously mentioned, Hayek argued that government should also supply services that the market does not. He viewed it as appropriate for government to provide services such as standard weights and measures, the monetary system, sanitation, health services, parks, museums, education, sports facilities, and roads. While he considered these products to be "public goods" that the private market has traditionally not produced efficiently, he thought that many of these services can best be provided at the local level. He also believed that government should not have a monopoly over the provision of these services. A government monopoly, according to Hayek, will deprive society of the entrepreneurial learning process. He also supported government regulation in the form of building and safety codes, although he was concerned that they would also produce inefficiencies such as increased costs and reduction in experimentation.

Hayek had the opinion that historical attempts to design a governmental structure around the principles that he thought were best have failed. While he thought that democracy is the optimal structure for governmental decision-making, with one of its main benefits being discussion and opinion formation, he believed that unconstrained democracy and majority rule lead to tyranny. He proposed that the legislatures' authorities be limited by a strong constitution. He envisions a constitution that divides the overall responsibilities of the two legislative bodies along specific functions. He proposed that the constitution include a fundamental clause directing the elected government to only coerce its citizens according to rules designed to protect their private sphere, and these rules would be established by what he terms the "legislative branch." Certain basic human rights, including the traditional rights of freedom, would be recognized, but the rules would not include social or economic rights. The legislative branch would be elected by popular vote, and its members would have long tenures to reduce the influence of shifting majority opinion. The other parliamentary body would also be elected by popular vote, have shorter tenures, and be responsible for all government operations except the ability to make coercive laws. A supreme court would have the responsibility to ensure that neither of the two legislative bodies overstepped their authorities under the constitution. He also favored some type of federalism, where many of the decisions unrelated to coercive laws could be made at the local level.

Hayek believed his proposed constitution would enhance the discovery of just laws and significantly reduce the influence of special-interest groups. He thought that it would lead to domestic governments acting in a way to retain existing citizens and attract new ones. As will be seen, the end state of multiple responsive governments envisioned by Hayek has some aspects that are similar to the key components of the solution to irreconcilable politics.

Hayek had fundamental philosophical differences of opinion with the views expressed by Rawls, Sen, and Harsanyi. These differences were not due to his personal situation nor to traditional concepts of selfishness. He simply did not seem to think that the other three authors' approaches to equality are in society's best interest. He thought that, for a society to be successful, people need the freedom to innovate and discover new things. He conceded that this could take time, but viewed this as a necessary cost. A key question is: How should we organize governmental decision-making when people have different levels of *patience* and *faith* about individuals' abilities to address societal problems without direct government intervention?

ROBERT NOZICK

Robert Nozick (1938–2002) provided his view of the moral justification for government and its "legitimate" functions in his book *Anarchy, State, and Utopia*.[28] He thought that a just government is coincident with the "minimal state," in which the government's scope is limited to defending its citizens from third-party threats and from each other. Nozick was an American scholar and Harvard University professor some considered to be one of America's foremost philosophers.[29]

He began his analysis of government in *Anarchy, State, and Utopia* by viewing everyone as being in John Locke's "state of nature," where government does not exist and individuals defend their own rights. He imagined that people in this anarchistic situation would have disagreements and be faced with numerous conflicts that would lead to various voluntary agreements not to fight. He did not think these self-enforced agreements would be continuously honored, making mutual agreements an unstable paradigm. In his view, this would lead to the development of a competitive market for protection. However, given the nature of coercion and violence, he argued that only one of the protective organizations in each geographical region will become the main or primary one.

Nozick considered a "state" as an entity that defends everyone in its territory. As presented, he did not view the "private" protection entity in each location as a state, since a private company will not normally defend people who do not pay for its services. To address the issues of public goods and "free riders" and to show how the private protection entity morphs into the minimal state, he developed the concept that people have morally sacrosanct rights represented by "side constraints" that prohibit certain actions by other people. From his perspective, nothing can justify a person or the state infringing upon these rights. This gives rise to the need for reparation for those whose rights have been violated.

He argued that the main protection entity, in its geographic sphere, would enforce its preferred justice procedures both on its customers as well as on any customer/noncustomer conflict. This does not violate the rights of the organization's customers, since they voluntarily choose it to represent them; however, for noncustomers, their rights may be violated if they prefer a different justice procedure. For Nozick, reparation requires that the protection entity must pay those whose rights have been violated. He suggested that the least expensive option is to have the entity provide defense services to nonmembers for any member/nonmember conflict. He also thought that free riders would not be an issue because almost everyone would want to be a customer of the main protection entity, since nonmember/nonmember conflict is not covered.

Nozick did not think that any government can justifiably have a broader scope than the minimal state. To attempt to prove this, he developed a philosophy for moral ownership of resources. He contrasted this, with its resultant complex distribution of resources, to other principles of justice, such as those preferred by Rawls and those characterized as communist. He argued that his philosophy would produce moral ownership of resources that is historical and not based on simple ex ante patterns. It may include ownership rights that have patterns but could also include those that do not. He also argued that other theories of ownership such as distributive justice require constant intrusion into people's lives, since citizens' voluntary acts of exchange and gifts would result in undesigned ownership.

Nozick was not in favor of taxation for purposes of redistribution, comparing it to "forced labor."[30] He viewed redistribution as also raising issues around immigration: people renouncing their citizenship as well as the definition of society. For Nozick, social cooperation does not create the need for distributive justice. He argued that a process of mutually agreed-upon exchanges would produce an appropriate set of ownership rights. Unlike Rawls, he did not have the view that the more well off should suffer the most from cooperation. He thought that Rawls was incorrect in reasoning that people behind the Rawlsian veil would agree to distributive justice. He argued that the philosophy of ownership he espoused is the fair basis of distribution, and that Rawls's maxi-min concept would result in complaints and charges of unfairness by the more advantaged. He did not believe that social cooperation is the sole source of just ownership, which led him to conclude that distributive justice is unjust. He imagined that a potentially better theory of distribution would be one in which people are rewarded for increasing societal resources.

Similarly, he argued against the concept that "society" owes a minimum standard of living to all its members. Since he viewed people as having a legitimate claim to their just ownership rights, a person in a society will only have a claim on other people's ownership rights if these holdings were inappropriately acquired. Unlike Rawls, he viewed people's natural abilities, work ethics, income, and inherited wealth to be justly obtained, unless you could go back in time and determine that people's forbearers had acquired resources through theft. To Nozick, people's random advantages, even those that are historically biased, need not be unjustly obtained.

He argued that any state broader than the minimal state raises the real possibility of having coercive government serve the needs of special interests, established firms, and the wealthy. At the end of *Anarchy, State, and Utopia*, he argues that people are all different, which led him to the conclusion that utopia would consist of many versions of utopia and what he deems as a "meta-utopia."[31] Interestingly, he considered the minimal state to be equivalent to this system of utopias, even though many people, like Rawls, Sen, and Harsanyi, would rather have a more extensive government. Nozick was also concerned about the role of the central government in this type of utopian environment. As we will see, addressing these last two issues is key to determining a just government for people with irreconcilable politics.

3

— ★ —

AMALGAMATING DISPARATE WORLDVIEWS

The authors discussed in the previous chapter are widely considered to be intelligent, educated, well read, and informed. The analysis underlying most of their arguments is logical and internally consistent. Their conclusions are powerful and persuasive, at least to some people. Even though some were born in different countries, they all had similar backgrounds and each made their home either in the United States or the United Kingdom for a large part of their life. None of their arguments appear to be the product of self-interest. They are all known as honest, rational, logical, and professional communicators. Yet they all disagreed. How could this possibly occur, and how do we resolve the inherent conflict between their various views?

Each of them qualifies as Smithian judges or *impartial sympathetic spectators* as described by Adam Smith, Amartya Sen, and John Harsanyi. Their writings show them each to be objective, and yet there is little consensus among them as to appropriate governmental policy. In fact, Sen and Harsanyi both utilize the impartial sympathetic spectator as a procedural device to determine just rules for a particular society, and yet they come to different policy conclusions. We know that the five theorists had read each other's works. Many of them even engaged in public criticism of each other's positions. From their extensive writings, it is fairly evident that no amount of public discussion or debate could have led them to reach a consensus view. They fundamentally disagreed. This clearly leads to the question of how to use the impartial sympathetic spectator procedure to make just societal decisions when the impartial sympathetic spectators disagree. Their debate obviously provides information for other people, but how should society make its decisions based on this information?

Each of them would also qualify as reasonable, at least from their point of view. However, of the five, only Rawls thought that the maximin principle is the guiding rule for a just society. Again, there was no consensus as to what reasonable behind-the-veil people would determine as the just guiding principles for society. John Harsanyi used a procedure equivalent to Rawls's original position and yet came to radically different governmental policy recommendations. This leads to the critical question of how to use the original position and the veil of ignorance procedure when there is disagreement between people in the original position. As stated in the prior chapter, Rawls modified the veil to hide people's philosophical views in an attempt to eliminate people's biases. But did he accomplish his goal? Are there remaining biases not filtered out by his procedure that lead people to choose justice as fairness?

Sen seems to disagree with Rawls's original view that there is a universal moral standard for all societies, irrespective of how the standard is determined. He argues that Rawls acknowledges this with his law of peoples, which does not presume that justice as fairness is appropriate for every society. He also suggests that Rawls's use of primary goods is not appropriate for everyone. Harsanyi thought that people behind the veil would determine a form of utilitarianism and not justice as fairness. He argued that Rawls made logical errors in his reasoning. Did Rawls's methodological procedures and assumptions effectively derive and confirm his own political philosophy instead of deriving an independent view? Did Harsanyi just produce his own ideology? If the original position and veil procedure are indeed scientific, logical, and unbiased processes, why doesn't everyone derive the same conclusions?

Each of them seems to be searching for a "just" resolution of the conflicts that they see in society. Even though people have different conceptions of what is fair, each of the theorists appears to agree with John Stuart Mill's maxims of justice: "The first appeals to the acknowledged injustice of singling out an individual, and making him a sacrifice, without his consent, for other people's benefit. The second relies on the acknowledged justice of self-defence, and the admitted injustice of forcing one person to conform to another's notions of what constitutes his good. The Owenite[32] invokes the admitted principle, that it is unjust to punish any one for what he cannot help."[33] While they may share these tenets, they also seem to interpret them differently. This caused the authors to differentially apply them to the world in which they lived.

Rawls perceived existing society to be unfair and permanently biased toward inequality. He viewed certain groups of people to be constantly disadvantaged relative to other groups, through no fault of their own. Applying Mill's justice maxims leads naturally to governmental policies aimed at reducing this injustice through focusing on the groups of people who are most disadvantaged. Sen focuses on people's differential abilities to use society's scarce resources and persuasively argues that a single-minded focus on growth of societal income or liberty will unjustly leave a tremendous group of deserving people behind. Harsanyi, similar to Mill, espoused a social decision-making rule that advocates policies that improve average adjusted societal utility, where utilities that involve antisocial tendencies have been excluded. Given his assumptions about people's underlying preferences and the similarity among people, his advocated policies are like Rawls's in directionality. However, he disagreed with his focus on societal differences. Robert Nozick argued that people's liberty is inviolate.

Sen and Hayek probably both agree on the ultimate desirable observable results from their preferred economic policies. For example, they seem to view high incomes, low poverty, wide opportunities, and low unemployment as desirable. However, they radically disagree over means to achieve these results as well as the acceptable level of relative suffering that people should endure along the desired path(s) of societal improvement. Their disagreements are unlikely due to their underlying ethics or morals. Hayek viewed governmental policies that attempt to correct for people's relative differences as potentially successful in the short run, but having medium- and long-term negative effects. He focused on the unintended consequences of government action. Sen forcefully argues that no one can predict all the consequences of their actions, but that does not mean that people cannot or should not make decisions. He appears to view societal decisions similarly. Even though the future is uncertain and the outcomes from societal actions are not completely predictable, society should make the most informed decisions possible. In effect, he seems to believe that we should have social policies that are well reasoned, even though we do not know all the effects of these policies.[34]

Hayek would have likely countered that this will probably cause the government to merely pick winners and losers. As stated earlier, he viewed society as continually adjusting to new information—some good, like inventions, and some bad, such as disasters. This new information will cause or allow people to adjust their plans. These adjustments are part of a process that Joseph Schumpeter famously named "creative destruction," which can lead to great wealth for a few and severe inequality, at least in the short run.[35] Hayek argued that policies that allow the process to be as effective as possible are the only way to accomplish societal progress. He viewed governmental policies that slow down this adjustment process as ultimately destroying the process, since those policies interfere with the necessary signals and incentives. Sen seems to have a difficult time accepting Hayek's fatalistic view that almost any governmental policy will destroy the process of societal advancement. Policies that allow people to have self-dignity and the opportunity for a fulfilling life appear in Sen's view, to be compatible with societal improvement.

Their differences do not arise from logical errors that they acknowledge. Instead, their policy conclusions likely arise from their differing concepts and assumptions of how people interact and how the world actually works. To provide a label for each of the authors' differing views on the various factors that determine their governmental policy approaches, we will utilize Immanuel Kant's concept of *weltanschauung* or "worldview."[36] "Worldview" has been used by many people over the past two hundred years and can have a variety of connotations. For the purposes of this book, worldview is a concept that captures the idea that everyone has a model of how the world works, of the numerous relationships, causes, and effects that logically lead them to various decisions, and of preferences over means to achieve various ends they favor. This is true in both their decision-making for their own personal ends and their desired social policies.

The objective world is too complicated for all its causes and effects to be correctly ascertained by every person and probably by any person. People develop simplified models of the world to guide them in their decision-making. These models are their representations of reality and differ from person to person. Many researchers, including Douglass North, have viewed people as using different models to evaluate the world and make decisions; North classified each person's model as their "ideology."[37]

Even though knowledge increases over time, differences in worldviews are likely to persist given the complexities of the interrelated environment in which we live. There are universal truths. Knowledge does exist. However, incorporating knowledge and new information into our worldview is a complex exercise and a highly personal endeavor.

Although everyone has a worldview that guides their decision-making, these worldviews will differ among people and not be consistent. Most people's worldviews will also contain some internal inconsistencies. To some extent, everyone makes logical errors in their reasoning. However, in the following chapters, we will abstract from reality and assume that people are more like the authors discussed in the previous chapter. Each of their individual worldviews are assumed to be internally consistent. Since people cannot determine the actual structure and "true" model of the objective world, they cannot convince others that their worldview is the correct one. Nor can they be absolutely certain that even their worldview is correct.

One conclusion of this chapter is that each of these authors had irreconcilable worldviews. No amount of discussion, information sharing, logical reasoning, reflection, criticism, or debate reconciled their views or would reconcile the models of those who share their worldviews. Nonetheless, each of the authors shared some under-standings. For example, each seemed to accept the necessity of gov-ernment and recognized the need for at least the "minimal state." There are obviously other people whose worldviews lead them to different conclusions.

The worldview concept is like Rawls's use of "comprehensive doc-trines" that he assumed everyone possesses.[38] For him, they served as guides to just actions and were the basis for people's opinions on appropriate social policies. However, they could all be different, since they were not produced by a just process. For example, he thought of utilitarianism as merely a philosophical view because, unlike his the-ory of justice as fairness, it was not derived from what he perceived to be a just procedure. Harsanyi would, of course, have disagreed.

The concept of worldview expands the definition of Rawls's compre-hensive doctrines by incorporating people's underlying views on how society should be structured. Worldview includes people's preferences for both the structure of government and specific policies of govern-ment not derived from a process that people with differing worldviews think represent the *truth*. As such, Rawls's worldview included his philosophical views as well as his views on justice as fairness and law of peoples. Neither of these were the "truth," from the other authors' perspectives. While Rawls thought that justice as fairness is derived from a "just" process that eliminates all biases, the other authors would disagree. Each of the authors firmly believed that his preferred policies were the optimal policies, given the world as he observed it. However, the authors were not able to systematically and logically convince peo-ple with differing worldviews that their views captured reality.

WHAT IS SOCIETY?

Each of these differing worldviews leads the individuals who hold them to varying conclusions about people's societal rights, individual rights, and social responsibilities. Interestingly and somewhat sur-prisingly, none of the authors has a "just" theory of societal formation. Sen emphasizes the differences in cultures, and Hayek distinguished between societies and governmental jurisdictions. Yet, neither of them seems to attempt to justify why governmental policies should be applicable to a specific individual. Rawls seems to argue that people in the original position will determine unique governmental policies applicable to everyone. However, he also argued that there should not be a universal government and developed a separate law of peoples applicable to other societies. Sen logically advocates governmental policies that encompass individuals outside the control of a specific government. His policies seem to be developed around the plurality of people and the impact their relative differences can have on each other. Nonetheless, he does not seem to develop a theory of justice that explains why some people should be under one governmental jurisdiction versus another one. Why should a person who lives in northern North Dakota "justly" be subject to different governmental policies than a person living in southern Manitoba?

From a theory of justice perspective, why isn't everyone part of the same society? Why isn't one übergovernment in the best interests of all people and the best societal construct? Is there some justifiable basis for limiting a specific government to a specific group of people or area of control, other than historical precedent? If the rationale is solely historical, then what is the moral basis for a person's social responsibilities to other people who happen to be citizens of the same government? Why should a person who lives in Del Rio in the United States have different responsibilities to other people in the United States than he does to people living a mile from him in Ciudad Acuña, Mexico? While these are obviously difficult questions, an approach to answering them will be developed in the next few chapters.

VOTING AS A POTENTIAL SOLUTION TO DIFFERING WORLDVIEWS

Each of the five authors likely thought his worldview was the most accurate assessment of how society actually works and the best blueprint for just governmental policies. However, none of their proposed procedures, including public discussion, the unbiased sympathetic

observer, or the veil of ignorance, produces unanimous societal decisions. A priori, it is not clear how to reconcile the different opinions and
conclusions held by these philosophers and economists. It is apparent
that through all the discourse and debate between them, their followers, and their critics, no one changed their fundamental point of view
or opinion. Although they are all logical and persuasive, they were not
able to convince the others to change their mind. They all wrote extensively. But logic, in the end, was not able to carry the day from any of
their individual perspectives. Is this a weakness in their arguments or
a weakness in their exposition? More likely it is a fundamental difference in their individual worldviews that discussion and debate cannot
ameliorate.

Given the diversity of opinion, how can we resolve their differing
views and determine the rules for a just society? More importantly,
if people have irreconcilable worldviews, what governmental actions
should they execute? How do we determine who is right and who is
wrong? Is one person right and everyone else wrong? Are they all
wrong? Does an average or median view have any relevance? If so, is it
better to differentially weight their views to determine a group consensus? If we decide to use differential weights, how do we determine the
weights for each author?

Voting is used by many governments and organizations to make
decisions. Let's examine voting to see if it can be used to try to reconcile their differing views. Properly constructed, majority voting
between the five will determine a unique answer. As will be discussed
in chapter 16, majority voting is an effective decision rule, although
in only rare circumstances will it coincide with the "group's will." This
is not one of those circumstances. Furthermore, as will be discussed,
in even rarer circumstances will voting produce the truth as determined by some omniscient power. While we do not and cannot know
how each of these authors would vote, we can be sure that their preferred rules for a just government are the ones they espoused in their
writings. Each of them prefers governmental rules and laws that are
the most consistent with his worldview. As previously stated, none of
these authors completely agreed with each other's views. Therefore, a
plurality voting procedure among them or among people who share

their views will not produce a winner. Each of them will presumptively just vote for their own view.

There are other voting procedures that will produce a winning view, including the Borda Count methodology, named after the eighteenth-century French mathematician Jean-Charles de Borda. To use this procedure, we hypothetically ask the authors, or people who share the authors' views, to rank each of the five philosophical views in order of their preference for the worldview that they would like to be the guide for governmental decision-making. A view that is ranked first receives four points (N-1), the second preferred view by each author receives three points (N-2), and so on. A winner is determined by adding the points for each view across the five voting authors. The winning author/worldview is the one that receives the most points. For example, we can imagine the preferences of those who share the views of each author for the worldviews expressed by each of the authors to be the following:

	N-1 (four points)	N-2 (three points)	N-3 (two points)	N-4 (one point)	N-5 (zero points)
RAWLS	*Rawls*	*Sen*	*Harsanyi*	*Hayek*	*Nozick*
SEN	*Sen*	*Rawls*	*Harsanyi*	*Hayek*	*Nozick*
HARSANYI	*Harsanyi*	*Sen*	*Rawls*	*Hayek*	*Nozick*
HAYEK	*Hayek*	*Nozick*	*Sen*	*Harsanyi*	*Rawls*
NOZICK	*Nozick*	*Hayek*	*Harsanyi*	*Sen*	*Rawls*

Given these imagined preferences, Nozick's views receive seven points and are the last-place preferences. The Borda Count winner is Sen's worldview, since it achieved thirteen points. Sen's worldview also wins in a bilateral vote against the other authors' views. Even though Sen's worldview is the imagined winner, is there any reason to believe that everyone would agree that his philosophical views should be the ones to govern the society in which they live? The minority voters, those who have views similar to Hayek and Nozick, would still disagree with any majority view, and it is not obvious why it is just to force the minority to accept the majority view. Voting, any type of voting, given the diversity of worldviews of the authors, is not a procedure for determining the just rules for society that the minority or potentially even the majority will accept, unless they believe there is some reason to compromise. But why should they compromise? And if they do decide to compromise, how will they compromise? As we will discuss, the answers to these questions are a key to addressing irreconcilable politics.

The other concern is that each of the voters is incentivized to vote strategically and not reveal his or her true preferences. This will be discussed in more depth in chapter 16. For example, those sharing Harsanyi's views and ranking Sen's worldview second help make Sen's worldview the winning one. It may be to their advantage to rank Sen's worldview last, even though they prefer Sen's worldview over all other worldviews except Harsanyi's. This would lower Sen's worldview point score and allow Harsanyi's worldview to be the winner. However, those who share the other authors' opinions would logically reason that Harsanyi's followers may not vote "honestly," causing the other authors' followers to also vote strategically. The incentive that diverse people have to vote strategically is an additional reason why they would not willingly accept voting by itself as a method of determining which worldview governs the laws for society.

The Condorcet Jury theorem is employed by some people to "justify" the use of majority voting. The eighteenth-century philosopher and mathematician Marquis de Condorcet was the first to establish that voting by individuals who are right more often than they are wrong on an issue, and whose beliefs are independent from each other will, as a group, have a higher chance of making the right decision than any of them would individually. As the number of voters increases, the probability that the majority will vote for the correct decision also increases. However, Condorcet's theory also requires that the voters have a common goal and vote honestly. For example, let's assume that either Hayek's or Sen's worldview is the one true worldview (presuming that such a thing is conceptually possible), that one of their worldviews is equivalent to the worldview of an all-knowing power. Let's also assume that we randomly pick a large number of additional economists and philosophers who, by majority, vote for Sen. Does this mean that Sen's views are right and Hayek's are wrong? If the procedure satisfies Condorcet's criteria, we can say that Sen's political philosophy is more likely to be right than Hayek's. However, the hypothetical voting procedure does not satisfy all of Condorcet's criteria and as such will not reveal the right or most accurate political philosophy.

First, it is not clear why either Sen's or Hayek's views are the "accurate" ones given the wide variety of potential political philosophies. Narrowing the choices to only two possibilities can lead to biases and voter incentive for strategic manipulation of their votes. Second, given the wide disparity between Hayek and Sen, it is not clear that their goals for society are the same given the differences in their worldviews. While both are intelligent, honest, and passionate for their fellow citizens, each of their worldviews leads to significantly different policy conclusions, at least in the short and medium term. Some voters, even if they believe that Hayek's worldview is correct, may weigh the short-term pain required by his policies more than the long-term gain. Therefore, voters choosing between Hayek and Sen may not be voting for the same objectives for society. If individuals are voting for different objectives and each is not completely accurate in deciding who is right, then it is not clear that majority voting is an improvement over the average voter, much less a method of discovering the truth.

The most critical assumption of Condorcet's theory is that people are right more than they are wrong in deciding for whom or what to vote. If everyone is more right than wrong on identifying the one true political philosophy, and everyone is identical and independently distributed, then their voting will follow the cumulative binomial distribution and majority voting will be a more accurate predictor of the true political philosophy than the political philosophy of any person picked at random. As the number of voters is increased, accuracy will increase and approach certainty with a sufficiently large voting population. The fundamental problem is that there is no reason to believe that all or any of the voters are more right than they are wrong on the issue of political philosophy. They may all be experts, but their opinions and voting need not produce the truth, since the accuracy of their individual worldviews is extremely unlikely to be the true model of how the world actually works.

Finally, there is the issue of the voter's independence. As traditionally formulated, each of the voters is assumed to independently decide for whom to vote. However, in the real world and in the example, voters are anything but independent. While they may vote honestly, the randomly picked sample of economists and philosophers, as experts, likely have all been influenced by Sen's and Hayek's writings. They have shared information and some voters have communicated with each other. They may all be sympathetic and seeking the truth, but they are not independent. Each of them, potentially, has a different worldview, which leads each of them to have different beliefs as to whether Sen or Hayek (or someone or no one) is right. As they gather more information, their beliefs may be adjusted to form a new modified belief. They may have strongly held views that cannot be modified by new information, causing their new beliefs to be the same as their prior beliefs. Given their educational backgrounds and communication with each other, it is likely that some or all voters' beliefs (both prior and posterior, as noted below) are correlated. Given the diversity of potential views, these correlations can be both positive and negative. That is, some agree with each other and some disagree.

If voters' views are not highly correlated, then they do not have to make independent decisions for the Condorcet theorem to hold.[39] However, the other assumptions behind the Condorcet Jury theorem still need to be true. At least half of the voters must have an accurate view of the world. That is, they must have worldviews that are consistent with the one true political philosophy. Since the voters are unlikely to think this is the case, they will not rely on the use of Condorcet's theory to determine the political philosophy that will govern their society.

CAN THE BAYESIAN PARADIGM RESOLVE DIFFERING WORLDVIEWS?

Another approach to group decision-making under uncertainty is the Bayesian paradigm. Harsanyi was at the forefront of the application of Leonard Savage's Bayesian decision theory to group decision-making.[40] Harsanyi assumed that everyone makes personal decisions that maximize their subjective expected utility. In the Bayesian tradition, everyone updates their subjective probabilities or beliefs (prior probabilities) as new information arrives to form updated beliefs (posterior probabilities) as if they followed Bayes's rule (conditional probabilities). In what has become known as the Harsanyi doctrine, Harsanyi argued that people must have the same beliefs.[41] He proposed that everyone has common priors and that the only difference between people's posterior beliefs is due to private information that they possess.

Can private information explain the difference among the authors? Above, the argument was made that the authors have different worldviews, not different information. Some psychologists, including Stephan Lewandowsky, et al., argue that people do not use all the information available to them in modifying their views.[42] This can allow misinformation to persist and cause people to reject other people's worldviews, since they might think that other people may have relied on misinformation in forming their worldviews. The Nobel Prize–winning economist Robert Aumann argues that individuals who act like Bayesians with common beliefs are incapable of "agreeing to disagree."[43] He shows that Bayesians with common priors also have common posterior beliefs, irrespective of their differences in information, if their posterior probabilities are common knowledge. The economists and professors John Geanakoplos and Herakles Polemarchakis continue Aumann's analysis to show that if individuals who act as if they are Bayesians and have common priors communicate their posterior beliefs, their belief systems will converge.[44] Therefore, in the medium or long run, Bayesian individuals who disagree must have either different beliefs or different internal models of how the world works.

Given different beliefs among a group, can that group make decisions based on the preferences and beliefs of its members, as if the group itself was Bayesian? If so, we can determine the optimal actions of the group by determining the acts that maximize the group's subjective expected value. Of course, this will also require knowing the preferences of each of the members of the group. Unfortunately, even if people's preferences are known, economists Aanund Hylland and Richard Zeckhauser show that there does not exist a group decision methodology that can be characterized as Bayesian when: (i) members of a group have different priors, (ii) one of the members is not a dictator, and (iii) actions by the group are weakly Pareto optimal (if all members prefer the same alternative, then the group's choice is that alternative).[45] Their assumptions hold for the group composed of the five authors. They all have separate beliefs. All of them are unlikely to accept one of them having the final decision. If they do agree on some issue, they will want that to be the group decision. Therefore, the authors' preferences and beliefs cannot be combined in a Bayesian fashion.

PROCEDURE TO DISCOVER THE SOLUTION TO IRRECONCILABLE WORLDVIEWS

Others have tried different approaches or procedures. For example, the political scientist Brian Barry proposed a procedure he called "justice as impartiality" to reach a consensus.[46] He argued that Rawls's process of reaching a consensus was not successful. To remedy this, he adopted a proposal by the philosopher T. M. Scanlon to modify the Rawls procedure and require a unanimous agreement among people who are knowledgeable and "reasonable."[47] From his perspective, the individuals in this situation will optimize their own best interests and pursue their view of what just rules for society should be. People who share the worldviews of the five authors satisfy Barry's conditions. The authors were all knowledgeable. They each had differing worldviews that they seemed to believe were correct. None of them had any superior bargaining clout. While it is not clear what exactly "reasonable" means, each of the authors would have likely accepted a consensus proposal that each of them found reasonable. Reasonable typically refers to a person's judgment and sense of fairness, both of which are affected by one's worldview. This, of course, implies that reasonable people will often disagree.

In this situation, reasonable people, who have the diversity of opinions of the five authors, will disagree. Barry's approach will probably not produce a consensus among the five authors, at least as interpreted by Barry, since he effectively states that Nozick's views are unreasonable and will not be considered. Under this condition, it is not very likely that people who view themselves as libertarians will accept the decisions reached by those with opposing views. Among the others, at a minimum, it is likely that people whose views are similar to Hayek's will also have a difficult time reaching a unanimous decision that does not involve compromise by people who share Barry's worldviews. Therefore, Barry's approach to resolving the dilemma of finding agreement between people who share the five authors' worldviews cannot be used.

His approach fails because he appears to try to force an agreement by limiting outcomes. Nonetheless, an agreement is potentially achievable if they all unanimously concur that some type of agreement is necessary to accomplish something that they all value. They can compromise and reach agreement if each of them benefits in some fashion. This requires an analysis of the costs of not reaching an agreement from each of their perspectives. The answer lies in identifying some common element in each of their worldviews that is enhanced by people of differing worldviews coming to a common agreement. We need to find a reason for some or all of them to agree to compromise. The existence of government is an obvious answer. Each author seems to believe that an entity that has the coercive powers normally associated with government is a necessity to furthering cooperation between people.

Nonetheless, they disagree on the most appropriate governmental policies and laws. To reach a common agreement and achieve the gains from government, they must negotiate governmental policies and laws that are acceptable to each of them. They must reach some type of compromise. This leads to the proposed procedure of bargaining—bargaining between people with different worldviews who desire to be citizens of a self-determined government. This is the same procedure Rawls proposed. However, as discussed in the prior chapter, he rejected it because he thought it was intractable. He is wrong. The bargaining analysis is somewhat complicated, but it is solvable.[48] It will lead to answers to the following questions:

- Will a group of diverse individuals who have the views isomorphic to those of these five authors voluntarily join a coercive entity that has the attributes normally associated with government?

- If so, what will be the resultant characteristics of that entity?
- How will that entity make collective decisions?
- What will be the structure of its decision-making apparatus?
- How will the group of people resolve their conflicts?
- How will they divide the gains from government?

In part six, the argument will be made that the attributes of a government determined by this approach are "just." Not only just, but it identifies the only just structure of government for a broadly liberal and diverse group of people. Even though no government has been formed by a group of independent people negotiating its formation, the following analysis will reveal insights into the nature of government that have been endlessly debated over the past few hundred years.

PART TWO

ANARCHY AND INTERPERSONAL CONFLICTS

4

★

INDIVIDUALS AND BARGAINING

BARGAINING PROCEDURE

The proposed bargaining procedure envisages people with the world-views of the five authors, in a stable original position, negotiating over the terms in which it is in their best interest to voluntarily join a newly formed entity that has the coercive powers that are normally associated with government. "Voluntary" implies that people have a choice. People will only voluntarily agree to join a coercive entity if the benefits outweigh the costs, from their perspective. To voluntarily join, they must accept a coercive entity's decision structure and expected policies. Unfortunately, bargaining between people with imperfect worldviews cannot determine social policies that comport to the truth. It can only determine the terms on which people with different worldviews will agree to participate in a collaborative effort for mutual benefit. However, as stated in chapter 3, the proposed bargaining procedure can reveal certain truths about government and can be used to design a just structure of government.

While no one has utilized the procedure of people voluntarily deciding to join a coercive entity to determine the just structure of government, the concept of using bargaining in a social contract setting has been tried extensively. As previously discussed, John Rawls considered bargaining and rejected it for the veil of ignorance. He viewed bargaining as the correct way for justice to be determined by people in the original position. However, since he could not see a way to model the complicated nature of the bargaining process, he proposed the veil of ignorance shortcut. But the veil of ignorance, as constructed by Rawls, is an ineffective procedure because it is not applicable to people with differing worldviews. As will be discussed in chapter 20, however, the veil of ignorance can be modified to accommodate differing worldviews. Correctly enhanced, it will produce the same results as the proposed bargaining procedure.

Interestingly, John Harsanyi, as one of the original contributors to game theory and bargaining, does not use bargaining in his utilitarian political theory.[49] Even though he acknowledged the fact that people have different views, his formal analysis presumes that everyone has the same social preferences. Bargaining is not necessary, since people have the same worldview and will automatically agree.

Important contributions to the analysis of individual decision-making in the context of government formation were made by the economists James Buchanan and Gordon Tullock, together and individually. They examined the constitutional contract between people in a specific society. In their path-breaking book, *The Calculus of Consent*, they presume that "uncertainty" about the future will cause everyone to come to a unanimous agreement on a constitution.[50] While it is possible that everyone in a defined group will unanimously agree to a constitutional contract, as we will see in part three, the unanimity criteria is not compatible with unlimited diversity. For some, the gains from government will be insufficient to overcome the compromises that they must make to be a member of a government with certain people. Buchanan and Tullock put the cart before the horse; the constitutional process helps determine the group that will form a common government. Every person will not voluntarily agree to be a member of the same government; a universal constitution is not achievable when people have differing worldviews. Furthermore, as will be seen, people can compromise on a constitution and about their rights and obligations even when the world is certain.

Two of the better-known bargaining analyses relating to political philosophy are due to David Gauthier and Kenneth Binmore. Gauthier, in *Morals by Agreement*, uses bargaining to provide a justification for the existence of morals.[51] Morals, in his theory, are a product of rational choice. He seems to use bargaining between logical, rational people, whose identities are obscured, to derive the moral structure of society. He proposes that people would recognize the benefits of cooperation, and that this requires that they would not take advantage of other people. He seems to think all rational people would agree to these conditions and would unanimously agree to divide the gains from cooperation according to a type of "relative concession." This is the same bargaining solution that two economists, Ehud Kalai and Meir Smorodinsky, had also discussed.[52] The results from the proposed bargaining procedure in the next few chapters are quite different than Gauthier's. For one, he appears to have implicitly assumed that people have the same worldviews. People with differing worldviews will not a priori agree on the optimal methods of engendering cooperation. Furthermore, they will not all agree to divide the gains from cooperation according to his principle of relative concession. Gauthier's bargaining analysis in *Morals by Agreement* has been criticized by some, including by Binmore.[53]

Binmore, a world-renowned economist and game theorist and one of the experts on the bargaining procedure that will be utilized in this book, uses bargaining to determine his version of a social contract.[54] He argues that life can be envisioned as a game in which cooperation between people is valuable but involves significant conflicts. He imagines and proposes that people in the real world simultaneously participate in a "game of morals" that leads them to a specific allocation of societal resources. The game of morals allows people who are at a disadvantage in the real world to go to Rawls's original position and bargain with the person who has a better position in life, assuming that both are behind the veil of ignorance. For Binmore, bargaining in the game of morals leads to a unique agreement to equally divide societal resources. He seems to believe that people who are better off in life are willing to participate in the game of morals and reach a more egalitarian division of resources, because over time and through repeated dealings with the disadvantaged members of society, they realize it is in their best interests. For Binmore, people's views of morals and fairness have developed in the medium run to help coordinate people's cooperative activities. The relatively well off seem altruistic in their willingness to abide by the game of morals, but for Binmore they are being reciprocal altruists, since he appears to view it in their best interest to voluntarily share their good fortune. In a two-person situation, Binmore's agreed allocation is equivalent to Rawls's maxi-min solution.

While many people will agree with Binmore's analysis, many other people will likely reject his definition of the social contract. They logically can do so because they have different worldviews than both Binmore and at least one of his bargainers. In his modeling of bargaining, people's worldviews seemed to have converged to some type of equilibrium opinion.[55] As argued in the previous chapter, the worldviews of people who share the five authors' ideologies will not completely converge. They appear to fundamentally disagree on the implications of various social policies. Even though many of their moral views may converge, their overall worldviews will not. They seem to perceive the world differently from each other and prefer different political policies.

For example, people who share the views of Robert Nozick or Friedrich Hayek are unlikely to agree that they are morally compelled to renegotiate their existing situation to make someone better off. While Hayek was in favor of a social safety net, he thought that a person's willingness to renegotiate their situation is dependent on fact and circumstance. Under no circumstances will people who share his views agree to a contract, enforced by others, that continually requires everyone to equalize their positions, irrespective of how or why those positions existed. Similarly, people whose opinions match Nozick's worldview will likely disagree with Binmore given Nozick's views on path dependence and history as an important element in any voluntary decision.

Binmore focuses on the division of the gains from cooperation but does not seem to address other disagreements that people will have in a cooperative venture. Bargaining among people with differing worldviews will not lead to a unitary worldview or moral outlook. However, it can lead to a compromise on the rules governing coercive collective action and an agreement on how to divide the resultant gains. As will be discussed in forthcoming chapters, the gains from cooperation can be large but are typically not so large that everyone will voluntarily compromise with everyone else. There is a limit to the amount of compromise that people will make to achieve a cooperative equilibrium.

Another significant distinction between the proposed bargaining procedure and Binmore's analysis is that the latter's determination of a just social compact seems to be based solely on a two-person world, which he uses to make judgments and recommendations about the complicated multi-person, multi-arrangement, multi-worldview environment that characterizes the world in which we live. Even though he recognizes the potential limitations of his analysis, he cannot find a multi-person solution that satisfies him.[56] The proposed procedure used in this book incorporates bargaining between more than two people. It allows coalition formation. Importantly, it does all of this for people with differing worldviews.

One of the notable points that Binmore discusses is that bargaining, by itself, does not have moral content. It is independent of one's ethics and value judgments. His bargaining analysis and the proposed bargaining procedure are effectively just logic applied to various assumptions. A bargaining solution states that people *will* make a certain decision instead of *should* make that decision. Therefore, most of the forthcoming analysis is objective instead of normative. It is concerned with people with differing worldviews recognizing the value of cooperation, compromising on their differing views, and bargaining for the gains from their collective action. The assumptions that are made can have moral content, especially the choice of the original position. As such, various original positions will be considered to reduce the moral dependence of the status-quo point. In chapter 20, the justice of using the proposed bargaining procedure to determine the structure of government will be discussed.

INDIVIDUAL DECISION-MAKING

Bargaining is a complex social arrangement. The results of actual bargaining are dependent on all the variables that affect the interaction among individuals. In making the analysis tractable, the bargaining environment will be greatly simplified from any real-world situation. Strong assumptions will be made concerning individual rationality and logical consistency. Actual bargaining between hypothetical people in the original position cannot occur. Nonetheless, simplified versions of people can be modeled, and their interactions can be analyzed in a controlled environment. This procedure may not be applicable to every situation. However, it is particularly suitable for determining the structure of a coercive entity by people with differing worldviews.

The bargaining process that will be used involves individual choice and decision-making. The approach is not traditional "methodological individualism," since people are assumed to be more complex than what is normally meant by this term.[57] Each person who is modeled may care about their own personal interests or about their fully considered worldview. The worldview they hold can be inconsistent with their own personal welfare. Alternatively, they can be self-interested. In either case, each person is assumed to want their way and will bargain from this perspective. Amartya Sen also employs an individual perspective in his analysis. In fact, his capability approach is based on each person's differing characteristics. He also does not seem to think that his analysis can be criticized as being "methodologically individualist."[58]

Although simplified models of people will be used, the analysis, for the most part, assumes that people's worldviews can overcome their own self-interest. As will be discussed in more detail later in the book, morals and behavioral norms are critical aspects of social cooperation. They are also important aspects of people's worldviews.

The four other theorists' views are also consistent with this approach. Analysis of individual behavior is at the core of the political and economic theories embraced by Nozick and Hayek. Harsanyi's social choice analysis incorporates individual decision-making. Similarly, people who share Rawls's views will agree with the use of individual choice, since he advocates the use of individual bargaining. Nonetheless, as Nozick points out, it is not clear that Rawls holds people responsible for all their choices given his views of the injustice caused by nature.

As mentioned earlier, chapter 20 is concerned with justness. To anticipate this, the proposed bargaining procedure will incorporate many assumptions that are not necessarily accurate representations of reality. For example, the imagined people under consideration will be free from many of the constraints that potentially allow citizens to be coerced within real-world society. While the analysis will incorporate diversity in individual worldviews and endowments, such as wealth, abilities, and desires, everyone will be assumed to be completely logical as it relates to bargaining. Each of the bargainers is assumed to be infallible in reasoning through the bargaining analysis. The "correct" or "true" bargaining decisions are much easier to ascertain than the ramifications of social actions. As such, everyone is assumed to agree on the optimal bargaining judgments and will not make logical bargaining mistakes. Stated differently, people are assumed to have common bargaining models and are thus incapable of agreeing to disagree on the optimal bargaining outcomes.

In addition, each person's bargaining decisions are assumed to be driven by the goal of having societal rules that are completely consistent with their individual worldview. As will be discussed in a subsequent chapter, people's worldviews can change. However, once bargaining begins, each person's worldview is assumed not to change until an equilibrium or bargaining solution has been obtained.

While each bargainer may have varying amounts of kindness and concern for their fellow man, they are assumed to make bargaining decisions solely based on their considered best interests and worldview. However, their worldview can cause them to prefer societal decisions that are not in their personal best interests. For example, wealthy people can prefer a tax system in which tax rates are severely graduated.[59]

5

———★———

THE WIDE, WIDE WORLD OF PHILOSOPHICAL ANARCHY

COOPERATION IN ANARCHY

The primary topic of this chapter is the theoretical pre-governmental stage. From a historical perspective, there may never have been such a situation, or, if it occurred, it happened early in the development of human society. Government is now ubiquitous. However, to determine the structure of government, a significant pre-governmental stage is contemplated. In this environment, people interact without the ability to use government. What if the institution of government had never been discovered? In the counterfactual world of people without government, what can happen?

Whatever the answer to these questions, the bargaining process over the structure of the coercive entity (government) is assumed to commence when people have reached some type of equilibrium in the absence of government. As will be discussed, people are assumed to have to commit resources to defend themselves in the absence of government. Throughout the book, we will use the term "equilibrium." It implies that the individuals under consideration have reached a point in their interaction where they have fully (or sometimes partially) adjusted to their circumstances. There are many different types or concepts of equilibrium. In this instance, equilibrium is the Nash equilibrium.[60] The Nash equilibrium is a concept where the individuals whose potential actions are being examined, knowing the decisions of others, have no reason to change their decisions. Stated differently, given the decisions or actions of others, people cannot gain more by modifying their actions. Once a Nash equilibrium is reached, it is changed only when conditions in the environment change. For the purposes of this chapter, the significant change will be the opportunity to form a government. These pre-governmental equilibria become the initial conditions or the original position of the bargainers. As mentioned earlier, the original position can be viewed as a theoretical way station before a government is formed. It may have been preceded by an initial point characterized by isolated people who do not cooperate with each other.

An important component of the model is the identification of natural forces that incent the simplified people in the pre-governmental environment to voluntarily band together and overcome their differing worldviews. For John Rawls, the incentive is social cooperation that he implicitly assumes can only occur in the presence of a coercive entity like government. Robert Nozick, on the other hand, assumes that some type of social cooperation is occurring before the dominant protective agency arrangement becomes the minimal state. This distinction is an important element of the bargaining process because it affects the gains from association that are the motivation to bargain over the formation of a government. Obviously, if there are significant gains from social cooperation, and all these gains can be attributed to the existence of government, then the incentive to form government is heightened and the division of these gains is critical. If, on the other hand, people can cooperate and benefit outside of government, then the gains from joining are less robust and the rationale to form the government is less compelling.

Many of the highlighted philosophers from chapter 2 implicitly or explicitly made different assumptions as to the pre-governmental starting points. Rawls and Nozick both start with John Locke's state of nature but deviate from there.[61] Rawls further restricts the state of nature by assuming people (at least the bargainers) are reasonable and that they are behind the veil of ignorance and in the original position.[62]

John Harsanyi and Friedrich Hayek appear to have a view that the pre-governmental state of nature is characterized by the constant threat of warfare. However, Hayek did not agree with Rawls that all social cooperation is due to the existence of government.

People are influenced by their environment. Therefore, it is probable that the bargainer's decisions can be affected by the specifics of the original position. The hypothetical anarchical situation that is assumed for each of the bargainers may have a significant effect on the bargainer's preferred governmental rules and laws. At one end of the anarchical spectrum is the environment envisioned by Thomas Hobbes, author of the influential book *Leviathan*, in which he focused on the role of government in protecting people from their base instincts.[63] Hobbes conceived of the commonwealth as being unanimously authorized by its subjects to defend them. He viewed each person as having irrevocably submitted their formerly independent will to the judgment of the commonwealth, irrespective of how the commonwealth makes decisions. While most people today will not completely agree with his views on government, his stated opinions on the state of nature are still held widely. He states that

> *during the time men live without a common Power . . . they are in that condition which is called Warre; and such a warre, as is of every man, against every other man . . . So the nature of War, consisteth not in actuall fighting; but in the known disposition thereto, during all the time there is no assurance to the contrary.*[64]

Moreover:

> *In such condition there is no place for Industry; because the fruit thereof is uncertain . . . no Culture of the Earth; no Navigation . . . no commodious Building . . . no Arts; no Letters; no Society; and which is worst of all continuall feare, and danger of violent death; And the life of man, solitary, poore, nasty, brutish and short.*[65]

Paraphrasing a statement from nineteenth-century German philosopher Carl von Clausewitz, Hobbes's view of anarchy is a place of violence where everyone is attempting to compel everyone else to fulfill his or her will.[66]

In the original position, which is like Hobbes's conception of the state of nature, the bargainers have little to lose by joining some type of government. The pre-governmental environment in which they find themselves is hellish, dangerous, and chaotic. While they have choice, government, almost any type of government, is preferable to the anarchy described by Hobbes. Not only is everyone incentivized to join or form some type of government, but also the relative gains from joining are significant.

The economists Winston Bush and Lawrence Mayer developed a model of "selfish" people and examined these individuals' incentives to escape Hobbesian anarchy and mutually agree to "ordered anarchy," where no one arms or engages in predation.[67] In this type of ordered anarchy, everyone will be better off. The savings from not arming and increasing productive activity are large and can be shared with everyone. There is a significant incentive for selfish people in this situation to cooperate and not arm themselves. But will they? Bush and Mayer determine that people may cooperate, but they view the agreements as unstable without some type of outside enforcement. Instability is due to the incentive that selfish people have to break their agreements, which lead them to choose not to enter into ordered anarchy in the first place.

The incentive faced by people to not cooperate in anarchy is analogous to many other social situations. The apparent paradox in which people will be better off cooperating, but do not cooperate because each person can gain from breaking the agreement, is called the "prisoner's dilemma." In the traditional description, two individuals have committed a crime together and have been arrested. The district attorney tells them that they can communicate with each other and that they will be offered a unique deal. If they stay quiet and do not confess, they will go free. Alternatively, if both confess, they will serve a medium amount of time in jail. If only one confesses, that one will be set free while the other will be incarcerated. Even though both will be better off by not confessing, a logical defendant will agree with the other one not to confess and then confess. Both will know that this is logically the correct answer and potentially not agree in the first place. Irrespective of whether an initial agreement is reached, the selfish logical person will decide to confess.

The prisoner's dilemma is present in every contractual situation where one person completes their side of the bargain and the other person has no incentive to complete their side of the actual or implicit contract. Each person logically reflects that the other has a reason to avoid honoring their agreement, which causes both parties to refrain from the cooperative arrangement. For example, if a person pays up front for an airline ticket, the airline has a strong incentive not to honor the ticket. Similarly, if the airline allows a person to fly before paying, the traveler has an equally strong incentive not to pay for the flight they took. As will be discussed later in the chapter, people can escape aspects of the prisoner's dilemma. But the incentives to break agreements are always present.

The political economist Michael Taylor seems to view Hobbes's conception of the state of nature as being more dire than is captured in the traditional prisoner's dilemma.[68] For him, Hobbes views people as being both egotists and negative altruists. Not only do they care about themselves, but they want to increase their position relative to others. This leads to very little cooperation without government enforcement. From this perspective, the state of nature and the original position are situations where self-enforcing agreements are not possible, violence is prevalent, and productive activity is virtually impossible.

ECONOMICS OF CONFLICT

Even though people have an incentive to deceive others, not honor contracts, and fight over resources as identified by the prisoner's dilemma, there are reasons that they may engage in some productive activity in the absence of third-party enforcement. There are significant benefits to everyone from the division of labor, and people have comparative advantages in cooperative production. These forces lead to a relative reduction in people's desire to arm and fight. Furthermore, the success of predation and violence is not certain. An area of research that formally addresses these factors is the economics of conflict.[69]

People, modeled as rational and selfish, are assumed to be able to engage in a variety of actions, including (i) productive activities such as producing goods and services that they value, (ii) violently taking property that initially was held by someone else, and (iii) investing in activities to reduce/prevent being attacked. The economist Stergios Skaperdas formally models a situation involving two people in a winner-take-all conflict that can invest their initial resources in productive activities, like producing additional food, and in conflict resources (weapons).[70] He assumes that the probability of winning the conflict or war is based on the relative investment in weapons. There are a variety of possible actions that each of the individuals can take. One possibility is that each person only invests in arms. This can be viewed as the Hobbesian equilibrium position where there is no productive activity.

Skaperdas shows that some amount of cooperation is possible in anarchy. This type of equilibrium is dependent on both the effectiveness of war and each person's trade-offs between investing in arms and production. People may find it optimal to arm and fight over resources. However, they may also invest some of their scarce resources in productive activities even though the other party may forcibly take those resources from them. People are incentivized to balance the relative probability of winning the fight over productive resources to the return from using resources in cooperation with others.

Michelle Garfinkel and Skaperdas, in their review of the conflict literature, develop a model where the equilibrium level of arms increases with the effectiveness of war and the amount of resources being fought over.[71] They also show that two people of equal ability, but with different levels of initial resources (if the differences are not too extreme), will both invest the same amount in unproductive arms. The economist Jack Hirshleifer labels this the "paradox of power," where the poorer person is incentivized to spend relatively more on arms, since his or her marginal return from latent violence is relatively higher than the marginal return from productive activities.[72] Everything else being the same, the less well-endowed side will have a higher special-ization in fighting. The weaker side is incentivized to try harder.[73]

Actual fighting, violence, or what the economist and Nobel laure-ate Thomas Schelling terms "brute force" is not the only outcome in anarchy.[74] Given the destructiveness and unpredictability of war, each person has an incentive to refrain from participating in violence and invest only in productive resources. In Garfinkel's and Skaperdas's dis-cussion of bargaining, every person determines the expected amount they would receive if they fought, as well as their total resources if they do not fight. They bargain over the gains from not fighting. They show that people can agree not to fight, but they will still invest in unproduc-tive arms as a method of enforcing their agreement. When bargaining is possible and war is sufficiently destructive, both sides will arm the same as if there were no bargain not to fight. They still invest in unpro-ductive arms to maintain the agreed equilibrium allocation.

A second possible strategic alternative for individuals in multi-per-son anarchy is to band together to increase the probability of winning any fight. While there are benefits from joining a group against a com-mon enemy, there are also significant impediments to a successful coalition. Selfish individuals have personal incentives that are not com-pletely compatible with the group's overall best interest. In a group, people have an incentive to "free ride." The economist Mancur Olson argues that overall group interests and the interests of individuals in the group are not the same.[75] He also argues that this conflict will cause people in anarchy not to act in concert without a "special device."[76]

In the context of anarchy, Garfinkel and Skaperdas model this incentive to free ride.[77] They show that within a group, each person has an incentive to reduce their effort in defending the group as the group size increases, which decreases both the incentive for others to contribute and the likelihood that people will form stable groups in anarchy. This cooperation paradox is comparable to the prisoner's dilemma discussed above. A priori, one would think that in anarchy, in the absence of government, people could find solutions to the con-flicts embedded in the free rider problem and the prisoner dilemma. It seems reasonable that people would naturally find ways to align people's individual interests to a group's interests. Stated differently, why doesn't Olson's "special device" exist?

The above discussion is based on the assumption that people are strangers. If people have repeated dealings with each other, they can develop mechanisms to limit or at least reduce predation and increase cooperation. This phenomenon can be examined in simplified settings through infinitely repeated prisoner-dilemma situations. If the prisoner's dilemma is repeated, people must consider the impact that their betrayal will have on their opponent's behavior in the future. In many situations, this continual interaction will lead each person to consider the negative effect their behavior has on the other person. Each person knows that they must be in the same situation, with the same person, the next time the game is played. They will factor this into their calculations for their optimal decision. There is a cost to breaking agreements, since the other person or persons will not cooperate with this type of person in the future. This is traditionally known as the "folk theorem."

Taylor analyzes anarchy as an infinitely repeated prisoner's dilemma and concludes that sanctions and threats can lead to voluntary cooperation. Contingent strategies are a necessary but not a sufficient condition for cooperation to be self-enforcing. The question about cheating and violence is whether people can earn enough value from cheating to overcome the penalties imposed on them by others. He views reciprocity and people's relative time preference as being crucial to engender cooperation. If people care a lot about the future, they will have a lower incentive to cheat. He argues that individuals will naturally find conditional strategies that will be effective. They will honor commitments if the downside from cheating is sufficiently onerous. Over time, people will discover methods that are effective at engendering cooperation, and others, who are similarly situated, will copy these methods. However, Taylor also seems to believe that as the size of the group or population increases cooperation will be more difficult, since conditional strategies require monitoring the behavior of others.

Applying the folk theorem to people in the initial position leads to increases in cooperation but typically does not lead to the elimination of all arming. Anarchy is potentially harsher than the situation faced by the prisoners in the prisoner's dilemma. Betrayal in anarchy can end the game for the other individuals. If warfare is sufficiently effective, people could still find it optimal to violate a contract and attack their opponent, even if they were not certain of victory. To prevent war, people must be able to commit to honor the peace.[78] In anarchy, people must arm themselves, since contingent force is the only believable threat. Therefore, even in repeated situations, anarchy will still lead to socially wasteful investment.

The one-shot prisoner's dilemma is near one end of the conflict spectrum. Other interpersonal conflicts are illustrated in simple situations, which are named the chicken game, the stag hunt, and the Nash demand game. The chicken game involves a conflict in which people need to act to accomplish a common goal. They gain from cooperating but gain more if the other person acts alone. For example, consider a situation where two people are concerned about a flood that would damage both of their properties. If they work together, they can prevent the damage by jointly filling sandbags. However, each selfish person would prefer that the other person perform all the work. If neither act, then their homes will potentially be flooded. Cooperation is not assured, but it is likely that one of them will act. In a repeated setting, the probability of cooperation is obviously higher but still not assured.

The stag hunt is named after a conflict described by the eighteenth-century political philosopher Jean-Jacques Rousseau.[79] He imagines a situation where a group of hunters are at their post hunting a deer when one of them spots a hare. Each hunter's share of a deer is more valuable than that of the hare, but capturing a deer is not assured. Rousseau reasons that the person who spots the hare will selfishly desert his post and capture the hare, causing the rest of the hunters to go hungry. The stag hunt model focuses on the importance of trust. How can one person rely on another when that person must rely on them? Without some assurance that the second person can be trusted, is it rational for the first person to put their well-being in the other's hands? In a setting of complete strangers who will never see each other again, they will either cooperate or not cooperate. Since a share of the stag is more valuable to each person than a hare, there are two pure Nash equilibria determined by people's beliefs about the potential actions of other individuals. It is not clear without more specifications which alternative is better for a selfish rational individual. Rational people do not always have to abandon their post as Rousseau imagines they will.

To resolve this indeterminacy, Harsanyi created the concept of a "risk dominated" equilibrium that he proposed as the unique equilibrium strategy.[80] In the case of the stag hunt, the risk-dominating strategy is for each of the hunters to capture the hare. Even though everyone will be better off if they all hunt the deer, their lack of trust could lead them all to choose the less risky and their less preferred alternative of hunting hare. However, in a repeated setting, cooperation is more assured, since a defecting hunter will probably not be counted on in a future hunt.

The final common conflict is known as the Nash demand game. This situation is at the core of the proposed bargaining procedure and is discussed in more detail in part three. Two individuals need to agree on how to divide a divisible good. If they do, they both receive their consensual share. If they cannot agree, then neither will receive any of the good. The conflict between the two individuals is complete. In this situation, there are an unlimited number of Nash equilibria. If one person's strategy is to propose three-quarters, then a response of one-quarter by the other person results in an improved situation for both people. Is there a unique strategy that rational people will follow? While it may seem that an even division of the good is the obvious answer, prior to Nash, no one could determine a rational way to determine a unique answer. If both agree to some division of the good, they are both better off. Why should an even split or any other division be the only logical answer? As we will discuss in the next chapter, under a few basic assumptions, a unique equilibrium division can be determined.

The naturally developed methods of increasing cooperation and reducing violence in pre-government environments as envisioned by Taylor are often labeled as "norms." Some norms, like driving on the left and language, evolve over time as people try to efficiently coordinate their activities. These types of coordination issues are not examples of prisoners' dilemmas, since an individual's noncompliance with the norm is internalized. He or she directly suffers from not being able to coordinate with other people. Driving on the right when everyone else is driving on the left puts the noncomplier at risk (as well as everyone else). Similarly, if a person is speaking a language that no one else can understand, his or her personal productivity suffers. On the other hand, emotions like guilt, shame, and altruism can address conflicts. They may not eliminate cheating and violence, but they may decrease the severity of the problem. For example, the historical custom of dueling has been widely identified as a norm that naturally developed to reduce the incidence of wider violence in a society.[81] People complied with the norm even though it potentially had severe personal consequences. They were incentivized to follow the "rules" for a variety of reasons, including the fear of ostracism and the loss of face. Economist Peter Leeson argues that there can exist a wide variety of common understandings among a group of people that provides tools to reduce antisocial behavior.[82]

ANARCHY BY EXAMPLE

It will prove instructive to review two historical examples of how people have coped with anarchical situations. In the situations, the focus is on people's abilities to be productive in the absence of governmental-enforced property rights and contracts. This will lead to insights on people's differing views on governmental policies as well as into the potential existence of production and exchange in the original position.

First, we will review the economic situation faced by a gang, in the modern United States, selling illegal drugs, which was examined by Steven Levitt and Sudhir Alladi Venkatesh.[83] The product the gang is selling, the arrangements it has with its customers and suppliers, the relationships it has with its competitors, and the arrangements it has within the gang are not protected by any government. In fact, from a gang member's perspective, the government is a hostile party and increases the overall costs of anarchy. Even though none of the gang's activity is protected by a governmental entity, it is successful at buying and distributing its product. The gang is productive, providing a product that customers want, and earning income for the members of the gang. The members find ways to be cooperative in a hostile and anarchical environment.

The gang members face many dangers. The data shows that the probabilities of being killed, injured, arrested, or imprisoned are quite high. Intergang rivalry and fighting is expensive in terms of potential death and in nonproductive activity. The gang spends a quarter of its collective time in battles, defending its borders, and in drive-by shootings. The gang uses its scarce resources to supplement its force by hiring mercenaries on a retainer basis. It also increases the wages of foot soldiers during active fighting. Furthermore, during active fighting, drug prices fall 20 to 30 percent, leading to significant reductions in revenues.

Even though its environment is hellish and the odds of survival seem unacceptable to most people, the gang and others like it are "voluntary" organizations. While the gang members' alternatives are poor, they have some choices. They can participate in an illegal enterprise where payments and working conditions are not protected by the government. Or they can join civil society by accepting legal employment or social welfare. Levitt and Venkatesh describe the gang as being organized like a modern franchised company where the local gang leaders pay a fee to the centralized leadership. In return for the fee they receive (i) protection, (ii) alliances with other gangs so that they can travel beyond their gang's border, (iii) access to drugs, and (iv) potential promotion into the group of central leaders.

The gang even offers some member benefits. For example, it provides money to the families of gang members who are killed. These arrangements are not legally protected. Families and gang members cannot sue the gang for failure to honor its implicit contracts. While each gang member is in an environment resembling Hobbes's description of the state of nature, it is not completely person against person. People cooperate inside the gang and some gangs cooperate with rival gangs. This allows both the gang and its members to have some level of productivity. Mutual need incentivizes the gang members to overcome various aspects of the prisoner's dilemma. Senior members of the gang benefit from more junior gang members and franchisees. Franchisees and foot soldiers benefit from the organizational structure of the gang.

That said, conflicts exist. For example, as described by Levitt and Venkatesh, junior gang members are incentivized to become involved in unnecessary and unsanctioned violence against other gangs as a method of establishing personal credibility.[84]

The gang environment is violent and unpredictable. Nonetheless, it is not as harsh as the anarchy envisioned by Hobbes. A strict interpretation of Hobbes's state of nature will lead to the impossibility of any kind of cooperative efforts in the original position. Gang members can overcome the limitations implied by the one-shot prisoner's dilemma. While they may have been egotists and negative altruists relative to some other gangs, they cooperate with each other and with other gangs.

The second example of an anarchical environment is complex equity trading in seventeenth-century Amsterdam examined by the economist Edward Stringham.[85] The ownership rights of physical shares were well established. There were explicit laws, upheld by the courts and enforced by the government, protecting buyers and sellers of shares. However, because of concerns that the government had about speculation, they prohibited complex transactions such as short selling; and laws concerning the enforceability of contracts on equity options were not clear.[86]

Governmental policy was conducive to people buying and selling equity. However, policy prohibited short selling, which is a situation where people sell stock they do not own on the hope that the stock will fall so they could profit by buying it later at a lower price. According to Stringham, the government did not seem to actively enforce the ban on short sales. Nonetheless, given their prohibition by the government, short sale agreements were not legally enforceable. This did not prevent a vibrant and complex equity market from developing. Brokers actively engaged in both short selling and options. Participants in these transactions recognized that the courts may not enforce their contracts. People were willing to buy shares in the Dutch East India Company and other companies from those who did not own the shares, fully aware that if the stock went up, the seller might claim that the contract was invalid. This one-way option, to avoid paying if the buyer is on the losing end of a financial contract, is the essence of the previously discussed prisoner's dilemma.

The market developed for the trading of short sales without the benefit of legally enforceable contracts because people thought that their counterparty would probably abide by the contract. The question is what gave market participants sufficient confidence that the sale contract would be honored? Economists have extensively analyzed market-based solutions to what Oliver Williamson, the recipient of the 2009 Nobel Prize in economics, has called "opportunism," which is essentially dishonesty in an exchange.[87] The exact nature of the various potential solutions is dependent on fact and circumstance. However, these methods to reduce cheating rely on identifying those people who have a lower probability of engaging in opportunism. Dishonest short sellers will drive out honest short sellers and a nongovernment-enforced market cannot develop.[88] But the illegal short-selling market did exist. Market participants used a low-cost solution: they used people's unique names. If sellers possessed unique names, then those who defrauded buyers could be blacklisted and potentially lose all future business.

However, it is not clear that a unique name plus the loss of future business is sufficient to guarantee contractual performance. Uniquely identified people can still profit from defrauding others; their profits are just curtailed. A viable solution to incentivize honest behavior from potentially selfish individuals requires that the loss of future business be more important than the gains from short-term cheating.[89]

Participants in the short-selling market, over time, likely invested in their reputations, which gave other people confidence to trade with them.[90] As a reputation for honest dealings increased, the transaction size and the amount of business likely rose. If the seller reneged on a contract, they may have gained on that contract but would have likely lost the value of all future income from securities trading. Opportunistic sellers could naturally be incentivized from cheating buyers, without the need of a third-party enforcer, by buyers discriminating between sellers based on their reputation. Each seller's name and reputation had value because potential counterparties could use it as an information variable; it signaled that the seller had a reduced incentive to cheat.[91]

Another potential concern for buyers of short-sold securities would likely have been that the seller could go bankrupt and, as part of the bankruptcy process, it might be determined that the short-sale contracts were not unenforceable. Given investment in their reputation and the value of future business, sellers had an incentive to manage their affairs to avoid declaring bankruptcy. However, the world was uncertain and bankruptcy was a possibility. Bankruptcy potentially produced a windfall gain for the estate of the short seller, since it may not have to settle unprofitable short sales. A natural solution that market participants may have used for this concern could have been to require a sufficient capital base from their counterparties. Liquid capital, that is not firm specific, would not affect the willingness of sellers to honor unenforceable contracts. However, everything else being the same, it would reduce the probability of bankruptcy. Even though Stringham does not discuss it, brokers potentially concentrated their legally unenforceable or legally uncertain contracts with dealers who had larger amounts of capital as well as historically successful businesses.

COOPERATION WITHOUT GOVERNMENT

The preceding discussion raises the important question of how successful individuals can be in solving the issues of violence, theft, and fraud without government. How extensive can society develop in the absence of government? Some think that government is entirely unnecessary and that, given sufficient time, people will naturally develop nongovernmental institutions to solve all cooperation and coordination issues. While there are many strands of thinking along these lines, two of the better-known advocates of this position are libertarian economists Murray Rothbard[92] and David Friedman.[93] Both are in favor of "anarcho-capitalism," which is the concept that private solutions will be found for nearly all social cooperation issues, and that private firms can even provide protection services, laws, and courts. They appear to believe that individuals directly or operating through private entities can fulfill all the services normally associated with government. To them, government regulations and laws are not necessary or desirable.

Rothbard and Friedman seem convinced that the private protection agencies discussed by Nozick are possible and that these agencies can also provide laws. People will be able to choose their favorite protection entity based on price, level of service, and the laws they support and enforce. Unlike Nozick, they do not seem to think the private protection agencies will find it profitable to fight each other, nor do they think that one of the private protection agencies will become dominant. However, Rothbard and Friedman seem to disagree over the ability of the private protection agencies to defend their customers from a powerful foreign government. Rothbard believes that foreign governments will not attack because in an anarcho-capitalistic area, there will be no central authority for the foreign power to commandeer. He believes the threat of potential guerrilla warfare will be an additional deterrent. Friedman seems to disagree. He does not see a natural deterrent that can prevent a determined foreign power from attacking and winning against a successful and relatively well-off area that is only defended by small private defense organizations. Friedman is obviously not alone in this view; most people will not accept Rothbard's belief that government is not necessary, including those whose ideologies are like those of the five authors. However, they will significantly disagree over most other aspects of government.

6

— ★ —

CONFLICTS WITHIN ORGANIZATIONS

Would anyone agree to a contract if a breach, even an inadvertent breach, could allow someone else to use violence to force them to pay or observe a previously agreed-upon penalty? Would someone voluntarily join an entity when failure to follow the entity's rules could result in fines, incarceration, or even death? Interestingly, many people voluntarily expose themselves to some of these risks in their everyday activities. The primary motivation for a person to submit himself to collective power is a common goal that is important from that person's perspective. If that goal is achievable or enhanced by certain restrictions on their behavior, the person can agree to those restrictions, if the goal is sufficiently valuable. This chapter will examine situations, some hypothetical and some historical, where people accept these risks in exchange for the benefits offered by joining an entity or from entering into a contract. Achieving these potential gains requires pre-commitment agreements and postagreement potential sanctions. Each entity, either directly or indirectly, can violently enforce its rules against its members or joiners.

A PRIVATE PARTNERSHIP

Consider a situation where ten like-minded individuals form Brown Eagle Investments, a private equity firm that invests in start-up companies. They know each other well, having either worked together at other firms or collaborated on complicated transactions together. Each person brings a wealth of experience and relationships to the common enterprise. While each person is different, all have determined that each of them is equally important to the success of the new firm. They respect each other and look forward to the mutual camaraderie of building a business together. They each think that there is a significant market opportunity to start and build a successful investment firm. While they realize that the venture is risky and will take years of effort to be successful, they believe the expected benefits make the commitment worthwhile.

As they contemplate their start-up, they agree to a written operating agreement, which documents how Brown Eagle will make decisions, to reduce misunderstandings in the future. They hold the view that the stability of the firm will require each of them to agree to certain terms, including restrictive covenants regarding future employment, restrictions on their ability to extract their capital and profits from the firm, and also on the use or disclosure of the intellectual property of the firm. Their consensus opinion is that building the company will be complex and difficult, and they want each member to commit in advance to both stay with the firm and to leave their capital with the firm for a certain period. Even though their personal financial situations vary, out of a sense of fairness, they each decide to invest the same amount of money in the enterprise. They also decide to retain a lawyer to write the formation documents and advise them on Brown Eagle's legal and tax structure. They want a governance document that is clear, is enforceable in a court of law, and reflects their business plan.

Pamela, the lawyer, informs them that a typical structure should include a board that is responsible for the overall decision-making for the firm and an executive officer reporting to the board with delegated day-to-day decisions. She also counsels them that board decisions are usually determined through various types of voting processes. After discussing the issue, the partners unanimously agree that Tom, the partner most respected by the group, will be the CEO, and that each of them will be on the board. However, they are uncertain as to what their other rights and obligations should be. They are also not clear what type of voting structure they should use. As any good lawyer could advise, Pamela suggests that they consider various hypothetical scenarios to help identify the pros and cons of different options.

She asks them to consider a situation in which the firm, after operating for a few years, receives a merger proposal from Platinum Stream LLC, a larger organization, that is worth a significant premium to each of the original members of the firm. There are, however, some drawbacks to the bid. It is not in cash, but instead is an exchange of their shares of their company for shares in a new entity. In addition, the proposal states that an outside CEO will be put in place and that the merger requires the firm to enforce each partner's restrictive covenants. These restrict their ability to (i) work in a competing business for a period of one year if they resign and (ii) withdraw their capital for five years. She tells them that they agreed to the employment restrictions because they did not want one of the original members to leave and immediately start competing with his or her former colleagues. They adopted the restriction on the removal of capital because the firm makes investments that take time to liquidate or sell.

Continuing with the scenario, Pamela asks them to imagine that they have agreed that certain corporate decisions including mergers or sales will be made by majority voting. After significant discussion, they reject the merger proposal by a vote of six to four. The six people reject it for different reasons, she explains. Some are concerned about enforcement of the restrictive covenants. Some by the dilution of their influence over the direction of the new firm. Others by concerns over the value of the overall transaction, including the value of their continued investment in the firm. The four directors who vote for the merger are, from their perspective, obviously worse off by the rejection than they would have been if the merger had been approved. They are worse off because Brown Eagle is *common* to each of the investors even though its shares are owned privately by each of them. The firm exists as a unique entity and has value independent of its members. The firm is an example of a "collective" or "common enterprise." It makes decisions that are potentially different than the decisions desired by each of its members. Even though it is common to each of the members, it has an independent existence through its decision-making process.

Pamela continues by suggesting that Platinum Stream modifies its offer by including some up-front cash to the partners and releasing everyone except the CEO from their employment restrictions. In this revised scenario, two members change their minds and vote for the merger. A majority of the board now supports the merger, and it is approved. The four members who voted against the merger and were originally in the majority are now worse off and are *forced* by the governing documents of the firm to sell their shares and be bound by the merger terms. Even though the four members may have the same concerns they had before about their personal situation, the direction of the firm, and the value of their investment in the firm, the majority forces them into accepting the merger. In this scenario, majority rule has made them worse off than they would have been if the firm had either governing documents that fully specified every decision for each potential situation or voting that required unanimity from its members. Majority voting allows the firm to make decisions, but it does not necessarily lead to the *right* decisions or to one that is *fair* from everyone's perspective.

Pamela tells each of the potential partners that unfortunately they are not always going to agree on the appropriate decisions for the enterprise. Not only that, but their personal situations are likely to change in the future so that a decision they prefer today may be different than one they prefer tomorrow. She states that a detailed initial governance document for the company will eliminate the voting inefficiencies discussed above. In fact, if it were costless to each partner (which it is not), each of them should agree in advance on each action the firm will take, in every possible scenario, for all time, prior to making the initial investment required to create the firm. These potential future actions will constitute the initial governing documents for the firm. It will specify the business's decision for every possible employment situation, financial arrangement, management structure, and personal financial situation. Unfortunately, since each of them has diverse views, it is unlikely that the prespecified decision matrix for the company will completely match the decisions that each of them will prefer the firm to make responding to each potential state of the world.

Because each of the members is expecting to receive some value from joining the firm, including camaraderie and anticipated returns on their time and capital, they may be willing to modify their preferred positions to match those of other potential members. Since the firm must choose one decision out of the set of possible decisions, every potential member's diverse view effectively imposes costs or constraints on other potential members. It is entirely possible that no individual prefers the ultimate decisions determined to be the best for the firm. The difference between the expected value of all the company's collective decisions, and the decisions an individual would have made as a sole proprietor for each state of the world, is a cost to each person who decides to join the firm. These psychic costs can be viewed as compromise costs. The presence of these costs reduces the incentive that members have to join Brown Eagle.

Each potential member will try to shape the pre-agreed decisions of the firm to maximize their expected value from joining the company— this is subject to the value they place on others joining the firm, and the value that others place on that person joining the firm. In choosing whether to join Brown Eagle, each person will consider the reduction in expected value of the firm caused by the divergence of the agreed-upon business's decisions from their own preferred decisions.

Unfortunately, the real world is too complex and unpredictable to draw up such detailed governing documents. Even though Pamela might like them to try, there are too many unpredictable variables. The limitations of language alone will make a full specification of every alternative impossible. Even a simple ten-person firm, with like-minded individuals, cannot fully specify every possible future decision in every possible future scenario.

Therefore, they must find another alternative. They need to decide on a collective-decision rule or rules. The "perfect" decision rule or voting method is one that exactly reproduces a pre-agreed-upon decision matrix. Even though each of them may disagree with the fully specified compromise document and conditional decisions, it is the optimal collective-decision mechanism. It allows each of the potential joiners to achieve their highest expected value from becoming a member or partner in the firm. A governing rule that approximates the decisions embodied in a fully specified decision matrix is the best they can achieve.

One potential governing rule is unanimous voting. Unanimity prohibits the firm from making decisions that are adverse to a member's interests. Since each member is a part of the firm until they exit, decisions by the company will impact them either indirectly through their ownership of the firm and the labor they are contributing or directly through the imposition of personal restrictive covenants. The unanimity decision rule protects each member of the firm from these potential costs. Unanimity also provides each of the members with some bargaining power.

However, the unanimous governing rule has certain costs and produces inefficiencies for the firm. A unanimity requirement will severely restrict the firm's ability to modify its choices and react to change. Unanimous agreement, after everyone has joined the firm, effectively gives every member a veto on every future decision the business faces.

Majority voting, either one vote per joiner or one vote per share of the firm, has some of the benefits of the unanimity rule because debate only occurs when there is a need for actual decisions and not for unlikely theoretical decisions. Furthermore, majority voting allows for the inclusion of information from the moment the firm is formed until the time of a decision. Majority voting has the additional benefit of being less costly than the unanimity rule, since it requires significantly less negotiation to reach an agreement. Majority voting also leads to the possibility of a dynamic firm, since a majority decision is achievable in every situation where there are an odd number of voters.

However, as was shown earlier, majority voting can impose significant costs on the minority. Without some restrictions on company decisions, each member can be significantly affected by future choices of the majority. The majority can decide to modify the initial governing document of the firm, fire existing members, add new members, require existing members to invest more capital, change the way the firm makes decisions, sell the firm, change another member's responsibilities, modify the firm's objectives, make investments, and hire employees. Even though the minority member invested the same amount of time and money into the firm, his or her desired decisions do not matter on that issue. The possibility that a member can be in the minority on an issue or series of issues important to him or her can lead a potential member to decide not to join Brown Eagle.

After examining various alternatives and conferring with Pamela, they decide to use five different governing rules.

The first rule is concerned with day-to-day decision-making. For efficiency purposes, they unanimously agree that CEO Tom will be given complete authority over these choices. They use a variety of methods to monitor Tom's actions, including periodic reporting to the board on the condition of the firm, internal and external auditors, and independent risk officers. The board is given the authority to make all decisions not delegated to the CEO. They agree that most of these decisions will be made by majority vote, including replacing Tom as CEO, if needed. In a tie, they agree to flip a coin. However, some decisions are viewed as so critical to some of the members that the status quo is better than allowing a small majority to make the decision for the partnership. For these types of choices, they require two-thirds of the members to agree ("supermajority" voting). These include decisions on selling the firm, merging with other firms, allowing individuals to withdraw their capital investment, allowing new members to join, and removing existing members.

During their debate and negotiations, they identify a separate class of issues viewed as so important that they are willing to allow a single member to unilaterally block decisions involving this set of issues. This unilateral set mainly encompasses issues that potentially have significant direct individual impacts on the members. These include a member's: (i) restrictive covenants, (ii) job responsibilities, and (iii) required addition of more capital to the firm. They are willing to give each member this right because the firm has the right subject to a supermajority vote to terminate any member. Each member is protected from some decisions of the majority (or supermajority), and the firm is protected from some of the unilateral decisions of its members. In addition, they agree that the original document can only be modified by unanimous vote.

INTRAFIRM CONFLICTS

This example of the formation of a simple partnership illustrates many of the issues that people seeking to form a government will face. The partners had to address three basic conflicts associated with diverse individuals joining an entity. These potential disagreements and conflicts occur in every collective arrangement. They are the essence of much of the debate about government.

The first type of conflict between the members only involves the firm or the collective. Each member of the firm or collective has a view on the various business decisions the firm needs to make, including the structure of its investments. There is no reason why each of the members will agree with each other's preferred decisions. Even though each of the members wants to see the firm succeed, they have differing views as to the best decisions that allow the firm to achieve its objectives. This type of conflict can be labeled "decision congestion." While each of the members can make their own individual decisions in their private lives, the firm is an entity and can only make one decision per issue. Firm decisions require some type of joint decision-making. Even if there are no other conflicts between the members, the fact that each member is not a dictator with respect to the firm's decisions produces a psychic cost for each member who joins the firm. This conflict is obviously exacerbated by the inability to have fully specified contracts. Delegation of some decisions to specific individuals coupled with some type of voting increases each individual member's costs from decision congestion.

The second type of conflict also occurs in every collective. The firm's interests do not completely align with each member's interests in every potential situation. While each member would like the firm to be successful, there are a variety of scenarios in which the individual is willing to sacrifice some company success for their own individual interest. Examples include personal working conditions, individual benefits, and dividend policies. Each member is concerned with their rights vis-à-vis the firm. Even though each of the members is an owner of the firm, each is not the sole owner, and therefore there are conflicts between each of the members through their relationship with the collective.

The third type of conflict, in its pure form, does not involve the firm or collective directly. It is concerned with each member's relative positioning. It is concerned with the allocation or distribution of power and profits. Each selfish member, everything else the same, will desire to have more influence over the firm's decisions as well as coveting a relatively higher share of the firm's profits. The firm, as an entity (or the members as a group), is indifferent to these allocations as long as each person's decisions are equally likely to result in efficient results and if profit allocations do not cause members to change their individual productivity. Selfish members will desire to have more personal influence over the firm's decisions, even if everyone agrees to the appropriate firm decision. Similarly, each of the selfish members will want to receive more of the firm's profits and have more options than other members. Each member is concerned with their rights vis-à-vis each other. In the above discussion, the members agreed to invest the same amount of money, and have equal voting rights and equal returns from their investments. This obviously is not the only possibility.

This conflict is the subject of most of the political philosophies around the *social contract* and *distributional justice*. However, the first two conflicts are just as real to the potential members. The existence and persistence of diverse worldviews is the primary driver for the first conflict and exacerbates the other two conflicts. The example also demonstrates the inefficiencies that exist in collective decision-making by diverse people.

THE COLLECTIVE ENTITY IS MORE THAN THE SUM OF ITS PARTS

In the previous discussion, recognition of potential conflicts led the members to agree to negotiate a written contract governing the firm as well as contracts documenting their individual relationships with the firm. A relevant question is why the ten prospective partners find the need to form a firm at all. Why don't they just verbally agree to coordinate their activities? Verbal agreements occur all the time. Ordering a pizza for home delivery is a verbal agreement. However, forming a firm is more complicated than ordering a pizza. It involves a myriad of issues, including the ones discussed above that need to be formally addressed. A written contract reduces the risk of misunderstanding, miscommunication, and poor memory. Therefore, it is unlikely that the members are willing to rely on verbal agreements, even if those agreements are legally enforceable.

Even if efficiency requires a written contract between the members, why do they need the government to enforce their agreement? As was discussed in the prior chapter, social pressure can be a viable enforcement mechanism to engender cooperation. However, its effectiveness is dependent on a variety of societal environmental conditions. The presence of government reduces the need for these conditions to exist and significantly weakens the incentive for them to develop. Government provides a set of tools and rules that can be utilized by other entities to increase their coordination and cooperation. The members will use social pressure but will not rely on it to enforce their mutual agreements. The use of contracts, contract law, corporate law, and rules against fraud, all enforced by an entity such as government, is more effective than just relying on social pressure to incentivize members to honor their agreements. The members in the hypothetical situation are not that concerned about unlikely risks such as theft or fraud. However, they are concerned about clear corporate governance, their responsibilities to the firm, their rights regarding the firm, and the possibility that facts and circumstances may cause members to change their views in the future. The use of government-enforced contracts significantly reduces these concerns. Failure by any of the partners or by Brown Eagle to adhere to their agreements allows the other partners or Brown Eagle to use the apparatus of government to punish noncompliance. This could result in fines and incarceration if they do not obey the court's decisions.

Again, why do they need to form an entity? Why don't they just enter mutual contracts with each other that specify all the conditions contained in the governing documents of the firm? Theoretically, the firm can be replicated by mutual contracts among its members. One reason for not having mutual contracts is that it would involve significant duplication of effort, as the terms governing the firm will need to be specified in each of the member's individual contracts and negotiated individually. Another concern would be how third parties would treat these mutual contracts. The individuals party to the mutual contracts will need bank accounts, office space, and customer agreements, which theoretically can be handled without an entity. But an entity significantly reduces the complexity. Certain types of entities may allow members to limit their liability from investment in the firm. The general partner in a partnership typically has unlimited liability. The members can potentially limit their liability by forming their firm as a limited liability company.

The economists Michael Jensen and William Meckling argued that firms are just bundles of contracts.[94] From this perspective, a firm or entity can be defined as a variety of long-term contractual arrangements among natural and nonnatural entities that have a common purpose.

While the Jensen-Meckling insight has significant explanatory power, viewing the bundled contracts as a separate entity provides a perspective that seems to be lost when just analyzing the contractual building blocks of the firm. Both a micro and macro view are critical in understanding the nature of an entity. For example, in chemistry, analyzing the atoms that make up a water molecule has explanatory power. Yet to just view the water molecule as atoms of hydrogen and oxygen ignores critical aspects of the water molecule. The firm formed by the members is distinct from their former relationships and broader than the contracts of which it is composed. It is in this sense that British economist Dennis Robertson's perspective on the firm as "islands of conscious" authority is important.[95] The potential members of the ten-person firm are connected by various moral and legal commitments before they form the firm. In coming together to form it, the members negotiate a governance document that binds each of them together more tightly than their preexisting relationships. The jointly owned and controlled firm potentially allows the members to be more productive and collaborate in a way that they could not as employees, contractors, or sole proprietors. The bundle of contracts that form the firm has higher cohesion than the individual contracts and commitments that the members have as a group not associated with the firm. There is a commonality at a firm or entity.

Robertson distinguishes a firm from the competitive market in which it is located and focuses on the "authority" aspect of the firm. This view of a firm has been extensively analyzed in the transactions-cost literature in economics. On the other hand, the economists Armen Alchian and Harold Demsetz concentrate on the *centralization* nature of the firm.[96] Actually developing a theory of the boundary of firms had to wait for the efforts of economists Oliver Hart, Sanford Grossman, and John Moore.[97] They use owner's control rights over assets, in the presence of incomplete contracts, to develop such a theory. They show that centralization does not solve the problem of incomplete contracts when there is specific investment. Under these conditions, ownership of the firm matters, even when everyone has the same worldview.

When viewing the firm as an entity, it is critical to acknowledge that there is a boundary to an organization such as a firm; inside the firm, resources are centrally coordinated according to the company's governance documents. Outside the firm are other entities and markets. The collective may have a decentralized organizational structure, but some decisions must be centrally controlled and planned. The firm may use market prices in its planning but cannot be run by a decentralized market process because of the lack of complete markets, for all the reasons previously discussed. The existence of firm-specific resources, not completely specified contracts, potential opportunistic behavior, and conflicts between the members imply that the firm will be more efficiently managed by the "visible hand" than through a market-price mechanism. The firm has a comparative advantage through its centralized control. However, as was discussed above, central decision-making has a cost to each of the members. Each member prefers that the firm's decision be their favored decision, instead of some type of joint decision. The only way for each member's preferred decision to always be their actual decision is if each of the members is identical (an impossibility) or if they do not form a firm.

Focus on the firm as an organization instead of simply as a bundle of contracts also provides insights into some of the conflicts that exist within the bundle of contractual relationships represented by the firm.

However, this perspective on the firm does not capture all the interrelationships and contractual arrangements between each of the members. The firm, as an entity, only captures those member relationships that are incorporated in its overall governing documents. The simple example of a private collective shows the wide variety of interconnections between the private interests of the individuals who agree to join a collective and the interests of the collective as a whole. The joiners are willing to voluntarily constrain themselves for the expected benefit of being part of the collective. Even though there may be a variety of scenarios in which joining the collective can be a personal disaster, the expected benefits outweigh those potential costs for the ultimate joiners. Similarly, the collective (or more correctly, the members collectively) is willing to constrain and modify its actions to entice individuals to join the group.

PIRATES AND SAILORS

Aristotle compared citizens of a society to sailors. He stated:

> *Like the sailor, the citizen is a member of a community. Now sailors have different functions . . . and while the precise definition of each individual's virtue applies exclusively to him, there is, at the same time a common definition applicable to them all. For they have all of them a common object, which is safety in navigation. Similarly, one citizen differs from one another, but the salvation of the community is the common business of them all.*[98]

As Aristotle recognized, being a sailor has many common attributes with being a member of an entity with a common mission such as a private partnership or even a government.

During the War of 1812, the United States provided commissions to private individuals and groups of private individuals to prey on British ships, both naval and merchant. Under US federal laws, these privateers were permitted to attack any British ship and retain anything of value. The American *Prince de Neufchatel* was one of the most profitable privateering ships during the war, successfully capturing numerous British ships, including nine in the British channel.[99] In October 1814, the ship was damaged in a battle with the British warship HMS *Endymion* off Nantucket. However, it was able to sail to Boston for repairs. While there, a syndicate of private individuals, including its captain, John Ordronaux, purchased the ship. As was typical, they entered a written agreement with the new crew as to the crew's rights, obligations, and compensation. Under the agreement, the owners received half of any revenues from captured ships as compensation for the initial provisioning and for providing the ship. The new captain, Nicholas Millin, and crew received the other half as their only source of compensation. From their allocation, the captain was entitled to twelve shares, the doctor six, the cook two, and ordinary seamen received one share each. The agreement also allocated an extra share to the first crewman to spot a vessel, two extra shares to the first two crewmen aboard a merchant ship, and six extra shares to the first two who boarded a warship.

Unfortunately for the owners and the crew, three British warships severely damaged and then captured the ship within eight days of exiting Boston. The only people who received compensation were the crew of one of the British ships who successfully boarded the *Prince de Neufchatel*.

The agreement between the owners and the crew of the *Prince de Neufchatel* can be viewed as forming an "entity" to accomplish the common goal of plundering British ships. The members of the crew willingly accepted the risk of death or imprisonment in a British jail for the potential benefits of being a member of the crew. They voluntarily agreed to place themselves under the command of Millin, for a minimum of four months, for the potential benefit of receiving a share of the bounty from their privateering. They also agreed to be paid differentially based on role, actions, and luck. The contract, like the organizational contract for the ten-person firm discussed earlier, was designed to address conflicts. It was also subject to the laws of the federal government. Could this same type of agreement occur in anarchy? Could sailors escape the conflicts discussed in chapter 4 and successfully organize themselves to accomplish a common goal without the aid of laws enforced by a powerful government like the United States?

The short answer is yes, which may be surprising depending on one's worldview. Pirating and privateering are almost equivalent enterprises, distinguished only by the latter being sanctioned by a formal government. A pirate is not protected by a traditional government. In fact, since they are essentially sea bandits, pirates are viewed as criminals. Nonetheless, as economist Peter Leeson suggests, pirates in the seventeenth and eighteenth centuries used various institutional arrangements, including voting and articles of agreement, to increase the efficiency of their common enterprise of plundering.[100] These arrangements were not aided by government. In some sense, these institutions essentially formed a pirate government.

Henry Morgan was one of the most successful pirates in the Americas in the seventeenth century, primarily preying on the Spanish. According to John Esquemeling, one of his crewmembers, Morgan, like other pirates, followed the rule of "no prey, no pay."[101] Prior to a voyage, Morgan and his crew would call a council to determine their objective and their obligations to each other. As part of this, they would set conditions about the division of any captured merchandise. A typical division would be an agreed share for the captain, a fixed sum for certain specialists such as the shipwright/carpenter and surgeon, and a fixed sum for people who were injured. These amounts would be subtracted from any booty, with the remainder being divided between the captain and crew. However, the captain would receive typically five or six times the regular crewman portion. Interestingly, this is a smaller portion than the captain of the privateer *Prince de Neufchatel* received. This differential likely resulted from the relatively higher power and importance of the pirating crew.

Morgan's agreements, which essentially formed a constitution among the pirates, were not unique. Bartholomew "Black Bart" Roberts, one of the most successful pirate captains in the eighteenth century, was elected by a majority of his crew, like many pirate captains. Prior to his election, one of the crew made the following statement on his behalf.

*That it was not of any great Signification who was dignify'd
with Title; for really and in Truth, all good Governments had
(like theirs) the supream Power lodged with the Community,
who might doubtless depute and revoke as suited Interest or
Humour. We are the Original of this Claim (says he) and should
a Captain be so sawcy as to exceed Prescription at any time,
why down with Him! it will be a Caution after he is dead to
his Successors, of what fatal Consequence any sort of assuming
may be. However, it is my Advice, that, while we are sober, we
pitch upon a Man of Courage, and skill'd in Navigation, one,
who by his Council and Bravery seems best able to defend this
Commonwealth.*[102]

From this pirate's perspective, they were in a common venture, a
commonwealth. To escape anarchy, they had to agree to place themselves under the power of a captain and agree to certain restrictions on
their individual freedoms. The pirate crew knew they needed to overcome their conflicts in order to be successful in their common quest.
The written and unwritten pirate articles were designed to address
three conflicts that are inherent in every entity.

One of the basic conflicts was the division of gains from everyone's common efforts. Captain Roberts proposed, and the crew unanimously accepted, an egalitarian division, much more egalitarian than
what was proposed by either the owners of the *Prince de Neufchatel*
or Harry Morgan. He proposed that he was to receive only two shares
versus an ordinary crewman's one share, which illustrates the relative power of the captain and crew. The ship they used was stolen and
effectively controlled by the pirates. The captain was popularly elected
and served at the crew's pleasure. If the division was too much in the
captain's and officers' favor from the crew's perspective, there would be
an incentive to depose the captain once any prize had been obtained.
On the other hand, the captain and officers had skills that the crew
valued, so they were willing to allow the captain and his officers to earn
slightly more than the average seaman. Roberts's articles, like Morgan's
articles before him, also entitled an injured person to a higher share of
the gains from their common effort. This right was not necessarily due

to the pirate's moral views but probably due to the incentive it gave to pirates to risk fighting and not shirking their responsibilities during an engagement. Interestingly, the owners of the privateer *Prince de Neufchatel* did not provide this same right to the crew but allowed the captain to award a higher share for an injured crewman. In addition, each of the members of the pirate crew agreed to be marooned or killed if they stole or did not turn over all captured merchandise.

Another potential conflict was the choice of mission and methods of achieving the determined objective. This was addressed in their articles of agreement. Unlike the privateers, the pirates used majority voting to determine their joint mission. Roberts's articles stated that "Every Man has a Vote in Affairs of Moment."[103] However, the elected captain had full responsibility when they were giving chase or in battle and had the accepted authority to deal harshly with any crewmember who did not obey his orders during any of these activities. The crew also elected a quartermaster who was effectively a magistrate or arbiter responsible for punishing petty crimes by the crew. Other decisions were decided by majority vote. Members of the crew who signed on to the voyage agreed to obey the captain and the quartermaster and abide by majority vote because that was the cost of potentially receiving a share of prizes. For example, one of the articles that they all agreed to was that "[t]o desert the Ship, or their Quarters in Battle, was punished with Death, or Marooning."[104] They gave up some of their freedom to make their own decisions and place themselves under the authority of the majority and particular individuals for the potential gains from pirating.

The remaining conflicts were associated with the potential differences between a single pirate's interest or small group of pirates' interests versus the interests of the pirate organization. Most of the articles were concerned with addressing these conflicts by compelling the pirates to agree to abide by the rules described in the articles and by informing the pirates of the rules. The specific rules for each pirating organization were different, since each group of pirates came to different conclusions as to the appropriate balance between individual freedoms and the behavior judged most effective for the crew to accomplish its common mission. While it is not completely clear why each of the articles was proposed and accepted, each served some purpose. For example, restrictions on gambling were designed to reduce dissension within the crew. Restrictions on candles and onboard fighting reduced the probability that the ship would be inadvertently damaged. Prohibition from desertion, commitment to the mission, and obligation to maintain weapons were aimed at eliminating shirking and improving the probability for a successful mission. It is doubtful that everyone ex ante agreed with the necessity for all of these restrictions; however, they all accepted them as a condition of being part of Roberts's pirating organization.

Did the pirate articles accomplish their task of increasing cooperation and enhancing the collective effort of attacking third parties? They seemed to be effective at reducing uncertainty and increasing the effectiveness of the organization. As Leeson argues, a critical element to their success was the division of power and authority within the pirating organization. The captain had ultimate power only under limited circumstances. When not engaged in action, the quartermaster had responsibility for maintaining order. The crew maintained its right to vote off a captain or officer they thought was not aligned with its best interests. These checks and balances tended to reduce opportunism by the captain, officers, and crew. Pirating in the Caribbean ultimately came to an end, not because of the deficiencies with the institutional structure of pirate government, but due to the superior military power and sheer size of the traditional governments. As will be discussed in the next part, the size of a government is an important element in fulfilling its role to defend its citizens.

PART THREE

THEORY OF VOLUNTARY GOVERNMENT

7

— ★ —

BARGAINING: A PRIMER

The previous three chapters laid the foundation for the analysis of how and why distinct individuals will agree to join one another in the pursuit of a common goal. In this pursuit, they sanctioned the potential use of violence against each other and third parties for violations of rules. Even the members of the civilized ten-person private equity firm agreed to the use of government coercion to enforce their mutual agreements.

People have divergent worldviews, especially concerning the issues of distributive justice and the role of government. Even though individuals can communicate, share information, and reason, they do not agree on the best method or methods to accomplish a common goal. Disagreement about means of reaching an ultimate common goal will lead to disagreement about not only methods but also subgoals that relate to the ultimate goal.

Chapter 5 discussed the difficulties that people have in cooperating "naturally." While they can reason through the overall benefits of cooperation, there are naturally occurring conflicts between people. These lead to the possibilities of latent violence, actual violence, and fraud. Over time, solutions can be developed to increase cooperation and decrease the incidence of violence and fraud. However, individuals with different worldviews will disagree on how successful these solutions can be in the absence of government. Each one of these different perspectives on what people can achieve in the theoretical pre-government phase of existence will form different "original positions" that will be considered in the next few chapters. They are the initial conditions that individuals will bargain to move away from by agreeing to form a government. In each potential original position, every individual is assumed to have reached an equilibrium. Each person begins in an environment characterized by no cooperation and potentially moves to a new position that is superior (from their perspective) to their beginning point. For a Hobbesian, the starting point and the original position are virtually identical. For example, if individuals cannot be productive without government, then each person in the original position will possess little, if anything. In the situation where people are assumed to be productive without government, the overall population is likely to be larger, and people's average material well-being will probably be relatively higher with higher variance. One question we will address is whether these differences in assumptions concerning the original position affect the nature of the government formed.

Chapter 6 analyzed the conflicts that exist between people when they pursue a complex common goal and form an entity. The three key conflicts that were discussed were: (i) disagreement about the preferred methods of achieving common goals, (ii) conflicts between the entity and each member's personal interests, and (iii) distribution of power and gains among the members. These conflicts can be addressed if the gains from forming the entity are sufficient.

This chapter begins the formal analysis of the situation where a group of people with different worldviews bargains over the formation of an entity that has the coercive powers normally associated with a government. However, expanding the insights from the last three chapters to the specific issue of determining a just structure of government will require a fairly rigorous use of bargaining theory.

RUBINSTEIN MODEL

Determining how two individuals will unanimously agree to divide the gains from government and effectively determine the initial allocation of property rights is a critical element of the analysis in the following chapters. The current standard approach to bilateral bargaining is a bargaining protocol originally designed by the economist Ingolf Stahl[105] in 1972; it was independently created, extended, and made famous by the economist Ariel Rubinstein[106] in 1982. It is called the alternating-offer protocol, since one individual proposes a percentage of the good or gain that he or she will take, and the other individual either agrees and bargaining stops, or disagrees and proposes the percentage that he or she will accept. The first person either accepts this proposal and bargaining ends, or makes a new proposal. Bargaining continues in this fashion until an agreement is reached. In Rubinstein's model, bargaining can theoretically last forever.

It has elements of many real-world bargaining situations although it assumes that the individuals are selfish and completely logical. "Logical" means that they can reason through the various alternatives, will not make analytical mistakes, and reason that the other person will "almost" certainly not make analytical mistakes. That is, each bargainer is assumed to have the same model of the world relating to bargaining strategies. "Selfish" implies that they want to maximize their share of the good or of the gains. Each person is also assumed to have complete information.

In determining their best strategy, each person will use backward induction in the way they would solve a dynamic programming problem or determine the solution to a maze. The use of backward induction leads to an equilibrium concept labeled as "subgame perfect" by Reinhard Selten in 1965, a German mathematician and Nobel-winning economist.[107] Through the use of backward induction, each individual will reason through their best option at each bargaining round or subgame, given the other person's best decision. The key to Selten's equilibrium concept is that the threats from the other person must be credible. For example, one noncredible threat would be a person claiming they will kill themselves if they do not get the allocation they want. Technically, a subgame-perfect equilibrium is a Nash equilibrium at each bargaining round or subgame.

Both people will reason through their strategy set and determine their decision at each bargaining round. Backward induction leads each person to reason through their optimal offer each period, given the optimal decision by the other person. The economists Avner Shaked and John Sutton showed that even though there are an infinite number of bargaining rounds to be considered in using Rubinstein's model, the decision tree repeats after the third round of bargaining.[108] This allows for a straightforward determination of the subgame-perfect equilibrium for each person.

Both people are assumed to (i) have a preference ordering over the alternative ways of dividing the good, (ii) want more of the good, and (iii) value the good more now than they value it in the future. This last condition is traditionally called "positive time preference." John Rawls, following Frank Ramsey, was somewhat critical of the way some people use the concept of positive time preference. Ramsey, an esteemed British mathematician, philosopher, and economist, argued that people do not necessarily value the future less than the present.[109] Many people agree with him, but people do typically value current possession more than they do future possession. This is true even when there is a price to current possession, such as storage costs or negative yields on bonds. Amartya Sen maintains that individual positive time preference could be due to people's decreased chance of being alive in the future.[110] Kenneth Binmore argues more broadly that delay is potentially costly because the future is unpredictable.[111] Even though most of the discussion in this book ignores the implications of mortality, the use of positive time preference does capture an element present in negotiations and bargaining: people's relative levels of patience.

Each person's time preference (future value of the good) is presumed to be positive and constant over time, and is assumed to capture all the characteristics of time relevant to that person. That is, each person's value of the good at the end of each bargaining period is independent of time. A higher discount rate signifies that the bargainer has less patience and desires the good relatively more now than in the future. Because both people are selfish, they are in complete conflict, since there is only a single good that they both want to fully possess.

The key to the Rubinstein model is that bargaining is costly to each of the individuals. Any delay in receiving the good negatively impacts both bargainers, although it negatively affects the person with the highest discount rate relatively more. In his protocol, bargaining can continue indefinitely if there is no agreement. In the traditional formulation, each bargaining round takes a specific amount of time, and one of the individuals is chosen to go first. Since each of the bargainers has a positive time value, the first person has a bargaining advantage.

Because we are interested in using this protocol to model bargaining between people as they contemplate exiting anarchy, the benefit of being the first to act will be an important consideration for each person. They will not agree to a procedure that they think is biased against them. Therefore, we will use a variant of the Rubinstein model that is unbiased and will label the resulting equilibrium result a "credible equilibrium." An unbiased procedure must treat each person symmetrically unless they have some distinguishing feature explicitly modeled. For example, people can differ in their preferences for time. A bargaining protocol that fully reflects this is not necessarily biased. However, there is no unbiased reason for one person to be "chosen" to be the first to propose a bargain.

There are at least two potential methods of removing the first-mover bias in the traditional two-person Rubinstein model. One, the model could explicitly incorporate the possibility that each person could be the first to act. That is, in each person's analysis of their strategy, they will consider two paths, one where they are the first person and one where they are the second. Each of these paths will produce a different subgame-perfect equilibrium result. Since there is nothing preventing either path from occurring, the nonbiased "credible equilibrium" allocation to each person will be the average of the two paths. The other method is a refinement of the Rubinstein model originally proposed by Binmore. He allowed the length of each negotiating time period to approach zero, which, in the limit, eliminates any bargaining advantage the first bargainer will otherwise possess.[112] The two different methods will produce the same equilibrium result.[113]

BARGAINING SOLUTION

Each person constrains the other from possessing the entire good. The agreement point is a credible equilibrium and, given the assumptions, it is unique. The bargainers do not actually bargain. They reason through their various options and, given the cost of delaying the bargain, they immediately consent to a specific percentage of the good. The agreed percentage incorporates their relative time discount rates. It's possible for them to split the good equally, but as will be shown below, they will only agree to an egalitarian allocation if they both have the same time preference.

In the general case, where the bargainers have different levels of patience, one of them will agree to receive a lower percentage. The rationale is straightforward. Since they both want to possess the entire good, the more patient bargainer can extract a premium from the other person, since they both realize that delay in reaching agreement will cost the more patient bargainer less than it costs the less patient party. The latter is willing to allocate the average of the weighted differences in their present values to the other person in order to reach immediate agreement.[114] Similarly, the more patient person is willing to accept the higher percentage and immediately agree, since the actual delay effectively reduces the present value of the good they are bargaining over. The person with the lower discount rate has a strategic advantage over the other individual, and since that person is assumed to be selfish, they will use this advantage to extract a higher agreed percentage of the good.

If the time between bargaining periods, in the limit, has been reduced to zero, each person will agree to a bargain in which they receive the percentage of the good equal to the other person's instantaneous discount rate divided by the sum of their instantaneous discount rates.[115] For example, if they have the same time discount rates, both will agree to an equal division. On the other hand, if one person has an instantaneous discount rate of 10 percent and the other person has an instantaneous discount rate of 20 percent, then they will immediately agree to divide the good two-thirds and one-third.[116] The person with the higher discount rate will agree to receive one-third of the gains.

Even though both people need to agree for either of them to receive any of the good, they unanimously agree that the more patient person will receive two-thirds of the good. Each agrees to an immediate uneven division of the gains because of the other person's believable threat of continual bargaining unless the division of gains accurately reflects their relative time preference. The less patient person is not able to bargain for an equal division of the gains because their relative time preference causes them to value the potential delay more than the potential delay is valued by the person with the lower discount rate. Each logical person knows this.

The bargaining protocol leads to a unique self-enforcing equilibrium allocation of the gains. Neither bargainer has any reason to modify their decision. The credible equilibrium agreed to by the parties allows each to achieve their goal of obtaining some of the good. Even though both are in complete conflict, they immediately come to an agreement on how to cooperate and divide their mutual gains. The protocol captures the real-world probability that one bargainer may have a bargaining advantage over the other individual. It allows one of the individuals to logically use their relative bargaining advantage against the other person to capture more of the gains from collective action. It does not impose any concept of fairness or justice to determine the equilibrium division of the good, except that people are assumed to be selfish and unwilling to use a biased bargaining procedure.

"Selfishness" is a strong assumption. While people can be selfish, they can also be altruistic. Nonetheless, Rubinstein's bargaining protocol sufficiently captures the bargaining dynamics of people who have different worldviews and want laws consistent with their own worldview. In the following chapters, people are presumed to be selfish, not necessarily in terms of a desire for material goods but from the perspective of attempting to obtain laws, rules, policies, and regulations they think are best.

8

— ★ —

COLLECTIVE DEFENSE

ANARCHISTIC DEFENSE

Government obviously has many different potential functions. External defense is a government function that the philosophers in chapter 2 seemed to agree is useful and necessary. This does not imply that government cannot solve other desired objectives. It also does not imply that individuals are correct if they think government's primary role is one of external defense. However, it does suggest that common ground among the five authors and people holding similar views is most likely to be found by focusing on the governmental function of external defense of its citizens or members. As such, each person examined in the following analysis is presumed to recognize that government offers certain advantages over the anarchistic environment of the original position in which they find themselves. However, government does not produce infinite gains. If people view the costs of agreeing with others on the formation of government as higher than their allocated gains, they will stay in the original position.

The first original position that will be considered is the Hobbesian environment where people need to independently defend themselves from violence and have been relatively unsuccessful at engendering cooperation. Each person is assumed to have done their best while in anarchy to achieve their objectives. Defense by individuals in the original position will be labeled as "anarchistic defense." To focus attention on certain key aspects of the formation of collective defense, and to assist with the concept of fairness that will be discussed in part four, each person is assumed to have complete information and be logical. We are interested in the decisions made by people who are somewhat more *perfect* than the actual average person. Complete information means that each person is fully aware of their own preferences as well as the preferences of everyone else. It also means that every person possesses full knowledge about all the actions and possible actions of other people. Their worldview is probably "wrong" in that it is not equivalent to the one "true" view on how human society actually works. But each person is assumed to have a "common" and accurate model of making decisions about bargaining and quantity of defense, given their otherwise "inaccurate" worldview.

In anarchy, each person will need to decide on the amount or quantity of defense to pursue as well as choose the type of defense to employ. People will decide on the type of anarchistic defense by analyzing the effectiveness of different approaches to defense through the filter of their worldview. Each person's worldview encapsulates their interpretation of the world around them. It includes their view of the engineering aspects of defense. Importantly, it also includes their moral views on using different types of defense. Some people will prefer to engage in armed conflict only when directly attacked; others may prefer to attack preemptively. Although different types of defense are likely to be more effective than others and, in anarchy, people may be incentivized to use techniques they find appalling, the analysis will be significantly simplified by ignoring these effects. To focus on people's worldviews and the difficulty or impossibility of proving that people are wrong about their opinions, each different preferred type of defense is assumed to be equally productive. This implies that there are multiple Nash equilibria (see chapter 5) in choosing the types of defense. There are many possible logical actions (apart from the quantity of defense) for people when defending themselves in anarchy.

This assumption has the added benefit of separating each person's demand (quantity) for defense from their choice of the *type* of defense. People's worldviews affect their choice of the *type* of defense to pursue;

each person has separate and independent preferences (but common models) about the amount or quantity of defense they prefer. For example, people must decide if they want to employ torture in their pursuit of defense. Some can argue that the use of torture increases the probability of defensive success. Others may disagree.

People will have different costs of defense, but again, for simplicity, the assumption will be made that the marginal cost of defense for each person is the same, and that it is constant. Effectively this implies that the total differences in defense costs between people are limited to differences in either fixed costs or to the quantity of defense they decide to pursue. Each person is constrained in their defensive efforts by their widely divergent original endowments and natural abilities. Individuals value defense in the original position, not because they can somehow consume it, but because of its usefulness in allowing them to pursue the life they want and value. That said, some people may enjoy participating in violent activities, and some people may be better at defense and violence than others. In either case, defense expenditures must compete with other priorities people value and want to pursue.

The overall Hobbesian environment is similar to the situation envisioned in the discussion of the economics of conflict. Each person needs to decide on the type of defense they want to pursue, and the amount they want to devote to defense, in order to survive and live the best life they can under the poor circumstances they find themselves. One person's action will affect other people's preferred actions. To focus attention on government formation and joint defense, a simple strategic environment is imagined. People are assumed to have diminishing marginal value from more defense expenditures. That is, each successive unit of defense is valued less than the one preceding it. They have been struggling in anarchy and have reached a Nash equilibrium where each person's marginal cost of defense is not affected by other people's actions. People are affected by the presence of other people and are required to spend their scarce resources on arms to defend themselves and survive, but their marginal or incremental expenditures are not affected by those expenditures of others. In addition, each person's marginal cost of defense is assumed to be the same, although their fixed costs of defense can vary within the population.

Each person is assumed to be selfish or value maximizing when determining their optimal expenditure on defense. However, their choice of approaches to the *type* of defense is based on their world-view and can be affected by their moral views. To further simplify the analysis, each person is presumed to have a positive constant value for other goods (such as food), summarized in a positive constant value for money. That is, each person is assumed to receive a constant increase in value from each successive unit of other goods. These selfish and logical people determine their optimal level of defense in the original position by maximizing their value from defense given the costs of defense and are constrained by their endowments.

Under these assumptions, each person optimizes their situation by picking the defense techniques that they most highly value through the lens of their worldview and choosing the equilibrium level of defense expenditures where the *normalized* relative marginal value from defense is equal to the fixed marginal cost of defense. Each person's marginal value from defense is normalized by their respective demand for other goods, such as food. Each person uses their scarce resources to provide for anarchistic defense, and will increase their expenditures on defense until its incremental value (weighted by the value of other goods) is reduced to the constant marginal cost of defense.[117] This implies that a lower constant marginal cost of defense will lead to a higher level of defense expenditures by everyone. Similarly, people with a higher value for other goods, such as food, everything else being the same, will spend less on defense. Each person is pursuing the amount of defense that is optimal from their perspective. Unless circumstances change, there is no reason for them to modify their actions. However, as was discussed in chapter 5, broadly viewed, resources are being wasted, since everyone must arm themselves because of the threat from other people. The threat from others can arise for many reasons, including desire for resources, power, and differences in religious or moral values.

QUANTITY OF COLLECTIVE DEFENSE

Let's now destabilize this equilibrium by introducing a new defense technology that is available to everyone. This new technology has lower fixed costs than individualistic anarchical defense but requires people to cooperate in joint defense. The more people who decide to participate in joint defense, the lower the overall fixed costs of defense. The joint defense production costs are assumed to be the same as the costs of anarchical defense except that total costs are reduced by a constant K for each person who agrees to participate in collective defense. To focus the analysis on certain key aspects of joint defense, two additional simplifying assumptions will be made. The first is that people who decide not to participate in joint defense can be excluded from collective defense. This can occur because: (i) everyone in a specific geographic area decides to join, (ii) geography is homogeneous and people who decide not to join will costlessly relocate, or (iii) the defense technology can discriminate between those who desire joint defense and those who are outside the defense collective. The second simplifying assumption is that the existence of people participating in joint defense does not increase the costs of defense for those who decide not to participate in collective defense. While both of these assumptions are somewhat extreme, they greatly simplify the analysis, and they do not change the overall conclusions. In parts four and five, the implications from somewhat relaxing these assumptions will be discussed.

Each person who is part of joint defense decreases the overall cost of defense when compared to the cost of anarchistic defense. That is, collective defense has increasing returns to scale. The total cost of collective defense is equal to the sum of the anarchical costs of defense for each person who participates in collective defense minus the product (in the mathematical sense) of: (i) the fixed productivity gain of K, and (ii) the number of people who participate in common defense.[118] One issue, which will be discussed later, concerns the methods that people use to reduce the possibility that the collective entity betrays some of them after they lay down their arms. For now, the assumption is made that some method exists, and any remaining uncertainty is fully reflected in the decreased fixed costs from collective defense. The collective defense entity or simply the collective can be viewed as a jointly owned and controlled entity that charges each of its members for the services of joint defense, and people bargain over the gains from association. Each person will only engage in joint defense if there is an increase in value from their perspective.

To determine the optimal quantity of defense for the collective, each person will reason through the requirements necessary to achieve each person's desired quantity of defense. This occurs when each person's normalized marginal value from defense is equal to the marginal cost of defense passed on to them by the collective. Each person will conclude that the optimal quantity of collective defense occurs when the *sum* of their relative marginal value of defense (relative to each person's marginal value of other goods) is equal to the collective marginal cost of defense.[119] The marginal cost of collective defense is equal to the product of the number of people who join in collective defense and the fixed marginal cost of anarchical defense. Since the collective production of defense has the same aggregate marginal cost as the sum of the marginal costs from anarchical defense, the amount of defense produced in joint defense is the same as produced by all the individuals in pursuing anarchical defense.

Under the simplifying assumptions, everyone concurs on the optimal quantity of collective defense. This is the "societal" optimal level of defense production. It is based not only on the given cost of anarchical defense but also on the value of defense of each person (who decides to join in collective defense). Society, in this context, consists of only those people who decide to band together for joint defense. The production of defense in anarchy is based on each person's marginal value of defense. It is the same for collective defense. Economist Paul Samuelson showed that the efficient or Pareto optimal level of production of a public good is produced when the sum of the marginal utilities of a good are equal to the marginal cost of that good.[120] In this context, Pareto optimality occurs when defense has been expanded to the level at which each person is satisfied, and a further increase will reduce at least one person's value. This is exactly the quantity of collective defense that will be produced by people voluntarily exiting anarchy and engaging in collective defense.

Defense is a public good that is normally viewed as having certain characteristics that make its production inefficient. Traditionally, it is considered to be nonexcludable, since the provision of defense services provides benefits for people who do not agree to pay for them and cannot be prevented from participating in them. Defense is also typically considered to be nonrivalrous, since consumption by one person does not reduce the amount available for consumption by someone else. These characteristics cause inefficient production of defense by competitive market forces, which is one of the conventional explanations for the existence of government. Given the conflicts discussed in chapter 5, people have an incentive to "free ride" on the production of common defense. People receive the benefits from common defense whether or not they contribute to its production, and their participation in these benefits does not reduce the overall level of defense. Rational people realize that these conflicts exist and have an incentive to avoid participating in the production of goods that possess these characteristics. Since free riding of defense is possible, it is not naturally provided by a competitive market. Therefore, the argument is made that government needs to provide the service and that people need to be forced to contribute to its production (including funding).

However, this introduces another inefficiency, since government is a *monopoly* producer of defense. A monopolist typically does not generate the societal optimal level of production. If the monopoly provider of defense services charges a common rate for defense, and acts like it is maximizing profits from providing these services, it will produce less defense than is socially efficient, which is a quantity that could be increased without reducing someone's overall value received from defense. Obviously, government does not have to act like it is maximizing profits. But if it levies taxes for the payment of defense at a level that does not equate to the socially optimal level, it will produce an inefficient amount.

Although defense is a public good, and the defense collective is a monopolist, it is naturally able to produce it at a socially optimal level. Selfish people, faced with the possibility of cooperating in joint defense they determine to be better than anarchistic defense, will cooperate and produce the quantity of defense that is optimal. As a group, given the simplifying assumptions, they can calculate the optimal level of defense for all those people who decide to join.[121] They will voluntarily agree to contribute to collective defense because that is the cost of getting other people to do the same. They will also consent to arrangements that penalize them if they attempt to free ride or do not contribute the socially optimal level of resources. Furthermore, unlike the situations discussed in chapter 5, where people cannot effectively reduce others' incentive to cheat, a defense collective has all the tools necessary to reduce the incentive to cheat to a level that allows people to band together in common defense. The defense collective is all about the production of violence, primarily for external defense, but obviously this violence can be used against its members to increase compliance with the jointly agreed-to rules.

COLLECTIVE DECISIONS CONCERNING POTENTIAL DEFENSE ACTIONS

An important debate during the eighteenth century concerning common defense was the appropriateness of maintaining standing armies.[122] During the ratification of the US Constitution, there was significant discussion around forming a permanent army. People's differing views were mostly philosophical and not related to cost. The modern view of maintaining a permanent military is based on the concept that discipline, training, and experience are crucial elements of a successful defense force. Many people shared this view in the eighteenth century, but others thought the benefits were outweighed by other factors. For example, James Madison was particularly concerned with the conflicts endemic to a professional military. During the Constitutional Convention, he stated, "A standing military force, with an overgrown Executive will not long be safe companions to liberty."[123]

Patrick Henry, during the Virginia debate on ratifying the Constitution, stated, "A standing army we shall have, also, to execute the execrable commands of tyranny; and how are you to punish them?

Will you order them to be punished? Who shall obey the orders? Will your mace-bearer be a match for a disciplined regiment?"[124] Madison continued his views from the prior year by stating, "[A] standing army is one of the greatest mischiefs that can possibly happen."[125] From their statements, both Henry and Madison were concerned with the conflicts between people serving in the army and the citizens they are supposed to defend. Their concerns affected their preferred strategies for common defense. Conflict exists in any situation where people's interests are not completely aligned. Even though the United States was not in a state of anarchy at the time of these debates, many people were concerned with these inherent conflicts. Now, imagine people considering the transition from protecting themselves under anarchy to relying on others in common defense: the issues of trust and betrayal are likely to be front and center. When people must rely on other people to defend them, who will defend them from the defenders?

While Madison and Henry recognized the benefits of a professional army over a militia, they feared the potential consequences of a standing army and concluded that the risks outweighed the efficiency advantages. They were convinced that a standing army was a real threat to freedom and liberty in times of peace. Other people disagreed. For example, James Wilson, a delegate to the US Constitutional Convention and one of the original Supreme Court justices, believed a standing army was vital. He argued that "the *power* of raising and keeping up an army, in time of peace, is essential to every government. No government can secure its citizens against dangers, internal and external, without possessing it, and sometimes carrying it into execution."[126] The facts were typically not in dispute, but people's worldviews led them to radically different conclusions. Some people were willing to take the increased risk of the army conducting a coup or being used by the government against its citizens for the decreased risk of foreign invasion.

The controversy continued after ratification of the Constitution, especially during John Adams's presidency, due to fear of a war with France. The House of Representatives authorized a buildup of the military in 1798. Two years later, they debated reducing the military. In those debates, John Randolph, a congressman from Virginia, stated

"I oppose the establishment of a standing army in this country . . . A people who mean to continue free must be prepared to meet danger in person; not to rely upon the fallacious protection of mercenary armies."[127] Henry Lee III, another member of Congress from Virginia, had a different view and, as it turned out, the majority view when he stated:

> *Gentlemen say regular troops are not necessary; militia, of themselves, are an adequate defence. This I deny; and as much as I wish to see our militia placed on a respectable footing, much as I count on their aid whenever danger approaches, yet I never can be brought to trust the defence of the country solely to them.*[128]

The controversy surrounding a permanent military was not solely concerned with effectiveness; John Randolph and others thought a free people should defend themselves.

While the question of a permanent military is no longer debated, there are a significant number of other controversies that continue to exist. For example, the use of a draft to supplement the military has been historically controversial. The United States has periodically used a draft but traditionally has allowed people various methods of opting out. For example, during the Vietnam War, men could defer service in the military by being full-time students. The rules allowed them to go to school until they were too old to be drafted. Approximately 1.9 million men were still drafted, a quarter of the men who served during the conflict.[129] Many people viewed the draft rules as unfair, including John Rawls. In 1967, he proposed that the Harvard faculty formally adopt a resolution opposing deferment, since he viewed the draft as discriminating against those less well off.[130]

The Vietnam draft was not the first draft that US citizens disagreed with. During the Civil War, there were demonstrations and riots by people against the draft. The Conscription Act of 1863 allowed men who were drafted to find and pay a substitute. Alternatively, it allowed draftees to pay $300 (approximately $6,000 in 2017 dollars) to the US Treasury. The fee acted as a ceiling on the payment that people could charge for being a substitute. Like the Vietnam deferments, many people thought these options were unfair and discriminatory against the poor. The question, of course, is: What is the optimal method the government should use to satisfy its need for troops? Even though younger males in the United States are required to register for a potential draft, the country currently meets its military needs through volunteers. But doesn't this have some of the same negative effects as the Civil War draft? James Tobin, recipient of the 1981 Nobel Prize in economics, thought so.[131] This view has led many people to propose compulsory governmental service for everyone. Of course, many also disagree with this concept.

As quoted earlier, Representative Randolph had a negative view about mercenaries and thought that citizens should defend themselves. The issue is still with us: Governments use private contractors and private security companies. They provide their services for a fee to supplement direct governmental resources. The location of military bases also leads to disagreements. Some people prefer these be located close to them for both defense purposes and the economic benefits that will flow to their local community. Other people want the decisions concerning bases to be made on strictly economic grounds. This issue becomes more acute when changing circumstances modify the need for military bases. The differences of opinion may lead to a continuation of the status quo and inefficient allocation of societal resources. As people in the original position consider banding together on collective defense, they will need to address these issues and determine how they want the collective to decide them, now and in the future.

Another issue Madison touched on is the question of when to use and threaten violence in defending the collective. Some people will prefer to be part of a defense collective that is isolationist. They would like a small military and only respond by force when third-party aggression is imminent. Other individuals prefer collective defense to be larger and more proactive. They favor a military strategy capable of projecting power. People also differ on when to deploy the military. Those considering collective defense may be relatively aligned about the preferred action when the collective is physically attacked.[132] However, people are likely to have significant differences of opinion concerning the use of force when the collective is not under imminent threat.

Potential members will have different views on the necessity of requiring soldiers to put themselves in harm's way in pursuing a military engagement that may not be necessary to ensure the continued viability of the collective. Others will view these risks and costs as acceptable in order to reduce the later probability of higher costs and losses. These differences of opinion are obvious in the debate over both the Vietnam War and the engagements in Iraq and Afghanistan. They also manifest themselves over differences in views over nuclear deterrence and the possession of nuclear weapons. For example, Amartya Sen appears to have had a negative view of India developing nuclear weapons. He argued that the weapons had moral costs, did not reduce the likelihood of war, and significantly increased the costs of warfare.[133] On the other hand, Rawls viewed nuclear weapons and other types of offensive weapons as necessary in a world where rogue regimes like Hitler's Germany exist.[134]

The discussion above is not exhaustive. There are many other questions and issues people will need to address in banding together for common defense. How does the potential collective balance out these differing opinions of its participating members? People are not forced to join in collective defense. They can remain in anarchy. They are incentivized to work together because collective defense has lower fixed costs than anarchical defense. However, in a collective, they may not be able to pursue the defense strategy that they prefer. In anarchy, they can utilize the strategy that provides the highest value. If people want to water board or behead those they disagree with in their pursuit of anarchistic defense, there is nothing others can do about it except to redouble their defensive efforts. In the equilibrium of the Hobbesian original position, everyone has reached a standoff in terms of the type of defense they are pursuing and the amount of defense that each person is producing. In no event are they required to adopt the tactics and strategies of others. In anarchistic defense, if some people want to pursue the moral high ground and not pursue torture, that is their prerogative. Circumstances are quite different when considering the strategies that people can use for common defense. People's relative values matter in joint defense.

A person who finds torture completely unacceptable will not join in collective defense if the rules governing the collective allow or encourage such treatment. Even though they realize that common defense is more effective at protecting them, the moral costs from their perspective outweigh these benefits. The Hobbesian original position is "brutish," but some people may view their own moral position on torture as more important. Do other people care that this person does not join? Potentially they do. If they do care, they may be willing to modify their rules so this moral person will find them acceptable and change their mind and join. But how does the collective decide on which defensive strategies to pursue given the differences of worldviews? How do people balance out the differing views of others when they need to ultimately come to a consensus?

People will negotiate with each other based on the relative importance they place on each of the possible actions that can be pursued in conducting common defense. They will try to communicate the importance they place on various actions and argue why others should share their views. However, people realize that not everyone can dictate terms and conditions to others in pursuing common defense. They will disagree on some of the points. Each of them must make concessions even when they feel strongly about a potential action.

INDIVIDUAL VALUATIONS OF COLLECTIVE ACTIONS

To model behavior and view the trade-offs people may be willing to make to agree to join with other people with whom they have conflicts, we will try to put these disparate items and decisions on a common footing. We need a mechanism that allows for intrapersonal comparisons. How does each person view the various trade-offs they may have to make to reach a consensus with other people? We also need to have interpersonal comparisons. We need to see how each person will compare the alternatives with each other. How will a person who does not want a military draft, but thinks that torture is fine, reach agreement with someone who thinks it is everyone's moral duty to fight for the collective, but believes that any type of torture is abhorrent? To simulate the conditions necessary for agreement, an assumption will be made that each person can value all the alternatives from his or her perspective, and that these values are in a common unit of measurement so the trade-offs between people can be compared.

Economists like to have as broad a view as possible concerning interpersonal comparisons of value. For example, in analyzing demand for consumer goods, economists use a methodology consistent with people behaving as if they had ordinal utility functions. That is, everyone is assumed to have consistent preferences for goods, but the amount that one individual values a good cannot be compared to the value that another individual places on that same good. Individual ordinal utility functions are sufficient tools for simulating how selfish people will act in choosing goods, but they cannot be used to determine the "values" different individuals have for a certain quantity of a good.

In bargaining analysis, economists typically assume people make decisions as if they have "measurable" ordinal utility functions.[135] That is, each person can have different values for disparate items, but these values are comparable across people because each person's value is assumed to be on a common unit of measure. Each person's value of a certain amount of a good is linearly related to another person's value of that same amount of the good. When people are presumed to have measurable differences in valuations, the assumption is that each person acts as if they can arrange the various alternatives in order of their preferences, and that their valuations of these orderings are comparable between each person according to an unknown linear scale. Without knowing the valuation scale, we cannot determine the intensity of how much more they prefer one good to another good.

The absolute differences between people's values for a specific amount of a good are only meaningful if we choose a particular scale. If everyone's values for an item are on the same known scale, then their differing values can be directly compared. We can then determine how much more they prefer a good or item compared to someone else. When this scale exists, the valuation is labeled cardinal valuation or cardinal utilities. Cardinal valuation implies that interpersonal valuations are similar to intrapersonal valuations. It means that the absolute amount of value that one person has for an ordered quantity of an item is directly comparable to the value that another person has for that same ordered quantity. The intensity that people have for goods or actions can be directly assessed. Cardinal valuation obviously requires much more information about people's valuations.

There are a variety of actions the collective can pursue in defending its members. Stated somewhat differently, there are many possible Nash equilibria both in the collective choice of the type of defense and in how to divide the gains arising from common defense. Without incorporating more information or structure, each of these potential actions is equally rational. Since people have different worldviews, they will prefer different actions for joint defense. This is consistent with the concept of each person having a different opinion and value on the possible actions. Individuals are not indifferent to the actual action chosen by the collective even though it was chosen from a set of rational actions. The problem remains as to how these individuals will resolve their differences.

The negotiation over the strategies for common defense can be incorporated into the overall bargaining problem facing the people who are deciding to join the collective. However, it is much simpler and more intuitive to separate the negotiation over defense strategies from bargaining over the gains from collective defense. Therefore, the plan of analyzing the choices people make is to assume they have cardinal values for each of the potential strategic actions for the collective and that these values are "transferable" between them.[136] These values are assumed to be in the same units as the cost of defense and their endowments. Each person may—and is likely to—have a different value for each potential collective action. In the next chapter, bargaining will be used to determine how people will decide to divide these transferable values, including the gains from the reduced cost of defense. This simplification obscures many of the nuances of bargaining but allows us to focus our attention on the larger picture of the chosen structure of the defense collective.

In simulating the trade-offs people will consider when negotiating over the strategies for the defense collective, the assumption is that there are a fixed number of potential decisions the collective can make, and a fixed number of actions people prefer for each decision. Each decision can have a different number of potential actions. Each person has a view of, or value on, each of these various actions for each decision and has a preferred action for each decision. These preferred actions for each person are those the defense collective would pursue if that individual were the dictator for that collective. In anarchical defense, each person pursues their preferred action. In collective defense, where people have different worldviews, not everyone can be—or act like—the dictator. The collective can only choose one action for each decision out of the multitude of potential actions. As discussed above, to simulate how people may address this conflict, we will assume that one's personal values on these actions are transferable to others.

Each person will place a zero value on his or her preferred action. Actions that are less preferred have negative values, with the least preferred action having the highest negative value. A value for a decision that is infinitely negative implies a person will not compromise on that decision. It infers that a person feels or thinks so strongly about a potential action that he or she must have his or her way. It represents the possibility that there may be certain issues that are not negotiable. A conundrum for the collective is trying to incorporate people with completely opposed views.

There are no assumed limits to the total values any one person can have for a particular action or to the total values for all the people considering joining the defense collective in aggregate. Theoretically, a person can have one preferred action for each decision with a value of zero and infinitely negative values for all other actions. Other people can have small differences between their values for the different actions. Some people may be opinionated and have high negative values for certain potential actions. Others may be indifferent to the choices between various courses of action. In which case, they will have small differences in their values over various potential actions. For example, one person can feel strongly that there should be strict rules prohibiting people from voluntarily abandoning the collective after agreeing to join. This individual may favor a rule that prohibits any land controlled by anyone who joins the collective from ever being withdrawn from the collective. This person can favor massive penalties for anyone caught attempting to withdraw their land from common defense or abandoning the collective to pursue another collective or to return to anarchistic defense. Another person can understand why that person feels the way they do but may value all these alternatives similarly. They may understand the benefits to the collective of having a stable group with stable land, but they may also value the flexibility to respond to an unpredictable future and may be indifferent to prohibiting people from leaving or seceding from the collective. Each person has complete information and knows their values as well as the values of everyone else. The relevant question is how these differences in values are utilized to decide the actions pursued by a group contemplating collective defense.

FREEDOM

There are a significant number of strategic and tactical decisions that the individuals participating in joint defense will want to address. The types of issues are broad and include questions such as whether the collective should:

- retain a professional military,
- implement a draft,
- be primarily defensive or project power,
- allow freedom of the press,
- offer people complete privacy,
- employ any type of torture,
- engage in spying on enemies and current allies,
- allow people to give up their membership in the collective once they join,
- allow people to remove their personal property (including land) from the collective once they join,
- allow immigration,

- allow for the death penalty for such offenses as desertion and treason,
- enact a self-imposed limit on the types of weapons employed, and so on.

No one "correct" answer to these considerations is applicable to every group of people considering joint defense.

Even though joining in collective defense is voluntary, given the diversity of worldviews, unanimity in the choice of actions for the collective is unlikely. People agree to join in collective defense because it has benefits for each person who joins. Otherwise they will stay in the original position. There is a cost to each person for every action the defense collective chooses that is not the person's preferred action. Each person thinks their preferred action is the one the collective should pursue. Unfortunately, the collective can only pursue one action for each decision, and this will cause psychological harm to each person who does not prefer the specific action chosen by the group. This effect is typically labeled as a "negative externality." That is, the group's choice of a specific action has an unintended negative consequence on members of the group. One of the inefficiencies of collective defense or of any type of joint decision-making is the logical requirement of having only one possible action. As was discussed in chapter 6, there is "congestion" in group decision-making that causes negative externalities to those who prefer different decisions. It is similar to the effect that people can have on each other on a crowded highway. If there are as many lanes on the highway as people, then people's actions do not negatively affect each other. However, if there is only one lane, then one person's actions or preferences can negatively affect everyone else.

"Freedom" is a word fraught with controversy. Most people want to be free and may want others to be free, but what does that mean? Depending on one's worldview, freedom has various meanings. At one extreme it means a person does not have any constraints. If a person has limited income or wealth, can they be free? If a person feels that some actions are prohibited by their moral beliefs, are they free? If a person has limited mobility or capabilities, can they be free? Is freedom an absolute concept or a relative one? What is the difference between liberty and freedom? Is the distinction between negative and positive liberties a relevant one? Does freedom convey certain moral duties, as Amartya Sen seems to forcibly argue? These are difficult questions.

"Freedom" in this book means that a person gets his or her way and, unlike typical freedom concepts, its definition is not determined by some political process. In the defense collective, it will be defined as the sum of the joiners' values for the defense actions ultimately pursued by the group. Mathematically, freedom can range from zero to negative infinity. Complete freedom occurs when the values' sum is zero. Alternatively, perfect "unfreedom" or lack of freedom is a situation where the values' sum is negative infinity. Under this definition, people in Hobbesian anarchy have complete freedom. The mathematical sum of their value of every action they take in pursuing anarchical defense is zero. Even though the environment characterized by the Hobbesian original position is brutish for everyone, and people are constrained by their limited resources and incentivized by the threat from everyone else to spend scarce resources on unproductive defense, each person who survives will be considered completely free. In Hobbesian anarchy, each person can follow their own preferences subject to their limited circumstances. In the Hobbesian original position, each person is constrained and influenced by others. However, given these conditions, they are completely free to make their own decisions and follow their own preferences.

Using this concept of freedom, some people can view the choice of moving to collective defense as unacceptable because of their loss of freedom. Even though collective defense has significant efficiency benefits over anarchical defense, it requires everyone who joins to sacrifice some of their freedom. They must accept the fact that the defense collective will not always and may never act the way they prefer. Their share in the gains from cooperation must be higher than the value they place on lost freedom (assuming the tax they pay the group is at least equal to their cost of anarchical defense).

This definition of freedom is significantly different than one where people have few constraints on their individual actions. A defense collective that has few laws that limit people's personal behavior is not necessarily a *freer* collective than a defense collective that places severe limits on what people can do or say. Under this definition, a person's freedom depends on how much the value of the defense collective's decisions differs from those preferred by that person. As such, a defense collective has complete freedom if its decisions are the preferred decisions of each of its members irrespective of the laws that limit their individual behavior. For example, a person will not have any loss of freedom from a decision by the collective to adopt a universal draft if the person prefers this rule.

Each person's total loss of freedom is equal to the sum of their values of the defense collective's chosen action for all the collective's decisions. For a person to be perfectly free when joining in collective defense, they will need the collective to choose all the actions that they prefer. If the collective has a diversity of people and a single dictator, the dictator will be the only free person in the collective. The total loss of freedom for the entire collective is the sum of each person's cumulative loss of freedom. The only way for the defense collective to be completely free is if all the actions chosen by the collective are each person's preferred actions.

FREEDOM-MAXIMIZING DECISIONS

If there are no net gains from cooperation, cooperation will not occur. This observation leads to some critical conclusions.

The first conclusion is that there is a maximum amount of diversity the two-person defense collective can withstand. For example, consider a person whose preferred action for the collective is to kill people with a specific ethnic background, and assume that she places an infinitely negative value on every other alternative. This implies that she will have infinite "freedom losses" from any other collective decision. Because K is finite, and by assumption is the entire gain from collective defense, this person will only join in collective defense if the collective pursues persecution of people with this specific ethnic background. Even if she were allocated all the gains from collective defense, the gains would not be sufficient to cover her freedom losses or loss in value that she would experience from any other decision. Now assume that the other person she is negotiating with is a person of that ethnicity. That person will probably value the prospect of being targeted by his or her own defense collective with infinitely negative weight. Since there are not sufficient gains to cover both people's freedom losses, these two people will not agree to be in the same defense collective.

Because freedom losses cannot be larger than zero as people exit Hobbesian anarchy, the maximum difference in total valuations of various actions to be undertaken by the defense collective is K. Any valuation differences higher than K will cause at least one of the individuals to decide not to join, since there are insufficient gains to cover both their freedom losses. In this situation, there are not any "net" gains from common defense. Similarly, if one person is the dictator and each collective action is his or her preferred action, then the largest amount of freedom loss that any other person will withstand to join in common defense is K. Alternatively, if some actions are preferred by one person and the remaining actions are preferred by the other individual, the maximum valuation difference they can have for each other's preferred actions is K, if they participate in common defense. The conclusion is that in a diverse world, a world characterized by wide-ranging worldviews and morals, not everyone will agree to be in the same defense collective.

Extending this line of reasoning leads to the observation that the larger the differences in people's valuations, the smaller the net gains from being part of the same defense collective. Each person will want to be the decision maker and choose all the actions for the collective. These actions will cause value destruction to the person who prefers a different action. If people have a choice of whom to collaborate with in joint defense, they would rather choose someone who has a worldview similar to their own. Similar worldviews will lead to larger net gains. If both people have exactly the same preferences, then the net gains are equal to K.

This observation seems to contradict the typical refrain that diversity increases productivity. Diversity in views has value under certain circumstances. In the situation where a decision maker is faced with a complex problem, diversity of views from his or her advisors, subordinates, or enemies can provide information and let him or her come to a more informed view. In theory, debate among a group of people with dissimilar views will allow the decision maker to come to a better decision than if he or she is surrounded by those who are effectively yes people. However, the decision maker will not be willing to concede decision-making authority to a person he or she disagreed with. The five theorists' arguments were honed by active debate with people who had different worldviews. However, at the end of the day, they all disagreed. None would be equally satisfied with the conclusions reached by the other authors.

Another conclusion is that the choice of defense actions is not purely scientific. There are many possible completely logical actions for the defense collective. While defense technologies will limit and affect the defense collective's actions, there are a wide variety of potential production possibilities. Similarly, there are many actions and strategies for the defense collective that are equally effective against external enemies. That does not mean that every conceivable action is logical. Some actions are inefficient. Not spending resources on collective defense in a hostile environment is not a Nash equilibrium. It is not the best response to those who are threatening the defense collective. However, there are many possible strategies that are rational. People, in the original position, who are considering entering joint defense, are not indifferent to these various alternatives. Each of them has preferred actions. Therefore, scholars and researchers cannot determine the actions chosen by the collective. Those choices are determined by the preferences and views of the people who join in collective defense. One two-person collective can act completely different than another two-person collective. The net gains from collective defense can be the same for two collectives that have the same productivity gains and yet pursue different defense strategies. The net gains are only affected by the relative differences in the members' values of the actions chosen by their collective.

TAXES AND COLLECTIVE DEFENSE

The optimal tax policy for a collective whose only goal is external defense, composed of people with differing worldviews like those of the five theorists, and where everyone wants to live under collective rules that they prefer, can be deduced in a variety of ways. However, given people's differing views, a simple method is to presume the group charges each person who wants to join in collective defense the most that person will pay. The highest amount each person will pay will maximize the gains to the overall group. If this rule seems harsh or too capitalistic, recall that each person will ultimately bargain over the overall gains from joining in collective defense. They will bargain over both the gains they receive from joining as well as their share of the gains from everyone else joining. If at the end of this bargaining process they decide not to join, then they have not lost anything except the potential gains. At the end of the chapter, we will discuss the possibility that people's worldviews, including their moral positioning, could override this decision rule.

By requiring every person to pay the most they will pay to be part of collective defense, the collective can provide the quantity of defense that everyone wants. This is what led to the earlier conclusion that people exiting the original position and cooperating in collective defense will produce the societal optimal amount of defense. Even though defense is a public good, by charging each person the most they will pay, the collective can economically produce the Pareto optimal amount of defense.

However, the collective can theoretically charge less than the most someone will pay and still produce the socially optimal level of defense. The minimum the collective can charge each person and still produce the socially optimal level of defense is the individual tax that equates the collective's marginal cost of producing defense with each individual's relative marginal value from defense (relative to the marginal value of other goods or money). This type of tax is known as a Lindahl tax, named for Swedish economist Erik Lindahl.[137] He was concerned with determining a just tax for the provision of public goods. He proposed a tax formula that allowed the allocation of costs of producing the

optimal amount of a public good to be based on the marginal benefits that citizens of a government were receiving from the public good.
This level of taxation will allow the defense collective to have sufficient
resources to produce the optimal level of the quantity of defense discussed in the first part of this chapter.

Any amount of tax in excess of this amount is not needed to cover
the group's costs of providing defense, but it will increase the gains
from collective defense that can be redistributed, through bargaining,
to the individuals participating in collective defense. The only way for
the group to benefit from those productivity gains is for those who
are benefiting from joint defense to fully compensate the group for
that joint defense. This will allow the group to collect the full gains
from each person joining. They then can bargain over these gains. One
potential bargaining outcome is that each person only pays the minimum (Lindahl) tax for being part of the collective. As will be seen in
the next chapter, this is an unlikely result.

Determining the maximum that people will pay is much easier
than in a real-world situation, since everyone is assumed to possess
complete information. The maximum amount each person will pay is
their opportunity cost of not engaging in collective defense. They will
not pay more than their next best alternative. In a simple two-person
world, this is each person's cost of anarchical defense. It is not their
marginal cost from anarchical defense, but the total cost of anarchical
defense or at least the cost they will forego by not having to be in anarchy. The two-person group will act like a monopolist and charge each
person joining in collective defense the full value of their next best
alternative.[138]

However, diverse people will not join in collective defense if they are
charged the costs they were paying to defend themselves. In Hobbesian
anarchy, each person has complete freedom of decision-making
(subject to the environmental conditions of the Hobbesian original
position). In joining in collective defense, they must accept defense
decisions that are not their preferred decisions. Therefore, the most
a person will pay to be part of joint defense is the full cost of anarchical defense minus their loss of freedom. Even though there could be
gains from joining, each individual will need to be compensated for the

decision externalities imposed on them. They will reduce the amount they are willing to pay to join by the full value of these externalities, which are their freedom losses. The aggregate loss in value that they experience from the group choosing actions they don't prefer reduces the amount that they will be willing to pay for joining the collective. The less they are willing to pay, the smaller the gains from joining the collective. Since each person wants to increase their net gains, both are willing to agree to collective decisions that are not their preferred decisions. Agreeing to the freedom-maximizing decision produces the optimal net gains from people joining the collective.

Given the simplifying assumptions that have been made, the maximum tax each person will be willing to pay is easily quantified. Recall that each person has the same marginal cost of defense, and that the productivity benefits of collective defense manifested themselves only through lower fixed costs of K. For these gains to be realized, each person must pay their full cost of anarchical defense.[139] This implies that the person with lower fixed costs of anarchical defense will pay less, everything else being the same. People, at a minimum, need to receive their freedom losses to induce them to participate in collective defense. Therefore, the maximum tax people will pay is their anarchical defense costs minus their freedom losses.

9

——— ★ ———

TWO-PERSON COLLECTIVE DEFENSE

BARGAINING OVER THE GAINS FROM COLLECTIVE DEFENSE

The prior analysis ignored an important element in each person's decision on whether to engage in joint defense. What are their individual gains? The analysis thus far has included the reasoning behind each person agreeing to maximize the overall gains from two-person collective defense. However, since each person is paying the maximum tax, they are receiving no personal benefit from joining in collective defense. As explained, the sum of these maximum taxes produces a net gain equal to the productivity gain of K minus aggregate freedom losses. These net gains are the inducement for people to engage in collective defense. But how are these gains allocated to each person? The property rights to these gains need to be established. Each person's personal gains will depend on the bargain that they can reach with the other person.

To examine the bargaining agreement, the alternating-offer bargaining protocol discussed in chapter 7 will be utilized. Each person is assumed to desire all the gains that accrue from joint defense. However, people need the other person to join in collective defense for either of them to escape the original position. As discussed above, each person agrees that the collective will produce the same quantity of defense that each was producing in anarchy. They agree that it is in their interests for each of them to pay the difference between each of their full costs of anarchical defense and freedom losses. This implies that the net gains from collective defense are equal to the fixed productivity cost savings of K minus aggregate freedom losses. These net gains create the conflict that needs to be resolved through bargaining. Each person wants all the net gains for themselves but needs the other person to agree to participate in joint defense, which requires agreement as to the share of the gains that each will receive from their joint effort.

The alternating-offer protocol requires that the analysis incorporates time. From the discussion in chapter 7, a key assumption is the bargainer's relative time preference, which is likely to depend on their borrowing costs and investment rates. The Hobbesian original position is one where cooperation is low and lending markets either do not exist or are not very efficient. Potential lenders will not be sure that people will be willing to return the borrowed funds. Lenders will charge a significant premium over their cost of funds to take the risk that people will pay them back. Recall that everyone in the Hobbesian original position is armed. A borrower who refuses to repay a loan cannot be forced to repay the borrowed funds. The only negative impact from fraud is reputational damage, which is not that valuable in an environment where cooperation is practically nonexistent. This implies that people's initial position and original endowments of resources will significantly affect their investment decisions. People's internal borrowing costs—which they can view as borrowing from themselves—are much lower than their external borrowing costs or the cost of borrowing funds from other people. People cannot lend their endowments to another individual without significant risk. The Hobbesian environment makes their own investments in arms and food seem more attractive (everything else being the same) than lending funds to other people.

Therefore, time is potentially less valuable for people with larger endowments: individuals with relatively larger endowments will be able to undertake more and larger investments than a person who has a smaller endowment. If there are different types of investments that people can make in arms and other productive activities, with differing rates of return, then people will pursue those investments with higher returns first. Each incremental quantity of endowment will allow each person to invest in activities with progressively lower returns. Everything else being the same, a person with more endowments or wealth can make more investments, and their marginal outlay will have lower yields. The poorer person will not be able to make these investments, and their marginal investment will have a higher yield. Therefore, everything else being the same, they will discount the future at a higher rate; they will have a higher time preference. This is the assumption that will be made in the forthcoming analysis.

In a dynamic context in which people's time discount rates are constant and do not vary with time, each person will optimize their value of the "flow" of defense. Based on the discussion above, the person who has a larger endowment is assumed to have a lower time preference, since they can move further along their investment horizon. The difference between the static analysis and the dynamic analysis is the impact of each person's time preference or their investment yield on the value of their defense and its effects on other things that each person values, including the gains from joint defense. Each person is assumed to want to maximize their constant per period values, which are just their static values discounted by their time preference.

If the two people can come to an agreement and collaborate in joint defense, they will also be able to potentially pursue other goals that have value to both of them. In particular, they will likely want to have rules against fraud and for orderly bankruptcy. They may also want to pursue certain social policies. These incremental goals are the subject of chapter 12. However, the current analysis requires an assumption of the impact the formation of the defense collective will have on the bargainer's relative borrowing rate and thus their relative time preferences. Each person's borrowing costs will be lower under collective defense than in anarchy, but for simplicity, the relative reduction caused by the movement from anarchy to joint defense is assumed to be the same for each person. In a bargaining context, this assumption eliminates the ability of one person to use the movement from anarchy to collective defense against the other person. It does not change the overall conclusion, but it does simplify the analysis.

Each person is assumed to have complete information about the other person's preferences, including their time preference. Each person has unique values for defense, for other goods, and for any net gains. From a bargaining perspective, none of these differences matter. Each person has power, since a bargain cannot happen without the consent of the other person. Bargaining requires unanimous agreement. Each of the bargainers will use backward induction to determine the other person's equilibrium response to their own potential offers and their equilibrium response to the other person's potential offers. As discussed in chapter 7, the two individuals will not agree to a biased procedure. Therefore, the bargaining protocol where the bargaining period between a bid and a counterbid approaches zero, in the limit, will be utilized. This leads to a bargaining equilibrium we have labeled a "credible equilibrium."

Bargaining can theoretically take time; that is, there can be more than one series of offers and acceptances. While they are bargaining, each person is still in the Hobbesian original position. Given their positive time values, each person is anxious to exit anarchy. However, the poorer person—the person with the higher time preference and less endowments—is relatively more incentivized to move from anarchy to collective defense. The richer person, or the person with the relatively lower time discount rate, recognizes the value of collective defense but is less motivated to join. Both individuals recognize this fact, which incentivizes the poorer person to immediately agree to give a higher allocation of the net gains to the richer person. The richer person has a lower time preference, which accrues to their benefit. A delay in agreement costs the richer person relatively less. The poorer person, the person with the higher discount rate, recognizes that the richer person will not agree to an even allocation of the net gains from their joint effort. Given that each person has a positive time value and wants to quickly exit anarchy, the backward-induction algorithm will lead to a unique credible equilibrium. The unanimous bargaining outcome is an uneven allocation of the net gains in favor of the person with the lower discount rate. The larger the differences in the two discount rates, the less egalitarian the division of the net gains.

The total gains of K are divided between the two people based on their relative freedom losses and their relative discount rates. The credible equilibrium allocation of the gross gains is for each person to receive their total compromise costs or freedom losses and then divide the remaining net gains based on their relative time preferences. Both will unanimously and immediately agree that the person with the lowest discount rate will receive a higher percentage of the net gains. If both have the same discount rate, they will agree to evenly divide the net gains, but the person with the highest freedom losses will still receive more of the gross gains. For example, assume that K is equal to 100 and that Sam has freedom losses of 30 and Sarah has freedom losses of 10. Out of the 100 of productivity gains, they will both agree to allocate each other their respective freedom losses to make them indifferent to accepting the freedom-maximizing decisions. If they have the same discount rate, they will agree to equally divide the remaining gains of 60 (100 minus the joint freedom losses of 40). Sam will receive 30 (his freedom losses) plus half of 60 and Sarah will receive a total of 40. On the other hand, if Sam's instantaneous discount rate is half of Sarah's discount rate, say 10 percent vs. 20 percent, then they will both agree that Sam will receive his freedom losses of 30 plus two-thirds of the net gains of 60. In this situation, Sarah's relatively high discount rate will reduce her credible equilibrium allocation of the gross gains from 40 to 30.[140]

While they *disagree* on collective defense decisions, given their differing worldviews, they will *agree* to these allocations as quickly as they can reason through the bargaining analysis. They can agree on the equilibrium allocation of the gains from collective defense because of the assumption that the bargaining analysis is simple enough that they can both logically ascertain the "correct" bargaining outcome given their differing worldviews and time values. In bargaining, unlike collective defense decisions, they cannot disagree on the implications of their potential actions.

REDISTRIBUTION OF ENDOWMENTS

The discussion has focused thus far on the narrow goal of external defense. There are obviously many other collective goals people will have as they exit the original position, including the problem of poverty and inequality of wealth. The Hobbesian original position is a dismal environment. Even though everyone is relatively poor (compared to other possible original positions), there will still be inequality. Many people will fail in the original position through no fault of their own. This fact will disturb many. As they find methods to work together and escape anarchy, opportunities that were not possible in anarchy will become feasible. Many individuals will want to help the less fortunate, given the power and the increase in societal income provided by the defense collective. People with varying worldviews will have different preferences over the methods of achieving external defense, but they will also have different ancillary goals for the defense collective as well as divergent methods of achieving these goals. These expanded goals are the subject of later chapters.

In the context of the simple goal of external defense, there are three types of decisions the defense collective could make that affect people's relative incomes or wealth. They are: (i) taxes or payments to the collective for the provision of defense services, (ii) relative allocation of the gains from joint defense, and (iii) reallocation of individuals' endowments and wealth. The first two were examined above under the assumption that people are selfish. The third one will be analyzed from a broader perspective where at least some people value equality of wealth and income because in their worldview, individual wealth equality improves collective defense. It is important to separate the desire for or against redistribution from each person's preference for a higher share of the gains; they are distinct preferences. The relevant question is whether a two-person defense collective composed of diverse individuals will agree to a condition that requires people who join in collective defense to equalize their wealth positions.

The issue of wealth inequality did not arise in chapter 6 about the financial services firm and pirates. Why didn't the ten individuals consider a rule that required them to equalize their net worths before joining together? Some of the conflicts were exacerbated by the differences in their income and wealth. Why didn't the pirates seek to equalize their wealth positions and appropriately adjust for their abilities before voluntarily signing on to multiple pirating trips? Why wasn't income and wealth inequality more directly dealt with during the founding of the United States? There are different answers to each one of these questions, but they all revolve around the amount of disagreement it would invoke. People recognize the potential costs of wealth inequality, but are the potential solutions too costly from at least some people's perspective to make equalizing wealth a desirable decision for achieving a common goal like external defense that is not specifically aimed at reducing inequality?

Some people favor reducing or even eliminating wealth inequality. That goal will be examined in chapter 12. The current discussion is concerned with the narrower question of whether it is a rule that would be adopted as part of the goal of common external defense by people who have the differing worldviews represented by the five authors. Even though their writings did not explicitly address this issue, one could imagine that people who share some combination of their views may think equal wealth could improve collective defense. A potential worldview may include a perspective that significant differences in wealth could lead to "envy" on the part of the poorer person, which could make a two-person collective among people of differing endowments less efficient. Rawls, who obviously favored significant redistribution, did not make this argument. While he acknowledged the existence of envy, his concept of justice is built on what he perceives to be a fairness concept and not negative emotions like envy. Nonetheless, in a sufficiently diverse population, there could be people who sincerely believe that reallocation of endowments will improve the stability of the defense collective. For example, a person could use utilitarian logic that redistribution improves aggregate welfare.

Of course, many people will have the view that redistribution is not a rule that should be enforced by the defense collective. For example, those whose worldviews are similar to Hayek's and Nozick's will not endorse this rule because they will not think there is any justification for equalization of wealth.

Which position will predominate in a defense collective? It depends on the diversity of the worldviews of the bargainers, which are theoretically independent of each person's endowment. For example, Nozick rejected both redistribution and other forms of government-enforced limitations on the ability of people to control their own property. However, he had a conflict with the author Erich Segal that belies his worldview. He rented an apartment from Segal and refused to pay more than was required under local rent controls even though he disagreed with that type of government policy.[141] Nozick was willing to make a decision that was completely against his worldview, either for personal gain or out of other principles. One's worldview need not be completely consistent with one's personal situation.

Nonetheless, let's initially make the traditional assumption that there is a positive correlation between one's personal situation and worldview. This means that the relatively poorer person, Paul, favors redistribution and the wealthier person, Rebecca, does not. The further assumption will be made that neither person is a zealot on the matter, and both are willing to compromise.

From the prior analysis, it is evident that if Rebecca's views against redistribution are stronger than Paul's views, then the defense collective will not have a rule for equalizing their wealth. In a two-person collective, each person is incentivized to agree to collective decisions that minimize the sum of each person's freedom losses, since the gains are reduced by each person's freedom losses. Because the wealthier person is assumed to care more about this issue than the poorer person, it is in both their interests to abide by the desires of the wealthier person. Paul will receive an allocation of the gains for his loss of freedom so that it is unimportant to him whether wealth is equalized, at least from its impact on collective defense. This transfer reduces the overall net gains. The remaining gains are then unevenly divided between the two people, with Rebecca receiving the larger share given her lower assumed discount rate.

It is possible that Paul could receive a larger allocation of the overall gains of K, since he is receiving his share of the net gains as well as compensation for compromising. Under this scenario, Rebecca is still receiving a larger increase in wealth from collective defense, since the allocation to Paul for his freedom losses simply offsets his feelings of envy produced by unequal wealth. The allocation of the gains for freedom losses does not increase his wealth; it is a payment for a dead-weight loss due to his view that the defense collective will be less effective if wealth is unequal. From the outside, just looking at the allocation of K, it may seem that Paul's wealth has increased from this allocation of freedom losses and that Rebecca is being altruistic in agreeing to this result. But that would be an inaccurate assessment. The allocation for this purpose does not increase his wealth, since compromise acts as a reduction in Paul's wealth. This payment simply gets him back to the value or wealth he possessed in anarchy. Rebecca accepts this reduction in the gains from collective defense because that is the cost of compromise. If Paul's view of the importance of wealth equality is lower than Rebecca's opposite view, but too high, then a defense collective between them may not be possible, since there will be no gains from association.

Another possibility is that Rebecca has a weaker valuation or intensity against redistribution to increase harmony than Paul has for it. Following the previous logic, under this assumption, the freedom-maximizing decision is for both to agree to wealth redistribution. It would seem that the logical decision for Rebecca would be to agree to redistribution and accept the allocation of the gains that equal her freedom losses from compromising. However, this alternative comes with other effects. For both people to agree to collective defense, they both must be at least as well off, measured in wealth, value, or utility, as they were in anarchy. This is the logic used for allocating part of the gains to the person who compromises. If they compromise and agree on redistribution as a requirement for collective defense, the transfer of some of her endowment is a cost to Rebecca relative to her position in anarchy. For her to be indifferent to joint defense, she must receive compensation for both her freedom losses and her loss in wealth from the transfer. Furthermore, logically, the redistribution of endowments is also an increase in wealth for Paul, since it is not a payment for his freedom losses. This means it will be considered as part of the gains from collective defense that are subject to bargaining. The implication of these various effects is that redistribution designed to improve collective defense is not achievable.

This leads to the conclusion that when people's differing worldviews are positively correlated with their economic situation, redistribution solely designed to improve collective defense will never be an equilibrium action. Even in the situation where people's worldviews and relative wealth are inversely related, the richer person's desire for redistribution to enhance collective defense will not lead to redistribution as the equilibrium decision, since the transfer is an increase in wealth for the poorer person and a cost to the wealthier person. Therefore, the only situation in which redistribution will be the collective decision is when both people have a worldview that redistribution improves collective defense, and this preference overcomes their desire for wealth and income. Any disagreement on this point will lead to the collective choosing the opposite action. Therefore, among diverse or selfish people, redistribution designed to improve collective defense will never be a collective decision.

OBSERVATIONS

One of the interesting conclusions to the discussion of joint defense is that the benefits from government create their own conflicts. In Hobbesian anarchy, people are isolated and in armed conflict. There is one large externality: people are potentially trying to kill one another. This incentivizes everyone to "waste" resources on defending himself or herself. The solution or partial solution, at least in the simple two-person example, is joint defense. However, joint defense introduces new externalities: decision conflicts. If people are too diverse, these conflicts will overwhelm the benefits of joint defense. If their views are not too dissimilar, then the benefits from eliminating (or reducing) one large externality offsets the many smaller externalities that are a necessary component of the solution. People accept decisions they themselves do not prefer because of the overall benefits of cooperative defense.

The second observation concerns the definition of society. These decision conflicts limit the breadth of joint defense and effectively determine the limits of society. From this perspective, society consists of those individuals who decide to join in collective defense. People engaged in different defense collectives are living in different societies. This will be more obvious from the discussions in chapters 10 and 11. If there are no decision conflicts and no loss of freedom, then everyone will be in the same defense collective. However, there are costs of being part of joint defense: people will not agree with every decision. In fact, people may not agree with any decision, yet they may still voluntarily join. If everyone has the same worldview, there probably wouldn't be a Hobbesian original position and there will only be one global defense collective. Since everyone possesses different worldviews, some more similar than others, there is a limit to the size of a defense collective. There is a maximum loss of freedom a defense collective can sustain and still remain viable, since the gains from collective defense are limited. The definition of society that many of the authors in chapter 2 struggled with naturally falls out of the analysis of joint defense.

The third observation concerns a question that was posed earlier: What effect, if any, would a different original position have on the structure of the defense collective? What impact would a more successful anarchistic environment have on people's decisions to join in collective defense? Given the prior discussion, it is difficult to envision anarchy where people are not incentivized to invest in self-defense. That same discussion could also easily lead one to conclude that people can find methods of cooperating in anarchy, given the significant benefits of cooperation.

These methods will probably involve some type of closeness and repeated interactions among people that will incent them to limit some of their antisocial tendencies. These naturally developed methods can be viewed as informal collectives. People must accept abiding by a certain code of conduct as a condition of cooperating with other people. They may accept these conditions because of the benefits of cooperation. This allows them to move from the Hobbesian original position to a more productive original position. For some people, there could be psychological costs of accepting these norms of behavior, which reduces the overall gain they achieve from moving from the Hobbesian original position. Stated differently, some people may have freedom losses in non-Hobbesian anarchy as they accept norms of behavior they disagree with as a precondition of cooperating with others. The increase in cooperation will lead to higher incomes for at least some people and to improvement in the overall standard of living. These improvements are unlikely to be uniform across people. These observations lead to the supposition that original positions that have more cooperation than the Hobbesian one are likely to have individuals with higher average wealth, more diverse wealth, more diverse worldviews, and a smaller proportion of their wealth invested in arms. Increases in the overall standard of living probably will also give rise to a larger anarchical population.

Everything else being the same, this implies that the productivity gains in moving from anarchy to joint defense will be smaller for individuals who live in non-Hobbesian anarchy. For people who willingly accepted the restrictions imposed by culture, tradition, and norms, the more cooperative original position will reduce the diversity in worldviews that can be accommodated in joint defense. On the other hand, those people who chafed at the restrictions imposed by the naturally developed cooperative methods may have freedom gains from joining in collective defense, since they may be able to jointly agree to rules they prefer over those that limited their behavior in the cooperative original position. These gains, together with the productivity gains, could increase the range of diverse worldviews. In either case, the basic structure of the two-person collective is invariant with respect to the original position chosen to begin the bargaining.

The fourth observation concerns the potential similarity between maximizing freedom and utilitarianism. John Stuart Mill calls utilitarianism the "Greatest Happiness Principle," which states that people from a moral perspective should follow rules that maximize everyone's aggregate utility.[142] Recall from the discussion of John Harsanyi's worldview that utilitarianism to him is where each person in society has an individual social welfare function that guides him or her in choosing decisions for society. He argues that each person's social welfare function is a linear function of other people's utility in society, from that person's perspective. He views people in society as sufficiently alike so that they could come to similar policy conclusions. According to this view, governmental policy should be set to increase the average utility for the average member of society. At face value, this seems somewhat akin to the concept of maximizing freedom. However, the only similarity between utilitarianism and freedom maximization is the concept of optimization.

One difference is the expansive view of government that is at the heart of utilitarianism. The utilitarian worldview views government as a tool for achieving a wide variety of social and personal goals. It essentially views government and individuals as existing in a complete symbiotic relationship. Government power is potentially available to everyone to enforce rules and make trade-offs between conflicted people based on what is best for most of the people. While the discussion of collectives will ultimately be expanded to include broader goals than just external defense, it is important to note that government for people in the original position is just a tool to accomplish some of their defined objectives. Its members set its goals. Government is just one part of each person's overall toolkit in attempting to improve his or her life.

In this chapter, every person's goal beyond external defense is retained and independently pursued by that person. The defense collective's only mission is to improve external defense for its members. However, there are some decisions that the defense collective will make that potentially intrude on each member's other goals. For example, each person could be required to defend the collective and be prohibited from exiting.[143] Since collective decisions are made by minimizing freedom losses, a person's ability to pursue other goals can be adversely affected. But, if they still decide to join in collective defense, they are willing to make this sacrifice because of their allocated net gains.

In the two-person defense collective, freedom is not a goal. It is a means of achieving the objective of defense. Freedom maximization is not a "moral" prescription. It is an *objective* method of determining decisions among people with diverse worldviews. There are no objective freedoms and there are no universal freedoms. Different defense collectives will pursue different actions because people who are members of those collectives value some actions for the defense collective over other possible actions. In Hobbesian anarchy, everyone is completely free. In entering joint defense, individuals willingly give up some of those freedoms to accommodate the views of other people. It is entirely possible that no one will prefer any decision that the collective makes. Decisions made by diverse people are all made through accommodation and compromise, but compromise is costly, since people who accommodate others must be compensated in some fashion. Compromise allows cooperation but decreases the gains from association. Maximizing freedom and choosing decisions that cause the least cumulative reduction in value also maximize the net gains from joint defense.

The two-person defense collective is the result of two individuals trying to improve their lives. Joint defense is pursued because it is more efficient than anarchy. The collective is not a goal of either person; it is a tool or means of efficiently achieving their objective of external defense. The two people who agree to jointly cooperate in defense have diverse personal goals and worldviews. They both agree they desire external defense, but they could and probably do differ in the amount of defense they want to pursue, in the actions they want to take in pursuing defense, in their material well-being in the original position, and in their other goals and objectives. The defense collective with its structure of freedom maximization, taxes, defense production, and allocation of gains is a better alternative than anarchy in achieving each of their objectives of external defense.

The defense collective is an organization similar to the entities discussed in chapter 6. While the defense collective is a means and not a goal, as an entity, it has a goal. Its objective, as determined by the two people who agree to cooperate, is to efficiently produce external defense. To accomplish this goal, it needs to make various strategic and financial decisions that affect the well-being of its two members. These decisions are made unanimously by both members, even though the decisions have nonegalitarian effects on them. The defense collective is an extension of each person's desire for defense; it is an important tool—arguably the most important tool—for each person to increase his or her welfare. The defense collective is not concerned with each person's overall utility or well-being. Its goal is narrow: to produce external defense as efficiently as possible given the diverse worldviews and defense desires of its members.

The journey through the logic of coercive collectives is partially done. However, there are quite a few loose ends. The two-person defense collective allocates most of the net gains from cooperation to the wealthier person. This seems logical but counterintuitive based on the discussion of pirates in chapter 6 and the proliferation of democratic voting. The more complicated goals of internal defense, fraud, and social concerns still need to be addressed. But first, the analysis needs to be expanded to include more than two people.

I O

— ★ —

THREE-PERSON COLLECTIVE
DEFENSE: COMPETING POLITICS

The next four chapters are concerned with the decisions made by multiple people as they exit anarchy and seek to form a multiple-person defense collective. The focus will be on the decision conflicts and the strategic positioning between the various potential members of the defense collective. The decision on the optimal quantity of external defense is unaffected by the number of people in the defense collective. Whether there are two people or two million, given the assumption from the prior chapters, logically they will all agree to produce the socially optimal amount of external defense and pay gross taxes equal to their anarchical cost of defense. Therefore, throughout the remainder of the book, we will take the quantity of defense and tax decisions as given.

COALITIONS

While a three-person defense collective does not capture all the aspects of a defense cooperative composed of hundreds of millions of people, it does provide some insights that will be useful when the interactions among a large group of people are explored. In fact, as we will see, in a variety of ways, a three-person collective is more complicated to analyze than a collective with a massive number of people. The analysis will continue under similar simplifying assumptions that were made in chapter 8, including: (i) gains from joint defense of K per person, (ii) complete information concerning people's worldviews, (iii) everyone uses a common bargaining model and does not make bargaining mistakes, (iv) people are selfish in desiring their worldview to be the paradigm in which social decisions are made, (v) everyone is also selfish in their desire for the gains from joint common defense, and (vi) each person has a positive and _equal_ time value.

The assumption that each person joining in collective defense reduces the relative costs of collective defense versus anarchical defense by K per person implies that the gross gains from three-person joint defense over anarchical defense are $2K$. The addition of the third person adds another K of defense-productivity benefits through a reduction in fixed costs. From the prior analysis of the two-person defense collective, the only variables that affect each person's net gains from joint defense are: (i) productivity gains of K, (ii) joint freedom loss, and (iii) relative discount rates. The potential three-person collective is more complicated because the loss of freedom for each individual, as well as the joint loss of freedom, is dependent on the specific individuals who are participating. In a two-person defense collective there are only two potential results: either both people remain in the original position, or they both agree to participate in joint defense. In the three-person collective, there are more potential outcomes. All three could agree to form a defense collective, they could all remain in the original position, or two of them could agree to form a two-person collective while the third person remains in anarchy.

Consider a situation in which hypothetical people, Cali, Layla, and Margaret, are considering exiting the original position. To simplify the discussion, three stereotypical worldviews will be used: conservative, liberal, and moderate. Cali is the conservative, Layla the liberal, and Margaret's views are moderate. Though they all disagree on various governmental policies, they are presumed to be sufficiently compatible so that each will agree to be in a two-person defense collective with either of the other two women. This implies that even the conservative Cali and the liberal Layla will have net gains from two-person collective defense. The three women are also assumed to be sufficiently compatible so that a three-person defense collective is possible. Layla and Margaret are assumed to be closer in agreement than Margaret and Cali. We will also assume that Cali has the highest freedom losses from agreeing to the freedom-maximizing decisions in the three-person collective, followed by Margaret and then Layla.

The gross gain from each two-person collective is the same and equal to K. The gross gains do not depend on the identity of the individuals, since each individual has the same productivity gain from exiting anarchy. However, the net gains—the gains after subtracting joint freedom losses from accepting the freedom-maximizing decisions from the gross gains of K—vary with the identity of the various members of each collective. The assumptions concerning the women's worldviews imply that there are higher joint freedom losses and smaller net gains in a two-person collective between the conservative Cali and the liberal Layla than in either of the other potential two-person defense collectives. There are also higher freedom losses in the three-person collective than in any of the two-person collectives.

The freedom-maximizing decisions can be different in each of these potential defense collectives. The decisions concerning joint defense that reduce the aggregate losses from compromise between Layla and Margaret can differ significantly from the decisions that will exist in the two-person collective consisting of Margaret and Cali. For example, one of many of the decisions that will need to be made is how to treat prisoners captured in war. The freedom-maximizing decisions between Layla and Margaret could be to prohibit torturing prisoners, while Cali and Margaret could compromise and agree that a wide variety of tortures are authorized, including water boarding and sleep deprivation. From the discussion in chapters 8 and 9, it is important to emphasize that these freedom-maximizing decisions are based on the women's preferences and on their intensity for these preferences. For example, Margaret can prefer not to torture prisoners but will compromise and agree to laws that allow torture in her defense collective with Cali if Cali feels more strongly that torture is an acceptable tool. In a two-person collective between Cali and Layla, the decision to torture is reached in the same way, although it is entirely likely that the joint freedom losses from the freedom-maximizing decisions are higher than in the other two potential two-person collectives, since Cali's and Layla's views are the most dissimilar. It is also possible that the freedom-maximizing decisions concerning external defense made in the three-person defense collective will be significantly different than those made in any of the possible two-person collectives. Continuing with the torture example, the three-person collective can decide to allow limited types of torture like sleep deprivation but ban tortures such as water boarding, which may be different than the freedom-maximizing decisions concerning torture in any of the potential two-person collectives.

Alternatively, although unlikely, it is also possible that the freedom-maximizing decisions in each of the potential two-person defense collectives involving a specific woman and the three-person defense collective are all the same. For example, this could occur in any of the collectives where Layla is a member if Layla has more negative views of each of the other member's preferred decisions than each of the other members have for Layla's preferred decisions. In this situation, the freedom-loss minimizing (freedom-maximizing) decision for each collective involving Layla is for each person who is a member of that collective and who disagrees with Layla to compromise and let Layla have her preferred decision be the collective decision. Under these circumstances, Layla does not have any freedom losses, and each collective's decisions are the same as if she were a dictator. This is an extremely unlikely result, since there are a vast number of decisions concerning rules that each collective needs to make with respect to external defense, and each of the women can have differing views regarding each one of these decisions. The women are willing to compromise in this way because it increases the overall net gains from collective action.

The relevant questions are whether a three-person collective will determine its decisions by maximizing aggregate freedom, and how the three people will agree to divide the gains from collective defense.

Of course, there is also the question of whether a three-person defense collective will form. Given different worldviews, is there a bargaining equilibrium that will be sufficient to induce the three women to leave the original position and suffer through the compromises necessary to participate in collective defense?

To answer these questions, a variant of the two-person alternating-offer protocol will be used. Much of the literature about bargaining between multiple people who follow this procedure analyzes the division of a single good by multiple people.[144] To produce a unique equilibrium for multiple-person bargaining, researchers modify the two-person alternating-offer bargaining protocol in various ways, including allowing early exit from bargaining and sequential bargaining. However, our bargaining problem is concerned with the question of the agreed division of joint gains from people adding incremental value to a cooperative effort. There is a significant difference between the situation in which multiple people are needed to accomplish a goal and negotiate over the gains from accomplishing that task, and one in which two people add value and each additional person adds incremental value, and they jointly bargain over the resulting gains.

The protocol that will be used is one where each of the women sequentially bargains, using alternating-offers, with one of the other two women, and if they reach agreement, they bargain with the remaining woman. The bargain with the first woman will incorporate the possibility of a completed bargain with the second woman. Alternatively, each woman can bargain with a coalition (defined below) of the other two women. Given the assumption of positive but equal time value, each person is equally anxious to exit the Hobbesian original position. As before, each will want to maximize her net gains from exiting anarchy and participating in collective defense. Each woman will analyze her strategy to maximize her net gains, which includes her desire for her worldview to determine all the rules that will be enforced by the defense collective once it is formed. They will all use backward induction to determine their optimal strategy. Given the assumption that the third person adds an incremental value of K to each two-person collective, each woman, everything else the same, will want the third person to participate in joint defense. Of course, everything may not be the same, since each person (i) has a different worldview, (ii) wants her worldview to prevail, and (iii) desires all the gains from collective defense.

To assist with the analysis, it is helpful to introduce the concept of a "coalition." A coalition is a pre-collective or a potential collective. It is a hypothetical possible collective used to illustrate the strategic possibilities open to each person as they consider joining in collective defense. In a coalition, individuals have reached nonbinding agreements with each other. A coalition may become a collective if every person under consideration has thought about every possible coalition structure, every possible coalition allocation and the interaction among the various potential coalitions, and then determines that a collective is in their own best interest. A coalition between various people may not be stable and can be affected and destabilized by the decision options available to other people or other coalitions. A coalition of all three people that becomes a collective is the "grand coalition."

There are six possible ways or "paths" of forming the grand coalition between the three women. For example, Layla can make an offer to Margaret that is accepted, and together they make an offer to Cali. Similarly, Layla can make an offer to Cali and then their two-person coalition can make an offer to Margaret to form the collective. Layla can also join the two-person coalition between Margaret and Cali. In addition, the order of offers can be reversed. Theoretically, each of the women can be in any of these situations. Along each of these paths there is a subgame-perfect equilibrium that each of the women will agree is in their best interest. However, as discussed in the prior two chapters, the women will not agree to a bargaining protocol that is biased against them. Unless one of the paths is in all their best interests, they will only choose a bargaining protocol that neutralizes any positional advantage anyone may possess.

From the prior discussion, we know that in the traditional Rubinstein bargaining protocol where each bargaining round takes time, there is a first-mover advantage. To eliminate this bias, the women can agree to average the subgame equilibriums of being the first to act or agree to a protocol where the length of each bargaining round, in the limit, approaches zero. Either alternative will produce the same equilibrium result. To simplify the analysis, we will assume that they have chosen the latter. The resulting credible equilibrium determined by backward induction between any two of the three women, ignoring the existence of the third woman, is a two-person coalition where (i) the decisions are made that minimize the joint freedom losses between the two women in the defense coalition; (ii) each woman equally divides the net gains, which are the gross gains of K minus each woman's freedom losses from accepting the freedom-maximizing decisions between the two of them; and (iii) each woman receives her freedom losses. This, of course, is the credible equilibrium that was determined in chapter 8 between two people who had the same time value.

By reducing the length of the bargaining rounds and producing symmetry with respect to being the first to act, we have reduced the number of unique ways that each of the women can join in collective defense, from six to three. For example, Cali can form a two-person coalition with Layla and then they can add Margaret. The bargaining result for all of them is the same whether Cali joins Layla or Layla joins Cali in their two-person coalition. However, the alternatives of Cali entering into joint defense with Margaret and then adding Layla, or Cali joining the two-person defense coalition between Layla and Margaret, can produce unique bargaining solutions.

PARTIAL CREDIBLE EQUILIBRIUM

Another term that will prove helpful in the following discussion is the concept of a "partial credible equilibrium." A partial credible equilibrium is an agreed allocation of the gains between one or more of the individuals from *one* of the ways of forming the grand coalition that fully incorporates each person's time value. It is a subgame-perfect equilibrium where (i) the length of each bargaining period is effectively zero, and (ii) each person's time value and other variables are properly incorporated into an equilibrium allocation of the gains, but it ignores other ways of forming the grand coalition.

Using backward induction, the partial credible equilibrium from Margaret joining the coalition between Cali and Layla incorporates the optimal collective defense decisions for the three women as well as an agreed allocation of the resulting gains. The optimal collective decisions are those that minimize the women's aggregate freedom losses. Since each woman wants to maximize the net gains from exiting the original position, they will all agree to accept the defense decisions that minimize their joint freedom losses. The net gains from adding Margaret are the incremental efficiency gains of K minus the incremental aggregate freedom losses. The incremental aggregate losses are Margaret's freedom losses plus Cali's and Layla's incremental freedom losses from accepting the freedom-maximizing decisions in the three-person coalition. Cali's and Layla's incremental freedom losses are the difference between their joint freedom losses from the three-person coalition versus their two-person coalition. If there are no differences between the freedom-maximizing decisions in the two different-size coalitions, then Cali and Layla will not have any incremental freedom losses. Under these conditions, the net gains from adding Margaret are equal to K minus her freedom losses.[145]

Alternatively, if Margaret prefers one or more different rules and feels strongly about her positions, then the freedom-maximizing decisions in the three-person defense coalition may be different than the optimal decisions in the two-person coalition that does not include her. These decision changes will lead to incremental freedom losses from Cali and Layla accepting the new freedom-maximizing decisions in the three-person coalition. The net gains from adding Margaret will then be the incremental gains of K minus the aggregate freedom losses from each of the three women.

Backward induction will also reveal the partial credible equilibrium allocation of the gross gains of $2K$ that will be agreed to by the three women. Margaret's allocation will be (i) half of the incremental net gains of her joining Cali and Layla plus (ii) her freedom losses from agreeing to accept the freedom-maximizing decisions among the three women.[146] She will bargain for half of the net gains because each woman is assumed to be equally anxious to exit anarchy. This is a partial credible equilibrium instead of a credible equilibrium because it ignores other options that the women have to form the three-person collective. If this is the only option available, this will be the credible equilibrium allocation that will be offered to Margaret, and Margaret will accept.

Cali's allocation of the efficiency gains of $2K$ from adding Margaret to her two-person coalition with Layla are (i) half of the net gains from the two-person defense coalition between Cali and Layla plus (ii) one-quarter of the net gains from adding Margaret to their two-person coalition plus (iii) her freedom losses from the three-person coalition.[147] The net gains in (i) and (ii) will be different because the aggregate freedom losses are different in each situation. The net gains in the two-person coalition are K minus Cali's and Layla's aggregate losses from compromising on defense decisions that maximize their joint freedom (ignoring Margaret's views). The net gains from adding Margaret are the efficiency gains of K minus Margaret's freedom losses and Cali's and Layla's incremental freedom losses from accepting the defense decisions that minimize all three women's freedom losses. It cannot be overemphasized that the freedom-maximizing decisions made in the two-person coalition between Cali and Layla can be significantly different than the freedom-maximizing decisions in the three-person coalition.

Layla's partial credible equilibrium allocation of the $2K$ of gross gains from this way of forming the three-person coalition is the same as Cali's allocation except that she will receive her own freedom losses. Layla will have the same allocation of net gains as Cali's allocation since they both have the same time preference and the bargaining protocol is unbiased. Layla, however, will receive less of the gross gains, since under the assumptions from above, she has lower freedom losses in the three-person coalition than Cali.

This, of course, is only one way of forming the three-person coalition. The other ways will lead to their own partial credible equilibrium allocations among the three women. All the equilibrium allocations will follow the same pattern that the two women who form the two-person coalition will each receive half of the net gains from their two-person coalition plus one-quarter of the net gains from adding the third woman. The third woman will receive an allocation of half of her incremental net gains. In addition, each person will receive her freedom losses from agreeing to the freedom-maximizing decisions in the three-person coalition. These compromise losses from the three-person coalition are invariant as to how that coalition is formed. However, as was discussed in the beginning of this section, the losses in each of the two-person coalitions are dependent on the identity of the two women. This implies that the incremental losses from adding the third woman will also differ between the three equilibrium allocations. The building blocks for determining the credible equilibrium among the three women have now been derived. It is evident that each of the women is in complete conflict with the other two women. No one has the bargaining power to incent the other women to follow the path of forming the three-person collective that is in her best interest. To prove this, we need to check whether one of the potential paths and resulting partial credible equilibrium allocations is in each of the women's best interests. If not, then they are all in conflict since each of them will then prefer a different path of forming the three-person defense collective.

Conflicts over the Preferred Path

Let's check whether one of these paths of forming the three-person defense collective is in each of the women's best interests. That is, do they all achieve their highest allocation of the net gains from the same way of forming the defense collective? If not, then they are in conflict and would prefer a different way of forming the three-person collective.

The first path we will check is the one where Cali joins the two-person coalition between Layla and Margaret. This two-person coalition provides Layla and Margaret with higher net gains than the other two potential two-person coalitions involving Cali since they are assumed to be the most politically compatible. Therefore, both Layla and Margaret would prefer the path where they first join in two-person collective defense with each other over the paths where one of them first joins with Cali. Let's make the additional assumption that both of them also prefer this path over the alternative of joining the two-person coalition between one of them and Cali. The question is whether it is possible for Cali to also prefer this path, under this new assumption.

For Cali to prefer this way of forming the three-person collective, the freedom losses from the two-person coalition between Layla and Margaret must be higher than the freedom losses from a two-person coalition involving Cali. However, the opposite is true. This implies that Cali would not prefer the alternative of joining the two-person coalition between Layla and Margaret.

The second path we will examine is the one where Layla is assumed to prefer joining the two-person coalition between Margaret and Cali. Under this condition, is it possible that both Margaret and Cali would find this method of forming the collective in their best interests? For this to be to Margaret's advantage, her partial credible equilibrium allocation from first forming a two-person coalition with Cali and then adding Layla must be higher than any other alternative. But it is not since she is more politically compatible with Layla and under these circumstances would prefer a different path.

The final way of forming the collective that needs to be checked is the one where Margaret joins the two-person coalition between Layla and Cali. For Margaret to prefer this path, it must have a higher allocation for her than being in a two-person coalition with Layla and having Cali join them. This can occur when Cali and Layla have high compromise losses from their two-person coalition, which is a distinct possibility. For Layla to also prefer this path, the freedom losses from being in a two-person coalition with Margaret must be higher than being in a two-person coalition with Cali. This is not the case. Therefore, Layla would not prefer this method of forming the three-person defense collective. They are all in conflict. None of the paths is in all of their best interests.

Unanimously Agreed Allocation of Collective Gains

Since they are all in conflict they will not agree to a biased bargaining protocol that favors one path over another path of forming the three-person collective. Nonetheless, the women's situations differ. While each person is equally productive in reducing the fixed costs of defense, they are not equally politically compatible since they have different worldviews. As we have discussed, this produces different levels of net gains, depending on the way the collective is formed.

In determining an equilibrium allocation, it will prove helpful to make the additional assumption that none of the women's freedom losses are sufficiently high to cause a path to produce a partial credible equilibrium allocation that exceeds K. As discussed above, they will not agree to use a bargaining procedure that is biased. As in the two-person situation, one unbiased protocol is for them to average the various paths of forming the defense collective. By equally weighing the various credible equilibrium allocations from each way of constructing the grand coalition, they can determine their credible equilibrium allocation of joining the defense collective. Therefore, each person will agree to an allocation of the gross gains of $2K$ where they receive the *average of their partial credible equilibrium allocations from the three different ways of forming the three-person collective*.[148]

This implies that the three-person collective will make the defense decisions that minimize aggregate freedom losses since this increases each of the women's net gains. It also means that each person will receive their freedom losses from compromising and accepting these decisions, plus one-third of the net gains from the different ways that they could have joined in collective defense. Each of the women will recognize that this is their best alternative and will immediately provide the offers and acceptances that are consistent with this credible equilibrium allocation of the gross gains from collective defense.

The three-person collective has almost all the properties of the two-person collective. Even though people have different worldviews and therefore have different preferred decisions as they relate to common defense, they are willing to compromise and accept decisions that they do not prefer because they are compensated for their losses from these compromise decisions and because they also receive an allocation of the net gains from common defense. Since each woman's preferred rules for defense cannot be the actual decisions that the defense collective adopts, they unanimously agree to the collective decisions that minimize their aggregate freedom losses because those decisions maximize their aggregate net gains. Given the assumptions concerning relative freedom losses, each person willingly leaves the original position for the benefits of common defense, willingly subjecting herself to coercively enforced rules concerning defense that are not her preferred collective defense actions.

However, there is one key difference between a three-person defense collective and a two-person defense collective. In the latter, where each person has the same time value, they agree to evenly divide the net gains. However, in the former where people have different worldviews and the same positive time values, yet prefer different paths to form the collective, they agree to unevenly divide the net gains. In the larger collective, the freedom losses that occur in each two-person coalition are a component part of the allocation of the gains in the credible equilibrium because each of the women achieves a different allocation in the different partial credible equilibrium allocations. The women have differential gains in the various two-person coalitions, which lead them to a preference over the ways of constructing the three-person collective. Under our assumptions, Layla will receive the highest allocation of net gains since the two, two-person coalitions that include her have lower aggregate freedom losses than the two-person coalition that does not include her. Similarly, Cali will agree to receive the lowest allocation of the net gains since the two, two-person coalitions that include her have higher aggregate freedom losses than the two-person coalition between Layla and Margaret.

This is an important point that will carry through the entire discussion of defense collectives with more than two people. In the two-person coalition, aggregate freedom losses are subtracted from the gross gains of K and the resulting net gains are equally divided. The person with the higher freedom losses, the person who suffered the most from compromising and accepting the freedom-maximizing collective decisions, has the highest allocation since she receives an equal share of the gains after deducting freedom losses plus her higher freedom losses. However, in the three-person collective, the person with the highest freedom losses may not receive an equal allocation of the net gains from each person cooperating in joint defense and agreeing to laws that she does not prefer. In fact, as we saw above, the person who suffers the largest compromise losses may have the lowest allocation of the net gains from collective defense. She may still have the highest gross allocation since she will receive her freedom losses, but this allocation is necessary to make her indifferent to exiting the original position and compromising on defense-related laws and rules.

FREEDOM LOSSES

As discussed in chapter 8, there are a wide variety of decisions that each defense collective and each potential collective or coalition will want to make. Some coalitions of people may decide to be primarily defensive while others will want to project power. Coalitions could also exist between these two extremes. If the method of deterrence is the only defense coalition decision, then each person will rather be in the defense coalition whose decisions concerning deterrence he or she agreed with the most. However, there are a number of other decisions that the defense coalition will make including issues of individual privacy, torture, press freedom, spying, interference with other collectives, immigration, and the use of a draft. In addition, there are also a wide variety of potential actions that a defense coalition can take for each decision it makes. This implies that it is unlikely that any two people will agree with every potential action for the coalition. It also means that each person will prefer to associate with people whose values on these possible actions are most similar to their values. The net gains from associating with people with comparable values are higher than the net gains from being in a coalition with people with widely different worldviews. However, as long as the net gains from adding another person, even a person with a significantly different worldview, are positive, then they will want to continue to expand their defense coalition. The decision that each defense coalition makes is dependent not only on the value that each member has on the decisions that are ultimately made, but also on their values for alternative decisions. The value that each member has for potential decisions are relevant to the determination of the actions by the defense coalition.

In the three-person collective above, the credible equilibrium allocation was derived. It is an average of each of the women's partial credible equilibrium allocations from each potential way of constructing

the three-person collective. The partial credible equilibrium allocation along each path of forming the collective is the one that each
woman will accept, using her relative bargaining advantages, assuming that each path is the only path. For example, if two people have
the same worldview as it relates to every defense decision including
torture, and they form a three-person defense collective with a person
with a different worldview, the credible equilibrium will be a higher
allocation of the net gains to the two people with the same worldview. These two people will also receive the same credible equilibrium
allocation. Irrespective of each of the women's freedom losses in the
three-person collective, the two women who have the same worldview do not have to compromise in their two-person coalition. Given
the unbiased bargaining protocol, this incentivizes the person with
the different worldview to agree to receive less than one-third of the
net gains from collective defense.

The decision on whether torture will be authorized in this defense
collective is dependent on the sum of the freedom losses experienced
by the two people with the same worldview from accepting the third
person's preferred position, as compared to the freedom losses experienced by the person with the different worldview who accepts the
other two people's preferred position. Let's simplify the analysis and
assume that the defense collective only needs to make one decision and
that decision involves torture of enemy combatants. Let's also assume
that the two people with the same worldview think torture is acceptable and that the third person disagrees. In addition, let's assume that
the freedom-maximizing decision for each of the two-person defense
coalitions is to torture enemy combatants. This implies that torture
will be authorized in the three-person defense collective, if the person
who thinks torture is unacceptable does not feel so strongly about not
allowing torture that her compromise losses exhaust all the gains from
collective defense. Assuming that there are net gains from collective
defense, the person who thinks torture is unacceptable is incented to
compromise and accept torture as a legitimate collective power, since
she receives her freedom losses plus a share of the net gains from collective defense. She will also agree to receive a lower share of the net
gains, which under these assumptions are the total productivity gains

of $2K$ minus her freedom losses from accepting torture as an authorized tool of the defense collective. Also under these assumptions, her credible equilibrium allocation of the total net gains is one-third of the difference between the total net gains and half of her freedom losses in the two, two-person coalitions. She receives the highest allocation of the gross gains since she is the only person who must compromise, but she agrees to receive a lower allocation of the net gains because of the other two people's relative bargaining advantage.

In deriving the credible equilibrium in the prior section, three important assumptions were made concerning the women's relative worldviews. First, they were all assumed to be sufficiently compatible so that a three-person collective was achievable; that is, there were positive net gains from collective three-person defense. Second, each of the two-person coalitions also had positive net gains. If the last assumption is relaxed, the derivation of the unique credible equilibrium allocation does not change if the net gains to each person in each of the partial credible equilibrium allocations calculated in the prior section are positive. However, if a path of constructing the collective has an allocation to any of the women that is less than her freedom losses, then that allocation is no longer credible or feasible. No one will accept that allocation; each person would rather stay in anarchy than accept that. Instead, the only credible allocation along this path is one in which each of the women receives an equal allocation of the net gains from the three-person coalition, irrespective of the net losses from the two-person coalition. In this situation, the extreme losses from the differential worldviews in the two-person coalition, from this way of constructing the collective, are so high that the partial credible equilibrium reduces to an equal division of the assumed net gains from the three-person defense coalition. If this is true for each path, then the credible equilibrium allocation for each person is her freedom losses plus an equal allocation of the net gains from the three-person defense collective.

The key difference between the two credible equilibrium allocations is the lack of any bargaining advantage in forming each of the two-person coalitions in the latter credible equilibrium. The credible equilibrium in the prior paragraph only occurs when the women have sufficiently compatible worldviews to form a three-person collective but not sufficiently compatible worldviews to have an advantage in forming a two-person coalition. Stated somewhat differently, the only instance when the credible equilibrium allocation among three people joining together in collective defense is an equal division of the net gains would be one in which no one has any advantage of first forming a two-person coalition. In this case, the way of forming the three-person defense collective does not matter. However, if the path of formation matters, then the credible equilibrium allocation will be an uneven division of the net gains from collective defense.

The third assumption was that none of the paths produced an allocation more than K. A path can theoretically produce an allocation to one of the women higher than K when the women are not that compatible, and one or more of them has high freedom losses in the three-person defense collective. It will only occur in one of the two paths where she is a member of a two-person coalition. An allocation more than K means that she is receiving more than her marginal contribution. She will not be able to use this as leverage against the other women. In determining the credible equilibrium, she and her partner in the two-person coalition will agree to cap her allocation along this path to K. It is this capped allocation that is then used to determine the credible equilibrium allocation.

This credible equilibrium agreement as to the division of the joint gains from collective defense is unanimously and immediately agreed to by each of the women. It is self-enforcing. That is, none of the women prefer a different allocation given the bargaining power and potential logical decisions of the other women. While the women are bargaining over the formation of a defense collective that has the coercive power to enforce all their agreements, they will not unanimously agree to the use of this coercive force until they have explored all their options and the collective is officially formed. That is, they will not agree to first form a two-person collective and then form a three-person collective. They will only form a collective once they all have reasoned through their strategy and determined a course of action that is optimal. In the case of the three women where their worldviews are not too dissimilar, this results in a unanimous credible equilibrium agreement to divide the net gains based on the average of the partial credible equilibriums. The agreement among the women will also include a provision that the defense decisions will be those that maximize their joint freedom. These two agreements are essentially the constitution for the defense collective, and the collective will use coercive force to enforce the constitution. Even though that constitution is unanimously approved, its terms are obviously not everyone's a priori preferred terms. At least one of the women may want to violate or change its terms after the formation of the defense collective. There is a cost to this for the other women, since they reached a finely balanced constitution in terms of rules and allocation of the net gains. One of the unanimously agreed rules will be coercive enforcement of the approved laws and allocations.

SHAPLEY VALUE

The analysis of the formation of the defense collective is in the tradition of "noncooperative" game theory where all agreements must be self-enforcing. The agreements and allocations are an integral component of the analysis and are internally determined by the participants' relative bargaining positions. "Cooperative" game theory, on the other hand, assumes that participants can somehow enforce all their agreements. One of the normative questions that people have asked in cooperative game theory is: What is a "fair" allocation if people can enforce their agreements? Lloyd Shapley, a Nobel Prize–winning economist, proposed an allocation. It has become known as the Shapley Value.[149] It is defined as the average of each person's marginal contribution to each potential way of constructing the grand coalition. It can be viewed as "fair" because it rewards members of the grand coalition for the marginal contributions they make to the overall gains from the formation of the grand coalition. On the other hand, it is not necessarily the same as an equal division of the overall gains, since it is possible that people have different marginal contributions, and for that reason, some will not view it as "fair."

The credible equilibrium allocation that was derived above for the three-person defense collective is equal to the Shapley Value, since each person receives the average of her net gains from each way of constructing the defense collective.[150] The agreed allocation is one in which each woman receives the average of her partial credible equilibrium allocations from forming the defense collective. It is equal to her freedom losses plus one-third of her specific net gains from each way of constructing the grand coalition. Each woman's specific net gains can differ because each of them can have different freedom losses from making compromises in each of the potential ways of constructing the three-person collective. If each of the two-person coalitions produces a net gain from the freedom-maximizing defense decisions, each woman's credible equilibrium specific net gains are the gross gains of $2K$ reduced by both (i) the aggregate freedom losses from the three-person collective and (ii) one-quarter of the total freedom losses in each of the two-person coalitions in which she is a member, plus one-half of the total freedom losses in the two-person coalition in which she is not involved.[151] Each woman will agree to receive one-third of her specific net gains.

As was discussed above, if none of the women have incremental value from first forming a two-person coalition, the partial equilibrium allocation along each path is the same for each and reduces to an even division of net gains. The agreed allocation in this special case is an even division of these equal credible equilibriums, which results in each person agreeing to receive one-third of the net gains from collective defense.

The Shapley Value is a normative concept, since it suggests a particular method of dividing the gains from collective action "if" people "desire" to achieve an allocation that has "certain" properties. The credible equilibrium, on the other hand, is a "positivistic" allocation, that is, unanimously accepted by each of the women irrespective of their individual views of fairness. It is a universal allocation, dependent on people thinking their views are the most accurate representation of the real world and on their unwillingness to engage in a biased bargaining procedure, but otherwise independent of any moral or ethical belief system. It arises because each of the women finds value in collective defense but is faced with decision congestion given their differing worldviews. They unanimously agree to the allocation that results from the credible equilibrium because each of them is selfish and wants their worldview to be the prevailing worldview for the defense collective.

In the credible equilibrium allocation of the net gains from cooperative defense, each person's marginal contribution to each way of constructing the defense collective is itself a product of a bargaining situation. Each person's marginal contribution is a partial credible equilibrium. Each partial credible equilibrium allocation is dependent on each person's relative level of freedom losses. The person with the highest overall equilibrium allocation will be the one whose net gains from all of their partial equilibrium allocations sums to a higher amount than those of the other women. The credible equilibrium allocation recognizes the incremental value this person adds to the formation of the defense cooperative—not by her imposing a solution, but by utilizing her bargaining advantage this incremental value provides to her and not accepting a biased procedure.

The three-person defense collective has elements in common with the two-person collective. The equilibrium defense actions are those that minimize aggregate freedom losses. Also, the allocation of the gross gains, K, in the three-person world, as in the two-person situation, is still dependent on relative freedom losses. However, the existence of the third person and the ability to form differing coalitions allows the person who is most politically compatible with the other two people to achieve a higher allocation of the net gains from collective defense. A critical question and one we have been leading up to throughout this part of the book is the impact on the equilibrium structure of the defense collective when the number of people cooperating in collective defense is in the millions. That is the subject of the next chapter.

I I

DEMOCRATIC DEFENSE COLLECTIVE

Thus far, the defense collective has only one goal: to defend its members from external threats. As we examine the impact on the structure of the defense collective from the presence of billions of people in the original position, we will continue with this simplification. As in the analysis above, each of these people will voluntarily leave anarchy for joint defense only if they perceive they will receive net gains for making that decision. That is, they will voluntarily abandon the freedom and inefficiency of anarchical defense for the potential benefits of collective defense if their allocation of the gross gains from collective defense is larger than their freedom losses from compromising and accepting the freedom-maximizing decisions in the collective they decide to join.

Given the wide range of worldviews in a large population, and the considerable, but limited, gains from collective defense, it is probable that people will determine their net gains are higher if not everyone joins one large defense collective. This is likely to be true even when the defense collective makes its defense decisions based on those that minimize everyone's freedom losses. The differing worldviews will cause people's freedom losses to increase exponentially as the number of people in the defense collective increases, while the productivity gains from additional people increase only linearly. This phenomenon

will lead to the formation of multiple defense collectives in a sufficiently large population. We will return to the impact this will have on
the characteristics of the defense collective at the end of this chapter.
For now, we are interested in only one of these potential defense collectives, and we will pick the largest one.

N-PERSON COLLECTIVE DEFENSE

This defense collective has N people, which is a subset of the total
population. Based on the analysis thus far, the total gross gains from a
defense collective with N people is one less than the total number of
people in the defense collective multiplied by the productivity gains
from each person of K. In other words, the gross gains for the N-person
collective is $(N - 1) \times K$. This is an intuitive formula, since one person
must associate with another person to produce any incremental value
over being in anarchy. As the defense collective expands, the gross
gains increase by K for each person who joins it in common defense.
The net gains for the defense collective are these gross returns minus
the joint freedom losses from everyone in the collective compromising
and accepting the freedom-maximizing defense decisions.[152]

The examination of the bargaining solution in the large defense
collective is simplified if two questions are initially addressed. First,
what is the maximum allocation of the gross gains from a credible
equilibrium that any member of a defense coalition, including the
grand defense coalition, can achieve? Second, what are the maximum
freedom losses that any member of a defense coalition or collective can
sustain and willingly join? The answer to both questions is the same,
and it is the incremental or marginal change in productivity from adding another person to the defense collective, K.

In a two-person defense collective, where each person has the
same positive time value and the same worldview, both people will
agree to equally divide the gross gains of K. If the aggregate freedom
losses are more than K, in a world consisting of only two people, then
neither person will willingly join in common defense, since collectively
they will need to receive more than K to be indifferent to remaining in

anarchy or participating in joint defense. However, the assumed gains from common defense are limited and equal to K. No one will be willing to join in collective defense if they sustain aggregate net losses. This result continues to hold in a defense collective of N people. The most that any one person can add in value to a collective is K. If they receive more than K, they are receiving more than their entire incremental value, which can only occur if someone is willing to subsidize them. Since the maximum gross gain from adding anyone to the collective is K, there is no reason for anyone or everyone to be willing to reduce their allocated gains to allow this person into the collective. Each person in a defense collective with $N - 1$ people would rather stay at that size than add anyone who requires or attempts to bargain for an allocation more than K. Nor would anyone join a defense collective when they do not at least receive their freedom losses, since in this instance they are better off in the original position (or joining another defense collective). If a person's allocation of the gains from joint defense is not sufficient to cover their costs from decision externalities, they will prefer to remain in anarchy.

Expanding the size of the defense collective from three to millions does not fundamentally change the conclusions from the prior chapter about how multiple people will unanimously agree to divide the gains from joint defense. We will continue the same assumptions that were made in the prior chapter, including that every person has the same positive time value, with two important exceptions. In a large population, the prior assumption that each of the potential two-person defense coalitions has net gains is too stringent. In a defense collective with a membership numbering in the millions, there will be as many worldviews. This will likely lead to many situations in which the worldview differences between any two people in the defense collective are larger than K. The people in this situation may be able to overcome the disadvantage and join the defense collective if their overall allocation of the gains from collective defense is sufficient to overcome these worldview differences with specific people. Therefore, the analysis needs to consider this potential outcome.

We also need to relax the assumption that no one had freedom losses that caused their allocation from any of the potential paths of forming the defense collective to be capped at K. In a large population, many people will have high freedom losses given the diversity of political views. This will lead to an imposition of an allocation cap of K on many of their potential ways of joining the defense collective.

Each person in the overall population, including the subset that joins the N-person defense collective, is assumed to want their worldview to be the accepted one that all the laws, rules, and procedures of the defense collective are based on. As such, each person will attempt to maximize their net gains from exiting the Hobbesian original position given their worldview, the worldviews of the other members, and the productivity gains from collective defense. This will lead them to use the backward-induction algorithm to reason through their bargaining strategy. Since no one will agree to a bargaining protocol that is biased, each will conclude that their optimal bargaining strategy is to unanimously agree to the allocation given by the credible equilibrium, which is equal to the average of each person's partial credible equilibrium allocation from each potential way of forming the defense collective. The credible equilibrium allocation to each person in the N-person defense collective is one where each person receives their freedom losses, plus the average of their marginal contributions to the overall net gains from collective defense as determined by the partial credible equilibrium allocations of the different ways of forming the defense collective. The N-person defense collective will choose its defense decisions based on those that minimize the freedom losses of its members, since those decisions maximize the aggregate net gains from common defense.

In the N-person defense collective, there are $(N - 1) \times K$ of total productivity gains from the N people participating in collective defense. Each person is bargaining over the allocation of these gains. But in the credible equilibrium allocation, no one will receive more than K or receive less than their individual freedom losses from being a member of the defense collective. Furthermore, the credible equilibrium allocation of the gains will only be to people who are members of the defense collective. These observations imply that the gross gains will be allocated to the N people with no person receiving more than K. The average allocation is therefore $((N - 1) / N) \times K$, which is less than K. However, as the number of people in the defense collective increases, the average allocation gets closer to K. For example, with two people, the average allocation is 0.5 of K. With three people, the average allocation is 0.666666 of K. With one million people, the average allocation increases to 0.999999 of K. This has the important implication that as the number of people in the defense collective gets very large, and as N goes to infinity (but still less than every person in the population), then the average allocation goes to K. Since no one can receive an allocation larger than K, this implies that in the limit, as N goes to infinity, the credible equilibrium allocation to each of the people in the N-person defense collective will be K. In the limit, each person in the defense collective, irrespective of their freedom losses, will receive the same allocation of the gross returns from joint defense that is equal to the marginal productivity gain from exchanging anarchical defense for collective defense.[153] A defense collective composed of people with differing worldviews that satisfies this property is a "democratic defense collective."

The two primary characteristics of a democratic defense collective are that every member has the right to have his or her worldview considered as a component part of the collective decision-making process, and each person equally benefits from the productivity gains from collective defense. The democratic defense collective is the limit of a multi-person defense collective. Stated differently, each multi-person defense collective approximates a democratic defense collective; the larger it gets, the better the approximation. The democratic defense collective is the result of a bargaining equilibrium between a large group of diverse people as they seek to achieve the gains from collective defense.

It embeds a certain type of equality, but maybe not the type of equality that any of the bargainers a priori think is "fair." For example, the members do not bargain for equal happiness, equal wealth, or equal opportunities. Instead, they bargain and reach immediate agreement with all the other members of the collective to receive an equal share of the productivity benefits. It is in each person's interest to accept this bargain if their freedom losses are less than or equal to the marginal productivity gains from collective defense, and there are no defense collectives in which they will have a higher net gain. If their only choice is between the democratic defense collective and anarchy, they will choose the defense collective if their net gains are not negative.

In terms of worldview, the type of equality that people bargain for in joining the democratic defense collective is one in which each person's worldview is considered but people's preferences are not equally weighted. The decisions made by the defense collective are those that maximize joint freedom or minimize aggregate freedom losses. As such, they incorporate each person's preferences as well as the intensity each person has for their preferences and for the preferences of every person. An individual who feels more strongly than another that a potential defense decision is wrong will have a larger impact on the final collective decision about that issue than the individual who does not feel as strongly. An opinionated person's worldview will be weighted more than a person who has views but does not feel as deeply about them. In a democratic defense collective, each person's views are considered, but those views that are held more strongly receive a higher weight in determining the collective defense decisions.

The equality of the democratic defense collective is such that each person agrees to an equal share of the gross gains. To many people this may seem "fair," since the total gains from collective defense are evenly divided between each of the members of the defense collective. However, this allocation implies that people with different freedom losses from compromising and accepting the decisions made by the defense collective will receive different net gains. Members of the democratic defense collective who feel strongly about a decision but decide to compromise (because in the aggregate others feel more strongly) will receive the same gross gains as those who feel strongly about a decision and do not have to compromise (because the collective adopts their preferred decision). Furthermore, members of the democratic defense collective who have strong views will receive the same gross gains as those who do not feel strongly about collective defense decisions.

To see the complete implications of an equal division of the total productivity gains, it is helpful to rank those in the democratic defense collective according to their freedom losses. Given the large number of people in that collective with differing worldviews, it is extremely unlikely that each person will have the same freedom losses from compromising and accepting the collective's decisions that maximize aggregate freedom. In performing the ranking, the person with the least freedom losses will be labeled as Person 1 and the person with the most freedom losses as Person N (for example, Person 251 million). Theoretically there can be ties, but it is unlikely that every person will have worldviews that will result in equal freedom losses. Person N, the person with the highest freedom losses, will not have losses in excess of K, since he or she will then have negative net gains and will not join this democratic defense collective. The person with the least losses may not have any losses but more likely will have some freedom losses that are less than K. This implies that the net gains for Person 1 will be higher than for Person N.

Recall that the credible equilibrium allocation to each person is his or her freedom losses plus the average of his or her marginal contributions to the aggregate net gains in the democratic defense collective as given by the partial credible equilibrium allocations from each way of forming the democratic defense collective. In that collective, each person's allocation is an equal share of the total productivity gains given by the marginal productivity gains of K, as well as an allocation determined by the credible equilibrium. Therefore, each person who has a marginally higher contribution to the collective's net gains will receive a higher overall allocation of the net gains. Freedom losses are effectively a cost of collective defense each person receives to make him or her indifferent from exiting the original position. Agreeing to actions for the defense collective that are not the person's preferred actions has a physic cost to each person and results in societal deadweight losses. People in the defense collective do not get any "satisfaction" from just receiving their freedom losses. People only gain from exiting anarchy if they receive an allocation of the net gains from collective defense. Therefore, Person 1 is the most "socially satisfied," since he or she, in the credible equilibrium, receives a higher allocation of the net gains. Person 1 may not be the most personally satisfied, or have the highest net worth, or be the most skillful person in the defense collective, but he or she is the person most content with the decisions made by the defense collective.

Person 1 can achieve this higher allocation because of the bargaining advantage given by his or her relative worldview compatibility with other people in the defense collective. The more compatible person has lower freedom losses and therefore higher aggregate marginal net gains, which the person can leverage into a higher equilibrium allocation of the net gains from collective defense. The person can achieve this allocation irrespective of people's views on "fairness," since each person wants his or her worldview to be the basis for all the rules that the democratic defense collective coercively enforces. The less compatible person, Person N, agrees to a lower allocation of the net gains and consents to suffer for his or her relatively higher level of freedom losses because he or she is at least as well off as being in the original position (or joining another defense collective).

A relevant question is whether this same result occurs in the democratic defense collective when people have different positive time values. As was discussed in some detail earlier, interpersonal conflicts will lead to economic inefficiencies in the original position, including the existence of inefficient capital markets. This could cause people with lower endowments and less wealth, everything else being the same, to have higher time discount rates than wealthier people. Even if it does not, it is unlikely that everyone will have the same time preference.

In the two-person defense collective, the person with the lower discount rate can achieve a higher allocation of the net gains, since both people realize that person is more patient. Both people are anxious to exit the original position, but if the poorer person is more anxious, the wealthier person can bargain for a relatively higher share. This also occurs in a defense collective consisting of more than two people, since those with lower discount rates, everything else being the same, can use their time discount advantage to bargain for a higher allocation. However, as the size of the defense collective increases, people with the highest discount rates continue to increase their absolute allocation of K. In the limit, in the democratic defense collective, the disadvantage of a higher discount rate is eliminated. Each person in the democratic defense collective is, by definition, already receiving the maximum allocation of the overall gross gains.

The existence of differing discount rates will not have any impact on the mutually agreed allocation of either gross or net gains in the democratic defense collective. The presence of numerous people in the multi-person defense collective provides a positive externality to people with less wealth and higher time discount rates. As more people join in collective defense, the average allocation of the overall gross gains increases. Since no one will receive more than K, those with the most patience ultimately see their advantage disappear. In the democratic defense collective, no one's time discount rate provides any differential advantage or disadvantage.

PERFECT VOICE AND PERFECT ENTRY

The economist Albert Hirschman discussed two forces common to almost any organization or social arrangement: the ability to exit a relationship and the ability to influence the decisions made by an organization.[154] Our discussion so far has focused on only one of these—voice. We have explored the decisions the democratic defense collective will make in the presence of differing opinions on the best laws and rules relative to collective defense. While each person's views will factor into the defense collective's decision, their views are not necessarily equally weighted. The analysis led to the conclusion that people voluntarily exiting the original position will unanimously agree to collective decisions that minimize aggregate freedom losses. Each will agree to have force used against them if they do not comply with these laws, even though they will a priori disagree with some or all of these decisions. They are willing to make this agreement because of the benefit each of them receives from participating in collective defense. Each person bargains for an allocation of the gross gains equal to their freedom losses plus the average of their net gains from each way of constructing the defense collective. In the democratic defense collective, this allocation is K for everyone irrespective of each person's freedom losses.

These conclusions are based on a few strong assumptions, including: (i) each person has perfect information about their own worldview as well as that same amount of information about every other person's worldview, including their preferences and intensities; (ii) every worldview can be directly compared with every other worldview; and (iii) people use the same bargaining model and do not make bargaining mistakes. These imply that each person who exits anarchy can accurately determine the optimal collective defense decisions, given every person's diverse views and opinions. There is "perfect voice" in the democratic defense collective. The defense collective perfectly listens to its members, accurately records their views, and flawlessly administers their decisions.

With perfect voice, the members of the defense collective do not need to rely on the pressure of potential exit to encourage the defense collective to make the optimal defense decisions. Nonetheless, exit is still an equilibratory force as people leave the original position. To join a defense collective, people must first exit anarchy. So far, the assumption has been that this exit is costless or "perfect," except for freedom losses. This implies that each person can easily enter collective defense with any other person. As everyone considers their strategy in the original position, they will want to join the defense collective that maximizes their net gains.

Everyone's desire to maximize their own net gains will lead them as a group to maximize aggregate net gains for everyone by forming different defense collectives and joining the collective that maximizes their net gains. If every person has the same worldview, then they will all join the same defense collective and aggregate gross gains will be the same as aggregate net gains. These gains will be equal to the number of people in the world minus 1, multiplied by the marginal productivity gain of K. Unfortunately, everyone has different worldviews, which leads to freedom losses, since each person has different opinions as to the most appropriate laws and rules for the defense collective. As discussed above, a sufficiently large diversified population, coupled with a finite productivity gain for each person joining the coalition, will incent people to join different defense collectives.

People disagree with each other. Look at the modern world in which we live and try to envisage everyone (or almost everyone) voluntarily agreeing to be in the same defense collective—not as a citizen of a country with a complex government that has varied objectives, but as a member of a simple collective with one goal of external defense. Some people can easily coexist with each other; others have such radically different views that voluntary coexistence is extremely difficult. For example, consider the disparate views of people of different religious faiths. Some people embrace tolerance of others' beliefs. Others persecute those who have different values. The productivity gains per person from joint defense must be extraordinarily large for a person to willingly join a defense collective with people who desire rules that do not equally protect them. People of different religious faiths can coexist and even thrive in the same defense collective, but the difference in their worldviews can also lead them to prefer to be in different collectives or to stay in the original position.

The desire to maximize net gains in the presence of diverse worldviews will lead to the formation of more than one defense collective, since there is a limit to the marginal productivity gains from exiting anarchy, and aggregate freedom losses increase as more people join in collective defense. Each person's desire to maximize net gains will also lead to people maximizing the net gains in each of these defense collectives. This will be accomplished by concentrating people into as few defense collectives as possible and will entail each defense collective enforcing only those rules that minimize the aggregate freedom losses of its members.

Each defense collective will continue to add people until no one else wants to join. Each person improves the overall productivity of joint defense efforts but only linearly. As more people join in common defense, the diversity of worldviews in the potential collective will increase, the freedom-loss minimizing decisions will likely change, and aggregate freedom losses will increase. People joining the defense collective of their choice produce both positive and negative externalities for each another. There are positive externalities from collective defense, but differing worldviews will lead to negative externalities as people are incentivized to compromise. These effects will cause people to sort themselves into the defense collective that maximizes their net gains.

Each defense collective will continue to expand until either (i) the marginal person, the person with the highest freedom losses, does not have any net gains, or (ii) no one is left in the original position. In a sufficiently large population of diverse people, the size of each of these defense collectives will expand until the marginal person has freedom losses equal to the marginal productivity gain of K. As the size of each of these defense collectives increases, the average gross gains in each defense collective will increase. In the limit, as an infinite number of people join each defense collective, every person in each of the collectives will receive the same allocation of the aggregate gross gains. Each person will receive K from exiting the original position. Given each person's positive time value, they will immediately and unanimously sort themselves into the various defense collectives where their net gains are the highest or, alternatively, remain in anarchy.

Even though each person in all of these diverse democratic defense collectives is receiving the same allocation of the gross gains, the different collectives can vary widely. First, each defense collective is likely to have a different number of people, since people will have different worldview compatibilities. This is true even for the democratic defense collectives, since there are many sizes of infinity. The ultimate size of the defense collective is therefore dependent on the size of the productivity gains of K and the relative compatibility of people's worldviews. As such, in the idealized environment we are considering, there will be many democratic defense collectives of differing sizes. This implies that the total productivity gains in each of these defense collectives can be materially different. Second, aggregate freedom losses can vary widely in each of the collectives. The closer people's worldviews, for a given level of K, the more people who will want to be in the same defense collective. Similarly, the higher the level of productivity gains, given a specific diversity of worldviews, the more people who will voluntarily join the collective. Recall that the value of K is dependent on the assumed economic efficiency of the various original positions. A highly diverse population that can have some level of cooperation in the original position is going to form smaller defense collectives than a diverse population of people who cannot cooperate at all in anarchy. Third, the allocation and dispersion of net gains can be markedly different between each of the collectives. Finally, not surprisingly, none of the defense collectives will have exactly the same rules.

The equilibrating impact of perfect exit and perfect entry has much the same impact on the characteristics of each of the defense collectives as perfect voice. Each person exiting the original position and entering the defense collective in which their net gains are the largest will cause each defense collective to choose those actions that minimize the aggregate freedom losses of its members. In the limit, as the number of people in each collective approaches infinity, this movement will cause its members to receive the same allocation of the gross productivity gains. These gains will be perceived differently by each of the members, since there is no force that causes or incents people to equally compromise.

However, it seems that only the marginal joiner in each of the defense collectives requires that his or her allocation of gross gains includes their freedom losses. As people reason through exiting anarchy and joining the democratic defense collective that maximizes their net gains, they do not seem to be attempting to extract their freedom losses from every potential coalition within the collective. People act as if they are ignoring their marginal freedom losses in each of the potential coalitions within the democratic defense collective that they join. Each person appears to be willing to accept his or her freedom losses as part of the cost of collective defense as long as each is a member of the defense collective where he or she has the highest net gains. This is an accurate assessment. Exit from the original position and potential entry into the various defense collectives is a type of macroadjustment that ignores the microforce of perfect voice.

The incentive force of perfect entry and exit makes the institutional structure of collective defense, in a world inhabited by people with diverse worldviews and positive time values, resemble a competitive market. Each of the democratic defense collectives is unique and a monopoly provider of collective defense to its members. However, as previously discussed, even though each defense collective is a monopoly, each provides the socially optimal amount of collective defense to its members. The structure between the various democratic defense collectives is competitive in the sense that each person receives the same gross gain irrespective of the personal value they receive from being part of collective defense. It is similar to a competitive market where each person pays the same price for a competitively produced good irrespective of their consumer surplus.[155]

Equilibrium defense collective decisions are those decisions that minimize freedom losses, which are determined through a dynamic process of people forming and being part of different coalitions on their way to forming stable defense collectives. People will reason that each person will change coalitions when the net gains from collective defense are higher in another coalition. The new coalition incorporates the new entrants' views in determining its freedom-maximizing decisions, and the old coalition drops the exiting members' views from its freedom-maximizing decisions. Differentially compensating people for agreeing to compromise, or charging people for benefiting from compromise agreed to by others, is not the equilibrium mechanism used by the force of perfect entry and exit for determining decisions in a democratic defense collective. Instead, people in a democratic defense collective find it optimal to internalize the negative externalities caused by people holding differing views, and to accept the uniform gross gains from coercive collective action.

Each person in the original position will use the forces of perfect voice and perfect entry and exit to maximize their net gains from the new technology of collective defense. This will lead to the world restructuring itself from anarchical defense and perfect freedom to a safer and more satisfied one consisting of many large defense collectives. A question we will address in part four is how close to a democratic defense collective people can achieve given the limitations of real-world processes.

SOCIETY

The five authors' political views did not seem to reveal a consistent definition of society. In some instances, they loosely employed the concept to capture the general interconnectivity of humanity. In other situations, they used it to refer to people within the same political sphere. However, none of the philosophers had a nonhistorical method of delineating the boundary between a group of people under the authority of one government versus people under the auspices of another government. They appeared to implicitly assume that people somehow found themselves under the control of some government. While this is a fairly accurate description of the real world, the analysis of people exiting the original position requires society to be an endogenous variable.

Society can be defined as all the members of a defense collective. However, it is not the collective; it is the members of the collective, viewed as a whole. This conceptual difference is important and similar to the historical difference between *societas* and *universitas* in Roman law. A *societas* was a partnership among people for the purpose of combining their resources for a common goal. It was not an entity and could not own or control property directly. The *universitas* was the forerunner of our modern companies and was an entity. Laws concerning *societas* only addressed the conflicts between partners or *socci* that arise from sharing the risks and rewards of their common goal. Laws concerning *universitas* addressed the broader conflicts that can exist between the partners and an entity. The concept of society captures the essence of partnership and commonality of goals between a group of people, while a collective refers more specifically to the entity the members have created to accomplish their common goal of joint defense.

Each person in a defense collective voluntarily chooses to be a member. They choose to associate with a specific group of people. They are willing to make certain personal sacrifices and accommodate the preferences of the other members because of the benefits of joint defense. However, they are not willing to make the compromises necessary to have this relationship with everyone. The members of differing collectives or societies are unique and have different worldviews. The compatibility and diversity of members' worldviews across the range of potential decisions and actions will lead some societies to be larger and more stable than other societies. A stable society is one where a small change will not cause significant dislocation.

The most stable society is one where everyone's worldview is the same. Everyone in this type of society agrees on the actions that the collective should pursue. A small change in one person's views or a small change in the membership of the collective will not cause whole-sale changes within the society. The freedom losses in this society are zero, and the gross gains from joint defense are equal to the net gains.

A stable society can also exist in a society composed of people with unique worldviews. Stability occurs in a diverse collective when there are small differences in the worldviews of people as they form successive coalitions on the way to forming the collective that suits them best. As each person and each coalition joins other coalitions, marginal productivity increases by K. In a situation where each incremental coalition merger absorbs the incremental freedom losses of the individuals merging to jointly defend each other, a bond forms between the individuals. Each successive merger potentially allows people with larger differences in worldview to band together in joint defense. A stable society can form if the freedom losses from adding large coalitions of people do not become too large. For example, there can be a large difference in the views between Person 1 and Person N, if the coalitions that link them together each have freedom losses significantly less than the marginal productivity gains of K. In this instance, a small change in one person's views on a potential action by the collective does not have a large impact on the membership of the collective. A new threat or a change in circumstances around an existing risk does not cause these people to group themselves into significantly sized factions. This type of society can be labeled as cohesive. It is stable because each individual's worldview is not positively correlated in a significant way with one large group of members and highly negatively correlated with another large group. As such, a change in conditions will only have a small impact on society's membership and equilibrium decisions.

Contrast this type of society to a more polarized one in which there are two "groups" of people with similar intragroup worldviews but dis-similar intergroup worldviews. A small change in circumstances or in the views of one group on one specific issue can prevent the two groups from joining another coalition to form a larger coalition, or a change in a view on a specific issue can cause a formed collective to dissolve. Interestingly, this type of society cannot necessarily be distinguished from the more stable society on end-state observations such as differences of freedom losses. Both societies can have exactly the same aggregate freedom losses and the same pattern and dispersion of freedom losses among the members of the collective.

To put some context around the issue, the assumption concerning people's knowledge of each other's worldviews will be somewhat relaxed. Let's assume terrorists or spies can exist who either disguise their own worldview to mimic the worldviews of members of another collective or pretend to be a member. The possibility that some members of the coalition may not be who they seem to be and may try to harm the other members can be dealt with in a variety of ways depending on one's worldview. For example, the members of one coalition may be so concerned with security that they are willing to significantly affect members' personal lives to detect the potential imposters. They may be willing to support invasive restrictions on travel and the flow of commerce. They may also require members to carry membership documents; establish a secret police force to root out potential spies; document and limit the sale of any product that can be used by a person to commit a terrorist act; incarcerate any person, even a member, who someone in the police force has reason to believe can be a terrorist; and centralize monitoring of all communication within the collective. Let's also assume that everyone in this coalition prefers this hard-line approach, has different intensities for non-hard-line actions, and views this issue as more critical than every other social concern.

The second coalition is assumed to have a materially different view of the risks presented by spies and terrorists. While they recognize the threat posed by terrorists, they are not willing to suffer the consequences of disrupting their lives and limiting their personal liberties to the extent that members of the first coalition favor. They each prefer some domestic safeguards but focus much of their effort on external monitoring and after-the-fact responses to domestic terrorism. The members of this one are also assumed to view this issue as the most important social concern and have different values for totalitarian approaches.

When the two coalitions decide to merge, they need to come to a consensus on every potential action for the defense collective. Given their different worldviews, this will cause freedom losses for at least the members of one of the coalitions and possibly both. For the merger to be viable, the marginal freedom losses must be less than the marginal productivity gains of K. Let's assume this leads to rules that are an accommodation between the two bipolar views on security. This will cause freedom losses for everyone in the combined coalitions. Each member in both coalitions may have a unique freedom loss, since each person is assumed to possess different negative intensities for security actions they do not prefer. On the surface, just examining the amount and dispersion of freedom losses, this merged coalition resembles a more stable coalition.

However, this type of collective is not stable. There could be a change in circumstances after the formation of the collective that causes the collective to break apart. For example, a serious terrorist event could occur that results in the death of many members of the collective. The hard-liners may blame the lax rules they agreed to as an accommodation to the former members of the other coalition. The new information may cause them to push harder for more totalitarian measures to prevent future attacks. The soft-liners would regret that the incident occurred but may not change their overall views. The differing views in reaction to the tragic events could lead to civil strife.

This contrived example of societal differences is not the most likely cause of disharmony in a society. Discord is more probable from differing religious beliefs. A society composed of large groups of people who hold religious beliefs that are intolerant of other people's views will be less stable than a society that embraces religious freedom. While it is difficult for groups of people with these contrasting perspectives to enter into joint defense, it is possible that the productivity gains are sufficient to overcome their differences. However, a small change in either defense productivity or in people's views could cause a formed collective to disband. Strong religious beliefs that are inimical to other opinions will, everything else being the same, lead to a smaller, less diverse society.

An often-asked question is why members of a society should or would agree to laws that seemingly require them to reduce their own welfare for the benefit of other people in society. The simple answer from our analysis is that selfish people will only agree to laws and procedures that limit their freedoms if they are gaining something of more value. Members of society are willing to agree to rules they do not prefer because that incentivizes more diverse people to join in the common goal of joint defense, thereby increasing their allocation of the gains from collective defense.

RELATIONSHIP TO ANARCHY

As was discussed in the two-person example, the non-Hobbesian original position has higher levels of cooperation than the more rudimentary Hobbesian original position. This implies that the productivity gains from moving to joint defense from Hobbesian anarchy are higher than the gains from leaving the non-Hobbesian original position. Everything else being the same, lower marginal productivity gains will incentivize fewer people to join each defense collective.

However, it is possible that some people can have freedom gains from joining in cooperative defense and exiting non-Hobbesian anarchy even though maximal freedom is assumed to have a value of zero. This can happen in a circumstance where they prefer some of the decisions made by the defense collective to the naturally developed morals and norms they are subject to in the more cooperative original position. It is also possible that people who have learned to be more cooperative may have worldviews that are more compatible, allowing a larger group of people to be members of the same collective for a given level of marginal defense productivity. People's moral backgrounds will affect their worldview and their preferred decisions for the collective. This implies that people's various original positions will have a persistent effect on the size, number, and policies of the newly formed democratic defense collectives.

Each defense collective will continue to exist in a sea of anarchy. People participating in joint defense exit anarchy, but each defense collective is in an anarchical position with every unaffiliated person and with every other defense collective. The diversity of worldviews causes people to choose different collectives or to remain in the original position. This causes and allows anarchy to persist. Each entity in anarchy, whether it is a real person or an artificial organization, like each of the defense collectives, must struggle with every other entity, without recourse to some more powerful external force to enforce agreements and promote the peace. In anarchy, each collective and individual can enter into treaties and nonaggression pacts with other collectives and individuals. Each entity has an incentive to abide by these agreements but, as was discussed in part two, there are incentives for everyone to violate the terms of their agreements. The five authors seemed to have different views about what people could achieve in the absence of government. However, they all seemed to agree that external enforcement would reduce the probability of cheating and lead to increased reliance on contracts and agreements. Interestingly, democratic defense collectives are more effective in operating without third-party enforcement than are unaffiliated persons.

While each collective has an incentive to cheat and break its agreements, these incentives are more muted in a diverse defense collective. Individuals have an incentive to break their agreements because they directly gain from not performing their part of the bargain while others abide by the agreement. Collectives need not have this same level of direct incentive. The gains from cheating on a contract are more dispersed in a defense collective and more direct between individuals. Furthermore, in a diverse population, there will be some people who will realize the value of upholding nonaggression pacts. It may be difficult for people to effectively discriminate between people with these views and people who are looking for a weakness to attack. Individuals who are trying to cheat other people will try to mimic the behavior of people who uphold contracts. A democratic collective composed of diverse people, some who want to honor nonaggression treaties and some who do not, will be a more predictable counterparty for other collectives. At a minimum, their debate and consensus process will give information to other collectives as to the types of people who make up the collective. This does not mean that democratic collectives will not violate their agreements. It does imply that anarchy between democratic collectives is more predictable and more productive than anarchy between individuals.

12

DOMESTIC COLLECTIVE GOALS AND METHODS

This chapter is concerned with collective goals beyond external defense. Logically, few people in the original position will agree to leave anarchy if they cannot at least be protected from fellow members of the collective. The economists and philosophers from chapter 2 materially disagreed on the appropriate goals of government; nonetheless, they all seemed to agree that government should have more responsibilities than just external defense. Even Robert Nozick, who had the narrowest view of the appropriate role of government, thought the coercive power of government should protect members of the collective from physical transgressions such as murder and assault, as well as theft, breach of contract, and fraud. However, even when each of the authors agreed on the appropriate goals for government, their differing worldviews led them to disparate preferred policies and rules for accomplishing these shared goals.

The analysis will begin by first discussing some aspects and controversies around a position held by almost every person—the prohibition of killing members of the collective. This will ultimately lead to a discussion of the implications for the structure of the collective when people in the same collective have differing views on morality, fraud, torts, and governmental regulation.

MURDER: SELF-DEFENSE

Prevention of murder is a near universally acknowledged role for government, but what is murder? Like most aspects of government, opinions vary. In 1993, Teresa Thomas was in court testifying in her trial for murdering her live-in boyfriend, Jake Flowers.[156] She claimed that she was acting in self-defense and that Flowers had repeatedly abused her. Thomas testified that over the course of their relationship, he was controlling and violent, and that she was repeatedly raped, including being sodomized two days prior to his killing. She also testified that he would frequently wake her up with his hands over her mouth, stating how easy it would be to kill her. He once pushed her so hard that she was admitted to the emergency room.

On the day of Flowers's death, she testified that he came home and he started yelling at her. She went to the bathroom and tried to escape, but the window in the trailer was too small and she could not exit. She then went into the bedroom and grabbed his gun out of the closet. She quickly moved to the kitchen where Flowers yelled at her and threatened to kill her. She fired two warning shots, and when he continued to threaten her, she fired two shots at him, which hit him in the arm and then entered his torso. The bullets caused him to fall, but he started to get up and she shot him two more times in his back. The cumulative effect of the shots to his back, chest, and abdomen caused his death.

At her trial, evidence was presented that she was suffering from "battered woman syndrome." A clinical psychologist testified that Thomas reasonably believed she was in imminent danger of death or serious bodily harm when she shot Flowers. The jury found her guilty, and she was sentenced to eighteen years to life.[157]

Thomas appealed the verdict and the Ohio Supreme Court heard her appeal. In their five-to-two ruling, they stated self-defense as a defense has three requirements, including "that the defendant did not violate any duty to retreat or avoid the danger."[158] The historical rationale for the duty to retreat is not completely clear. Some people have conjectured that it arose out of English statutes that assigned the king monopoly over peacefulness and was aimed at the overall reduction in interpersonal violence. Irrespective of its historical origin, at the time of the court ruling there was an exception to the duty to flee if a person was in his or her own home. The court stated that

> *this exception to the duty to retreat derives from the doctrine that one's home is one's castle and one has a right to protect it and those within it from intrusion or attack . . . the rationale is that a person in her own home has already retreated "to the wall," as there is no place to which she can further flee in safety . . . thus a person who, through no fault of her own, is assaulted in her home may stand her ground, meet force with force, and if necessary, kill her assailant, without any duty to retreat.[159]*

The justices went on to state:

> *In Ohio, one is not required to retreat from one's own home when attacked by an intruder; similarly one should not be required to retreat when attacked by a cohabitant in order to claim self-defense . . . accordingly, we hold there is no duty to retreat from one's own home before resorting to lethal force in self-defense against a cohabitant with an equal right to be in the home.[160]*

The court reversed the verdict, concluding that the trial judge gave improper instructions to the jury by not informing them that Teresa did not have the duty to retreat. In her retrial, she was acquitted.

Even though nearly everyone will agree that they want to be protected from murder, that preventing murder is a desirable social goal, and that murderers should be punished, there are a wide variety of views around various aspects of murder. The issue of self-defense is controversial. Thomas used a handgun to kill her boyfriend. Does the individual possession of guns improve safety, or does it lead to increased violence and death? Again, people have significant differences of opinion. In a 2014 Gallup poll, 63 percent of people responded that guns increase the safety of homes.[161] In their 2016 poll, 39 percent of the respondents had guns. Fifty-five percent thought that laws governing the sale of handguns should be stricter, but only 23 percent thought that handguns should be banned.[162] If Thomas had not had access to a gun, would Flowers still be alive? For that matter, would Thomas still be alive? Given significant differences in worldviews, what would people in the original position agree to on gun control in forming the defense collective?

Let's return to the other issues raised by Thomas's situation. Will everyone come to the same conclusion as the court on the social "duty" to retreat further? People with different worldviews will disagree about rules and laws over self-defense, the duty to retreat, and the potential use of violence. Some people will prefer laws designed to reduce violence to the utmost and that require people to retreat in the face of violence, if possible. Other people view people as having more social rights in their home. They prefer and support rules, like the "castle doctrine," that allow a person to stand their ground in their own home. However, that was not the real issue that the court addressed. The Ohio law, while allowing people to stand their ground in their home, was silent on the rights of cohabitants and invited guests and on the obligations a person may have to these people in their home.

The court ruled that Thomas did not have an obligation to retreat, since "there is no rational reason for a distinction between an intruder and a cohabitant." Not every rational person would agree with them. For example, the Rhode Island Supreme Court, a few years earlier, had a significantly different view. They stated that

> we are of the opinion that a person assailed in his or her own residence by a co-occupant is not entitled under the guise of self-defense to employ deadly force and kill his or her assailant. The person attacked is obligated to attempt retreat if he or she is aware of a safe and available avenue of retreat.[163]

Their rationale for this conclusion is "due recognition to the value of human life while recognizing that the right of self-defense is born of necessity and should terminate when the necessity is no more."[164] Obviously, the Rhode Island Supreme Court seem to have had a different view than the majority of the justices on the Ohio Supreme Court on the trade-off between potentially unnecessary violence and people's rights to defend themselves. The statutes in both states were similar in allowing people to stand their ground in one's home, and both left unspecified the rights and responsibilities against co-occupants. The Rhode Island justices understood other jurisdictions had previously ruled that co-occupants do not have the duty to flee. Nonetheless, they appear to have preferred a law that required co-occupants to flee their home because they viewed that requirement as reducing the future loss of life. In designing the rules of the collective as people exit anarchy, some people will prefer rules that provide more rights to cohabitants, while others will not.

Differences of opinion on these issues are not limited to these two states. There is little uniformity in the laws over the right to stand your ground in the United States. Some jurisdictions, like the District of Columbia, require a person claiming self-defense in their own home to take reasonable steps to avoid another person's death if these steps are consistent with one's own safety. Many state legislatures have a broader view of potential victim's rights and have expanded the traditional castle doctrine used in Ohio. They have removed the duty to retreat and allowed people to stand their ground in a wide variety of places, including one's car and place of employment. Other states have self-defense laws that no longer require evidence that a person was in fear of their life when they killed someone, and the jurisdictions have expanded the right to not retreat to include public spaces. Many of these laws also allow relief from civil lawsuits. Given a choice, some people will prefer laws that have liberal views on people's obligations regarding self-defense. Other people will feel safer and will prefer laws and rules that severely restrict people's ability to claim self-defense. The question for those considering exiting anarchy is what impact these differences of opinion will have on the defense collective. Will they feel compelled to compromise and suffer a loss of freedom, or will they only associate with those who have similar views and suffer a reduction in the gains from association by being a member of a smaller collective? Is there an alternative? Is there decision congestion in a defense collective negotiating over people's rights and responsibilities with respect to self-defense?

MURDER: PREVENTION AND PROSECUTION

People in the original position will want to prevent themselves from being murdered, and many will want to prevent others from being killed. In anarchy, they need to allocate their own resources to protect themselves. As they contemplate exiting anarchy and joining with others in collective defense, they will want to protect themselves from external invaders but also from murder by their fellow members.

Completely preventing murder is impossible. The United States is a modern government with sophisticated machinery for the prevention of murder, yet according to the Bureau of Justice Statistics, in 2015 there were 15,696 homicides in the United States or 4.9 homicides per 100,000 people.[165] This is a significant reduction from twenty-four years earlier when there were over twice as many homicides per 100,000 people.[166] The United States is not alone in being unable to prevent murder. In fact, the homicide rates in some countries are much higher than in the United States. For example, in 2014, Honduras had seventy-five homicides per 100,00 people; El Salvador, sixty-four; Venezuela, sixty-two; and South Africa, thirty-three. Other countries have lower rates, including Chile, Czech Republic, Saudi Arabia, and Japan. Two of the countries with the lowest murder rates are Switzerland with 0.7 and Singapore with 0.3 murders per 100,000 people.[167]

These statistics point to the difficulty of eliminating all murders and the diversity of murder rates across locations. Research on differential murder rates focuses on the potential influence of a variety of factors such as ethnic diversity, education levels, laws, and law enforcement. Murder rates are also impacted by people's various religious beliefs and the development of different moral philosophies. Even when religions are consistent, for example in their disdain for murder, their definitions of murder and their preferred penalties for murder can be radically different.

Most people, including the five reviewed theorists, seem to hold the view that the prevention of murder is enhanced through collective effort. Collective effort involves legislation and laws defining and prohibiting murder, enforcement of these laws, utilization of methods and techniques to determine the guilt of the potential murderers, and application of some type of penalty. However, people with different worldviews will disagree on the social and environmental causes of murder as well as on the best methods to reduce it. They will differ in their views on the appropriate laws involving murder as well as various aspects of law enforcement, including penalties. As illustrated in the prior section, they will even disagree on the definition of murder.

Bruce Benson, a libertarian economist at Florida State University and legal scholar, appears to think that the current concepts of police and criminal processes are inefficient.[168] He argues that victims in most countries and particularly in the United States are not incentivized to cooperate with the police. He seems to have the view that existing public law enforcement does not solve many of the interpersonal conflicts discussed in chapter 5, leading to crime victims being less willing to testify, excessive plea bargaining, crowding in jails, and early release from those jails. Benson appears to think the modern view of crimes as a negative activity against society has gone too far, and that crime prevention and enforcement should be aimed at helping victims. He favors some privatization of the justice system. Benson advocates a system that gives victims rights to restitution as well as some private policing. He argues that a more private justice system will increase the likelihood that crimes are reported and that perpetrators are successfully prosecuted. While many people probably disagree with Benson, a number of people in the theoretical original position may share his views.

Important aspects of legal design are the methods of prosecuting and determining the guilt of an alleged criminal. While processes continue to evolve in most countries, and differences exist across jurisdictions, most countries currently use one or some combination of three approaches: common law, civil law, or Sharia law. The latter type of law is based on the Quran—the various teachings and ways of the prophet Mohammed, as well as interpretations and application of these principles by learned Islamic scholars. The other two approaches to the law are not associated with a specific religion and are the predominant form of legal structure currently used in non-Islamic countries. Legal theorist Mirjan Damaška has characterized common law as focused on "conflict resolution" and civil law on "policy implementation."[169]

Most countries are civil-law countries. Civil law, which has its origins in Roman law, typically has extensive codes and statutes, and depends on the state or government to formulate detailed rules. Common-law countries like England and the United States have laws often established by judges as they resolved legal disputes. Economists Edward Glaeser and Andrei Shleifer, in their research on legal origins, distinguish between the characteristics of each type of law. They view the key elements of common law as including "oral argument[s]," "trials," and "precedents." Civil law to them is characterized by written "evidence," review by a "superior" court of lower court judgments on the law and evidence in the case, and the ability of a judge to simultaneously be the "prosecutor."[170] Modern common-law countries obviously have laws established by their various legislatures, but these laws are often written broadly, allowing for refinement and interpretation by judges. An obvious example is the discussion in the prior section on different views of self-defense. Economist Rafael La Porta and his colleagues argue that differing "legal rules" will affect economic development.[171] They contend that civil-law countries have higher levels of government regulation and that common-law countries are better at enforcing contracts and securing property rights. Whether their analysis and insights are correct or not, it is evident that one's preferred legal design can be affected by one's worldview.

People in the original position will prefer a legal approach that most conforms to their worldview. A person's worldview shapes how they think others in society will interact with each other. Their worldview will affect their desired rules as well as the methods, if any, that they prefer to shape social behavior. Some will prefer an approach that enforces God's law as interpreted by them or their religious leaders. Some could go so far as to view the central function of government as the enforcement of God's law. Others, like Friedrich Hayek, will prefer laws that "naturally" evolve and will want a legal system designed to enhance this natural process. Still others will prefer a more hierarchical and centralized approach to the law from a nonreligious perspective. The economic literature discussed above on legal design argues that there is a correlation between the desired goals of government and the legal design for accomplishing these goals. It suggests that people who share John Rawls's views and prefer a more extensive government will also prefer a civil legal structure. Alternatively, those who share Hayek's views will prefer a common-law approach. Differences in worldviews lead to differences in preferred legal approaches, which implies that diverse people in the original position will differ in their preferred approach to legal design.

As discussed in previous chapters, people will also differ in their views of the level of cooperation that can or will occur in the absence of government. This may influence their judgment as to the type of law that the imagined people in the original position will choose. Many people will view the Hobbesian original position as the only possible environment in anarchy. Other people will view cooperation as imminently feasible without the institutional arrangement of government. Since a person's environment has some influence on their opinions and worldview, people who believe that only a Hobbesian original position could exist are also likely to imagine that people who are in the original position and contemplating leaving anarchy for collective defense will probably prefer a more hierarchical legal system. Individuals in the original position that conforms to the Hobbesian view of violence have never witnessed cooperation and are not likely to trust the other members of the collective. They are more likely to prefer, at least initially, government control and codified rules. Juries may not be trusted. General principles governing laws may be viewed with suspicion. People who have never witnessed others voluntarily cooperating may consider a legal system to be safer and more predictable when judges are given detailed rules and instructions and when judicial decisions are reviewed by other judges for errors concerning the facts and the law.

Alternatively, a person in a more benign original position, in which some level of cooperation exists, where they have experienced non-governmental methods of cooperating, may be comfortable with more of a common-law design. They may have more confidence that juries can be impartial and unbiased, and that judges interpreting the law will be fair and balanced and determine a predictable outcome. For example, according to Bryce Lyon, it took five hundred years from the time juries were first introduced in 1159 for the English to design a jury system that people viewed as impartial.[172] While people differ in their preferences over legal systems and processes, one of the most significant differences in opinion occurs over punishments and penalties for convicted criminals.

MURDER: CAPITAL PUNISHMENT

Differences in people's worldviews will lead them to have potentially significant differences of opinion over the rationale for punishments, as well as the effectiveness of various types of penalties. For some people, the appropriate penalty for various crimes is significantly influenced by their views on concepts such as justice, fairness, and retribution. This will cause them to disagree over the appropriate penalties for different types of crime. The majority of people in the United States currently view capital punishment as a just penalty for premeditated murder.[173] Others view capital punishment as too harsh a penalty and prefer that murderers serve a significant amount of time in prison. As we contemplate the discussions among a large number of people in the original position, it is unreasonable to believe they will all prefer the same penalty for murderers.

Two examples of differing religious positions on capital punishment are those of Catholicism and Islam. The Roman Catholic view, as expressed by the pope John Paul II in his *Evangelium Vitae* in 1995, is to accept capital punishment but only for the most severe crimes and then only when there are no realistic alternatives.[174] Alternatively, Sharia law views capital punishment as an appropriate punishment for murder. Murder is punished by retaliation, effectively a life for a life. However, unlike most common-law and civil countries, Islamic law considers murder a private crime, not a public crime. As such, the victim's family has the right to decide on the appropriate punishment for their murdered relative. They have the right to decide if the convicted murderer will be executed, set free, or made to pay a fine to them. Many people not of the Islamic faith also hold this view. They think that victims, and their families in the case of murder, should have some rights. Of course, the more common view in most countries today is that murder is a crime against the public, that the public peace has been violated. From this perspective, victims' families have no more rights than any other person.

Unlike Catholicism, which makes a distinction between civil law and church law, Islam holds that civil law should enforce God's law. Those who follow Islam will have different views on appropriate civil laws than will Catholics. Not only is it likely that Catholics and Muslims will have moral differences, but, also, people with the same religious views can have widely different ideas on the application of their personal moral views to determine the laws enforced by their government. Given these differences, it is also likely that many of the imagined people in the original position will have different views on the separation of religion and government.

Some people in the original position will think that criminal penalties serve as a form of retribution for the offender. This is often associated with Aristotle. However, some will view crime and criminal penalties through an economic lens. People with this opinion will think that punishment "should" be aimed at reducing the incidence of crime and "should" be no harsher than necessary to accomplish this goal. Cesare Beccaria, an Italian philosopher and jurist who lived in the eighteenth century, was one of the first to espouse this view. He perceived most punishments, in his time, as too severe and was against capital punishment for any crime.[175] Gary Becker, a US economist and winner of the 1992 Nobel Prize in economics, argued that criminal behavior can be accurately modeled by assuming that people are, at least on average, economically motivated.[176] He asserted that a significant percentage of people contemplating criminal activity are rational and selfish, and that increased probabilities of conviction and harsher penalties will reduce the incidence of crime. As such, police resources and criminal punishments should be set appropriately to reduce crimes to levels desired by society. He argued that even though society wants to reduce crime, because of cost considerations people are unwilling to reduce the incidence of crime to zero.

Richard Posner, a US federal judge and legal theorist, argues that the common law has developed as an efficient response to potential criminal activity.[177] For him, societal resources are used to detect, prevent, and punish criminals because crime itself is socially wasteful. Penalties such as prison or death sentences are efficient methods of reducing criminal activity. For example, he argues that fines cannot be the only penalty because most convicted criminals will not be able to pay a fine that is sufficient to materially reduce the criminal act. He suggests that high fines will be a sufficient deterrent for the financially well off, but that the average person will not be able to pay, and therefore fines will be ineffective. He also argues that insurance markets will not develop to cover a criminal's fine because of moral hazard. Payment of a fine by an insurance company will not be a deterrent; therefore, insurance companies will not write these types of policies. He models required penalties as equal to the benefit to the criminal (or harm to the victim) divided by the probability of indictment. Crimes such as murder that have extremely high value loss to the victim will need to have equally high penalties even if the likelihood of conviction is high. His approach seems to be a form of utilitarianism advocated by John Harsanyi, since it requires placing societal-wide values on gains to criminals and losses to victims. It appears to assume that society has developed a unified view on the cost-benefit trade-off between extra resources to increase the probability of conviction and the desired criminal penalties.

Posner's analysis supports the use of capital punishment with some restrictions. First, no legal system is perfect in determining guilt and innocence. There are two types of errors: type one—incorrect rejection of the true "null" hypothesis, and type two—failure to reject a false null hypothesis. If the null hypothesis is that the person on trial is innocent, then most people and most legal systems probably would rather have a type-one error than a type-two error. They would prefer to let a murderer go free rather than convict an innocent person. As such, some people may not approve of the death penalty, since it is irreversible and adds to the costs if a type-one error is made by the judge or jury. Posner also focuses on the critical issue of marginal deterrence. His thesis is that capital punishment should be used for only the most severe crimes because there is no incremental deterrent effect for additional crimes committed by that person.

Many people will reject the use of the death penalty even if it can be economically justified, viewing it as immoral and barbaric. Most countries in Europe have entered a common treaty on human rights that bans the use of capital punishment.[178] Only Belarus has opted out of the prohibition of the death penalty. Switzerland, a country with one of the lowest murder rates in the world, has made capital punishment unconstitutional.

However, the death penalty continues to be legal in other parts of the world. Singapore, which also has a low murder rate, credits its severe penalties, including the use of corporal punishment and the death penalty, for contributing to its lack of crime. Most US states have laws that allow for the death penalty under certain circumstances. Interestingly, the European countries are more aligned with each other on the issue of the death penalty through treaty than are the US states.

The death penalty is obviously controversial. Nozick views "retributive punishment" as a type of signal by society to the person being penalized that his or her action is unacceptable. He does not endorse capital punishment but thinks that it could be appropriate for certain people like Adolf Hitler. Rawls thought that the death penalty could be derived through procedural justice. Gallup polls illustrate the level of disagreement over the use of capital punishment in the United States. Respondents in Gallup polls over the years were asked if they supported capital punishment for those "convicted of murder." In 1937, 60 percent of the people said yes; by 1966, the percentage saying yes had fallen to 42 percent. However, it rose to 80 percent in 1994 and fell back to 60 percent in 2016.[179] People who favored the death penalty in 2014 gave a variety of reasons for their preference. The three main reasons were "fits the crime," expense of incarceration, and the belief that it was warranted. People who opposed the death penalty were asked for their reasons. The top three were killing is "wrong," the possibility that convicted people could be innocent, and "religious belief."[180]

The US Supreme Court has reviewed the use of the death penalty numerous times and has consistently viewed it as not a per se violation of the "cruel and unusual" prohibition in the Eighth Amendment to the US Constitution. However, there has been an intensely held minority view of the court that it is both cruel and unusual.

In 1971, the Supreme Court considered two cases involving the constitutionality of the death penalty.[181] In one of these, the defendant was on trial for shooting his wife of four months in the face as she sat on the toilet. The jury convicted him of murder and did not recommend mercy. The argument was made that his rights had been infringed because there were no standards at that time in Ohio governing the imposition of the death penalty, and because Ohio allowed the jury to decide the verdict and the penalty at the same time ("unitary hearing"). Some states had a bifurcated process where a verdict was first determined and then a sentencing proceeding would be held, at which time evidence that had been excluded by the court at the trial could be heard.[182] In a single proceeding, the jury may not be aware of evidence that may have modified its view on the appropriate penalty. Furthermore, the defendant may be reluctant to invoke his Fifth Amendment right to not incriminate himself in a unitary hearing.

The court held, in a six-to-three vote, that the defendant's rights were not infringed and that a single "guilt and punishment proceeding" was constitutional.[183] Justice John Marshall Harlan provided the majority view. He suggested that juries had rebelled against the mandatory death sentence required by many states in the late 1800s and refused to convict people whom they believed were guilty. The incidence of "jury nullification" led the legislatures in the various states to modify their laws and give juries discretion over sentencing. The court held, "in light of history, experience, and the present limitations of human knowledge, we find it quite impossible to say that committing to the untrammeled discretion of the jury the power to pronounce life or death in capital cases is offensive to anything in the Constitution."[184]

The next year, in a five-to-four decision, the Supreme Court seemed to reverse itself and held that the Georgia law concerning the death penalty was unconstitutional, violating both the Eighth and Fourteenth Amendments.[185] Justices Potter Stewart and Byron White, who had voted in the prior year that the Ohio procedures were constitutional, appeared to change their minds and voted that Georgia's capital-punishment statutes, which were substantially like Ohio's laws, violated the defendant's rights. Two new justices joined the court, Lewis F. Powell Jr. and William Rehnquist, and both voted the same as the justices they replaced that the death penalty as practiced by Georgia did not violate the constitution. Interestingly, there was no majority opinion. None of the judges who voted in the majority seemed to agree on the rationale for their decision—all nine justices wrote their own opinions.

Justice William O. Douglas stated, "There is increasing recognition of the fact that the basic theme of equal protection is implicit in 'cruel and unusual punishments' . . . The President's Commission on Law Enforcement and Administration of Justice recently concluded . . . the death sentence is disproportionately imposed, and carried out on the poor, the Negro, and the members of unpopular groups."[186] Justice Stewart wrote:

> *These death sentences are cruel and unusual in the same way that being struck by lightning is cruel and unusual. For, of all the people convicted of rapes and murders in 1967 and 1968 . . . many just as reprehensible as these, the petitioners are among a capriciously selected random handful upon whom the sentence of death has in fact been imposed . . . But racial discrimination has not been proved and I put it to one side. I simply conclude that the Eighth and Fourteenth Amendments cannot tolerate the infliction of a sentence of death under legal systems that permit this unique penalty to be so wantonly and so freakishly imposed.*[187]

Justice White wrote:

> *I do not at all intimate that the death penalty is unconstitutional per se . . . For present purposes, I accept the morality and utility of punishing one person to influence another. I accept also the effectiveness of punishment generally, and need not reject the death penalty as a more effective deterrent than a lesser punishment. But common sense and experience tell us that seldom-enforced laws become ineffective measures for controlling human conduct.*[188]

Justice Thurgood Marshall, who was consistently against the death penalty, quoted a prior chief justice, stating the "cruel and unusual language 'must draw its meaning from the evolving standards of decency that mark the progress of a maturing society." Thus, a penalty that was permissible at one time in our Nation's history is not necessarily permissible today." He suggested that the death penalty had its origins in "private vengeance" and stated, "As individuals gradually ceded their personal prerogatives to a sovereign power, the sovereign accepted the authority to punish wrongdoing as part of its 'divine right' to rule. Individual vengeance gave way to the vengeance of the state, and capital punishment became a public function." He continued, "Retaliation, vengeance, and retribution have been roundly condemned as intolerable aspirations for a government in a free society . . . The history of the Eighth Amendment supports only the conclusion that retribution for its own sake is improper." He then addressed the issue of deterrence and argued, "They have succeeded in showing by clear and convincing evidence that capital punishment is not necessary as a deterrent to crime in our society. This is all that they must do . . . I see no alternative but to conclude that capital punishment cannot be justified on the basis of its deterrent effect." He stated that it "violates the Eighth Amendment because it is morally unacceptable to the people of the United States at this time in their history." He argued that people are not well informed on all the issues surrounding the death penalty, and that if presented with the facts, "the great mass of citizens would conclude on the basis of the material already considered that the death penalty is immoral, and therefore unconstitutional."[189]

Following the Supreme Court ruling, most states continued to have a death penalty, and most of these modified their statutes concerning capital punishment to align with the guidance given in many of the justices' opinions. Various states interpreted the justices' opinions somewhat differently, but they typically changed their procedures by incorporating sentencing guidelines, bifurcated trials, automatic appellate review, and review of sentences for evidence of disparate impacts. Four years later, the Supreme Court heard *Gregg v. Georgia* and held that Georgia's new laws and procedures concerning the death penalty were constitutional and did not violate the Eighth Amendment.[190] The vote was seven to two, with only Justices William Brennan and Marshall dissenting. Justice Stewart announced the majority opinion. He stated that

in a democratic society legislatures, not courts, are constituted
to respond to the will and consequently the moral values of the
people . . . Retribution is no longer the dominant objective of the
criminal law . . . but neither is it a forbidden objective, nor one
inconsistent with our respect for the dignity of men . . . Statistical
attempts to evaluate the worth of the death penalty as a deter-
rent to crimes by potential offenders have occasioned a great
deal of debate. The result[s] simply have been inconclusive.[191]

The Supreme Court and diverse groups of people in the various
potential original positions will struggle to agree on appropriate penalties for crimes. They will disagree on the effectiveness of sanctions
such as the death penalty for preventing severe crimes like murder.
Many people will agree with Justice Brennan in his dissenting opinion
in *Gregg*:

The fatal constitutional infirmity in the punishment of death is
that it treats "members of the human race as nonhumans, as
objects to be toyed with and discarded" . . . Justice of this kind
is obviously no less shocking than the crime itself, and the new
"official" murder, far from offering redress for the offense com-
mitted against society, adds instead a second defilement to the
first.[192]

Other people in the original position will think that convicted
murderers like Johnny Kormondy, who was found to have killed
Gary McAdams by shooting him in the back of the head and raping
McAdams's wife with the help of two accomplices, should be executed.[193] Others will want to live in a collective that executes people like
Charles Frederick Warner, who was convicted of raping and killing a
girl who was eleven months old.[194] Some people in the original position
will favor rules that allow the collective to execute a person many may
think is intellectually disabled like Warren Hill, who was indicted for
beating a fellow prisoner to death with a board studded with exposed
nails.[195] At the time, he was serving a life sentence for murdering his
girlfriend. Still others will feel safer in a collective that executes people

like David Zink, who was convicted of raping and murdering nineteen-year-old Amanda Morton.[196] Zink was on parole after serving twenty years for rape and kidnapping. He accidently rammed into Morton's car while drunk and, fearing that his parole would be rescinded, kidnapped and raped her. He killed her by tying her to a tree in a cemetery, snapping her neck, and using a knife to sever her spinal cord.

In addition, some people in the original position, who are giving up the right to unrestricted self-defense and agree to be protected by the collective, may want crimes besides murder to be punished by capital punishment. For example, many people may want a crime such as child rape to be punished by the death penalty. They would be unhappy with the current majority decision of the Supreme Court that it is illegal to punish someone with the death penalty for a crime against an individual that does not involve murder. For example, the Louisiana legislature was of the majority view that it was legal and appropriate to punish convicted child rapists with the death penalty. The Supreme Court, in a five-to-four decision, held that the death penalty could only be applied to crimes against people when someone had been murdered, and that the Louisiana law violated the Eighth Amendment.[197] The court allowed for the possibility that crimes against the state such as treason, terrorism, and "drug kingpin" activity could be penalized by death. It based its decision on a new concept of a "national consensus." Justice Anthony Kennedy provided the court's opinion and argued that only six states had statutes allowing capital punishment for child rape, and therefore the Louisiana statutes were not supported by a national consensus and violated the prohibition against "cruel and unusual" punishment.

People in the original position will have a similar debate as did the Supreme Court. As such, there can be people who want child rape to be punished by death. The "collective consensus" may be similar to the majority view of the US Supreme Court. However, unlike the people of Louisiana, those in the original position, who have deeply held views different than the "collective consensus," have a variety of options. If they feel strongly that child rape should be punished by penalties more severe than imprisonment, they can stay in anarchy and continue to practice self-defense; they can also join a smaller collective with people who have similar views to their own, where their views are the "collective consensus." Both options have costs, since the larger the collective, the higher the gains from collective defense. Nonetheless, some people may have strongly held views so different than the majority of others' that they are unwilling to be in the same collective as that majority and are willing to suffer the consequences. The question for each person exiting anarchy is how to associate with others in joint defense when people have such diverse views on critical issues, including murder, capital punishment, and self-defense. Are they doomed to be in small collectives with like-minded people? Alternatively, are most of the gains from collective defense eliminated by freedom losses through accommodating other people's worldviews?

The discussion by the justices in these various cases raises two other critical issues that people in the original position must face. One is the inadequacy of language. It is extraordinarily difficult to be completely precise and communicate exactly one's thoughts and desires. All communication is subject to interpretation. Constitutions and statutes will not have the same meaning to everyone, especially over time. The discussion in the prior chapters on the rules the defense collective would choose implicitly assumed that those rules could be elaborately spelled out so there would be no disagreement. Theoretically, if writing and discussion are costless, it would be possible to list every conceivable scenario so that people in the original position could give their views and decide on the appropriate defense collective to join. However, even then, it is possible that people could have different interpretations of what was originally agreed. They would need some mechanism to mediate differences in interpretations. They would need courts and judges. And they would need to give instructions to these jurists on how to interpret their written agreement forming the defense collective.

The second point is a related one. In a more real-world setting, the imagined people in the original position would find it impractical to spell out every theoretical possibility. They would be specific on some issues and set broad principles on others. They could easily disagree on the level of specificity that their agreement should entail, since there are costs to higher specification as well as costs to lack of specification.

The latter occurs because it may be impossible to return to anarchy after people agree to join in collective defense. If they think there is a meaningful risk that their agreement to join the collective will be incorrectly interpreted, they may be less willing to join. They may have an incentive to be in a smaller, more cohesive collective where there is less conflict between worldviews and less need for interpretation of the preestablished rules. At the margin, "interpretation risk" acts like a loss in freedom.

The justices had (and seem to still have) significant disagreement over the interpretation of the Eighth Amendment and the role of the court. People in the original position who believe they made an agreement to allow capital punishment in certain circumstances would want to protect themselves from "new" rights that people who commit those crimes are determined to have by a judge or judges who conceive that those rights were implied by the original agreement. People who commit crimes are obviously better off by this new interpretation, since they will no longer be subject to the death penalty. However, people exiting anarchy who felt that the collective was safer from the periodic imposition of the death penalty would feel less safe if the collective is determined to be unable to enforce that rule. The interpretation that the death penalty violates people's rights would be perceived as a loss of freedom by those who thought that the use of capital punishment had been agreed upon as part of the grand bargain in forming the collective.

ABORTION

For many women, one of the most difficult decisions they will face in their lives is whether to abort an unwanted or unexpected pregnancy. It is a permanent and irreversible decision wrought with uncertainty and potential regret. If they decide to continue with the pregnancy and ultimately give birth, their life is permanently altered. If they decide to abort the pregnancy, they run the risk of complications from the procedure. Many may think that the abortion decreases the probability of successful future pregnancies, and for some women there is the risk of guilt. In addition, some women are subject to laws that make it illegal to have an abortion.

Nineteen-year-old Tegan Leach was living in Queensland, Australia, in 2009 with her boyfriend Sergie Brennan. They had no plans to have a child, but she thought she might be pregnant and checked it with a home pregnancy test, according to news reports.[198] It was also reported that at that point in her life she was not prepared to be a mother and that Brennan did not want to be a father, since he had the view that he could not provide his "kid the best."[199] They decided to terminate the pregnancy, but she did not want to have a surgical procedure.[200] Instead, she purportedly decided to take two drugs that are widely used to induce a miscarriage, Misoprostol and Mifepristone.[201] Both drugs are generally viewed as safe. Some women experience some negative side effects from taking these drugs, but only in rare circumstances have they been serious. The drugs did not harm Leach, and the abortion was successful.[202] In taking the drugs, however, she violated the law, according to prosecutors in Queensland.

Several of the abortion laws in Queensland still existed from 1899. These laws permitted an abortion only under certain circumstances such as protecting "the mother's life."[203] Leach was charged with inducing her own miscarriage by using a "noxious thing" with a penalty of seven years in jail.[204] Brennan was charged with assisting in an illegal miscarriage with a maximum jail term of three years.[205] They both pled not guilty to the charges. The trial judge determined that the prosecution had focused on the drugs being "noxious;" a crucial part of the case seemed to be the jury's views on whether the drugs were indeed "noxious."[206] The jury of four men and eight women quickly determined that both Leach and Brennan were not guilty.

Why do communities have laws against self-induced abortion? Some people favor these types of legislated rules because they believe that people may harm themselves by attempting to self-induce a miscarriage. They may think that people do not have a sufficient level of information to make an informed decision, or they may think that the drugs or procedures are too risky and require the involvement of a certified expert. From this perspective, laws against self-induced miscarriage act as a signal to people in the community that their potential actions are risky. The penalties are designed to make people modify their decision to induce a miscarriage. Of course, if the penalties are too severe, the jury may be unwilling to convict people.

Some people may favor this type of law because of what they perceive to be potential adverse effects of an abortion on the woman. For example, in a discussion of the Leach abortion trial, the president of a local chapter of an association[207] concerned with both abortion and euthanasia was quoted as saying that she supported the law because an abortion "does harm."[208] She seems to express concern not only for the potential riskiness of the procedure but also its effect on the psychological well-being of the potential mother.

Other people who favor laws against abortion probably do so because they believe that abortions are morally wrong and are essentially a form of murder. As was discussed earlier, almost everyone agrees that killing another human being is wrong, except in certain circumstances such as self-defense and capital punishment. However, the question of murder hinges on the definition of a person and a determination of the beginning of life. When does life begin? Does it start at conception, or when the fertilized egg reaches a certain level of physical or mental development, or at a specific point in time like the end of the first trimester, or when the fetus is viable without the mother, or when the fetus is born? Even if one views the fertilized egg as having rights, how are conflicts between it and the woman carrying it resolved? What if the woman is a victim of rape? What if her health is threatened? What if there is a risk that the child will be deformed? What if she is not ready for a child? People's views differ, and because people's views differ, should a community express its "collective" view through a defined statute, or allow the woman to make her own personal choice? As we all know, there is significant and heartfelt disagreement about these issues.

Pope John Paul II, in the same *Evangelium Vitae* mentioned earlier, strongly expresses the view that life begins at conception and that there are no circumstances, not even those allowed under Queensland law, under which abortion is acceptable. To him, it seems to always be equivalent to murder. Catholicism, unlike Islam, makes a distinction between civil law and God's law and traditionally does not advocate laws that enforce its moral teachings. However, the Catholic Church thinks that the issue of abortion is such a grave "sin" that civil laws that allow it are "unjust" and should not be supported.

In the United States, as in most other countries, abortion is controversial. Per the Gallup poll, only 29 percent of the people surveyed in 2017 thought that women should have the right to have an abortion under any circumstances.[209] Prior to 1973, most states had abortion laws like other governments' laws that made it illegal to have an abortion unless the health of the woman carrying the fertilized egg was in jeopardy. In 1973, the US Supreme Court decided in a seven-to-two vote that women had a "liberty" by the "due process clause" of the Fourteenth Amendment to have an abortion within the first trimester of pregnancy.[210] This invalidated the states' laws against abortion. Almost twenty years later, in the case of *Planned Parenthood v. Casey*, a significantly different Supreme Court voted to modify their prior decision.[211] In a five-to-four vote, they upheld a woman's right to an abortion, but removed the absolute trimester right and agreed that the states may regulate abortion. Justice Antonin Scalia, who was part of the four-person minority of the court, stated that abortion "is not constitutionally protected—because of two simple facts: (1) the Constitution says absolutely nothing about it, and (2) the long-standing traditions of American society have permitted it to be legally proscribed."[212]

Many people in the original position would want to allow women the right to have an abortion. Even people who disagree on a wide variety of collective decisions can agree on social issues such as abortion. For example, in 1997, Nozick participated with Rawls and four others, including Ronald Dworkin, in an amicus brief to the US Supreme Court advocating the constitutionality of euthanasia. They noted that they disagree on many issues but jointly supported the court's *Casey* decision to permit abortion.[213]

While Nozick and Rawls agreed on euthanasia and abortion, many other people in the original position would have views on abortion like the legislature in Queensland or the Catholic Church. Abortion, like the issues of external defense, self-defense, and capital punishment, will cause people considering joint defense to disagree. However, abortion is a somewhat different concept and issue than these other goals, in two fundamental ways. First, the fertilized egg is not a deciding person. Women pregnant at the time of deciding to exit anarchy would be making the decision for the fertilized egg. Second, the issues surrounding the concept of abortion are moral concerns and do not involve interpersonal physical conflicts between existing people in anarchy. Each person in anarchy chooses his or her own view on abortion. People in the original position can have an abortion whether or not other people in anarchy disagree with them. People can disagree with other people's choices, which can lead to conflict and violence in anarchy. However, the assumption has been made that violence and physical disputes in anarchy have reached a level of equilibrium, irrespective of the cause of violence.

This does not imply that people's actions in all possible original positions with respect to abortion cannot be influenced by other people's views. In the Hobbesian original position, the fact that someone wants other people in anarchy to behave differently costs people resources in defending themselves. But it does not necessarily change their behavior. People in Hobbesian anarchy do not have to modify their actions to suit other people. If they decided to accommodate some people's views and choose not to have an abortion in the desire to reduce the resources they are committing to defense, they will open themselves up to attack from someone else for some other reason. In anarchy, they need to spend sufficient resources to defend themselves. This expense reduces their standard of living but allows them to live and make their own choices. In Hobbesian anarchy, each person is "free" to have an abortion for whatever reason she wants. The person carrying the egg makes the final decision on how to resolve her conflict with the fertilized egg. In Hobbesian anarchy, each person's worldview, and no one else's, determines whether she will have an abortion. The fertilized egg only has rights if the person carrying it thinks it does.

However, people in original positions where there is some level of cooperation may be incentivized to accommodate other people's views. For example, prohibition of abortion could be part of a broad moral code that people have accepted as being part of a community that has found methods of cooperation and interpersonal exchange while still in anarchy. The price of cooperation is to abide by the moral code. In the absence of defense collectives, people may have decided it is in their best interest to accommodate the views of other people with whom they are cooperating. Breaking the rules and having an abortion can lead to people no longer trading and cooperating with that person as a way of enforcing that society's rules. The cost of having an abortion in this type of social situation is a reduction in the standard of living of all those involved in the activity. They effectively can be required to move from the original position that has some level of cooperation and a higher standard of living to the Hobbesian original position where they are "free" to make their own choices.

As people contemplate entering a defense collective, the worldviews of others in the collective matter, irrespective of what type of original position people find themselves. Some people may feel so strongly about the abortion issue that they will not want to be in a collective with people who do not share their views on abortion. Other people will view it as one other decision that needs to be resolved in addressing the goal of preventing murder. People will need to decide if they are willing to give up the ability they had in Hobbesian anarchy to make their own decision as it relates to abortion and accommodate other people's views. A person who thinks abortion should be against the collective's rules may agree to a law that allows it in the first trimester but only under certain conditions. For example, they may want women to hear the heartbeat of the fetus prior to the abortion. They may want to ensure that partial-birth abortions are banned and that the collective never subsidizes an abortion.

COLLECTIVE RULES AND MORALS

The issues raised by abortion are part of a broader group of goals that some people would want to pursue as they contemplate moving from the original position to a collective. They would want the collective to have rules against behavior and actions that conflict with their moral position. Some people would feel strongly that laws should be devised to prohibit or at least limit activity that they feel is "wrong," such as euthanasia, pornography, prostitution, premarital sex, homosexuality, blasphemy, gambling, polygamy, same-sex marriage, using contraception, taking drugs, and using alcohol and tobacco. Other people may view these activities as immoral, but they do not want to impose coercive collective rules and penalties on people engaging in such behaviors. Still others may not find any of these activities objectionable.

A large group of diverse people would differ in their moral beliefs as well as in their views of both the breadth and depth of collective rules governing people's behavior given the same moral beliefs. For example, some people would want to prohibit the consumption and production of all alcohol, as the United States did during Prohibition and as some counties in various states do today. Other people may want to control its consumption by regulating aspects of its sale and distribution. They may agree with the current policies of Sweden, which require all packaged alcohol above 3.5 percent by volume to be sold by government-owned stores that limit their hours of operation. Some people will want to control alcohol by restricting the age that people can legally consume and purchase it. Other people may want to limit its consumption by heavily taxing its production and sale. Some people may want strict penalties for public drunkenness. Still others may be fine with no controls over its consumption and distribution. Given these potential differences in views, what would a group of diverse people considering banding together in joint defense decide to do about the consumption of alcohol by its members?

Each of these potential moral issues will increase the overall aggregate diversity of opinion within a given collective. The issues raised by prostitution are illustrative. Some people would want to prohibit all types of prostitution, viewing it as demeaning for all participants as well as reducing the overall morality of the community. Some may want to follow rules like those throughout the United States (absent a few counties in Nevada) that ban and criminalize any type of participation in prostitution. Some people may favor the approach taken by Sweden that allows prostitutes to solicit but criminalizes the procurement of sexual services. Other people would not want to ban or put any controls on prostitution. Others may want to allow prostitution but would want prostitutes to be employees of state-run brothels, as

Germany does today. Other people may want to emulate Argentina and Denmark and allow individual prostitution but prohibit brothels and pimps. Other people could agree with the legislature in New Zealand and the Netherlands, by allowing prostitution and attempting to protect prostitutes with various regulations. People exiting anarchy would also have different views on "softer" forms of prostitution like striptease. Some people may agree with the legislature in Iceland that prohibits all forms of striptease, viewing it as exploiting women.

As people contemplate exiting the various original positions, they would be confronted with differing moral views. Some may share Hayek's thinking that there are three levels of moral beliefs in conflict: (i) innate morals typically localized around one's family, (ii) evolutionary morals that occur through traditions and group selection, and (iii) morals developed through human design and intellect. Others may view morals as handed down by God. Some may think that there are universal morals, and of course other people may have the opinion that there are a wide variety of legitimate moral codes. Some may share the distinction that Australian philosopher J. L. Mackie makes between morals as an overall guide to acceptable behavior versus morals as a limit on people's base desires.[214]

Many people in the original position who accept Mackie's distinction would also agree with the views of Patrick Devlin, a judge in the United Kingdom, who argued that morals legislation is in the public interest, since it increases the "cohesion" of society.[215] He shared the opinion that society exists because of collective views and communal standards of behavior and that the cost of being part of society is being "bound" by laws that enforce these standards.[216] The important question, for those people in the original position who do not share Devlin's views, is why they must pay this cost. Why do they have to sign up for "bondage?"

Those who share Devlin's ideology must consider whether they would only associate with people with similar views or whether they could somehow be part of a larger collective of diverse people. At some point, as the collective expands among a population of diverse worldviews, people must contend with others who have different moral views as well as people with different views on imposing their moral views onto others.

Devlin's opinions seem to be particularly applicable to people in non-Hobbesian original positions where strong moral or religious codes have allowed a high level of cooperation to exist in anarchy. Many people exiting anarchy would continue to think that these shared traditions and moral views are important and will argue strenuously that they should be enforced by the coercive powers of the new collective. The fact that the new technology of the coercive collective can improve cooperation without the need to coercively enforce all or many historical moral rules may be viewed negatively by people who share Devlin's views. Other people would completely disagree with Devlin and perceive people who share his worldview as "conservative," desiring to cling to the past. Dworkin and Herbert Hart criticized Devlin from this perspective.[217]

While people who share Devlin's ideology may prefer the existing practices regarding their morals, they are not irrational. They just have a different worldview. They make different assumptions and judgments about human behavior. They may desire to live in a community that acts like a family and has a civil code based on what Hayek has characterized as "innate" morals. This view is often associated with Aristotle. He viewed each "polis" as unique and having the purpose of improving the moral life of a certain select group of its members. Alternatively, some people will hold Hayek's second view on morals and believe that their historical moral traditions have been a critical reason for the success of their community and society. As they contemplate leaving anarchy for joint defense, they will not want to take the risk that either their life or their family's life will be injured by the immoral behavior of other people.

This type of belief by people contemplating joining in collective defense seems to be like the view of Robert George, a legal scholar and political philosopher at Princeton University. In his defense of morals legislation, he argues that it protects members of society from the negative effects of "vice."[218] George maintains that morality is a public good and that immoral behavior is effectively a negative externality like air pollution, especially as it relates to one's "children."[219] People in the original position who agree with his opinions would argue that collective rules that enforce morality improve society.

Some people in the original position would want to go a step further, like those who follow Islam, and insist on collective rules that are all encompassing, governing all aspects of people's lives. Others, who share the view that the collective should have rules against "immoral" behavior, would think that the collective should not or could not prohibit all "vices." They would have a view like those of Saint Thomas Aquinas who wrote, in the late thirteenth century, that civil law should not address all sinful behavior, since most people will be unable to live a righteous life.[220]

George appears to agree with Aquinas that not all immoral behavior should be illegal. People in the original position who share their opinions would favor governmental rules concerning ethical conduct they think most people will obey. However, they would want some "vices" to be illegal given their presumed impact on the overall moral environment of society. Many of these same people would think that repressing industries that cater to unethical behavior and punishing the aiders and abettors would have a similar positive impact on the collective they join. As cooperation expands in the collective and the natural phenomena of comparative advantage and the division of labor increase, collective rules preventing the provision of unethical services may be an attractive option for many people who want to prevent moral misbehavior. One of the problems, of course, is that making an activity illegal does not eliminate the activity but pushes it into the "black market." Societal resources are then spent on enforcing the rules of the collective. This can occur even in a collective whose rules were unanimously agreed to as part of the bargain of joining the collective. Some people will deliberately break the rules they did not agree with but were somehow incentivized to accept in joining in collective defense.

Of course, other people in the various original positions would disagree with Devlin and followers of Islam and may strongly believe that most morals legislation is unnecessary and undesirable. Like political philosopher John Stuart Mill, they might think civil laws should only address actions that could cause "harm to others."[221] Or they will agree with Herbert Hart in response to Devlin that laws must acknowledge "individual liberty."[222] Alternatively, many may have opinions similar to Nozick. Not surprisingly, he also disagreed with Devlin, stating that governmental laws should only prohibit behavior that violates what he calls the "ethics of respect" that naturally developed to improve trade and cooperation.[223] This ethic is narrow and essentially covers what many mean by "natural rights."

In some ways, these disagreements over morality are like the disagreements about external defense or murder legislation. However, there is one significant difference. Everyone who participates in joint defense will agree that joint goals for both external and internal defense exist, and that joint defense has value over individual defense. They will recognize that joint defense has costs in the form of decision congestion when combined with differences in opinions on various actions by the collective. However, as we have seen, many people would disagree with the entire concept of morals legislation. Like Nozick, many people would not think that any of these types of rules are necessary or desirable. Unlike the earlier issues of external defense and murder that everyone in the collective embraced as a joint goal, the issue of morals legislation is not a jointly shared goal. This is a critical issue for the structure of the collective that people agree to form because there are no gains from morals legislation for some people who want to exit anarchy.

The important question people would face as they exit anarchy is why they should be willing to suffer a loss of freedom from morals legislation when they do not receive any gains from this legislation. In a large population of diverse people, the marginal joiner of the defense collective, whose net gain from joint defense is zero and who disagrees in any way with the moral rules agreed to by the defense collective, would not be willing to join that collective.

Interestingly, people who exit anarchy from original positions that have some level of cooperation may be able to increase their level of freedom by joining a collective that does not have coercively enforced rules corning morality. A collective allows them to at least achieve the degree of cooperation they had in anarchy. The rules for the cooperative can be materially different from the moral or religious codes they are subject to in anarchy. If their worldview differs from the worldview embedded in the moral code of their anarchical society, they could increase their level of freedom by associating with like-minded people. The ability of the collective to coercively enforce its rules that these people prefer over their anarchical moral code decreases their freedom loss. People in these non-Hobbesian original positions would still have freedom losses, since they are in a collective with people with differing worldviews, but they may have smaller freedom losses than they had in anarchy.

COLLECTIVE RULES AND FRAUD

An issue almost everyone is concerned with is potential fraudulent behavior. Behavioral modification caused by moral beliefs obviously reduces the incidence of fraud. And as discussed in chapter 6, people will use "good will" and "reputation" as fraud-reducing devices. Required investment in developing friendships and in building a "name" internalizes the costs that a person committing fraud imposes on other people.

Another method or device that people may use to reduce the incidence of fraud is through cooperation with people or entities that have been "rated" or "reviewed" by someone they trust. For example, the magazine *Good Housekeeping* early in the twentieth century set up a testing station that reviewed household products and allowed those products that passed their tests to advertise in their magazine. It guaranteed consumers their money back for any defective product that advertised with them. Over time its "Seal of Approval" earned a high reputation with consumers, which caused manufactures of consumer products to want to have their products rated. Underwriters Lab was founded in 1894 to test the safety of electrical devices. Today they test, validate, and certify a wide variety of products. Roughly twenty-two billion products worldwide carry the UL mark.

The five theorists were probably aware of these methods to reduce fraud, but like many other people, they did not seem to think these "naturally" generated approaches are sufficient in and of themselves to reduce the incidence of fraudulent behavior. Even Nozick was in favor of state- or government-enforced rules concerning fraud. Many people exiting anarchy, even if they are in original positions where cooperation exists, will want collective rules against dishonesty in transactions. However, even if they agree on the need for collective enforced rules, people will disagree on the specific rules and on the best approach the collective should pursue to reduce fraudulent actions. The various coercive actions the collective may pursue against those who commit fraud can be broadly grouped into three types: criminal, tort, and regulatory.

Criminal fraud is like other crimes. The collective decides that it is illegal and uses its resources to prosecute those thought to have defrauded other people. Different states in the United States and different countries have varying definitions of fraud and apply a variety of penalties. In the United States, criminal fraud typically involves a jury deciding beyond a reasonable doubt that a person deliberately misrepresented a situation and that the representation was relied on by someone who suffered a loss. Convicted fraudsters include Bernie Madoff, who was convicted of conducting a multiyear Ponzi scheme in the magnitude of $65 billion. He was sentenced to 150 years in jail. Frank Abagnale was convicted of forgery and passing fake checks. He served four years of his twelve-year jail sentence. Bernie Ebbers, the CEO of WorldCom, was convicted of accounting fraud and sentenced to twenty-five years.

Fraud can also be a "tort," a civil violation where the collective enforces the judgment of a court or jury that fraud has occurred. The penalties are typically monetary and accrue to the person who was defrauded. The tortfeasor can be assessed penalties equal to his or her victim's loss plus punitive damages. Many people in the original position would desire that tortfeasors pay high punitive damages as punishment for their actions and as a deterrent to other people who may be incentivized to commit similar acts. The loss suffered by their victim(s) can be much larger than the tortfeasor's gain. Since it is a civil issue, the typical level of proof is much lower than in criminal cases with either a jury or judge making a judgment on the "preponderance of evidence." One prominent example of a difference between approaches to fraud as a tort is that in the United Kingdom, the tortfeasor is required to pay his or her victim's attorney's fees while in the United States each person pays his or her own attorney.

Some people may be so concerned with potential fraudulent actions that they will not want to rely solely on the disincentives provided by making fraud a crime and a tort. Even though collective resources would be used to prosecute fraudulent behavior, and people who are defrauded could potentially sue the entity that defrauded them, some people who are considering joining a collective may want a more ex ante active approach to deterring fraudulent acts. This typically involves some type of regulatory scheme managed by the collective. While there can be significant differences in people's views over different types of laws and penalties to apply to fraud, these differences are dwarfed by the differences of opinion that exist over regulations designed and administered to prevent fraud.

The controversy surrounding breast implants is illustrative. The US Food and Drug Administration (FDA) estimates that it currently regulates 20 percent of consumer spending in the United States.[224] Its current mandate includes being "responsible for protecting the public health by ensuring the safety, efficacy, and security of human and veterinary drugs, biological products, and medical devices; and by ensuring the safety of our nation's food supply, cosmetics, and products that emit radiation . . . speed innovations that make medical products more effective, safer, and more affordable."[225] The FDA received authority to regulate breast implants in 1976 through the Medical Device amendment to the 1938 Food, Drug, and Cosmetics Act.

The first breast-implant operation to use silicone, a product designed by Dow Corning Corporation, was performed in 1962. Mariann Hopkins, in 1976, had breast implants following her double mastectomy for cancer, according to court records.[226] Both implants were designed and manufactured by Dow Corning. A few weeks following surgery, she experienced complications from her left implant. She had both implants replaced with Dow Corning–manufactured silicone implants. Two years later she was diagnosed by her doctor with an incurable autoimmune disorder resembling rheumatoid arthritis.[227] In 1986, an implant was discovered to have ruptured, leaking silicone into her body, and again she had both replaced with two new implants manufactured by Dow Corning.[228]

Somewhat later she learned that other women were suffering from the same symptoms she had, and that her connective-tissue disease could be caused by leaking silicone. She asked her rheumatologist if the leaking silicone from her previous implants could be the cause of her disease. According to her, the doctor effectively told her people look for a scapegoat and that she should resign herself to having the disease.[229] After consulting with a lawyer, she sued Dow Corning for causing her illness. The jury found Dow Corning liable for fraud and malice and awarded her $7.3 million. Dow appealed the verdict, but the appeals court concluded that "given the facts that Dow was aware of possible defects in its implants, that Dow knew long-term studies of the implants safety were needed, that Dow concealed this information as well as the negative results of the few short-term laboratory tests performed, and that Dow continued for several years to market its implants as safe despite this knowledge, a substantial punitive damages award is justified."[230]

At the time, Dow Corning was one of the largest companies in the United States with global sales of nearly $1.8 billion. It produced approximately five thousand products, had forty thousand global customers, and eight thousand employees.[231] By 1991, there were approximately two million women who had received silicone breast implants, and Dow Corning was the largest producer with a significant market share. Dow Corning charged on average $195 for each implant and had total revenues from implants of $12.7 million in 1990.[232] The sale of breast implants was less than 1 percent of its total sales, and according to its vice president and chief financial officer Edward Steinhoff, had been an unprofitable product since 1986.[233]

In March 1992, the new CEO of Dow Corning announced that they would stop manufacturing and selling breast implants, and the subsidiary of Dow Corning that previously produced the implants, Dow Corning Wright, would be sold (although the liabilities from the sale of implants would be retained). Even though Dow Corning and the other manufacturers of implants won many of their court cases, the torrent of fraud claims from women who asserted they had been grievously injured by the Dow Corning implants caused the company to voluntarily enter Chapter 11 bankruptcy in 1995.

While Dow Corning was suffering from tort legislation, what was the FDA doing about breast implants? The FDA was concerned about the potential negative health effects from leaking implants. While it received authority to start regulating implants in 1976, it did not classify implants as Class III devices (like heart pacemakers) until 1988. The classification required all manufacturers of implants to file a premarket application demonstrating the safety and effectiveness within thirty months. In 1991, it issued a ruling requiring all manufacturers of implants to file a premarket application or cease selling the product. Dow Corning filed an application and submitted fifty thousand pages, which included information about its manufacturing process, product designs, and various safety studies it had conducted over the past thirty years. The FDA asked a panel of outside experts for their recommendations. The panel advised the FDA to seek more information about safety but recommended that silicone implants continue to be sold.

Dr. David Kessler, the FDA commissioner, was apparently troubled by the negative internal Dow Corning documents that were part of the discovery in the Hopkins trial as well as clinical information on ruptures and the possibility that leaking silicone could be linked to autoimmune disorders. In January 1992, he asked every manufacturer for a "voluntary moratorium" on selling silicone implants. In announcing the moratorium, he stated that the FDA's role was to ensure that implants are both safe and effective. In April of that year, he lifted the moratorium but made it illegal in the United States to receive a silicone implant for cosmetic reasons. Until then, approximately 60 percent of all implants were used for breast augmentation.[234] Only those women who required reconstructive surgery or who were parts of a clinical trial could legally receive a silicone implant following the FDA decision. The FDA continued to allow saline implants, which were a small part of the market. Dow Corning had decided to exit the business a couple months earlier and withdrew its premarket application two days before the FDA's April decision.

While the FDA was not alone in banning cosmetic silicone implants, most countries continued to allow them for cosmetic reasons. The

European Union (EU) conducted a variety of studies and established different working groups and concluded that they should not ban silicone implants. The British medical-device agency, in response to the FDA decision, also established an expert panel who recommended against a ban, since in their opinion "no evidence" was available to justify such a decision. In 1994, after reviewing all available data, they confirmed their earlier conclusion that there was no evidence of silicone breast implants causing autoimmune problems.[235] The approach of the regulatory authority in the UK was radically different from the FDA. The FDA seemed to want proof, from their perspective, that implants were safe, while the UK appeared to want some evidence that they were unsafe.

In 1994, the *New England Journal of Medicine* published a paper by the Mayo Clinic that did not find a connection between connective-tissue illnesses and implants.[236] One year later, a study at Harvard medical school on nurses came to the same conclusion.[237] Numerous studies in Europe concurred with this assessment. In 1999, the Institute of Medicine published a report for Congress that concluded that silicone was used in a variety of products including hypodermic syringes, that it was not toxic, and that implants that used it did not raise "health concerns."[238] In 2006, fourteen years after making them illegal and eleven years after Dow Corning's bankruptcy, the FDA approved the marketing of silicone breast implants for cosmetic reasons for people over the age of twenty-two, viewing them as reasonably safe and effective.

People with different worldviews will obviously come to different conclusions about the entire issue of breast implants. Some will view US laws on discovery, jury decisions, and torts as highly effective in punishing people and entities that commit fraud. Others will view the US system as inefficient and unpredictable. Some people will view the FDA's actions as appropriate given the lack of information and uncertainty over the long-term impacts of breast implants on health. Other people will view the FDA as being too conservative, effectively stopping all women in the United States from having a cosmetic procedure that was widely available to women worldwide. Some people will question the FDA's "value" judgment of viewing silicone breast implants as safe and effective for women who had had mastectomies, but not safe and effective for women who wanted to enhance their breast size for cosmetic reasons. Those same people may also disagree with the FDA's decision to allow breast augmentation for women who are twenty-two years old but not for women who are twenty-one.

The political issues around breast implants are not unique; people's worldviews will lead to significant disagreement about government regulation. These disagreements would also occur among people in the original position. Some people would favor extensive regulation because they want a high level of confidence that products and processes are safe and effective. They may be much more concerned with type-one errors, the approval of an unsafe or ineffective product, than a type-two error, the nonapproval of a safe and effective product or process. Other people would have the opposite view. For example, Milton Friedman, the Nobel Prize–winning economist, argued that government regulators are potentially biased because the approval of unsafe products is observable while preventing a safe and effective product from being marketed is not readily apparent.[239]

While his criticism has some validity, it is not dispositive in a world of multiple jurisdictions and different points of view. People who are subject to the FDA's rules receive valuable information from the activities of jurisdictions not subject to the FDA's restrictions. The information that a product is seemingly safely used in another country will put pressure on the FDA and regulators from other countries to approve that product. However, as we saw in the controversy over breast implants, this pressure may not be successful in convincing the FDA to agree with regulators from other countries. Nonetheless, this pressure will be particularly powerful if almost everyone agrees that the product will significantly enhance at least some people's lives. Pressure will also be intense on the FDA to approve the use of controversial products for people who have little to no downside risk from using the product. The obvious examples are people who have life-threatening diseases such as AIDS or Ebola.

Information that other jurisdictions have deemed a product as unsafe may also be used by critics of the FDA and other regulators that the agency is too liberal in its approval of products. Regulators such as the FDA may be accused of allowing unsafe and ineffective products to be sold. It may also be accused of being slow to admit its mistakes and of keeping unsafe products on the market.

The FDA was established in 1938 over safety concerns of various consumer products. In 1962, Congress significantly expanded the FDA's scope from the issue of safety to the broader concern over the effectiveness of drugs. Unfortunately, establishing that a drug or product is "safe" is not just a matter of science. As we have been discussing, it is a complicated process fraught with value judgments. Determining effectiveness is even more challenging. Since people obviously differ in their desires for a safe product versus the potential benefit from the product, as well as in their views on the trade-offs between effectiveness, price, and availability, how should a regulator make these decisions? It is an especially difficult question for products that affect the human body, given our current level of understanding.

Government regulation can be controversial for other reasons. For example, it can be viewed as decreasing competition and increasing prices. Drug prices in the United States can be substantially higher than the prices for the same drug in other countries, since each distributor in the United States must be licensed. Some states have tried to give their citizens more choice by passing legislation to make it legal for them to purchase drugs over the Internet from select countries. Maine passed such a law. Various pharmacy groups sued Maine and in 2015 a federal judge overturned the Maine law, holding that it violated federal law. The judge ruled that the law prevents the central government from having "one voice" over imports.[240] As people decide to exit anarchy and join a defense collective, would they want the collective to have one voice? Would they have a choice? Some people would want more flexibility than having their actions limited by a regulator like the FDA, which has the power to establish rules for the entire defense collective. Would these people always need to compromise and accept collective-wide regulation for goods such as food, cosmetics, and drugs?

13

—★—

DOMESTIC GOVERNMENTS

MULTIGOAL COLLECTIVES

People differ in the goals they want a collective to address. They will also disagree over the best methods and procedures to accomplish jointly agreed goals. The relevant question for us is: What impact do these various disagreements have on the membership and structure of the defense collective?

External defense is the foundational goal of any defense collective, since failure to protect the members of the collective from external threats would lead to dissolution of the collective. The collective is an entity in an anarchical environment. In a world of selfish people, it would need to spend the scarce resources of its members both to protect the well-being of its membership and to ensure that collective decisions of the membership are executed. The successful performance of the goal of external defense would allow the collective to pursue other goals.

Given the discussion in the prior chapter, it is evident that people in the original position would want to pursue collective goals beyond that of external defense. These incremental goals include preventing murder, theft, and fraud as well as various moral and social objectives. A person who prefers that the defense collective pursue these incremental goals would do so because he or she values those goals and views the collective as being more effective at accomplishing these objectives than that individual can in anarchy. To analyze the impact of these new aims on the structure and formation of the defense collective, many of the simplifying assumptions from chapter 8 will be incorporated. These include the assumptions that each person in the original position: (i) utilizes the same bargaining model and in doing so does not make mistakes, (ii) is selfish with respect to his or her unique world-view, and (iii) possesses complete information on people's worldviews.

It will prove helpful to divide the various potential goals into two types. The first includes those such as the prevention of murder and theft where people in the original position use scarce resources to protect themselves. These goals will be analyzed in a similar fashion to the goal of external defense. The joint or collective provision of these goals is more efficient than people can achieve in anarchy. This is represented by a reduction in fixed costs when two or more people decide to cooperate. As with external defense, the assumption will be that each person adds the same amount of transferable incremental efficiency to the collaborative arrangement. However, the amount of the fixed cost reduction can differ from goal to goal.

The other types of goals are moral and social objectives that people may have individually pursued in anarchy. While it is possible and maybe likely that some people would use their resources in the original position to attempt to force other people to adhere to their moral or religious beliefs, the analysis is concerned with people who have a broadly liberal worldview. This type of person may have strong moral, ethical, and social views, but will stop short of violence or latent violence to enforce their worldview onto others. Broadly liberal people include the five theorists. They may have significant differences of opinions on moral and social issues. However, they may be willing to support collective enforced laws concerning moral and social issues that others may not prefer if these laws are produced by a process that they view as legitimate.

Therefore, at least for people with these worldviews, the analysis can be simplified by assuming the various moral and social goals do not add any incremental value to anyone in the original position. People's desires for these goals would be modeled by associating them with the goal of public safety, and assuming moral and social goals simply increase the number of decisions people would want to make concerning public safety. Given differences of opinion on these social goals and on how to pursue them, this would lead to incremental freedom losses from the collective goal of public safety.

Many people in the original position would share the views of the various judges, legislators, and scholars reviewed in previous chapters. Some will like to live in a collective with rules that narrowly define self-defense. Others will like to live in a collective that prohibits guns. Others will prefer rules that allow people to own guns and for people to use a gun in broadly defined self-defense. Some people in the original position will like to live in a collective with substantial resources dedicated to enforcement of the jointly agreed rules and significant penalties for violating various rules. Some people will favor the death penalty for a wide variety of offenses. Other people will want to restrict the death penalty to only the most significant crimes such as multiple murders. Others can view the death penalty as barbaric and unacceptable under any circumstances. Some people will want the right to have an abortion. Other people will want to severely restrict this right or eliminate it entirely. People exiting the original position would have differing opinions on the rules and restrictions that should apply to activities such as pornography, prostitution, gambling, and using drugs and alcohol. Unfortunately, the joint effort to accomplish these various incremental goals in the presence of differing worldviews has the same type of negative externalities involved in the prior discussion of joint defense.

Coordinated effort leads to decision congestion and a need for people to reach a consensus. In a coalition or collective of diverse people, accommodating the views of others by accepting decisions on the appropriate goals and methods, and pursuing jointly agreed goals that are not consistent with each member's worldview, is a costly process. Consensus and agreement among people with diverse worldviews lead to freedom losses. The incremental goals of public safety, fraud, and theft prevention would lead to incremental collective gains, but at the same time they would also lead to an increase in aggregate freedom losses.

As each person in the original position contemplates their strategy to exit anarchy, they will consider the worldviews of every person and the bargaining options that each person possesses. Their logical analysis will follow the lines of reasoning in chapters 10 and 11. The only differences are that each person will factor in the impact of (i) the potential gains from coercive collective action being higher, since each of these new goals would lead to higher aggregate gains as more people pursue them; and (ii) aggregate freedom losses also being higher, since people have differences of opinion on both how to pursue these goals and whether to pursue them. As before, this would lead each person to conclude that they will all agree to jointly form the minimum number of collectives that can incorporate their various worldviews. Given a large number of people, each collective would continue to expand until anyone left in anarchy has net losses from joining a coercive collective. Each person in a diverse collective would reason that everyone in their and similar collectives will unanimously agree that people will receive differential net gains based on their individual freedom losses from accepting the collective decisions that minimize aggregate freedom losses.

The addition of each person to each multigoal collective would increase the aggregate gains from collective defense, public safety, fraud prevention, and other collective goals because of the enhanced efficiencies of collective action assisted by coercively enforced rules. Each additional person adds more incremental gains to the multigoal collective than they did to the single-goal defense collective. However, each of these people who join the multigoal collectives have different worldviews. They all have different opinions on how best to pursue these various goals, including the controversial goal of morals legislation. Each person who agrees to be a member of a multigoal collective would consent to compromise and accept the decisions that minimize the aggregate freedom losses with respect to each of these goals individually and in total. For example, the prohibition of the death penalty would be the compromise decision in a collective if people's preferences against the death penalty, weighted by the intensity for those that hold this view, are greater than the weighted preferences of those people who desire a death penalty. People with strongly held views can affect the decisions made by the collective. A controversial law over which some have strong views on both sides of an issue would lead to high aggregate freedom losses plus high freedom losses for all of the individuals who compromise and accept it.

People in the original position would join the multigoal collective that maximizes their net gains. This implies that a person who prefers being a member of a collective that allows the death penalty would compromise and accept a law that prohibits the death penalty if that law minimizes the aggregate freedom losses in the collective that maximizes their net gains. They are willing to compromise on this law and other laws because the gains from collective action, assisted by the coercively enforced laws and rules of the multigoal collective, are sufficient to overcome their psychic losses from making this and other compromises, and they cannot do better by joining a collective with other people. Alternatively, if a person feels strongly that the death penalty is necessary and cannot locate a collective where their overall net gains are at least zero, then that person would decide to remain in the original position.

The compound effect of all these different views on diverse and controversial issues would cause those decisions that minimize aggregate freedom losses to rise more than linearly as more people join each collective. That is, as the size of each of these collectives increases, the aggregate freedom losses in each of these collectives will rise faster than the aggregate collective gains. This implies that the average net gains decrease as more people join each collective. Given a sufficiently large population in the original position, the marginal person in some of the multigoal collectives would have no net gains.

Except for having multiple goals, these broader collectives have the same characteristics as the single-goal collectives from the prior chapters. However, if we make a plausible assumption that the gains from collective defense are larger than the gains from any other collective goal, and that the differences of opinion concerning defense are not greater than the differences of opinion concerning other goals, then other conclusions can be drawn. The first is that, for a given population of people, there will be more multigoal collectives than would have existed if external defense were the only goal. These multigoal collectives will also be smaller and less diverse. This occurs because the large number of people in a single-goal defense collective will have negative net gains if they pursue domestic goals. This will incent them to form smaller, less diverse multigoal collectives.

Freedom losses from the pursuit of multiple goals by diverse people will be much higher than the freedom losses from collective defense. Even though the gross gains will also be higher, these additional gains are swamped by the psychic losses from the differences of opinions about all the decisions that people want to make concerning these additional objectives. This will, on average, cause people to associate with others who have similar views about nondefense issues. The multigoal collectives would all pursue defense, since that is a foundational goal, but each of them would expand to a point where there are aggregate net losses from the pursuit of the nondefense-related goals. This would cause each of them to be somewhat smaller and less diverse as the gains from collective defense must cover the net losses from these other goals. These net losses have the effect of a reduction in the net gains from collective defense, incenting fewer diverse people to join the multigoal collective.

So, is this it? Have we determined the structure of government that a diverse group of people seeking to exit anarchy would form? Would people who have all the assumed advantages of complete information, inability to make bargaining mistakes, and the capability to perfectly specify and anticipate every possible contingency form numerous, relatively small, and somewhat homogeneous governments? The simple answer is no.

NESTED COLLECTIVES

The members of each of these multigoal defense collectives have other degrees of freedom. The foregoing analysis treated domestic goals the same as external defense, allowing only one collective domestic action for every domestic decision. For external defense, the members must agree to the decisions that the collective will pursue. Is this also true for all domestic decisions? Are there methods that can be used to limit the decision externalities in the collective and reduce the overall level of decision congestion within the collective? Yes.

In the multigoal collectives analyzed above, freedom losses expanded significantly as more people joined the collective. People's differing worldviews led them to disagree about the best methods and procedures to reduce the negative impact that some people can have on other people, as well as the best ways to encourage collective behavior. In general, people disagreed over the responsibilities that members should have to the collective. They disagreed over the rights that members should have from the collective. They also disagreed over the rights and obligations that members should have to each other. Everyone in the multigoal collective was subject to the same coercively enforced rules with respect to every goal that that collective decided to pursue.

However, why does the collective need to have uniform rules for all goals? Why does everyone need to have the same rights and responsibilities with respect to every social goal, including the goals they completely disagree with? For example, why must everyone in a collective be subject to the same laws on abortion or to the same criminal penalties? People in different multigoal collectives are subject to different rules. Why doesn't that apply to rules within a collective?

Uniform rules are required for external defense because the collective is an entity established to defend its members. It cannot logically pursue different actions for the same required decision. But this limitation does not exist for all the collective's domestic goals. It could logically make different decisions for the same nondefense-related goal. The members of a multigoal collective could reduce their aggregate freedom losses and entice new members to join by allowing differential rules with respect to domestic issues. This is true even if the assumption is relaxed that joint defense has larger gains than any domestic goal. The formation of one or more "nested collectives" is an institutional structure that people in the original position would consider as part of their strategy to maximize their net gains from coercively assisted collective action. A nested collective is a domestic coercive collective whose members are simultaneously members of a defense collective. Nested collectives include regions, states, provinces, cantons, counties, cities, and towns. However, as will be discussed in some detail later, the governance structure of nested collectives and their relationship with other coercive collectives are potentially much different than these characteristics of traditional domestic governments. A person who exits anarchy would be a member of one defense collective but could potentially be a member of many nested collectives. Nested collectives are an institutional method of addressing differing worldviews with respect to nondefense goals for members of a defense collective.

A nested collective is an entity that its members can join to enhance their collective efforts to accomplish a goal or goals beyond external defense, using unanimously approved force or coercion. Like a defense collective, each nested collective is an entity and, as such, it can only pursue one action for each decision. For example, people can be members of a nested collective that has a law against abortion. The law can (i) only allow abortion in the first trimester, (ii) prohibit abortion entirely, (iii) permit it only if the mother's life is in danger, or (iv) be like the laws of Queensland in 2005, but not all four simultaneously. The members of this nested collective will choose the rule on abortion that minimizes their freedom losses. However, they do not have to conform this rule to the worldviews of other members of the defense collective.

Given diverse worldviews and the complexity of the issues surrounding abortion, people in a nested collective who hold similar views on abortion are unlikely to agree on every potential rule. For example, should a nested collective that allows abortion require parental consent or notification for underage mothers? If so, at what age should notification be required? What rules, if any, should govern the use of fetal tissue? What penalties should be imposed on people who break the rules? People will disagree. This would cause freedom losses in each nested collective, as those members must accept rules and laws they do not prefer in order to receive the benefits of being a member of that nested collective. The existence of freedom losses reduces the membership of each nested collective and would lead people to form more than one nested collective. These losses may also incent some members of the defense collective who do not want any rules on abortion to decide not to be part of a nested coalition (a pre-collective) that focuses on abortion, preferring to make their own abortion decisions unrestricted by the views of other members.

Nested collectives reduce decision congestion in the defense collective because they allow for different sets of governing rules for domestic goals. The reduction in decision congestion naturally leads to a decrease in freedom losses. Nesting is an institutional answer to diverse worldviews. It allows for the existence of multiple sets of rules throughout the collective for domestic goals. Such collectives enhance the willingness of people to be part of the same defense coalition when they have compatible worldviews on external defense but significantly different views on domestic issues such as abortion. Given these worldview differences, there will still be freedom losses from collective-wide rules on external defense and from nested collective rules on domestic issues. But the freedom losses would be less than they would have been if the collective enforced the same rules about every domestic goal.

Nested collectives reduce dissonance caused by differing worldviews. They allow a larger number of diverse people to be members of the same defense collective. As discussed above, even the seemingly universal desire to prevent murder is not without conflict. Some people will, like the justices on the Rhode Island Supreme Court, want laws that do the utmost to preserve life. Others will prefer laws that allow people to "stand their ground." People will disagree over the appropriate penalties for breaking a collective law, even the law against murder. Some people will prefer strong laws against the possession of guns. Other people will believe that possessing a gun makes them safer. Given the differences in people's views and the nearly endless number of decisions involved with the multiplicity of potential goals, there is almost a continuous gradation of the population.

DEFENSE COLLECTIVES AND MULTIGOAL NESTED COLLECTIVES

Each person in the original position would incorporate the potential use of nested collectives as they examined their strategy to maximize their net gains from the new technology of coercive collectives. The result of this deliberation would be a unanimous agreement between everyone in the original position for most of them to join various defense collectives. The members of most of these defense collectives would pursue multiple collective goals. Many of these people would also become members of various nested collectives. The equilibrium properties of these more complex defense collectives would have characteristics like those of the democratic defense collective that have been analyzed previously.

Decisions made in each of the defense collectives would be those that minimize the aggregate freedom losses of its members. These decisions would be applicable to every member of that defense collective. Similarly, the domestic decisions made by each of the nested collectives would apply to each of the members of that nested collective. However, each of the nested collectives could have different rules and goals. In a diverse nested collective, these decisions would be made in the same way in which they are determined in the defense collective— by choosing those actions that maximize freedom. Each defense collective would continue to add people until the marginal person's allocation of the gross gains from the defense collective and the various nested collectives they belong to is equal to their psychic losses from accepting the decision of these entities. Since the marginal gains are finite, everyone has a unique worldview, and total gains increase at a slower pace than the associated freedom losses, there is a limit to the size of each defense collective and each nested collective.

The allocated gains from being a member of these more complicated, diverse multi-person defense collectives are calculated in exactly the same way as they were in chapters 10 and 11. In the limit, as the size of each of these approaches infinity, each person receives the same allocation of the gross gains and must absorb the freedom losses that resulted from their acceptance of the laws of the defense collective. Those people more politically compatible with others will receive higher net gains. In addition, members of the defense collective will receive an allocation of the gains from each nested collective in which they are members. The determination of these gains can vary among the nested collectives, since these nested collectives may be less diverse. For example, there could be a nested collective dominated by people who share Rawls's opinions. Given his philosophy, they would likely divide the gains produced by that nested collective differently than determined by bargaining among more diverse individuals in the defense collective.

Each person's strategy would include the possibility of joining a nested collective, and they would do so if that decision maximizes their net gain after incorporating the optimal strategy that everyone else will employ. Everything else being the same, people will have higher gross gains if everyone in a defense collective joins the same nested collective. Of course, in this case, no one will need to be in a nested collective. They can just pursue the goals of the nested collective in the defense collective. People sort themselves into one or more nested collectives because they disagree on issues associated with domestic goals. They sacrifice the gross gains from joining a larger nested collective because of their reduced freedom losses from having to accept laws they do not agree with. The ability to be a member of a nested collective would allow many people (but not necessarily everyone) in the original position to increase their net gains and be part of a larger defense collective. The credible equilibrium allocation that would be unanimously agreed to by each person in the original position, even those who remain in anarchy, would incorporate the use of nested collectives. People who are broadly liberal and members of a sufficiently diverse defense collective could form many nested collectives and would form at least two, because of the diversity of their domestic views. One of these would be organized around a central goal like income equality while the other would appeal to those whose views are like Nozick's.

The members of a diverse defense collective would not all join the same nested collective unless defense and domestic goals are inextricably related. To prove this, let's assume that people want to pursue a variety of goals, and they are in one nested collective because there is some cost to being in multiple collectives. Will they do so? Will the members of a nested collective always pursue other nondefense-related goals with the same members? Unlikely, for the same reason there are nested collectives. People's worldviews differ. As the goals pursued by a nested collective increase, everything else being the same, freedom losses will rise faster than the gains from the collective pursuit of these goals. Given a wide diversity of worldviews, some people will experience net losses from the pursuit of every domestic goal with the same group of people. This will incent them, even in the presence of disaggregation costs, to form or join another nested collective.

This does not imply that there won't be multiple-goal nested collectives. It just leads to the conclusion that everyone will not find it in their best interest to be in the same nested collective with the same people. Even people who have similar worldviews will disagree over the best approach to various collective problems. This will cause some of them to want to pursue collective goals with different people. John Rawls and John Harsanyi agreed on many social and philosophical issues, but they still had many differences of opinion. Would each of them prefer to reach a consensus answer with each other on every domestic issue, or would they prefer having the flexibility of reaching a consensus with other people on some issues? Now add hundreds of thousands or millions of people who have similar but distinct worldviews. What is the likelihood that each of them will determine it is in their best interests to have to reach a consensus with this same group of people on every decision, for every collective goal they want to pursue? The probabilities are extremely low. Given sufficient diversity, the probabilities approach zero.

AGREEMENTS BETWEEN NESTED COLLECTIVES

Using nested collectives, many collective goals can be pursued without any member experiencing net losses from that goal. If they experience an overall net loss from collective action, they will join a different defense collective or stay in anarchy. If they have a net loss from a domestic goal, they can join another nested collective with members of the same defense collective or decide not to participate in collective action with respect to that goal. However, as we will discuss in part four, there are reasons why people may want to be in a nested collective that is pursuing multiple goals. As such, it is entirely possible that some members of these multiple-goal nested collectives will have net losses from some of these jointly pursued goals that are effectively subsidized by the net gains from other collective goals. Is this also possible for the defense collective? Will members of a defense collective find it optimal not to utilize nested collectives for some nondefense goals or issues? Stated differently, are there certain uniform rules unrelated to defense that could occur in a defense collective?

In forming the diversified defense collectives, uniformly applying domestic laws throughout a sufficiently large diversified defense coalition would cause some of its members to have net losses from some nondefense laws. This would incent these people to exit and join another defense coalition that does not have these uniformly applied domestic laws. It would also incent everyone in the defense coalition to compromise and agree that these people will not have to be subject to these uniform rules. However, this raises the question of whether there are some domestic issues that everyone feels so strongly about that they will agree these should apply to everyone in the defense collective. Theoretically, there could be many, but two of these seem likely for people whose worldviews are categorized as broadly liberal. But before examining these, it will prove illustrative to discuss various conflicts between the differing nested collectives.

Let's consider the goal of preventing murder. Each nested collective focused on public safety would protect its members from murder by enforcing agreed-upon rules and imposing certain agreed-upon responsibilities on its members. As stated previously, these rules can differ between the various nested collectives. Each nested collective would have been authorized by its members to use coercive power over them to prevent murder, given the perceived benefits of the collective prevention of murder. But what about the potential threat from people who are not members of their nested collective?

The defense collective is designed to protect each of its members from the threats imposed by nonmembers. The public-safety nested collective is designed to safeguard each of its members from being murdered. However, thus far, the discussion has been about the agreement between the members of a nested collective not to murder each other and the jointly agreed laws and procedures designed by them that accompany this agreement. But who or what protects members of the various nested collectives from the threat of murder by members of the defense collective who are not also members of their nested collective? The members of each nested collective would not ignore the threat from other members of the defense collective. They could attempt to address this threat either through the use of some type of defensive arrangement or through the employment of mutual agreements. The first approach is conceptually like the situation in which the overall defense collective finds itself with other defense collectives. This approach presumes that each of the nested collectives is in some type of conflict with other nested collectives within the same defense collective that requires the potential use of force. While differences between the nested collectives may exist, armed conflict is costly, which implies that each of the nested collectives would prefer reaching some type of agreement with each other to prevent the murder of its members by the members of another nested collective.

The members of each of the nested collectives would want to design their mutual agreements to give them the same level of protection that they expect to receive from their own nested collective. However, each person has a different worldview. Members of the defense collective effectively sort themselves into the optimal public-safety nested collective by joining the collective that has policies that most conform to their own preferred policies. This can lead to significant differences in policies, laws, and procedures concerning murder in each of the nested collectives. The agreements between the nested collectives must either establish which nested collective has jurisdiction or determine different rules and procedures for the murder of a member of one nested collective by the member of another.

Agreeing to a jurisdiction is the far simpler approach but it requires, under certain conditions, the members of the various nested collectives to submit themselves to the policies and procedures of another nested collective. For example, one potential jurisdictional agreement could be that a murdered person's nested collective's rules and laws are used to capture, prosecute, and punish the murderer. This agreement may fit many people's worldview concerning murder, especially those who think that retribution is important. However, it subjects a "potential" murderer to the procedures and penalties of another nested collective that they had decided not to join. This is a simple agreement, but it has obvious weaknesses.

Let's assume that Robin is in the original position and is considering joining a defense collective with multiple nested collectives. Robin considers various what-if scenarios, one of which is a situation like that of self-defense presented in the prior chapter. Let's also assume that Robin prefers being a member of a nested collective that has rules like those articulated by the Ohio Supreme Court. If she is ever in a situation where she kills a cohabitant, she does not want to have had a duty to retreat. She wants to have a solid defense in claiming that the killing is self-defense. On the other hand, if Robin supports the internested collective agreement that the nested collective of the person she killed has jurisdiction, she may not be able to claim self-defense. If the person she killed is a member of a nested collective that has a rule favored by the justices on the Rhode Island Supreme Court—that co-occupants have a duty to retreat—then Robin will be prosecuted for murder and will not be able to claim self-defense. While this agreement may be acceptable to many people, others will find its asymmetric treatment of people as troublesome. It also has severe knowledge requirements. Given the potential wide variance in rules and procedures among the various nested collectives, people will not know the laws governing their behavior unless they know the membership of all the people with whom they come into contact. It can lead people to favor laws that prohibit visitation by people from other nested collectives, since the more visitors that are in their nested collective, the less effective are their preferred laws.

The jurisdictional agreement we are most familiar with is one involving location. Governments are traditionally associated with a specific geography. They control a specific place on a map. There are obvious reasons associated with defense that explain why this has historically occurred, and there are other logical cost reasons that will lead a government and a nested collective to have control over a specific piece of physical territory. However, the space they control need not be compact or even connected. If the public-safety nested collectives each control a specific location, then a simple jurisdictional agreement between the various nested collectives could be one where jurisdictional responsibility rests with the nested collective where the killing took place. Under this agreement, neither the membership of the person who is killed or their killer is important. All that matters is where the killing takes place.

Under this jurisdictional agreement, asymmetric treatment of people can occur but not within the same nested collective. The knowledge requirement is less, since one only needs to know the rules and laws of the nested collective in which they are currently located. The agreement to vest jurisdiction with the nested collective where a killing occurs does not provide all the protection that a member of a nested collective has within their own nested collective. However, if they physically stay within their own nested collective, they can assure themselves that they will be subject only to the laws concerning murder that are most compatible with their own preferred laws. If everyone restricts themselves to their own nested collective, they will achieve some benefits from cooperation with other people but will suffer from the lack of cooperation with the large number of people in other nested collectives within their defense collective, as well as members of other defense collectives. The benefits of that cooperation plus the perceived benefits from visiting other places will incent many people to leave the comfort and protection of their nested collective.

They may willingly subject themselves to the laws of another jurisdiction. However, this is not without its costs. Visitors to other nested collectives effectively suffer incremental temporary freedom losses by accepting the rules of nested collectives that are different than the rules of their preferred nested collective. They willingly suffer these freedom losses because they are achieving some type of gain from physically associating with the members of other nested collectives. The members of the nested collectives being visited by members of other nested collectives also gain from increased trade and physical collaboration. This has the interesting incentive for the various nested collectives to enact similar laws. The rules within each of the nested collectives do not need to be the same, but the closer they are to their potential visitor's preferred rules, the higher their visitation rate. If many people do not feel safe visiting a particular nested collective, on average there will be less visitation to that nested collective.

The promise of increased trade and connectivity between the members of the differing nested collectives would incent each of the members of the nested collectives to modify their preferred rules to accommodate the preferences of nonmembers. Differences would still exist, given the differences in worldviews, but the expectation of the benefits from collaboration would lead to amelioration of the more radical laws for many of the nested collectives. Those nested collectives that do not modify their laws to accommodate the worldviews of large numbers of nonmembers would suffer from lower levels of physical collaboration. For example, if most nested collectives have procedures concerning due process, then those nested collectives that do not protect their members by enforcing due process will suffer from reduced visitation.

Are incentives and agreements between the nested collectives sufficient for members of the defense collective to feel safe from nonmembers of their nested collective? What are the consequences of the nested collectives breaking their agreements with other nested collectives? What do nonmembers of a nested collective do if that collective refuses to enforce its laws against murder for nonmembers? What are their options if one of the nested collectives in their defense collective refuses to extradite a person who has escaped their nested collective's jurisdiction and is accused of murder within their jurisdiction? What happens if one of their members is kidnapped by members of another nested collective and killed, and the other nested collective is unwilling to prosecute its members or extradite them? Conceptually there are three possibilities.

One possibility is that the nested collectives effectively become mini defense collectives, using force to protect their members from the members of other collectives. While this is theoretically possible, it is the least likely solution given its inherent inefficiencies. Another possibility is that the nested collectives could use the defense collective to enforce their various agreements. As discussed at the end of chapter 11, defense collectives exist in an anarchical environment. There does not exist an organization that has coercive power over the various defense collectives that can force them to abide by their agreements. This is not true for nested collectives, since they can submit their agreements to the defense collective. There is also the option that nested collectives could have their agreements between each other adjudicated and enforced by a neutral third party. Failure to comply could be met with various sanctions from the other nested collectives.

In joining a defense collective, people are willingly abandoning unrestricted self-defense for the benefits of collective defense. Will they voluntarily associate with people in joint defense who will not prosecute their murderer? Not likely. People will place a near infinite weight on not being murdered. People benefit from the existence of nested collectives because no one in the defense collective has to suffer the freedom losses from having to reach a consensus with everyone in the defense collective over every domestic law and domestic goal. However, many people are likely to insist on certain defense collective rules concerning the behavior of the various nested collectives that are part of their defense collective. The narrower the list of these demands, the higher the average net gains for members of the defense collective.

At the beginning of this section of the book, we mentioned the existence of two domestic laws or rules that broadly liberal people are likely to agree will apply to everyone in the defense collective. The first concerns persecution. People of sound mind will not join a nested collective focused on public safety that persecutes them. Irrespective of their worldview, the purpose of this type of nested collective is to defend its members from other members. Policies, laws, rules, or processes that encourage or allow the nested collective to persecute any of its members for any reason, including race or religion, will receive a weight of near infinity by everyone. This implies that every member of a public-safety nested collective will be defended by that nested collective. But what about nonmembers?

As previously mentioned, nonmembers can potentially indirectly influence the policies of nested collectives in which they are not members through bilateral and multilateral agreements. However, with respect to an issue such as persecution, it is unlikely that anyone will compromise and join a defense collective in which any of the other nested collectives can legally persecute them or people like them. As stated above, everyone is likely to place near infinite weight on these anti-persecution preferences. Broadly liberal people would likely unanimously support the adoption of a defense collective's rule that prohibits any nested collective from persecuting nonmembers. They will not join a defense collective with people who desperately want to persecute them and do not agree to this rule.

Another defense collective's rule people are likely to unanimously agree to enforce is that everyone in the defense collective must join a nested collective focused on public safety. Some people who want to join the defense collective may want to stay in an anarchical situation with respect to preventing murder. They may suffer sufficient freedom losses from joining any of the defense collective's public-safety nested collectives, so that they find it preferable to provide their own protection from other members of the defense collective. This may not be acceptable to the other members of the defense collective. As was discussed in chapter 11, collectives are more likely to keep their agreements than individuals, since the gains from breaking agreements are concentrated with individuals versus being dispersed in collectives. Unaffiliated individuals are unlikely to surrender themselves if they are accused of murder by a public-safety nested collective. This will undoubtedly lead to a paucity of agreements between individuals and nested collectives and instability within the defense collective as nested collectives seek to defend their members against unaffiliated individuals. The unaffiliated persons are effectively imposing a negative externality or cost on other members of the defense collective. This could cause all broadly liberal people to compromise and accept a defense collective's rule that everyone must join a nested collective focused on public safety—one of sufficient size where their individual interests are dispersed.

NESTED COLLECTIVES: SOME CHARACTERISTICS

Much of this chapter has been focused on the use of nested collectives to reduce freedom losses from the pursuit of domestic goals. Are there other potential solutions to irreconcilable politics with respect to domestic issues? Yes, in a world of fully prespecified decisions for every possible contingency, the members of the defense collective can synthetically create the nested collectives by simply entering a broader defense collective agreement that incorporates all the terms in the agreements between the members of each of the nested collectives. The agreement can have common rules for defense and varying rules for domestic goals. In this type of environment, the need to form a nested collective is muted. However, in the more realistic scenarios that are the subject of the next few chapters, where people cannot pre-specify every possible decision, nested collectives allow their membership to preserve their decision-making ability independent of the views of other members of the defense collective. Nested collectives are the preferred method for diverse people exiting the original position to achieve the collective life they would like to lead in the presence of incomplete contracts. By forming nested collectives, they can protect themselves from having to conform to the domestic views of every member of the defense collective.

The boundary of governments or coercive collectives, including nested collectives, is defined by power or control over the decisions of government. This is consistent with the theories of the boundaries of firms as articulated by Oliver Hart, Sanford Grossman, and John Moore. The boundary of a defense collective, in terms of its membership, is determined by the interaction of the gains from collective defense and people's differing worldviews over collective defense decisions. Given the nature of external defense, these decisions must be controlled by a coercive entity, since there is not a universal government to enforce contracts even if contracts were complete. The boundaries of nested collectives, on the other hand, exist because contracts or constitutions cannot be complete. People want their worldviews to determine their collective rules, both over collective defense and over domestic laws. Given limited gains from domestic coercive action and differing worldviews, people will find it optimal to be subject to differing domestic rules. As will be seen in chapter 18, only separate domestic entities allow people to have control over their domestic laws when constitutions are incomplete.

The introduction of nested collectives complicates the analysis of the taxes that people would agree to pay as they exit the original position. Recall from chapter 8 that each person in the simple two-person defense collective effectively pays taxes equal to their costs of anarchistic defense minus their allocation of the gross gains. This holds true for a diverse multi-person defense collective. However, the members of different nested collectives could have widely varied tax policies, since their worldviews can affect their preferred tax policy and could be less diversified than the worldviews of the members of the defense collective. For example, the members of some of the nested collectives could easily agree to tax policies designed to reduce inequality. As such, people's overall tax burdens are dependent on the nested collectives they decide to join and the worldviews of their members.[241]

Finally, we should discuss at least some impacts that different types of original positions can have on the series of defense and nested collectives. People in original positions in which cooperation is greater than in the Hobbesian original position would have relatively lower productivity gains in joining collectives. However, some people could prefer the man-made rules of their chosen defense and nested collectives to some of the inherited norms and morals of the non-Hobbesian original positions in which they found themselves. For example, someone may want to be a diamond merchant. In his original position, the role of diamond merchant could require people to be members of a certain family or religion as a method of reducing fraud. By joining a nested collective that coercively enforces fraud laws, a person who is not a member of that family or religion may be able to convince people to trade with him. Another example is a person who wants to marry someone of the same sex and happens to live in an original position where the culture prohibits same-sex marriage. If she breaks the inherited rules, she may be ostracized, essentially causing her to move to the Hobbesian original position that has lower levels of productivity. By joining a nested collective that allows same-sex marriage, she could reduce her freedom losses or increase her level of productivity.

In addition, many people in non-Hobbesian original positions would have learned traits that allow them to cooperate with other people. These norms of behavior may cause their worldviews to be more correlated, allowing more people to be in the same defense and nested collectives for a given level of marginal productivity gain. Since people's backgrounds and learned behaviors matter, the different original positions would have a lasting effect on the structure of the world, even after the introduction of the new collective technology. An individual's learned norms will have some effect on his or her preferred collective goals and preferred collective decisions to achieve these goals. These norms will also affect the policies of the coercive collectives that the individual decides to join. People from non-Hobbesian original positions could have a long-lasting advantage over people who find themselves in the Hobbesian original position. This agrees with conclusions drawn by Italian economist Guido Tabellini, who argued that people may not adopt the most efficient laws and processes because they have been conditioned by their historical environment to accept "ineffective government."[242]

PART FOUR

COLLECTIVE RULES, SERVICES, AND DECISIONS

14

---★---

COLLECTIVE RULES AND TYPES OF
VOLUNTARY GOVERNMENTS

The new technology of using coercive collectives to improve coordination and cooperation allows people exiting the original position to pursue goals and produce products and services more efficiently than is possible in anarchy. Almost every good and service is more effectively produced through some type of cooperative process. People may find methods of collaboration in anarchy, but cooperation is enhanced by the introduction of defense and nested collectives that have delegated coercive powers to enforce agreed-upon laws. People exiting the original position would have differing views on the best methods of producing goods and services that they value, the best procedures for encouraging the introduction of new methods of producing these goods, and the best processes for encouraging the development of new technologies, products, and services. Many would be concerned with the negative effects of the production and consumption of various products including impacts on workers, consumers, the physical environment, and the social environment. Diverse worldviews would lead different collectives to pursue different strategies in addressing these various concerns.

The defense and nested collectives previously analyzed were structured by diverse people in the original position who wanted their worldviews to be the paradigms for governmental policies and therefore
wanted to increase their gains from collective action. This diversity
and "selfishness" for their worldview led these imagined individuals to
use freedom-maximizing decisions to make social preferences and sort
themselves into multiple defense and nested collectives. They also led
to equal sharing of the gross gains among the members of each of the
diverse defense collectives (at least in the limit). Each member's relative wealth level did not affect the allocation of either the gross gains
or net gains from the defense collective. The defense and nested collectives discussed in the prior chapters all produced nonnegative net
gains for each of their members. As such, no member's wealth declined
from joining a collective. The broad societal trade-offs envisioned by
utilitarianism that were discussed in the review of John Harsanyi's
views in chapter 2 did not occur in these diverse collectives. However,
less diverse coercive collectives can exist.

GENERAL COERCIVE COLLECTIVES

For example, it is possible for the freedom-maximizing decisions in a
coercive collective to be those that conform to John Rawls's worldview.
The Rawlsian collective, given the overarching goals of its less diverse
membership, would have coercively enforced rules that require members to subject their pre-collective possessions and abilities to accomplishing the collective goal as a condition of membership. Members
may still have equal political power, but they would voluntarily give
up their bargained share of the gross gains to benefit the least-well-off
members. To the extent that it helps these members, they would even
agree to collective rules that require them to reduce their wealth and
endowments that existed in the original position.

The Rawlsian collective would be less diverse than the defense collectives discussed in earlier chapters, but it can still have a somewhat
varied membership. It would consist of people with similar worldviews
to Rawls, as well as those selfish people who think that they will be

socially and economically better off in a collective whose main goal is enhancing the life of the worse-off members of the collective. If there are enough people who share Rawls's exact opinions, then the structure of the collective can follow the structure of government envisioned by Rawls. Recall from chapter 2 that he favored four branches of government. In his view, government should not directly make every decision that affects the members of society. He supported a concept of government that enforces private property rights, where single members or a subset of members can establish entities that produce goods and services. However, he thought that private enterprise will, in many instances, lead to monopoly power, which caused him to argue for the establishment of a branch of government to regulate the market, including prices. He also thought that a part of government should increase the probability of full employment. His other two branches focus on what he thought of as the primary purpose of government, insuring that wealth and power are distributed in ways that improve the overall welfare of the least-well-off members of the collective.

This specific structure for the coercive collective is dependent on the freedom-maximizing decisions of the collective being completely consistent with Rawls's vision. If members of the collective basically agree with Rawls, but have views that somewhat differ from his, then it is unlikely that the freedom-maximizing rules for the collective will be exactly the laws and regulations that Rawls proposed. The resultant laws could still conform to the overall philosophy of dedicating one's life and collective resources to helping the least fortunate, but in a way that does not exactly match Rawls's proposals.

The Rawlsian collective is an example of a "general coercive collective." It uses coercive force to enforce laws and rules designed to regulate and control a broad range of its members' activities. It has few if any limits on its *scope*. A general coercive collective can be established to pursue a wide range of goals for its members, but it does so in a manner that leads it to regulate a substantial portion of its members' activities. Alternatively, like the Rawlsian collective, it could have an overriding goal so extensive and pervasive that accomplishing it requires an all-encompassing structure that regulates a significant amount of its members' actions. The Rawlsian collective is primarily concerned with inequality among its members, which requires it to have rules to reduce inequality, unless inequality benefits the least-well-off members.

Another example of a general coercive collective is one that may be established by followers of Islam. As discussed in chapter 12, Islam is an all-encompassing religion that typically does not distinguish between civil law and religious law. As such, people in the original position who are devout followers of Islam may decide to form a *general* coercive collective. The collective would establish rules and laws based on Sharia law that would regulate broad aspects of its members' lives, including the coercive enforcement of the Islamic moral code. People with non-Islamic worldviews may perceive a pure Islamic collective as pursuing multiple goals, even though the members of the pure Islamic collective would all view the pursuit of these goals as part of a unifying vision of the world.

Both the Rawlsian collective and the Islamic collective can be nested collectives whose members are also members of a larger, narrowly focused defense collective. This will, of course, only occur if each of the members of the Rawlsian and Islamic collectives determine that this maximizes his or her net gains. Peaceful coexistence as part of the same defense collective is possible if (i) the members of both nested collectives' worldviews concerning external defense are sufficiently compatible, (ii) the conflicting views on domestic rules that apply to every member of the defense collective are not too disjointed, and (iii) the rules for both nested collectives are broadly liberal. There is nothing inherent in Rawls's philosophy and in the beliefs and teachings of many strands of Islam that will make their coexistence in the same defense collective impossible. However, if the members of the Islamic collective favor laws that are not broadly liberal and strongly believe they should use force to compel others to follow their religion, then coexistence in the same defense collective will not occur.

In a sufficiently large and diverse population, there is likely to exist a substantial group of people whose beliefs are not broadly liberal. A crucial component of their worldview may lead them to believe they cannot peacefully coexist with any nonbelievers or with people with specific worldviews. Their strongly held views would cause them to prefer rules and laws concerning external defense and offense that are inextricably intertwined with other domestic laws. People with these worldviews will tend to prefer to be in a general defense collective that does not support the existence of multiple nested collectives. A recent example of this type of worldview is radicalized Islam, which is manifested in ISIS. Violence and external defense are core components of their overall belief system. Their worldview will lead them to have negative freedom losses from almost any type of compromise with people with different worldviews. The collectives formed by people with this type of worldview will not be diverse. They would not make the compromises necessary to be in a collective with those with differing beliefs and values.

Another example of a general defense collective is one formed by people in the original position who have a unifying philosophy that Rawls termed "outlaw states."[243] People with this worldview have a goal of using force to conquer other defense collectives and subjugate unaligned persons. Its members are driven by the overriding goal of war, which leads to nationalistic and mercantilist practices. All other potential goals anyone in this society may have are subordinate to the overall goals of a strong and powerful defense collective. Interestingly, most modern national governments are effectively general coercive defense collectives even though their citizens (members) are not necessarily aligned on an overarching goal of world domination.

While it is possible that the members of the Rawlsian and Islamic collectives, whose laws are broadly liberal, can be in a single nested collective or can be members of a defense collective without nested collectives, these structures are unlikely to maximize each person's net gains. Given their differing worldviews, compromising on domestic laws is likely to lead to a reduction in average net gains. Forcing the members of both collectives to live by the same domestic rules would lead to a desire by at least some of them to exit. Coexisting as members of the same defense collective, but in separate nested collectives, has many benefits. It allows the members of both nested collectives to capture the benefits of being a member of a large defense collective. It allows them to live by differing domestic rules. As we discussed in chapter 13 and will discuss in detail in later chapters, domestic conflicts will still exist. Addressing these will lead to incremental freedom losses, but compromising on a few domestic issues without needing to agree on every domestic issue will increase average net gains. As members of separate nested collectives, they can compromise and agree on certain critical domestic and internested collective conflicts such as a requirement that the nested collectives do not persecute nonmembers. Furthermore, the two nested collectives can have various mutual agreements on reducing the conflicts between their members without having to agree on each domestic rule.

LIMITED COERCIVE COLLECTIVES

A different type of coercive collective is a "limited coercive collective." It uses its coercive powers to enforce rules to pursue specialized goals. A limited coercive collective has limited *scope*. The defense collective discussed in prior chapters is a limited coercive collective. Its coercively enforced rules are those designed around the narrow goal of external defense. A limited coercive collective may have multiple goals, but none of these goals either independently or in combination are so broad that the collective will have rules and laws that regulate most of its members' other activities.

The agreed rules of the limited collective such as a defense collective may and probably will include provisions that are much more comprehensive and restrictive on each member's actions in an emergency. For example, if a defense collective is in a war of survival with another defense collective, it is easy to imagine that members with differing worldviews will have agreed in advance to significant restrictions on their individual actions. These rules can give the limited defense collective broad powers during times of emergency and supersede the rules of the various nested collectives. Under these circumstances, the limited defense collective can have powers isomorphic to those of a general defense collective. However, once the emergency is at an end, the defense collective's rules would revert to ones that are more focused and limited. The end of the emergency would also lead to the reestablishment of the differing rules of the various nested collectives.

People in the original position who share Rawls's views would join a limited defense collective while simultaneously joining a general nested collective focused on domestic issues. People who share Robert Nozick's views would form limited nested collectives that focus on domestic concerns while joining a limited defense collective. The goals pursued by limited nested collectives could be quite broad, including rules and laws concerning public safety, food, drugs, the physical environment, occupational safety, employment, retirement, welfare, and health care. Given the assumptions that all land is homogeneous and there are no moving costs, people could choose these collectives based solely on the worldviews of other people. The question of the relationship between these various nested collectives and the defense collective is the subject of part five.

A coercive collective is not the only institutional tool people will use to increase cooperation. In a desire to produce goods and services, some will prefer that one or more of the coercive collectives directly produce goods and services. Others will think that almost all goods and services should be produced by "private entities," whose primary goal is to maximize the profits for their owners. The five authors disagreed over many issues, but each of them thought that the existence of private enterprise would enhance the welfare of society. Each also seemed to think that private enterprise needs rules and laws enforced by a coercive government to flourish. These regulations include property rights, contract laws, bankruptcy laws, and corporate laws.

While they agreed on the need for these laws, they disagreed on the best rules that should govern the behavior of these private entities, including the broadness and expansiveness of laws affecting private production and consumption. People in the original position would have these same disagreements. As each person considered their strategy and the possibilities offered by exiting anarchy, they would deliberate over different laws as well as different approaches to producing the laws necessary for private enterprise to prosper. This would include having these laws produced by limited or general collectives, but it also may include the use of one or more "transactional coercive collectives."

TRANSACTIONAL COERCIVE COLLECTIVES

A transactional coercive collective establishes a framework supporting various voluntary activities that it offers to its members and to non-members for a fee. For example, a group of people in the original position could agree and compromise on a set of rules and laws they think will enhance the formation and management of private entities. They could form a transactional coercive collective to enforce these rules, which could include specialized courts to interpret the use of the collective's rules.

The transactional collective offers these bundled services for a fee to both members *and* nonmembers, which is somewhat different than nested and defense collectives. The only benefit of being a member is an ability to have a transactional collective's rules incorporate each member's worldview and an allocation of the net profitability from the provision of services. As part of its enforcement of its laws and statutes, it is probable that the transactional coercive collective will require the users of its services to be members of a public-safety nested collective that acknowledges its jurisdiction over violations of the rules concerning entity formation and management.

In a dynamic environment that is different than the one we have been considering, the various transactional collectives could produce excess returns for their members. Over time, the transactional collectives most responsive to the needs of their clients may tend to build up expertise and dominate the provision of these services. These types of collectives could also be part of a nested collective pursuing other goals for its members. Modern US states allow individuals and entities to form new entities like corporations, whose internal governance structure is regulated by state laws. Many of these states provide these services to entities that do not have any operations in that state and to people who are not citizens of the state. People decide on the jurisdiction that has authority over their new entity based on cost, flexibility, simplicity, responsiveness, and consistency. As such, they may choose states that they otherwise do not have a connection with. For example, Delaware has gradually replaced New Jersey as offering the package of laws and procedures that people most prefer to govern the formation of corporations. Other states have been unable to displace Delaware's dominant position for a variety of reasons, including its willingness to be at the forefront of innovation related to corporate governance and its specialized corporate legal processes and professionals.

Rules governing entity formation are not the only laws that states offer to nonresidents. Many allow and encourage the use of their proprietary laws as the governing law for private contracts, irrespective of the domicile of the contractors. For example, many people utilize New York law for their private contracts even though none of the parties to the contract reside in New York. In addition to being subject to the laws where they live, nonresidents of New York who use New York law voluntarily subject themselves to the coercive power of that state.

LOCAL COERCIVE COLLECTIVES

An important type of coercive collective, and the final one that will be discussed, is a "local coercive collective." It is the opposite of the transactional collective, since its defining characteristic is the gain that its members receive from being geographically close together. For a variety of economic, geographic, or social reasons, which will be discussed more thoroughly in the next chapter, people may receive gains from being geographically near to one another. While this physical closeness provides certain benefits, it also increases interpersonal conflicts. Geographic proximity increases externalities and causes seemingly unrelated conflicts and issues to be connected. Instead of people pursuing goals in separate limited nested collectives, they would be incentivized to address them within the same nested collective. Even people who have worldviews like Nozick or Friedrich Hayek may decide to join local coercive collectives to focus on a variety of local issues. Examples faced by people who decide to settle in a similar location include laws that may address noise, pollution, communicable diseases, physical privacy, fire, prostitution, alcohol, drugs, poverty, homelessness, and zoning.

This type of collective can be viewed as limited, since it is focused on collective issues caused by location. However, these locational conflicts tend to be broad, which can lead local coercive collectives to pursue a wide variety of goals and enact extensive rules and regulations. Everything else being the same, people in the defense collective who decide to locate close to other people would want to be members of local coercive collectives with people who have similar worldviews with respect to local issues and conflicts. However, there could be overriding reasons that cause them to join a local coercive collective with people who have very different worldviews. The locational gains may be so significant that people willingly suffer large freedom losses and join local coercive collectives with people who have a substantially different worldview. Nonetheless, freedom losses caused by membership in a collective with people of widely varying worldviews would incentivize them to try to capture the economic benefits of geographic closeness with people who have more similar worldviews.

The overall impact of incentives associated with geographic closeness would increase the equilibrium diversity within an average local community and increase the likelihood that there will be many coercive collectives with multiple goals. While these are general equilibrium tendencies, the observed outcomes in a large, diverse population are likely to be quite varied. There can be local coercive collectives that are wholly part of a general collective; local collectives in which everyone is a member of different nested collectives; local collectives in which everyone is in the same limited nested collectives; local collectives composed of people who are not members of any other nested collective; and local collectives that are a mixture, in which the various nested collectives have made exceptions to some of their rules. Finally, there can even be metropolitan communities composed of a local collective for a centralized part of a geographic area surrounded by a group of local collectives with differing rules and laws.

Our historical experience leads us to expect local communities to be part of a larger political entity, with everyone in a local community subject to the same rules and laws. While the theoretical analysis of coercive collectives supports this, it also supports the existence of local communities composed of people who are subject to different laws. How is this possible? How can neighbors be subject to different rules? Before addressing this question more thoroughly, it will prove helpful to examine a less theoretical example of neighbors being subject to different laws and protected by different police forces.

New Jersey is currently made up of over five hundred municipalities and twenty-one counties, with each municipality in one county only. Each citizen of the state is a citizen of one of these municipalities and a citizen of one of the counties. There are no unincorporated areas where a person is not subject to the laws and ordinances of a municipality. New Jersey is a "home rule" state and allows its local communities and counties to make some of their own laws. This "right" is not part of the US Constitution or the New Jersey state constitution, but it has been continually supported by the state legislature. As such, each municipality and county has different management structures, laws, ordinances, taxes, law enforcement, and courts. While most people in the state will be neighbors with people who are in the same county and municipality, and therefore subject to the same laws and police, this will not be true for all neighbors. The five-hundred-plus municipalities have many common borders, and therefore many citizens of the state are neighbors with people who live in different municipalities and different counties. This implies that neighbors can be, and often are, subject to different laws, ordinances, procedures, taxes, school systems, police, and courts. Issues involving domestic abuse or theft in a home in one jurisdiction will be handled by different police and courts than if those incidents occurred in a neighboring home in another municipality.

The township of Closter, New Jersey, has approximately eight thousand residents and incorporates 3.3 square miles in Bergen County. It is surrounded by six other municipalities: Norwood, Emerson, Harrington Park, Haworth, Demarest, and Alpine. Like other states, New Jersey has a state law that prohibits alcohol consumption by anyone under twenty-one. These states have similar laws because each of them has responded to a federal regulation that reduces their highway funding if they allow underage drinking. New Jersey, being a home-rule state, allows each of its municipalities to have differing statutes concerning alcohol, as long as they do not conflict with state law. Not surprisingly, given people's differing views, many municipalities can have varying laws and regulations concerning the consumption and sale of alcohol.

Many of the citizens of Closter appeared to be concerned about underage drinking and teenage parties. As such, they passed a municipal ordinance that seemed to allow police to enter private homes without a warrant, under some circumstances, if the police suspected underage drinking, and to arrest any underage person.[244] The ordinances in neighboring towns do not have to be consistent with Closter's municipal ordinances. People in those towns may feel that allowing police to enter their homes based on local officers' judgment is an invasion of privacy. They may also think that arresting teenagers for being at a peaceful party, where some underaged people are consuming alcohol, may have an unacceptable detrimental effect on some of the teenagers' future education and job prospects. Therefore, it is possible that there could be two homes, side by side, that are in different municipalities where underage drinking is treated significantly differently.

The citizens in the neighboring communities may have different views on the soundness of allowing adjacent municipalities to have their own rules concerning teenage drinking because there are potential spillover effects from these differential rules. Teenagers from Closter appear to be incentivized to party in the neighboring municipality that has laxer laws on underage drinking. Some citizens of Closter may be fine with this potential side effect of the differential laws. For example, they may have supported the ordinance because of the noise and congestion from teenage parties. The movement of parties to another town satisfies their goal. Some Closter citizens may not agree with the legislation and may like the choice in laws because they prefer an ordinance that reduces the probability of teenagers being arrested for underage drinking. However, some Closter parents may feel their children are more at risk because of the more liberal rules in a neighboring town. People in the adjacent towns may be negatively affected by the Closter laws due to the potential increase in noise and congestion from Closter teenagers traveling into their town to attend drinking parties. These various possible spillover effects illustrate the fact that local coercive collectives are not completely independent, and that people that are members of one local coercive collective are potentially affected by the rules enforced by other local coercive collectives. Furthermore, spillover effects are not limited to local coercive collectives but apply to other coercive collectives, including defense and nested collectives.

What conditions are necessary for the credible equilibrium to be one in which neighbors are subject to different rules and laws? There is obviously some cost to having different rules and ordinances. In a more real-world setting of nonhomogeneous land, differential rules can develop because of unique aspects of geography. However, even in an environment of homogeneous land, people with different worldviews will have varying views on collective goals and on the optimal methods of addressing common goals. Given the complexity of the world, it is impossible for everyone to have completely accurate internal models of the implications of the various potential methods of organizing social conduct. People will not be able to convince other people that their worldview is inaccurate. These potentially vast worldview differences would lead to a credible equilibrium in which people exiting the original position compromise and unanimously agree that there will be different laws and rules.

As previously discussed, the presence of differential laws requires methods of determining which law and coercive procedure is applicable to each person. People exiting anarchy would seek effective and low-cost methods of determining jurisdictions. Physical location has historically been such a method of making this determination, but obviously other means can occur through technological advances. The enforcement of many laws and rules are more cost-effective when there is critical mass. Critical mass does not require continuity or mathematical compactness, but local enforcement is more effective if there are many people subject to the same laws and courts. Finally, coordination among the various collectives would improve efficiencies. This will be discussed in more detail in chapter 16 when the assumption that all rules and laws can be prespecified is relaxed.

The overall conclusion with respect to local coercive communities is that people in a local community can be members of different nested collectives that have different laws concerning, among others, self-defense, murder, criminal procedure, police powers, sentencing guidelines, and the death penalty. People can be members of different nested collectives that have differing rules on prescription drugs and safe foods. They can even be members of different nested collectives that have different rules on income taxes, poverty, social equality, and income equality, as long as the local effects of these various differing rules do not cause aggregate freedom losses larger than the rationale for people to locate in the same local community.

COMPLEX WEB OF COERCIVE COLLECTIVES

The "big bang" caused by the introduction of collective technology to a large diverse population in a world of homogeneous land and zero moving costs will result in people forming and joining a varied group of coercive collectives. Many people will decide to become members of more than one coercive collective. People's diverse worldviews will incent them to form many large defense collectives to increase their net gains and reduce their freedom losses. Most of these defense collectives will, in turn, have members that form smaller coercive collectives. Many of these smaller coercive collectives will have a local geographic aspect, since people want to locate together for a variety of economic, geographic, and social reasons. The members of these various local collectives can also be members of various nested collectives, including general and limited collectives. Many people may also subject themselves to specialized transactional coercive collectives to accomplish certain desired goals.

15

★

COLLECTIVE SERVICES AND NONCOERCIVE ORGANIZATIONS

SYMBIOSIS BETWEEN GOVERNMENT AND NONCOERCIVE ENTITIES

The formation of coercive collectives occurs because of people's desire to more efficiently cooperate and collaborate. However, as discussed in the prior chapter, people exiting the original position will form entities other than coercive collectives. These noncoercive entities will utilize and be subject to the jurisdiction of various coercive collectives in accomplishing the goals of their members and owners. For example, people can form for-profit entities such as corporations and partnerships to produce goods and services their owners and managers think people desire.

An entity producing these goods and services can utilize the authority of one or more coercive collectives to enforce agreements that it has with its owners and investors. The partnership between the ten people that was discussed in chapter 6 is an example of this type of agreement. People voluntarily subject themselves to incremental rules as a condition of being an owner or investor in the private entity. Failure to obey the conditions of the agreement will allow the noncoercive entity to use the procedures established by the relevant coercive collective to enforce that agreement. The relevant rules will depend on the worldviews of the members of the coercive collective and of the owners of the noncoercive entity. Some of these rules will be civil and involve monetary penalties for failure to follow the contractual obligations. Some rules will be criminal, while others will be torts. The coercive collective will enforce its rules through a variety of sanctions, including incarceration. People subject themselves to these incremental laws and the risks from disobeying them for the same basic reason they join coercive collectives with people who have differing worldviews. They expect to gain from being associated with the entity. They expect to receive gains that exceed the anticipated costs, including the costs of breaking the laws they voluntarily accepted.

Each private noncoercive entity will likely also utilize the power of one or more coercive collectives to enforce its contracts with its customers, suppliers, and employees. People who enter these contracts subject themselves to the relevant rules and procedures of these various coercive collectives. Some of these contracts may be standardized and a condition of engaging with the entity. For example, the freedom-maximizing rule for a coercive collective can be one where employees of a private organization owe it a fiduciary duty, which requires each employee to put the interests of the entity ahead of their own interests. The act of being an employee of a private association that is subject to a coercive collective with this type of rule automatically subjects each employee to the power of the coercive collective.

Many private organizations will want to borrow funds to accomplish their goals. The ability for creditors to use rules enforced by a coercive collective to increase the probability of being repaid will have a significant effect on the equilibrium terms of borrowing money. This will incent borrowers to voluntarily subject themselves to the power of a coercive entity. Private entities will also be subject to the power of various coercive collectives whose members think that private organizations may be capable of actions detrimental to their interests. For example, the freedom-loss minimizing rules for a coercive collective affecting private entities can include laws related to consumer protection, fraud, pollution, and employment issues. Failure by an organization to obey these various rules can subject it, its owners, and its employees to various civil and criminal penalties.

Even though these profit-oriented entities are technically private and noncoercive, they have a symbiotic relationship with one or more coercive collectives. The rights and obligations of a profit-oriented entity are dependent on the members' worldviews of these various coercive collectives. Similarly, the rights and obligations of other entities and people that interact with each profit-seeking organization are also completely dependent on these members' worldviews. As diverse people exit the original position, the credible equilibrium will include a wide variety of rules applicable to private enterprise. Laws will differ between the various defense collectives, as well as between members of the large diverse defense collectives that utilize nested collectives. This implies that a large diverse defense collective, through its members' various nested collectives, will have a variety of laws and rules concerning consumer protection, employment, bankruptcy, banking, and pollution. These differing rules, procedures, and laws will increase the costs for those private organizations subject to different jurisdictions. The costs of complying with these different rules and regulations will be absorbed by the individuals and organizations associated with these noncoercive entities.

These duplicative compliance costs will incent some of the nested collectives to somewhat harmonize their laws. However, the credible equilibrium will still be a world of differing laws because members of the coercive collectives do not agree on the best laws and rules. Multiple rules and costs of complying with them are an equilibrium byproduct of differing and irreconcilable worldviews. Many people will think that inefficient laws are an acceptable price to pay for some higher value. For example, John Rawls explicitly acknowledges that his preferred "just society" will not be meritocratic or the most efficient.

VARIETY OF NONCOERCIVE ENTITIES

Entities such as corporations and partnerships are not the only noncoercive organizations that people exiting the original position will use to enhance cooperation and produce desired goods and services. They will also form noncoercive collectives such as societies, cooperatives, and mutual companies. These types of entities, like coercive collectives, allow their members to capture the gains from pursuing a joint goal in which the members are involved in the production or consumption of certain types of goods and services. Like corporations and partnerships, they can also utilize the power of coercive collectives to address the conflicts between their members.

There are a wide variety of noncoercive collectives. For example, in the financial services area, there are mutual savings banks, credit unions, building societies, mutual insurance companies, and mutual funds. Given the potential diversity of views and circumstances, there will be disagreements and freedom losses as members compromise. Conflicts will naturally arise between various members. These conflicts will not result in the freedom losses that members of most defense and nested collectives must endure, but they can lead to people preferring to be in different private collectives.

For example, in 1781, the Philadelphia Contributionship, the first mutual fire insurance company in the United States, adopted a rule where it would no longer insure homes with nearby trees.[245] Some members did not like this restriction, so they formed a second mutual insurance company, which they named Mutual Assurance Company. This mutual insurance company agreed to insure its members' homes even if trees were close to their buildings. It stayed in business for over two hundred years. The members who formed Mutual Assurance achieved net gains from their perspective, even though they were part of a smaller insurance company, because of the flexibility of being able to retain trees close to a building. They would have been worse off, from their perspective, if the city of Philadelphia, the state of Pennsylvania, or the United States had a law or rule that prohibited members from forming a new mutual fire insurance company.

Another example of a noncoercive mutual entity is the Shore Porters Society that was formed by porters in 1498 in Aberdeen, Scotland. While it is a private partnership today, it was created by porters who banded together to unload ships in Aberdeen Harbor and agreed to divide the revenues from such activity. A further example is the Fenwick Weavers' Society that was formed in 1761 by weavers to jointly buy yarn and sell cloth. The society allowed the weavers some level of economic power over both their costs and sales. As part of the society, they established a bank and retail store for members.

As with any collective, there will be conflicts between the members of cooperatives, which will be exacerbated as the number of members increase and with increasing diversity of the members. For example, many grape producers in Germany are members of cooperatives to gain economies of scale and enhance their economic or pricing power.[246] These cooperatives potentially struggle with issues involving adverse selection, since it is difficult for each of the cooperatives to determine the quality of the grapes delivered by their members. Economists Jon Hanf and Maximilian Iselborn argue that producer cooperatives need a variety of controls to protect the members as a whole from the possible selfish actions of individual members.[247] In addition, they mention research by others where moral constraints like "trust and loyalty" are important elements in collective coordination. These concerns will also exist for members of coercive entities.

Many people in the original position will decide to form and join various types of "consumer" cooperatives to gain buying power and reduce the effects of monopoly or oligopolistic supply. Depending on technology, types of consumer services that may be produced by a cooperative include water, sewage disposal, and distribution of electricity, natural gas, and cable television, as well as the ownership of telephone landlines and roads. The production and distribution of each of these goods and services have economies of scale and a "local" or geographic character to them that leads to a monopolistic element, at least in their distribution. The economies of scale occur because the distribution of each service has certain fixed costs, which causes average costs to decline as more people are added to the various networks. However, there is a limit to these cost reductions, since there are also physical congestion costs associated with their production or delivery. Furthermore, once the distribution network is in place, the service provider can charge monopoly prices to consumers of these services. For these reasons, people who are geographically close to one another have an incentive to form one or more cooperatives to provide at least the distribution of these services to themselves. They can participate in a collective and capture all the benefits of producing these services for their members.

CLUB GOODS

These types of goods are examples of "club goods," which were first analyzed by James Buchanan, the Nobel Prize–winning economist who was quoted in chapter 4.[248] At the time, he was looking to fill in the gap between the traditional view of pure private goods such as a personal haircut and a pure public good like external defense. He showed that, in a homogeneous population, a public good such as a swimming pool can be efficiently provided through voluntary action and did not require the direct intervention of a coercive government. Club goods are often referred to as "impure public goods." They have three characteristics. First, their production or consumption exhibits increasing returns to scale. That is, as more members are added, the average cost of production is reduced. They also have some type of congestion cost; as more members join, there are crowding effects. The third characteristic is that nonmembers can be excluded from the use of club goods. These three characteristics, applied to an entire population, lead to an optimal size of each club and a division of the overall population into various clubs. Even though club goods have some nonrivalrous consumption, their production can be efficiently handled by a voluntary economy. Buchanan's concept has spawned a massive body of literature as researchers have explored various aspects of clubs and impure public goods.[249]

Many authors in the club literature draw a sharp distinction between pure public goods and club goods. For example, in the review of club theory by Todd Sandler and John Tschirhart, the authors view joining a club as a voluntary activity while the consumption of a public good is nonvoluntary.[250] They do not seem to think that "pure public goods" like external defense are subject to congestion costs. Furthermore, in their paper, Sandler and Tschirhart view people as voluntarily sorting themselves into various clubs, but they argue that this does not occur for pure public goods. Their analysis and statements do not appear to capture the environment of people with differing worldviews. As diverse people bargain to exit anarchy, their differing views on political decisions impose crowding costs on each other. Some of these compromises relate to what are traditionally viewed as "pure public goods." As such, "pure" public goods do not exist as people transition from anarchy.

There is decision congestion in every entity that has members or owners with differing views. The act of compromise causes freedom losses to the person compromising and effectively turns what many people view as a good that has no crowding costs into a costly good. As people exit anarchy for the gains from coercive collective action, they want their worldview to prevail. As such, people will negotiate with everyone else to sort themselves into various coercive collectives to pursue goals such as external defense and public safety. The compromise rules are ones that minimize aggregate freedom losses for the members of the various coercive collectives. People in the original position voluntarily and unanimously agree to the credible equilibrium because it maximizes each person's net gains. The existence of diverse worldviews causes pure public goods to essentially have all the characteristics of a club good or an impure public good.

Buchanan's congestion-cost concept is directly applicable to the psychic costs people experience as they exit the original position. Diverse people will form different types of entities to improve cooperation and enhance their lives. They will form various types of coercive collectives to address interpersonal conflicts. They will not find it optimal to be in the same defense collective with every other person in the population. Nor will everyone in the original position want every collective decision to be a consensus decision with each person in their defense collective. This leads to a compromise structure of government where members of a limited defense collective form general nested collectives, limited nested collectives, transactional collectives, and local coercive collectives. In addition, some people will form noncoercive entities such as corporations, sole proprietorships, and partnerships to produce goods and services that they think others will value. Some people will also form noncoercive collectives like cooperatives and mutual entities to assist in the production and consumption of goods with certain characteristics. None of these noncoercive collectives exists in isolation; they involve interaction with various coercive collectives. The nature of this interaction is completely dependent on the worldview of the members of the various coercive collectives. Some people will prefer that all goods and services will be produced by noncoercive entities. However, given differing worldviews, others will disagree.

COERCIVE COLLECTIVES, GOODS, AND SERVICES

Buchanan's swimming pool example is a useful tool to illustrate some of the various methods that people exiting anarchy can devise to produce goods and services. One possible method is that a small group of people form a corporate entity to own the pool, and charge daily and seasonal rates to people who want to use the pool. The owners take the risk that people will sufficiently use the pool to make it worthwhile for those owners to go through the expense of providing the service. Potential swimmers have the option of only paying when they want to use the pool.

A more aligned method is one where the owners of the pool offer "memberships" to pool users that give them long-term rights to swim, as if they were members of a collective. Daily-use fees will likely be charged to reduce congestion issues. However, these pseudo membership rights are not ownership rights, but only contractual rights. As part of the membership agreement, the owners of the pool can reserve the right to shut down the pool and sell the underlying land and facilities. The division of the sale proceeds and the return of some or all of the membership fees will be part of the membership contractual agreement. This method provides a different level of risk and return for both the owners and the users of the pool than the daily-use arrangement would. An alternative method is that a group can organize a pool collective in the form of a mutual entity or club to provide the pool services to its members and their invited guests. The members contribute to the construction of the pool and pay periodic payments for its maintenance. They are likely to charge themselves usage fees to reduce conflicts caused by physical congestion. Another possibility is that at least some people exiting the original position may view a swimming pool as a valuable asset for their local coercive collective. They may think their local government can manage it as well as a private entity, and that a "public" swimming pool adds to the overall quality of their community. They may hold this view even if they do not personally use the pool. As such, they may also be willing to subsidize its use by other people.

The potential provision of services other than laws by a coercive collective will be considered by each person in the original position as they reason through their bargaining strategy. Many people in the original position may think that a wide variety of products, including goods and services such as utilities, education, recreational facilities, libraries, public health, museums, public landscaping, parks, roads, arts, unemployment compensation, and social security, are better provided by a coercive collective than a private entity or an entity that does not have coercive authority.

Many of these types of goods and services have shared consumption. Physical proximity leads to production efficiencies but also to conflicts. Depending on people's worldviews, they may view a coercive collective as the best organization able to manage these conflicts. People decide to locate close to one another for a variety of reasons, including the physical environment, transportation, economic benefits, and family. As discussed in chapter 14, physical proximity will cause people to form local coercive collectives to produce rules. It can also incentivize some people to agree that their coercive collective will produce goods and services. This can occur even if all land is initially homogeneous. Once people exit the original position and form various coercive and noncoercive entities, different locations will be perceived differently by members of a defense collective. For example, as people exit anarchy and significantly increase their level of cooperation, population density will increase and cities will develop. Large cities typically have urban agglomeration benefits. These cities exist and expand because of increasing returns caused by a variety of complementary forces, including concentration in knowledge, labor quality, customers, and supplier concentration. They have higher output per capita than smaller cities or unincorporated areas. Their inhabitants also have, on average, higher real incomes.

Economists Kristian Behrens, Gilles Duranton, and Frédéric Robert-Nicoud argue that cities are the result of "agglomeration economies."[251] They develop a model in which population density gains exist and people sort themselves based on expected entrepreneurial return and wage levels. People who have more natural abilities are incentivized to locate to these population nexuses. The economists' analysis can be expanded to include other probable impacts. Large cities likely develop because they export various products to other cities. The resulting increase in population will also provide opportunities for people to produce locally consumed goods and services including retail, construction, transportation, utilities, and real estate. These industries will lead to an even larger city as population density lowers the costs of production for these services. As the population of the cities increases, the residents become more self-sufficient, consuming a higher percentage of their own production and becoming less dependent on imports. The fully developed large cities include a vast array of products and services, including intermediate goods, such as service businesses like accounting, legal, transportation, banking, and advertising that are used in the production of exported goods. Migration and interaction among the residents of the city will lead to differential abilities, aspirations, income, and wealth.

The benefits provided by these large cities will incent people of differing worldviews to locate within the same city. However, given their varying political views, they will want to form independent coercive collectives within the city such as districts, towns, or boroughs. Each of these smaller local coercive collectives is likely to have at least some unique rules. Each can be of varying size and provide different levels and types of services to its members. Some of them can share services, and each of them can subscribe to various intergovernmental agreements concerning jurisdictional issues and conflicts.

Let's examine a hypothetical borough whose members all have some combination of Robert Nozick's and Friedrich Hayek's worldviews. The members need to decide how local public goods will be provided. One of these is sewage services. Let's assume that the freedom-loss minimizing decision is to prohibit the use of latrines or individual septic systems and require all members to use a central septic system. Centralized sewage disposal is a club good with monopolistic elements, which will incent the members with these types of worldviews to settle on three possibilities: (i) allow private companies to compete to build and supply the sewage services but regulate their activities, including the prices they can charge; (ii) competitively bid out the development of the septic system and treatment facilities, but have the resulting system managed directly and owned by the borough; or (iii) competitively bid out the building of the septic system and then have it managed and owned (including the pipes) by a new noncoercive collective.

All three options are in use in the United States to provide a wide range of goods and services, including water, electricity, and natural gas. The first option is effectively a "public utility," where the good or service is provided by a private entity whose actions are regulated by some governmental entity. The second is a "municipal corporation" where the municipality or borough directly controls all aspects of the provision of these services. Many citizens of the borough may want the borough to directly control the provision of sewage services as well as provide various local public goods, including recreation facilities, parks, libraries, museums, and other local utilities. The final option is typically viewed as a "utility cooperative," where the gains from producing the activity for the local community are internalized and shared with the members of the collective. As previously discussed, a cooperative allows its members to reduce the costs of monopoly provision. The sewage cooperative can include the members of the borough or, if the gains are sufficient, it can also include the members of other boroughs. This type of collective is effectively a private entity and does not have direct coercive power. If users of the service do not pay their bills, or violate rules of the collective, it cannot directly use force against its members. It has no more authority than any other private entity to enforce its rules. It relies on the rules of the borough or a nested coercive collective to enforce the agreements it has with its members.

Each of these methods of supplying local public goods and services has different costs and benefits. An extensive body of literature has developed concerning the benefits and costs of the different approaches. Not surprisingly, given different worldviews, there is still disagreement over the best method of providing even a simple service like sewage. Many of the disagreements involve differing views on the optimal approach to reducing conflicts between the entity and the people it is serving. Even people who have worldviews that are some combination of Hayek's and Nozick's will disagree on the best method of providing local public goods.

Another set of decisions that residents of the borough will consider concerns housing. There are, of course, a wide variety of different rules the borough can adopt to regulate local housing. One alternative is that the borough allows its residents to join a noncoercive collective that owns contiguous land and rents, leases, or sells individual parts of the land to its members. This type of collective is a housing cooperative, housing co-op, or housing club. It is likely to have some type of zoning or architectural rules that restrict its members' abilities to construct housing, including rules concerning building height, property type, property setbacks, color, and types of materials. Each of the members will be subject to these restrictions as a condition of joining the collective. The cooperative may also have a wide variety of rules on such issues as noise, minimum wages for the employees of the cooperative, welfare contributions, vagrancy, solicitation, water pollution, air pollution, dress code, drug and alcohol use, and prostitution. The rules of the housing collective are in addition to the rules and laws of the borough, which has members in common with the housing collective. Failure to follow any of the rules of the housing collective can result in fines, loss of membership, and loss of the property a member has leased or purchased from the cooperative. Similarly, failure of the cooperative to enforce these agreed-upon rules will give members a cause of action against the cooperative. The borough or some other coercive collective picked by the members of the cooperative will enforce these various rules.

The housing co-op can also own land in common that it uses to provide various community necessities, including sewage, water, recreation facilities, public landscaping, fire departments, roads, schools, libraries, and hospitals. It can use this land to directly provide service businesses like stores, restaurants, and banks. Alternatively, the housing club can sell or lease property to private third-party entities that want to provide some of these goods and services to the members of the cooperative, all subject to the rules of the cooperative. The members of the cooperative may view these third-party providers as more efficient at offering these services than the collective might be. The choice in rules and provision of services will depend on a multitude of factors, including the worldview of the membership of the cooperative.

The housing co-op can be organized as a commune where all the services are directly provided by the membership. However, given the laws of cooperative advantage and division of labor, the cooperative will likely determine that it is more efficient to purchase at least some goods and services from people and entities that are not members. This will require payments by the housing collective to third parties, which will in turn require it to charge its members for the services it provides. These charges will likely include a combination of up-front fees, periodic assessments, and usage fees dependent on a wide variety of circumstances, including the financial condition of its members, the services provided, and the members' worldviews. The various decisions made by the cooperative, including its rules, provision of services, and the methods of providing and paying for the services, will affect the value of the members' property, cooperative lease rates, and the value of membership. A housing co-op can be viewed as a noncoercive cooperative inside the borough where the members of the housing collective are also members of the borough.

Of course, a housing collective is not the only method of structuring housing. A borough can have rules that allow individuals or private entities to also directly own land and build either single-family or multi-family homes. The owners and renters will have conflicts and desire services. The members of the borough will adopt rules to address these conflicts and either directly or indirectly provide services. As such, a borough can be considered a broad housing cooperative or club with coercive powers.

A borough whose members have worldviews that are a combination of John Rawls's and John Harsanyi's is likely to be a mere agency of a larger, general coercive nested collective focused on reducing the inequality of people's capabilities and incomes. The existence of cities and their tendency to exacerbate inequality will be an important issue for their overall nested collective. The Rawls-Harsanyi borough may not be independent, but it may be delegated some local decision-making within the broader rules set by the general nested collective, since it may be viewed as having more local information and knowledge to implement the nested collective's goals. Conceptually, the Rawls-Harsanyi dependent borough can be adjacent to the Nozick-Hayek independent borough.

Many people are convinced that the potential returns to scale from the provision of local public goods will lead to a merger of these different boroughs. For example, the economists Oded Hochman, David Pines, and Jacques-François Thisse argue that geography leads to local governments providing a full range of local public goods, and that some form of larger government is needed when the costs of local goods exceed user payments.[252] Similarly, the economists Duncan Black and Vernon Henderson maintain that there is a role for larger governments in the provision of local goods because of spillover effects.[253] However, these costs of local collective decision-making are likely to be more than offset by the freedom losses from consensus decisions on a variety of issues when people have significantly different worldviews. Centralization is not the only method people can use to address spillover issues. Repeated interaction between the members of the different boroughs will incent the boroughs to reach agreement on their various conflicts. At least some of the boroughs are likely to find it less costly to address various spillover effects and potential conflicts through bilateral agreements or through standardized agreements that can be adjudicated by some agreed-upon third-party coercive collective. For example, in the United States, many local communities have entered medium-term contracts with other local communities concerning a number of services, including public safety, fire, ambulance, snow removal, libraries, and schools. These contracts are typically negotiated by the individual municipalities to reduce their costs. They are enforced by the state of their incorporation.

The freedom-maximizing decisions for some coercive collectives can include directly producing private goods. For example, the members of a coercive collective can agree to restrict the consumption of alcohol. They may have the freedom-maximizing opinion that complete prohibition is impossible, and that attempting to prohibit its production and distribution will lead to black markets, increased crime, and a general reduction in the respect for the rule of law by members of the collective. These negative consequences can occur even in a collective where prohibition is part of the collective's founding constitution and unanimously agreed to by its members. Each person agrees to collective rules, not because the rules are their preferred ones, but because they are a member of the collective that maximizes their net gains, and the collective follows rules that minimize aggregate freedom losses. People who desire alcohol will view its prohibition as a psychic cost of joining with other people in the pursuit of some common goal. Obviously, if people have sufficiently negative intensities for this type of law, they will join another collective or stay in the original position.

After joining the collective, the members who do not prefer prohibition (and maybe some members who do) can decide to break the law and consume alcohol if the costs of consumption or production are not too onerous. To reduce the risks and societal costs from complete prohibition, the collective that wants to control liquor consumption can mandate that the only distributor of alcohol for the members of the collective is a collective-owned and collective-operated enterprise. The direct ownership of the distribution of alcohol allows the collective to directly control the price of alcohol, the locations in which it can be sold, the time of day it can be sold, and the days of the week it can be purchased. Given people's differing worldviews, the collective may use alternative methods of controlling the distribution of alcohol. Instead of direct ownership of the distribution channel by the collective, the collective can allow private entities such as corporations and cooperatives to distribute alcohol while imposing a variety of liquor-oriented regulations on the distribution entity and its owners.

16

★

MAJORITY VOTING AND FREEDOM-MAXIMIZING DECISIONS

INEFFICIENCIES OF MAJORITY VOTING

In chapter 6, the impracticality of fully specifying every collective decision for every possible future eventuality was discussed in the context of ten people forming a private equity firm. There is extensive economic literature on incomplete contracts and their impact on firms.[254]

Complete specification of every decision contingent on future events is even more difficult to envision for a coercive collective or government. The inability of each person exiting anarchy to know the decisions that each of the collectives will make in every future situation has negative repercussions. People will still be incentivized to form and join coercive collectives given the significant advantages that the collectives offer over anarchy. However, collective decisions in the absence of perfect voice will cause incremental freedom losses as people exit anarchy. This will lead people to devise institutional structures that approximate a fully specified constitution with provisions that minimize aggregate freedom losses.

In the discussion in the prior chapters, where perfect decision pre-specification was assumed to exist, people maximized their net gains by sorting themselves into coercive collectives. The combination of perfect exit and perfect voice allowed each person in the original position to achieve the most he or she could, given the diversity of worldviews and the limits to coercive collective action. However, the inability to fully specify all future decisions for each collective potentially causes this logical and naturally occurring sorting process to break down.

If a person in anarchy does not know the rules and laws of a coercive collective under different potential circumstances, he or she will be unable to determine if exiting the original position is in his or her considered best interest. Without pre-specification, the collective can potentially impose certain obligations that a person exiting anarchy may find unacceptable. People exiting the original position will want to know (i) what the collective they are joining is attempting to achieve, (ii) their obligations to the collective and to their fellow members, (iii) their rights from the collective and from their fellow members, and (iv) their allocated share of the gains from joining in coercive collective action.

In the idealized environment of complete decision pre-specification, existing members of a collective can still regret their decision to join the collective if situations occur in the future that they thought were improbable. However, without complete pre-specification, people exiting anarchy not only do not know what events will occur in the future, they will not know how the collective will respond to those future events. The collective may respond in ways that would have incentivized some of the members to join another collective or to stay in anarchy, if they had known the collective would make those decisions.

By comparing people's net gains under two alternative realities, we can examine the impact of the inability to determine in advance all the coercive collective's decisions. The people under consideration are assumed to have different worldviews and to be picked randomly from a large population. Under one alternative, they are initially placed into a coalition or pre-collective where pre-specification of every future decision is possible and where perfect entry and exit into a final collective exists. This coercive coalition will be labeled the "Voluntary Coalition." The other alternative is one in which they are directly placed into a coercive collective whose membership cannot be altered and that uses majority rule, with one vote per person, to make all decisions. It will be called the "Leviathan Collective." Under each alternative reality, the members need to only make one common decision: What should be the rule on capital punishment? They have three options—A: no death penalty; B: death penalty only for murder; or C: death penalty for murder or rape.

Initially, the assumption will be made that both coercive entities will choose A instead of B if these are the only two alternatives. They will also choose B instead of C in the same scenario. And A over C. This implies that both entities will choose A—no death penalty—for the following reasons. For the Voluntary Coalition, A is chosen because no death penalty is the freedom-maximizing decision. The decision to avoid a death penalty has lower freedom losses than the other two alternatives. The Leviathan Collective chose A because most of the people preferred it to either of the other two options. In this instance, majority voting has exactly produced the freedom-loss minimizing decision. It has done so with much less information about the members than is required by the freedom-loss minimizing decision process. Majority voting only records people's preferences. Unlike the freedom-maximizing decision framework, it does not utilize the negative value that people place on their nonpreferred decisions. It does not capture the intensity each member has for collective decisions that are different than their preferred decisions.

For majority voting to reproduce the freedom-loss minimizing decision, the value or intensity members have for that choice cannot alter the coalition decision. This can occur under a variety of scenarios, but it typically requires that the differences in value that members have for alternative decisions are relatively balanced across the membership. People can disagree, but the intensities of these disagreements need to be relatively uniform for majority voting to produce the freedom-maximizing decision. The information deficiency that is an integral component of majority voting implies that majority voting will not always determine the trade-offs and compromises that a diverse group of people in the Voluntary Coalition will make when negotiating a set of rules and procedures for pursuing a collective goal.

For example, if a minority of the members prefer capital punishment and the majority of members view the death penalty for

murder as highly unacceptable, then majority voting can be an efficient mechanism of producing the freedom-maximizing decision.
However, if the majority views no death penalty as preferable to
either of the other alternatives, but does not strongly hold this view,
and the minority members have strong views that the death penalty
is an important punishment for certain crimes, then majority voting
will not produce the freedom-maximizing decision. In this situation,
the Voluntary Coalition will make a collective decision different than
the decision preferred by the majority. Even though more people prefer not having a death penalty, the strong minority view will lead to
the freedom-maximizing decision of capital punishment for certain
crimes. Under these conditions, the Leviathan Collective will not make
the freedom-maximizing decision. Therefore, majority rule does not
always result in decisions that minimize its citizens' freedom losses. It
will not be the collective-decision mechanism that people will choose
if they have the option of perfect voice. Just as importantly, people will
never be able to determine if majority decisions are optimal unless they
can somehow quantify the intensities the citizens have for alternative
collective decisions.

   Another possible preference pattern is that in two-choice majority
voting, the Leviathan Collective votes for A over B, B over C, and C over
A. That is, the majority prefers not to have a death penalty when comparing it to the choice of the death penalty only for murder. However,
in this example, they also prefer the death penalty for murder and rape
instead of the alternative coalition decision of not having a death penalty. When this preference pattern occurs, the Leviathan Collective is
unable to determine a unique decision supported by a majority. French
philosopher and mathematician Nicolas de Condorcet first identified
this majority-voting inconsistency in 1785. More recently, it was the
subject of Nobel Prize–winner Kenneth Arrow's path-breaking book
Social Choice and Individual Values.[255] His "impossibility theorem"
implies that entities such as the Leviathan Collective, where members'
worldview preferences are unrestricted and a simple collective-decision
process such as majority voting is used, cannot eliminate inconsistent
voting or "cycles."

When the members of a coalition or collective have these types of preferences, coalition decisions made by majority voting can be influenced by the order of voting. This inconsistency also implies that majority-voting decisions can potentially be manipulated. That is, the process that determines the order of voting can affect the outcome of the election. Economists Allan Gibbard and Mark Satterthwaite proved that the assumptions underlying Arrow's impossibility theorem also incent members of entities such as the Leviathan Collective to lie about their true worldview preferences.[256] Therefore, not only does majority voting not always produce freedom-maximizing decisions, the members of coercive collectives or governments who rely on majority voting to make all coalition decisions cannot rely on other members to honestly vote their true worldview preferences. Their decisions can also be influenced by the process that underlies majority voting.

Majority voting does not necessarily use and reveal each member's true preferences in determining a collective decision. The freedom-maximizing decisions process (if it were available) does not suffer from these issues because it uses both the preferences and the negative values that each member has for his or her nonpreferred choices in determining coalition decisions. Therefore, the Voluntary Coalition will still choose the freedom-loss minimizing decision over the other alternatives even when its members' preferences exhibit voting cycles.

In summary, majority voting may produce the freedom-maximizing coalition decision, but then again it may not. In a diverse membership, the freedom-maximizing coalition decision can be significantly different than the majority view. In many coalition decisions, the intensities the members have for alternative decisions are critical in determining the freedom-maximizing decision, preventing voting cycles, and eliminating dishonest voting.

BENEFITS OF FREEDOM-MAXIMIZING DECISIONS

The freedom-maximizing decision is used by the members of the Voluntary Coalition, not because of one person's worldview, and not because it is moral, but because it is an efficient mechanism to increase the net gains of people as they exit the original position. As discussed earlier, freedom is not a goal of every collective. It is not, as proposed by Robert Nozick, a universal side constraint imposed on all members of every collective. It is simply a means of efficiently achieving each collective's objective. In the case of the Voluntary Coalition, whose assumed goal is to defend its membership from each other, freedom maximization increases its members' net gains. Coalitions composed of different people will pursue different actions because members have varying worldviews. In Hobbesian anarchy, everyone is completely free even though they must spend their scarce resources on defending themselves. In voluntarily engaging in collective action assisted with potential coercion, individuals willingly give up some of those freedoms to accommodate the views of other people.

It is entirely possible that no one will prefer any decision that the coalition makes. Decisions made by diverse people are all made through accommodation and compromise. But compromise has a psychic cost to those who compromise. It decreases the net gains from association. Maximizing freedom and choosing various decisions that cause the least cumulative reduction in value maximizes the membership of the Voluntary Coalition and increases the average net return for them.

Unlike the members of the Leviathan Collective, the members of the Voluntary Coalition can exit and join another coalition or return to anarchy if they so wish. The initial members of the Voluntary Coalition will remain in the coalition if (i) each person's allocated gains from remaining are greater than his or her freedom losses from accepting the decision that there is no death penalty, and (ii) there is no other collective in which a member can have higher net gains. If there is a coalition that can be created where a subset of the members of the Voluntary Coalition can have higher net gains, they will exit the Voluntary Coalition. Similarly, if nonmembers can achieve a higher net gain by joining the Voluntary Coalition, they will join it. Since the Voluntary Coalition was randomly chosen, it is likely that its membership will change as it morphs into a collective, since people both in and out of the Voluntary Coalition will sort themselves into the collective that maximizes their individual net gains. In the credible equilibrium, the membership of the Voluntary Coalition will likely be significantly different than the randomly chosen membership of the Leviathan Collective.

This adjustment process focuses attention on the crucial distinction between the two types of coalitions or collectives. People's intensities about alternative collective decisions are crucial not only for determining the optimal *decisions* for a collective but also for determining the optimal *membership* of the collective or collectives. Information on members' relative intensities is insufficient to produce the decisions that people exiting the original position will choose for themselves. People exiting anarchy will use information on everyone's intensities to sort themselves into the collective that will provide them the highest net return. They will join collectives with people who have similar worldviews as determined by each person's preferences for collective goals, by their preferences for collective decisions in pursuing these goals, and by the negative intensities they have for alternative collective decisions. In the process, each person will join a collective that uses all its members' intensities about alternative collective decisions to determine the final collective decision.

SEN'S LIBERAL PARADOX AND FREEDOM-MAXIMIZING DECISIONS

The ability for people to sort themselves into differing governments based on their preferences and intensities allows people to address Sen's "liberal paradox."[257] In his research on social choice, Amartya Sen analyzed a problem where a person in a two-person social situation has complete authority over one decision. He shows that this can lead to inconsistent societal decisions if the other person in that same society has a view that is opposed to those of the decision maker. The analysis in this chapter is consistent with Sen's paradox. People in both the Leviathan Collective and the Voluntary Coalition will have differing preferences and may not be able to make any decision unilaterally and may have views completely opposite those of other members. However, people in the Voluntary Coalition, with completely opposite preferences, will remain in the Voluntary Coalition only if they do not have sufficiently strong negative intensities for the compromise decision to overcome the benefits of being a member of the collective.

In his 1998 Nobel laureate address, Sen seems to propose a solution to his paradox that incorporated people's views on the appropriate balance of rules limiting their actions and those promoting their wants.[258] This is a component in the determination of governmental rules by people exiting anarchy. The use of people's intensities about alternative collective decisions, together with the ability to form both defense collectives and nested collectives, allows those exiting the original position to address the issues raised by Sen's paradox. People will sort themselves into the coercive collectives that offer them the highest net gain, which depends on both the gains from collective pursuit of a common goal and the worldviews of potential members.

Since the gains from collective goals are *limited*, there is also a *limit* to the diversity in worldviews that can be in one collective. Not everyone will determine that it is in her or his best interest to be in the same collective with every other person. The ability to form new coalitions and ultimately form different collectives with differing membership and varying goals allows people to improve their positions. The diversity of collectives, both defense and nested, seems to enable people in the original position to escape Sen's paradox, or at least reduce its effects.

People will form collectives with others whose views are sufficiently like their own so that each person's freedom losses are no larger than the allocated gains from collective action. This implies that the range of preferences weighted by each person's negative value for the nonpreferred collective decisions is restricted. However, that does not mean that the range of unweighted preferences is restricted. A collective can have members with opposite preferences as long as those members do not have strong negative reactions to the agreed collective decision that is not their preferred decision. The voluntary formation of coercive collectives does not necessarily group people in a way that eliminates Arrow's voting cycles. That is, the use of majority voting by people who have sorted themselves into the collective of their choice based on complete information on everyone's worldview can still result in voting inconsistencies.

Nonetheless, collective formation does place a limit on individuals' negative intensities for their nonpreferred decisions, if those decisions are the ones used by the collective. Each person's negative views for the collective decisions are limited by the perceived gains from joining the collective. This implies that people who place an infinite negative weight on their nonpreferred collective decisions cannot be in the same collective with people who have equally strong but opposite views. It also implies that collectives in which the gains from collective action are relatively smaller will have less intensity-weighted divergence of opinions.

The members of the Leviathan Collective are likely to be in the "wrong" collective from their perspective, since they are randomly chosen out of a large diverse population. It is likely that both the majority decisions and the freedom-maximizing decisions will incent some of the members of the Leviathan Collective with sufficient freedom losses to exit the collective if they could. It is possible that the freedom losses are so large that they exceed the gains the members receive from the collective. However, without the ability to join another collective or return to anarchy, these members must suffer through the imposition of other members' worldviews. As discussed above, this is not the case with the Voluntary Coalition. Each member who stays or ultimately joins and allows it to become a stable collective does so because it is in his or her considered best interest, considering all the other alternatives. Members of voluntary collectives undoubtedly have freedom losses, but they have optimized them in pursuit of gains from coercive collective action.

MAY'S THEOREM PROVES INADEQUACY OF MAJORITY VOTING

The comparison of the Leviathan Collective to the Voluntary Coalition illustrates the inadequacy of majority voting as the sole process of determining collective decisions for people exiting the original position. Another method of coming to this same conclusion is through the use of May's theorem. In 1952, a mathematician, Kenneth May, proved that majority voting is the collective-decision rule a group of people will use if they want their joint decision rule to satisfy four properties, two of which are that people's intensities do not matter and that each collective decision is independent.[259] He also showed that majority voting is the only collective-decision process that satisfies these four criteria. Using his theorem, people in the original position who can fully prespecify every potential collective decision will only choose majority voting if they do not want their preference intensities to matter and if all collective decisions are independent.

However, for those in the original position who have varied worldviews, their intensities matter, and political decisions are not necessarily independent. People will use the freedom-maximizing decisions to sort themselves into the optimal coercive collective(s) and to maximize their net gains from coercive collective action. This procedure incorporates each person's intensities for decisions that he or she does not prefer. Furthermore, the goals that people will want to pursue will require multiple decisions and many potential actions. The marginal joiner of the defense collective will have aggregate freedom losses from all these potential actions and decisions that are exactly equal to his or her net gains. Since people exiting the original position will want their strongly held views over social preferences to matter, and all political decisions are not independent, majority voting is not the sole method people will use as they exit anarchy and pursue collective action, even if they cannot prespecify all future decisions. They will supplement voting with the existence of multiple independent coercive collectives, including independent nested collectives.

MAJORITY VOTING AND DELEGATION

The need to delegate decision-making is another fundamental issue that arises out of the comparison of the Leviathan Collective with the idealized Voluntary Coalition. This issue was also discussed in the analysis of entity formation in chapter 6. While pre-specification of every decision is impossible, so is the likelihood that every person in a large coalition or collective can vote on every prospective decision. This will lead each coalition and each collective to decide on some form of delegated decision-making. Some members (and potentially some nonmembers) will need to be chosen to make some decisions for the collective. Each collective must have a process to determine who will manage its affairs. This process must also address how the delegates are determined and what types of controls are placed on the delegates, as well as the specific types of decisions that are being delegated.

Unfortunately, delegation leads to new conflicts. The interests of the delegates, the collective, and other members of the collective are not always perfectly aligned. These types of conflicts arise in every multi-person organization. It is often referred to as the principal-agent problem. The very reason that defense collectives and nested collectives exist—conflicts between people—gives rise to new conflicts as most of each collective's decisions are delegated. The existence of non-aligned interests does not imply that every delegate in every potential situation will use their delegated power of decision-making for their own personal ends at the expense of the collective. However, it does imply that this possibility exists and that processes and procedures will be considered by the members of the collective to reduce the negative effects of these types of conflicts.

Some of these conflicts will arise even in a collective where each major decision can be prespecified. This occurs because of the division of labor and the law of comparative advantage. Each collective will find it advantageous to delegate the execution of its decisions to some of its members (or nonmembers). However, these conflicts are exacerbated when the members delegate the more extensive decision-making required, if pre-specification does not exist.

Let's consider mutual insurance companies to examine the consequences of some of these nonaligned interests. The production of insurance services involves an insurance entity issuing policies to people or other entities that entitle the insured to some level of compensation in the event the client suffers some specified loss. The insurance entity charges up-front and ongoing fees, which it invests for its own benefit. After purchasing the policy, the insured is dependent on the insurance company's willingness and ability to pay a claim. This presents a potential conflict between the policyholder and the insurance company, which can be addressed in a variety of ways. Policyholders can reduce fraud by requiring that the insurance policy is subject to the jurisdiction of some coercive collective and by purchasing insurance from reputable entities. They can reduce their exposure to bankruptcy risks of the insurance company by some combination of (i) purchasing a policy that has financial covenants that restrain the activities of the insurance company, (ii) transacting with only those companies that have high equity relative to their risks, or (iii) buying insurance from an entity regulated by some coercive collective. In addition, some policyholders may decide to rely on the desire by the insurance company to continue to write new policies, which will only occur if the insurance entity maintains its financial condition. The conflicts can also be addressed through organizational form.

Mutual insurance companies combine the functions of ownership and the consumption of insurance services. This incentivizes the mutual insurance company to maintain its credit worthiness so that it can pay all claims when due. Alternatively, insurance companies can be organized as stock companies. This structure separates the ownership of the company from its policyholders. Given the fixed payments to the potential policyholder claimants, this separation leads to an incentive by the stock insurance company to take more financial risk than a mutual insurance company as it attempts to achieve returns for its stockholders. Policyholders of stock insurance companies are essentially senior bondholders, whereas stockholders receive the residual returns after paying policyholders' claims. While no stock insurance company intentionally wants to default on its claims, everything else being the same, it potentially has an incentive to pursue strategies and tactics that result in a higher risk of default. Since future events are not completely predictable, this implies that policyholders of stock companies may have a higher chance that their claims will be unpaid than if they had been members of a mutual insurance company. Given these risks and conflicts, why do stock insurance companies exist? In a competitive market, why aren't all insurance companies mutual?

Economists David Mayers and Clifford Smith Jr. address this question.[260] They argue that mutual companies have a competitive advantage in controlling the policyholder and owner conflict while stock insurance companies are more adept at addressing the conflicts between management and owners. Both types of firms use boards of directors to supervise the managers of the companies, but stock companies have other devices to address the principal-agent concerns unavailable to mutual companies. Stock insurance companies have shares that trade so that stockholders, potential stockholders, and directors have real-time information as to the market's judgment about the prospects of the company. Stock companies are also subject to takeover by other firms and proxy fights. Furthermore, management of stock companies can somewhat be tied to the performance of the firm through compensation in the form of restricted stock and stock warrants. Each of these characteristics of a stock insurance company allow it to be more effective than a mutual company at reducing opportunistic behavior by management and employees of the firm.

Mayers and Smith postulate that in a competitive market, both types of insurance companies can coexist. They argue that mutual firms will be relatively more involved in insurance markets like life insurance, where management judgment is less critical. They also contend that mutual insurance companies, for these same reasons, will have less product scope than stock insurance companies, and that management of mutual companies will be lower paid, but have higher perks. In 1999, J. David Cummins, Mary Weiss, and Hongman Zi tested these suppositions by analyzing the historical behavior of mutual and stock insurance companies in the United States.[261] They found that mutual companies focus on products that are relatively simple and homogeneous. They also discovered that these types of organizations are not as cost conscious as corporations. Interestingly, they concluded that mutual insurance companies are somewhat superior to stock companies in less complex businesses. However, this decreased as the size of the mutual company increased. Their analysis is not determinative. Large mutual insurance companies can exist and both types of entities can be preferred by their policyholders. However, it does point out some of the issues that people in the original position will consider as they put institutional structures in place to protect themselves from potential opportunistic behavior by both their delegates and the employees of the collectives that they decide to form and join. These structures are even more important for coercive collectives such as the defense collectives and the nested collectives, given their delegated power.

The defense and nested collectives are coercive collectives. They enforce their rules through the threat and use of physical force and coercion. The members' delegates to each of the collectives will decide many of these rules and, either directly or acting through or with other people, will be the actual enforcers of each of the collective's laws. These people have all the same strengths and weaknesses of other members of the collective and can theoretically utilize the coercive power of the defense and nested collectives for their own purposes. This potentiality is one of the reasons why Nozick's concept of private firms—which are controlled independently by one or more people—as the primary source of external defense is not a logical outcome of people exiting the original position. The conflict between the controllers of an entity and the consumers of the entity's services are at its most extreme in the provision of defense and public safety. The economists Oliver Hart, Andrei Shleifer, and Robert Vishny reach this same conclusion.[262] People will not voluntarily submit themselves to the coercive power of entities unless they have methods or procedures they believe have a reasonable likelihood of eliminating or significantly reducing the power of a coercive entity to inappropriately exercise their delegated coercive power.

People exiting anarchy will not rely on the "purchase" of protection. Instead they will form coercive collectives such as defense and nested collectives as an institutional device to reduce the conflicts between the ultimate controllers of the coercive entity and the people these entities are designed to protect. They may decide to supplement this protection with other types of safeguards such as guns, locks, and private guards. However, they will not rely solely on these noncollective efforts to enhance protection. This institutional structure allows people to capture all the gains from the various goals assigned to each coercive collective. Nonetheless, there is a residual cost to the collective form of institutional structure. It still relies on delegating at least some decision-making power to other people. For coercive collectives to successfully achieve the goals assigned to them by their membership, methods need to be utilized to control the potential opportunistic behavior of their management and employees.

In the economic study of government, the logical implications of these types of conflicts have been a central focus of the extensive "public choice" literature whose pioneering studies include works by James Buchanan, Gordon Tullock, Mancur Olson, William Niskanen, William Riker, and Anthony Downs.[263] This body of work has been supplemented in recent years by the analysis of the ramifications of incomplete contracts, notably by economists Gene Grossman and Elhanan Helpman.[264] This research focuses on the myriad of conflicts people in the original position will be concerned with as they structure the institutional apparatus of the coercive collective. These include division of power, special-interest groups, rent-seeking behavior, protectionism, and bureaucracy and cannot be eliminated. All that the members of each collective can do is to put in place controls and processes to reduce the inefficiencies and costs from these delegation conflicts. The costs of these controls, plus the residual costs from the remaining delegation conflict costs, reduce the overall gains from collective action. In equilibrium, it will cause people in the original position to form smaller and less worldview-diverse collectives, since the marginal joiner's net gains from joining each collective is reduced by these conflict costs.

Typical institutional structures involve one or more boards of people who are picked by the members of the collective as well as the senior manager of the collective who can be chosen by the members or the board members. The more coercive power that is invested in the collective, the more importance members will place on division of power and authority. Members can use other devices, such as limiting the scope of the coercive collective, even if there are underlying reasons to have multigoal collectives. Given the difficulties that a large membership will have in controlling the potential excesses of both their delegates and their employees, restricting the scope of the defense or nested collectives can be a method that many people exiting anarchy may prefer. Everything else being the same, general coercive collectives, such as the collective preferred by John Rawls, will have more principal-agent issues than would more limited nested collectives. This can lead people who are otherwise indifferent to the type of collective to prefer being members of limited collectives.

The members of each collective will want the "optimal" structure around the delegation of decision-making and the execution of these decisions, since this will increase net gains. However, like every other collective decision, people's differing worldviews will lead them to diverse opinions as to the best structure of managing the collective and controlling their delegates. Differing worldviews will also cause people to have varying perspectives on the extensiveness and pervasiveness of the problems associated with these conflicts. These differing views on the best method of controlling delegation conflicts will lead to increased freedom losses by the average member of each collective and a further reduction in the equilibrium size of each collective. It will also lead to different policies and procedures by the various collectives as they seek the optimal methods (from their perspective) to align the interests of their delegates with the interests of the collective.

Delegation combined with the inability to prespecify every decision raises other conflicts. How do the delegates ascertain the collective desires of the members? As previously discussed, majority voting may not produce the freedom-maximizing decisions and may not even produce a consistent decision. Members' negative intensities for their nonpreferred decisions are critical pieces of information that the members need to sort themselves into the appropriate collectives and to determine the optimal decisions within these collectives. Unfortunately, member intensities are not readily observable by the delegates. Even if the delegates want to make the decisions that the members want, how do they determine what these decisions are? Furthermore, since it is impossible for anyone to determine the freedom-loss minimizing decisions, it is also difficult to determine if the delegates are substituting their worldview for the "undetermined" worldview of the membership. It is possible under these conditions that when people decide on their delegates (maybe through majority voting) they will pick those they think have worldviews most like their own. However, potential delegates may be incentivized to "hide" their true worldviews to increase their chances of being chosen as a delegate. Once chosen, they may decide to make decisions differently than they indicated they would. Potential members of the various collectives will consider all these possible conflicts as they seek to improve their environment by joining in coercive collective action. They will want to design and utilize various institutional structures to limit the negative effects of these costs.

Another conflict exacerbated by the principal-agent issue is the potential opportunistic behavior of some of their fellow members. Each member has an incentive to convince the delegates and employees of the coercive collective to pass laws and regulations that benefit that member at the expense of the collective. The intramembership conflicts that exist in every collective are magnified by both the existence of delegated decision-making and the power of a coercive collective to make and enforce rules and laws. People with diverse worldviews will prefer different approaches to reducing these conflicts. However, given people's incentives and cleverness, these conflicts cannot be eliminated, only reduced. Mancur Olson argues that over time institutional processes to limit or control people's ability to enrich themselves at the expense of society become ineffective.[265] People who have this perspective will prefer being a member of a nested collective that allows and encourages dynamic institutional formation to address economic corruption.

BENEFITS OF A CONSTITUTIONAL PROCESS

The preceding discussion has demonstrated that majority rule in and of itself is an inefficient decision-making process for diverse people as they form coercive collectives. People exiting anarchy will naturally seek a different process, a more robust procedure than just reliance on majority voting. If possible, each person will seek to use information on every other person's worldview preferences as well as the intensities of their preferences. Without an ability to prespecify every potential decision, each person needs something other than majority voting to efficiently decide which collectives they should join, as well as to determine if they should even engage in collective action.

One possibility is that the people exiting anarchy can voluntarily share their preferences and their values for alternative decisions with the other people leaving the original position. Unfortunately, people have an incentive to lie not only about their preferences but also about their intensities. For example, people may misrepresent their world-views to induce more people to join a collective, and then through majority voting, after people have joined, change the decisions of the collective to more fit their "true" preferences. Through this type of preference misrepresentation, people can find themselves in the "wrong" collective through no fault of their own. People also have an incentive to overstate their negative intensities for every potential collective decision that conflicts with their preferred decision. These misrepresentation incentives will cause people exiting the original position to seek some type of process to filter out the lies from the truth concerning potential members' worldviews. Furthermore, without some procedure that can place people's valuations on a common scale, it is impossible to completely compare people's worldviews.

Alternative collective actions need to be compared by each person and between everyone. How will a person who does not want a military draft, but thinks that torture is fine, reach agreement with someone who thinks it is everyone's moral duty to fight for the collective but believes that any type of torture is abhorrent, especially when that person can lie and use strategic manipulation? The assumption that people have transferrable values allowed us to simulate the conditions necessary for agreement and compromise. It allowed us to forego an all-inclusive bargaining analysis.

Regrettably, people in the original position cannot use this shortcut. They need to bargain over the conditions of their exit from anarchy, not just about how to divide the gains from collective action. The product of their bargaining will be an initial or foundational agreement, a constitution. This agreement cannot specify every possible decision for every possible contingency. It can, however, specify some of the decisions of the collective, including goals, some rights members have with respect to each other, some rights they have from the collective, some responsibilities they have to one other, some obligations they have to the collective, methods of choosing delegates, and methods of managing the conflicts endemic with delegation. The constitutional process—the negotiation process of agreeing to a constitution—is a partial solution to the problems presented by majority rule and lack of information concerning people's intensities.

The constitutional process has three important elements. First, it involves complex discussion—the sharing of ideas and viewpoints among potential members of each coalition and collective. This allows the potential members to convey information about their worldview preferences and the strength of their convictions. The process incentivizes people to share information and attempt to convince others why their worldview is comparatively better. It causes and encourages extensive dialogue among people with differing worldviews.

Second, the constitutional process requires an agreement. To reach agreement, people with diverse worldviews must make trade-offs and are forced to compromise. Attempting to reach an agreement causes people to compare their relative preferences, as well as to compare the intensities of their preferences to the intensities they think others have for their worldviews. Agreement among people with differing worldviews will require a process of proposals and counterproposals. People will debate and negotiate words, sentences, and paragraphs to cause the agreement to match their preferred collective decisions. They will argue and cut side deals, and may even threaten other people, all in an attempt to have the ultimate agreement mirror their worldview. However, the ultimate agreement requires everyone who enters it to voluntarily consent to each of its terms. Failure by a potential member to reach agreement with one group of people will cause that person to try to reach accord with other groups and form other coalitions.

Complete failure by a person in the original position to reach agreement with anyone will cause them to remain in anarchy and forego the significant advantages of coercive collective action. This incentivizes diverse people to compromise. A person will concede some issues to incent others to give in on issues they feel or think are more important. In so doing, they compare the intensity they feel for the potential collective decisions with how they think others feel for these decisions. This process allows and causes people to attempt to put everyone's intensities on a common scale. The estimated scale will obviously not be perfect and is subject to significant error, but people are highly incentivized to attempt to determine the truth about other people's preferences and the intensities they have for alternative collective decisions. Compromise provides the common scale for people to make the necessary interpersonal comparisons of value.

Third, each of the members agrees to be bound by the terms of the constitutional agreement, including the agreement to have the collectives they join use coercive force to attempt to compel compliance with the agreed terms. This has two important ramifications for the potential members. It reduces the incentive for potential members to mislead others as to their preferences and intensities. As part of the negotiation process, people may attempt to convey the impression that some potential decisions are unacceptable even though they are willing to compromise. However, other people with differing worldviews will attempt to extract some concession for agreeing to these decisions, whether or not they are heartfelt by potential members on the other side of the issue. The overall negotiation process will severely restrict people's abilities to hide their true preferences and intensities. Also, being bound by the agreement protects potential members from changes in the agreed decisions after they have joined. They will still be at risk for unspecified decisions, but the range of uncertainty about future decisions of the collective has been reduced.

This last point has an important corollary. The completed constitution serves as an approximation of an unbiased and honest signal to other potential joiners concerning the worldviews of the members of the collective. People who agree to the constitution are bound by it, and therefore it is an honest indication of a person's worldview. It is not necessarily a complete or perfect representation of the initial members' worldviews, since the negotiation and compromise process is inherently imperfect at eliminating strategic manipulation by the participants. However, given the assumption that everyone in the original position is rational, each person will use their best efforts, as part of the overall negotiation process, to have unbiased errors in their estimation of other people's worldviews. The constitution incorporates its members' best efforts to reach a consensus worldview and informs other potential members of the unbiased consensus worldview of the collective. Each ratified constitution naturally limits the range of worldviews of its members who will agree to its terms. Stated differently, people with diverse worldviews will negotiate constitutions with varying rules and procedures. As such, it informs both the membership and anyone who decides to join the collective of the range of possible future decisions the original members will prefer that are not specified by the constitution.

Since a fully specified constitution is not feasible, it will enumerate certain key (from the perspective of the joining members) decisions that are either conditional or have limited conditions so that members can identify and then commit themselves to a consensus worldview. As such, it will include rights and responsibilities the initial members believe are important and will not change over time. It will state how collective decisions other than those in the constitution will be made. It will specify how the delegates are determined and their length of service. It will determine a process for handling different interpretations of the wording of the constitution. Finally, it will specify how the constitution can be modified.

The constitutional process will provide people in the original position with information on other people's worldviews to allow each of them to determine if the expected benefits of exiting anarchy are greater than the expected costs. If they decide to leave the original position, the constitutional process will provide information so they can sort themselves into the collectives that are most compatible with their worldviews and maximize their net gains. The process will not be perfect, since people's preferences and intensities cannot be perfectly observed and people have some incentives to mislead. Nonetheless, the overall constitutional process reveals aspects of people's worldviews that allows for sorting to occur and for people to somewhat protect themselves. The result, given the diversity of worldviews, will be a plethora of collectives. The size of the collectives will be smaller than the collectives that would have been formed if people could fully pre-specify all potential decisions. However, people will still form various defense collectives and will join nested collectives under the protection of the defense collective they join. They do so because of the expected gains from coercive collective action. Their behavior is enabled by the worldview-revealing ability of the constitutional process.

17

★

TIME AND COLLECTIVE ACTION

The passage of time is a critical variable for people in the original position. So far in the analysis, its effects have been incorporated only through its impact on people's motivations to conclude bargaining over the gains from coercive collective action. People's positive time discount rates incentivized them to reach an instantaneous bargaining solution. However, the passage of time can have other significant effects on the membership of each collective and on the decisions each collective will make. The potential future actions of the collective and its members will affect its current laws and policies. Similarly, economists Daron Acemoglu, George Egorov, and Konstantin Sonin seem to argue that the current policies of an entity like the defense collective can have an effect on the entity's "future" actions, and this effect must be considered by the entity today.[266]

CHANGING WORLDVIEWS

One aspect of time is that some of the members' worldviews can change. With time, people learn, gather new information, and question previous theories, all of which can cause them to change their views.

What impact does this possibility have on people who are contemplating leaving anarchy for the benefits of collective action? In the original position, people can change their views and act upon their new view without consulting others. In a collective, each person's ability to have their modified views affect the collective's decisions are constrained by the pre-agreed constitution and the worldviews of the other members of the collective. The constitution, subject to its procedures for modification, codifies certain collective decisions. The probability (from each member's perspective) that each of the members will change his or her worldview and the frequency (again from each member's perspective) of these potential changes will be factored into the negotiated constitution. It will affect both the preferences that some members have for certain constitutional provisions as well as the preference intensities some potential members have for alternative constitutional terms. If a member does not think his or her worldview is stable, is subject to significant change, that member will want a constitution that does not specify many decisions. He or she will also prefer a constitution that can be easily modified. This type of person will still value being a member of a stable defense collective, but will want as much potential future flexibility as possible.

Potential members who think their worldviews will not change over time can also be negatively affected by people modifying their worldviews. Even though they originally sorted themselves into the coercive collectives where their net gains were highest, with people who had compatible worldviews, over time—as people's worldviews change—their original net gains can be reduced. People can find themselves in collectives with others who have significantly different worldviews as those other people's worldviews change. This will increase the probability that future collective decisions will not be their preferred decisions, as well as increase the chances that some of these collective decisions will be unacceptable. In effect, they can find themselves in the "wrong" collective. Their worldview may have remained constant, but the consensus worldview of the collective, as expressed by the future decisions of the collective, may have radically altered from the original consensus worldview.

This possibility will affect some people's preferred constitutional terms. Everything else being the same, people who think their views are stable will prefer a more detailed and all-encompassing initial constitution. They will prefer a constitution that is difficult to modify and whose provisions are biased toward the status quo. They will also want the decisions of the initial delegates to be difficult to modify. In addition, they will prefer to incorporate some type of conservatism into the speed of change of the rules and procedures of the various collectives in which they are members.

The likelihood that the original members' worldviews will change is impossible to determine. The five reviewed theorists may not be completely representative of the members of a large diversified defense collective; nonetheless, the probable stability of their views is of interest. Based on their biographies and published works, their worldviews seemed to be stable. John Harsanyi's fundamental worldview did not appear to change over time, even when his views were criticized by other scholars. Similarly, Amartya Sen's and John Rawls's philosophical views did not seem to change as they aged. Both Friedrich Hayek's and Robert Nozick's views did change, but not after they received their doctorates. In college, each of them was a socialist. Nozick, after discussions with friends and academics, including Murray Rothbard, whose anarchistic views were discussed at the end of chapter 2, became a libertarian. Similarly, Hayek's views were affected by his relationship with Ludwig von Mises,[267] a leading Austrian economist.[268]

Some people will view the relative stability of the five scholars' views as consistent with the potential changeability of the worldviews of a broader group of people. Professors Benjamin Page and Robert Shapiro argue that American views have been relatively stable over the past fifty years.[269] However, their detailed analysis and conclusions have been criticized.[270] Judgment of the potential likelihood of changes in members' worldviews over time is another differentiating factor in people's preferences and intensities for specific collective rules and procedures.

The potential for members' worldviews to change over time (if there is some stability to these changes) also increases the benefit that people exiting the original position will receive from the existence of multiple defense collectives and nested collectives. Everything else being the same, the ability to change membership decreases the freedom losses for the average member, since people can re-sort themselves into the collectives that most fit their new worldview. People who significantly disagree with the decisions of the collectives in which they are members can seek out new collectives whose collective decisions are more aligned with their own worldviews. This re-sorting benefits members who move, since they can join collectives with laws that cause them less freedom losses. It benefits the collective they join because their joining increases the gross benefits from collective action. It also potentially benefits the collective they leave because their negative influence over the decisions of that collective has been eliminated. The members of the collective they leave hope that other people with more similar worldviews will decide to join. Existing members can also view the change in other members' worldviews as negative externalities if enough people change their views and modify the collective's decisions in such a way as to increase their freedom losses.

SORTING AND THE TIEBOUT HYPOTHESIS

Gerald Wright, Robert Erikson, and John McIver argue that there are significant interstate political differences among citizens in the various American states.[271] Interestingly, Paul Brace and his colleagues conclude that these differences have been stable over time.[272] If these arguments are accurate, they imply that if states are constitutionally permitted to have different laws, then they will have different laws if they are sensitive to their citizens' views. They also imply that people who have strongly held views and disagree with their state laws may be incentivized to migrate to another state jurisdiction. This adjustment process of moving to another state, and the adjustment process of voluntarily exiting a coercive collective and joining a new collective—in an attempt to be governed by laws closer to one's worldview—are like the phenomenon of "voting with your feet" that was first studied by the economist Charles Tiebout.[273] He hypothesized that local communities that provide services such as municipal golf courses, public beaches, education, and public hospitals compete with other communities, and people are incentivized to locate to the community that offers the package of local public goods that best satisfies their preferences. He argued that people can influence the provision of public goods through sorting themselves into different local communities, which can theoretically lead to the efficient production of local public goods. His research has been controversial for a variety of reasons, including its emphasis on the decentralized provision of local public goods versus a more centralized approach.

Tiebout assumed that everyone moves and sorts themselves into various local communities based *solely* on the communities' tax policies and provision of local public goods, which will lead to relative homogeneity within communities and heterogeneity between communities. Economists Paul Rhode and Koleman Strumpf show that the opposite has happened in the United States between 1850 and 1990.[274] They argue that even though moving costs have significantly declined over time, communities are more diverse, and the dispersion between various community approaches to the provision of public goods such as education have narrowed. They do not deny that local public-good policies matter to people; they only argue that people's views on them have not been the dominant reason for migration.

Their analysis illustrates some of the difficulties of using econometric methods to corroborate one's worldview. For example, their conclusions are not surprising given the discussion of agglomeration effects in the formation of cities. People relocate for a wide variety of reasons, including geography, employment, and family. Everything else being the same, this will cause a drift toward homogeneous policies between communities if people have different worldviews but on average move for other reasons. However, their analysis doesn't appear to imply that local public goods are not the dominant reason for *some* people to move to other communities. Their observations relate to the *majority* of people, not the *minority*. Some people relocating because of local public goods and their tax consequences seems to be entirely consistent with their analysis. As they acknowledge, their approach also potentially suffers from the traditional criticisms of time-series studies that are unable to control for changes in people's preferences and institutional change[275]. For example, a key proxy they use for local community decision-making is spending on education, which has increasingly been influenced by both federal and state rules.

One of the potential weaknesses of both the pure Tiebout hypothesis and some criticisms of the hypothesis, as applied to the world in which we live, is the presumption that local communities have the independent ability to make their own provision of local public goods. In the United States, local communities, municipalities, cities, towns, and counties have no independent existence besides those granted to them by the various states in which they reside. In 1903, the US Supreme Court ruled that public entities such as municipalities

are the creatures—mere political subdivisions—of the states, for the purpose of exercising a part of its powers. They may exert only such powers as are expressly granted to them, or such as may be necessarily implied from those granted. What they lawfully do of a public character is done under the sanction of the state. They are, in every essential sense, only auxiliaries of the state for the purposes of local government[276].

All the states have added state constitutional provisions that provide some type of equal education for its citizens. This has, over time, caused state governments to exert more control over spending on local public education. In addition, the federal government has also increasingly exercised influence over state government policies on local education through various spending initiatives and the delegated responsibility concerning equal protection, which has led to homogenization of state approaches to local education. These centralized policies have led to local educational spending becoming more uniform across communities and may lead to a bias in the education spending proxy.

Even though education is supported by various federal and state polices on spending and taxation, there are still differences between many communities concerning local property taxes and education. This will lead to the phenomenon, which occurs in some New Jersey communities, where families put their homes up for sale as soon as their youngest child graduates from high school. They sell their houses and move to towns that have lower real estate taxes. These people did not move earlier presumably because they believed their children's school system was worth the higher real estate taxes.

Some will argue that people's abilities to escape taxes, rules, and laws by changing location is an inefficient adjustment mechanism because of the externalities discussed above and perceived spillover effects. This will lead them to prefer centralized control and large general collectives. It can also lead to some in the original position preferring certain constraints on people's abilities to move between defense collectives and within defense collectives. For example, the Chinese government has historically restricted migration between the countryside and cities. Many city residents do not think that new entrants fully internalize the costs they impose on existing city residents. Concern over migration is also one of the reasons for Brexit, Britain's planned exit from the European Union. These types of issues will incent some people in the original position to strongly prefer rules that restrict migration.

Of course, other individuals in the original position will favor constitutional provisions that mandate free movement of people at least between nested collectives within a defense collective. The US Constitution, as currently interpreted, and the agreements underlying the European Union contain this type of provision. Many individuals think there are significant economic and social costs to immigration restrictions. For instance, the economists Chun-Chung Au and J. Vernon Henderson determined that in China agglomeration effects are significant and that government-imposed limitations on internal migration have caused many cities to be inefficiently small.[277] Given the difficulty in changing constitutional restrictions, people holding either view may not want to have the movement of people addressed by the constitution, leaving the mobility decision unspecified and subject to periodic review.

People's ability to re-sort themselves after the formation of the various collectives is helped by the existence of a constitution that conveys the consensus worldview of the various collectives. However, the constitution is not the only source of information for people not satisfied with the laws of their current collective; people will base their decisions to change collectives also on their estimate of the culture, institutions, and current decisions of the other collectives. While there will be interaction between people in different defense collectives and in different nested collectives within the same defense collective, interaction is on average more intense between people in the same collective. People will use methods other than official laws to engender cooperation. The citizens of each collective will develop their own beliefs, customs, habits, idioms, morals, and methods of accomplishing collective goals. In a word, each of the various collectives will develop their own culture. On average, the members of a defense collective, irrespective of their parallel membership in various nested collectives, will have more interaction than they will with members of other defense collectives. This will result in different cultures between each of the defense collectives. It has the further important implication that the cultures within each of the various nested collectives, within a defense collective, are more similar than the cultures either between the various defense collectives or between the nested collectives pursuing similar goals in different defense collectives.

People will only voluntarily change collectives if the expected costs of doing so are lower than the expected benefits from such a change. The potential expenses of changing collectives may include physical moving costs. Even though people are physical beings, not all coercive collectives govern a physical area. Collectives can exist that are extra-territorial. An example is a transactional collective. Nonetheless, many coercive collectives will be responsible for a specific area, and these areas can overlap between collectives with different goals. For these types of collectives, people can incur a variety of moving costs. Beside physical costs, they may have to incur the psychic cost of exiting the membership of multiple collectives even though they are unsatisfied with the laws of only one of the overlapping collectives. Finally, they must adapt to a new culture, which can include learning a new language, as well as complying with cultural mores that change slowly over time. These costs will on average be higher for exiting a defense collective than for exiting one or more of the nested collectives within a defense collective.

Given the current state of technology, collective external defense is enhanced by control over physical territory. As such, each of the defense collectives is likely to claim jurisdiction over unique, nonoverlapping territory. Therefore, exiting a defense collective will typically require a physical move. It will also necessitate that people stop practicing their historical culture and learn the culture of their new defense collective. In addition, exit will also entail resigning from the membership of the various nested collectives (at least the ones that govern a physical area) and join new nested collectives within the new defense collective. Withdrawing from one or more of the various nested collectives, without exiting the defense collective, has lower costs because people can retain the culture of the defense collective. Also, the physical moving costs on average are likely to be lower when only exiting a nested collective.

GENERATIONS AND DIVERSE WORLDVIEWS

While potential changes in members' worldviews is an important consideration for people as they contemplate joining in collective action, an even more significant effect of time on people contemplating exiting anarchy is that sooner or later the entire membership of each surviving collective will change. People do not live forever, which will potentially change the consensus worldview of each of the collectives as original members die.

People also have children. Offspring pose many new questions that need to be answered by people contemplating joining a collective. Will members' children automatically be admitted as members and, if so, at what age? Will children's taxes be different than the taxes of the original members? If they are admitted as members, how are their unknown future worldviews factored into the initial constitution that forms the collective, if at all? People will obviously have different views on these questions. However, people typically have a natural affinity for their family. Desire for their protection is a reason that many people will find it advantageous to join in collective defense and join coercive nested collectives. As such, they will want their family members to be protected by the collective and to become full members.

Members' children may not want to become members of their parents' collective(s). An important variable in their preferences over staying in the collective(s) will be their worldview compared to the consensus worldview of their parents' collective(s). If their worldview is not sufficiently compatible, they will want to join another collective. Everything else being the same, the original members of the collectives will want their children to join and contribute to the collective effort, since this will increase the gross gains from collective action and reduce or eliminate the losses from the death of the original members. As such, there is an incentive in large collectives designed to last multiple generations, such as the defense collective, for newcomers such as children to be taxed the same as the original members. The addition of children obviously has a potential downside for existing members, since each of the children's worldviews can be different than their parents' worldviews, and they may be able to significantly affect decisions not specified in the constitution. However, if there is free movement of people, including children, then the potential negative effect children could have on other members of the collective can be reduced.

Most parents will attempt to convey their norms and values to their children. In addition, some parents will also attempt to fully imprint their worldview on their children.[278] These efforts, if successful, have two potentially positive benefits for people exiting the original position. First, children who adopt their parents' worldviews will be more satisfied staying in their parents' collective, since their worldviews will be similar to other members' views. Second, children who can be convinced that their parents' worldview is the most accurate representation of reality will not generate a negative externality for the original members of the collective. However, it is not at all clear that parents will be able to permanently imprint their worldviews on their children, especially as their children encounter other worldviews and ideas.[279]

The inability of parents to completely indoctrinate their children is potentially positive, since it leaves open the possibility that children can independently reason and develop a more accurate model of how the world works. However, it may have negative consequences for the existing members of the various collectives, especially since children may have significant moving costs in relocating collectives. The presence of migration costs implies that children will remain in their parents' collective even if the gross gains they receive from the collective exceed their freedom losses. Children may decide to stay in their parents' collective even if they detest the collective's existing laws and there are other collectives that have laws more compatible with their worldview. Everything else being the same, the greater the moving costs, the larger the freedom losses children will sustain before deciding it is in their best interest to move, and the potentially greater negative externalities they will have on other members of the collectives in which their parents are members. The potentially extensive freedom losses suffered by children staying in their parents' collectives will incent them to attempt to modify the rules and laws of those collectives to ones more in keeping with their own worldviews. Over time, the original consensus worldview of the collective can change, and the original members can find their worldviews in the minority. There is a limit to these changes, which depends on the extent of the children's exit costs and the pace of births and deaths. Nonetheless, these potential changes may cause some people to favor constitutional provisions that codify specific rights and obligations.

As discussed above, the costs of exiting a nested collective or a series of nested collectives and remaining a member of a defense collective are significantly lower than the costs of exiting a defense collective. The nested collectives within a defense collective will have at least some common unofficial societal rules. They will have elements of a common culture. Moving between nested collectives and staying in the same defense collective has costs, but they will typically be dwarfed by the costs of exiting both a nested collective and a defense collective. This implies that members of a broad general collective are at more risk to changes in the consensus worldview than members of a narrowly focused defense collective that has multiple types of nested collectives. It is less expensive to exit one of the nested collectives than exiting the general defense collective. For this reason, many people leaving the original position will favor constitutional agreements that specifically limit the *scope* of the defense collective. The existence of nested collectives reduces the future freedom losses of people as they exit the original position and also reduces their freedom losses and the freedom losses of their children as they and their children are affected by the passage of time.

COLLECTIVE STABILITY

Each person who leaves anarchy will want to join a defense collective that has a high probability of stability and will support constitutional measures that support this stability. If a person joins a defense collective that fails, they will either perish or involuntarily become part of another defense collective with rules and laws that are less optimal from their perspective. Furthermore, their children can be significantly adversely affected by the failure of the defense collective. People exiting the original position will have a lower likelihood of living the life they want to live if the defense collective they join fails. This does not imply that each person will prefer to join a defense collective that maximizes its defense expenditures or will seek to join a general defense collective that sacrifices all other collective objectives in the pursuit of collective defense.

The power and allure of the benefits from cooperation, even among different defense collectives, will encourage nonaggression between many of the defense collectives. As previously discussed, coercive collectives have lower incentives to engage in opportunistic behavior than each of their members experienced in the original position, since the gains from opportunistic behavior are socialized. Coercive collectives are also unlikely to always be on the knife-edge of annihilation by one or more hostile defense collectives, since their structure encourages productivity increases and buildup of excess resources. All-out continuous war between each of the various defense collectives is unlikely to be the equilibrium condition. A more likely scenario would be periodic wars and large periods of peace. This implies that people can pursue goals other than collective defense without the constant threat of extinction. It also gives rise to an increase in diverse views on defense expenditures and strategy, since people will have different views on the probability of being attacked and the advantages of attacking and threatening other defense collectives.

Decentralized coordination is very difficult in anarchy for all the reasons that were outlined in chapter 5. However, the possibility of decentralized coordination between coercive collectives is much more likely than between individuals. As discussed in chapter 11, collectives reduce many of the negative aspects of opportunistic behavior. The defense collectives can have mutual agreements and form societies of defense collectives to address conflicts. While there is no global power to govern their agreements, compliance with the terms of treaties and agreements will be significantly higher than if the defense collectives were individuals. Nested collectives can also enter into agreements with each other to address their conflicts. In addition, they can delegate a third party, including the defense collective, to enforce their agreements.

PART FIVE

— ★ —

CONSTITUTION FOR THE BROADLY LIBERAL FEDERAL GOVERNMENT

18

—— ★ ——

CENTRALIZATION AND
COMPOUND GOVERNMENT

COMPOUND COLLECTIVE

The constitution of a coercive collective delineates the collective's governance structure. It may also address the goals of the collective, methods of addressing these goals, limits on the collective, and rights and responsibilities of its members. Importantly, it provides information to people in the original position, allowing them to better sort themselves into the defense and nested collectives that optimize their net gains from coercive collective action.

This chapter is concerned with the constitutions for defense and nested collectives whose members have diverse and broadly liberal worldviews. The members of each of these collectives are assumed to have sorted themselves into the collective of their choice, based on their various worldviews. The fundamental question is whether there are logical divisions between the defense collective and the various nested collectives. Members' worldviews affect most aspects of the various collectives; do they also affect the dividing line between the defense collectives and the nested collectives? Asked somewhat differently, will broadly liberal and diverse people exiting the original position agree to a certain set of goals for the defense collective, irrespective of their worldviews? In addressing these questions, it will prove helpful to analyze the impact that majority voting has on decisions made by the various coercive collectives in the presence of concurrent powers.

To assist the discussion, we will consider a special type of coercive defense collective whose constitution has four simple provisions. The first is that each collective decision is made by majority vote. The second provision is that there are few limits to the *scope* of the defense collective; it can pass laws on many domestic issues that have majority support. The third provision is that the various nested collectives can pursue any collective goal their members want, except for external defense (concurrent and exclusive powers provision). The final constitutional clause allows the defense collective's decisions to be dominant if there are conflicts between the defense collective and any of the nested collectives' decisions (supremacy provision). The government with this type of constitution, where people are members of a large general defense collective and members of different general nested collectives, will be labeled a "compound collective." It tends to meet the definition of a compound government, as analyzed by the political economist Vincent Ostrom.[280]

To explore some of the deficiencies in this type of government, the political decision on whether to enact minimum-wage legislation will be examined. The members of the compound collective are assumed to: (i) have differing worldviews, (ii) possess perfect information as to people's worldviews, (iii) vote in conformity with their worldviews, and (iv) be a member of the nested collective whose expected policies cause them the least expected freedom losses. Given their differing worldviews, each member of the compound collective will have different opinions on the benefits or detriments of minimum wages. Everything else being the same, this will result in different minimum-wage programs in the various nested collectives.

Some people are likely to think that minimum wages are justified. Their reasoning may be based on various factors, including their belief that a minimum wage (i) reduces inequality, (ii) increases workers' economic security, (iii) increases disposable income for some members of the nested collective, (iv) improves lower-paid employees' sense of self-worth, and (v) does not reduce the number of jobs. People may be persuaded by academic research, like the analysis of respected economists David Card and Alan Krueger.[281] They found that the 1992 minimum-wage rate increase in New Jersey did not decrease employment in the fast-food industry. Some people who favor minimum wages may think that employers have some monopoly pricing power over their low-paid labor force. Others may believe that employers have more information on wages than lower-skilled workers, allowing employers to exploit the workers' information gap and pay people less than they would if knowledge were more dispersed. Any of these views, together with people's sense of fairness, will lead people to vote for the imposition of minimum wages.

However, other members of the defense collective may believe that minimum wages do more harm than good. They may hold the opinion that the market for unskilled and less-skilled workers is reasonably competitive, which will lead them to conclude that minimum wages will contribute to lower employment. Some people may think minimum-wage laws will reduce employment opportunities for lower-skilled workers, including people new to the labor market. For instance, economists David Neumark and William Wascher found that approximately two-thirds of the academic research supported the claim that there is a negative effect on employment from an increase in the minimum wage, and that this impact is more significant for those with fewer skills.[282] People in the various nested collectives who believe this line of reasoning will either vote against a minimum wage or prefer a minimum wage that is low. Of course, some people prefer not to enact a minimum wage because they are personally paid relatively high wages and are selfishly concerned that high minimum wages will increase the prices of the goods and services they purchase.

These differing views on the benefits and costs of minimum wages will cause people in the various general nested collectives to vote for different levels of minimum wages. This will result in differential minimum-wage laws among the nested collectives. Since the minimum-wage laws are adopted through majority voting, there can be many people in each of the various nested collectives who prefer a different minimum wage. Some may prefer a higher rate while others prefer a lower one. The various minimum-wage laws are unlikely to be the freedom-maximizing laws, since the members' intensities with respect to their preferences are not considered as part of the overall decision-making. Nonetheless, since people sorted themselves by worldview and can freely move between nested collectives, they will join the nested collective in which their expected net gains are highest. The ability to be a member of nested collectives with different minimum wages will reduce freedom losses as people exit the original position, even if each of the collectives they join uses majority voting to make collective decisions. Perfect exit and entry reduces the costs of inefficient and imperfect voice.

But the analysis of voting on minimum-wage legislation in the compound collective is not complete. The members of the various nested collectives also have a right to vote as members of the defense collective. Since it is a general collective with few restrictions on its *scope*, let's assume that it has the delegated authority by its constitution to also make decisions on minimum wages. The members of the defense collective who have strong views on high minimum wages will want a defense-collective rule that mandates relatively high minimum wages. They may be in the minority in their nested collective and want a defense-collective law to trump their nested collective rule. Alternatively, they may be satisfied with their nested collective rule but think the minimum wages established by other nested collectives are too low and unfair to their low-paid workers. They may also think that nested collectives with no minimum wages will cause negative spillover effects. That is, they may be concerned that the absence of minimum-wage legislation will incent the businesses regulated by their nested collective to change collectives, reducing the overall effect of the minimum wage imposed by their nested collective. Given the constitutional provision of supremacy of the defense-collective decisions, these various concerns will incentivize the members of the defense collective to put the question of the defense collective's rule on minimum wages to the overall membership.

If most of the nested collectives have some form of minimum-wage legislation, majority voting by the members of the defense collective will lead to the imposition of a minimum wage for the overall defense collective that is somewhere between the highest and lowest passed by the various nested collectives. Members who prefer minimum wages at least as high as the defense collective's rule will vote for the legislation because they are no worse off. If they are a member of a nested collective that has a higher minimum wage than the defense collective's minimum, they can continue to live in a nested collective that imposes these higher minimums. If they are in the minority of a nested collective that has a lower minimum wage, they will be more satisfied with the higher defense collective's minimum wage.

The majority members of those nested collectives that had minimum wages below the defense collective's minimum-wage levels will not vote for the defense collective to have minimum wages higher than the rate in their nested collective. However, they are in the minority in the overall defense collective, and their preferences will be overridden by majority vote. The supremacy rule for the defense collective will require the nested collectives with minimum wages below its own to increase their minimum wages, subjugating the preferences of most of the members of the affected nested collectives to the majority views of the overall membership of the defense collective. They are worse off by the passage of the defense collective's rule. The imposition of minimum wages by the defense collective will increase freedom losses, since it reduces the choice available to members of some of the nested collectives. It makes voice less efficient and negates the benefits of exit and entry.

Economists Jacques Crémer and Thomas Palfrey rigorously analyzed a similar situation.[283] They argue that when people have unique policy preferences (but equal worldviews) and when an entity such as the defense collective does not have an efficiency advantage, in the absence of spillovers, the ability of this organization to overrule the preferences of the citizens of other domestic governments affects more people negatively than positively. They also conclude that this effect can occur and even potentially be exacerbated when a government like the defense collective is more efficient at providing the public good. In addition, they reason that this same effect will occur in a representative democracy in which citizens first vote for their representatives, and the representatives pass laws based on majority vote.

Unless the defense collective's rule is set at the minimum wage adopted by the nested collective with the lowest minimum wage, some members of the defense collective are worse off by having the larger collective overrule their nested collective's decision. Concurrent powers and the supremacy rule will produce laws that lead to excess central intervention, since the majority has an incentive to use majority decision-making rules to accomplish their preferences. This occurs even if everyone agrees that there is no logical reason for central involvement.

The unchecked ability for the defense collective to override the preferences of the members of the nested collectives acts as a negative externality and will affect the decisions people make as they contemplate exiting anarchy. The compound collective effectively increases the net losses for many people, since their views on domestic issues can differ from the average worldview of members of the defense collective. The majority view can override their preferences, not only on defense decisions but also on nondefense issues. Concurrent powers and supremacy of the defense-collective decisions negate many of the benefits of nested collectives. Compound governments are effectively general defense collectives even if their members are also members of nested collectives. If people exiting the original position cannot somehow restrict the overall breadth of decision-making of the defense collective, many of them will be incentivized to join smaller defense collectives. A restriction that all governments are compound governments will cause the credible equilibrium to be one in which the average membership size of defense collectives is smaller, as would be the overall net gains from coercive collective formation.

Each person who joins a coercive collective has an incentive to use the collective's decision-making process—its institutional structure—to have the collective execute his or her worldview. If people join a defense collective that has the authority to override the decisions of nested collectives in which they are not members, they are incentivized to use their voting power to achieve that objective. This authority benefits people who are in the majority of the defense collective with regard to domestic decisions. This power effectively increases the size of their nested collective, and their net gains, at the expense of those who have minority views. Those people who are in the minority on domestic issues will want to protect themselves from majority decisions. They can do so by joining a smaller defense collective whose membership is more aligned with their views. However, they have better options. They can agree to a constitutional provision for the defense collective that restricts the defense collective's future actions with respect to domestic activities. By negotiating and joining defense collectives that limit their own authority to override the domestic decisions of the various nested collectives, they can increase their overall net gains from collective action. These restrictions will restore the value of nested collectives and allow the equilibrium size of defense collectives to increase. Aggregate freedom losses will be lower.

While many people may be better off with a defense collective that has unlimited scope, others will be worse off. Those who are worse off are incentivized to negotiate constitutional provisions that restrict the scope of the defense collective. This will allow more options and choices. People in the original position are not forced to join unrestricted defense collectives. They have the strategic option of joining smaller defense collectives. Those who may have gained from the lack of restrictions will be left with the strategic choice of joining smaller unrestricted defense collectives or larger defense collectives that have restrictions on domestic decisions. The credible equilibrium will be the latter option. Individuals whose worldviews incent them to be members of diverse defense collectives will choose to be members of the type of defense collective that has limits on its scope of nondefense decisions, since they gain from being part of the larger defense collective.

In an environment where people cannot agree in advance to every potential collective action, where people's worldviews may change, and where the members of the collective change over time, the constitutions of the various collectives provide valuable information to people in the original position. A constitution for a defense collective that does not restrict the collective's own activities, and allows its majority members to overrule the majority preferences of the members of the various nested collectives with respect to domestic issues, will inform potential members that they are joining a general defense collective that regulates both defense and domestic issues. Without more specification of goals, rights, and obligations, members are completely subject to overall majority preferences as those preferences change over time. People who join defense collectives that allow for independent decision-making by nested collectives have the enhanced ability to escape being subject to the preferences of the overall membership on nondefense issues. They can subject themselves to the majority preferences of a subset of the overall defense membership, which they can choose based on an estimate of relative preferences. As such, the credible equilibrium defense-collective constitution for diverse people will include restrictions on the authority of the larger collective to overrule the domestic decisions of its members' nested collectives.

CENTRALIZATION

But what about potential conflicts between the various nested collectives such as spillovers and externalities? These occur when the actions of one nested collective or the actions of their members have a negative impact on the members of other nested collectives. Without central intervention, nested collectives are not required to consider the impact of their actions on others. The prior discussion, in chapter 14, of differing laws concerning teenage drinking in New Jersey is one example of governmental policy spillovers. Another example can be found in differing policies on minimum wages.

What if the members of one nested collective prefer not to have any rules concerning a minimum wage, and this causes businesses to relocate to that jurisdiction and potentially reduces employment in one or more of the other nested collectives? This could reduce the standard of living in the affected nested collectives and decrease the effectiveness of their preferred rules concerning high minimum wages. Wouldn't the defense collective need to intermediate? By establishing rules that are applicable to everyone in the defense collective concerning minimum wages, it can reduce some of the negative effects of differential laws. While this is obviously one method of managing conflict between members of the defense collective, it is not the one that diverse people exiting the original position will choose.

Spillover effects can incent people in the original position to join larger nested collectives than they might otherwise join, but it will not cause everyone to join a defense collective that has the delegated power to overrule the decisions of nested collectives in which they are members. The ability to form large independent nested collectives, including large local collectives with independent decision-making authority, is a freedom-loss reducing option when compared to joining a compound government. It allows its members to directly address negative externalities in the same way the larger defense collective does. However, since almost all these conflicts do not involve everyone in the defense collective, people with diverse worldviews will not want to join defense collectives that treat every domestic collective decision as one that requires or involves every member of the larger collective.

Even though centralization within a large nested or local coercive collective has lower freedom losses for a diverse population than centralization within a general defense collective, joining large nested collectives as a method of reducing externalities between smaller nested collectives is not the only option people in the original position will pursue. Expanding the scope and breadth of a coercive collective that makes its decisions through majority voting has certain costs.

First, since marginal freedom losses increase with a larger membership, externality costs will be affected by the size of the coercive collective. Everything else being the same, a small local collective is more likely to expand its membership because of a given spillover than might a large regional nested collective. This does not imply that large nested collectives will not have conflicts with other nested collectives; it simply suggests that the costs of resolving the same type of externality through consolidation is more expensive for the members of a large nested collective than for members of a small local collective.

Second, as was discussed in chapter 16, even if people can sort themselves into the optimal coercive collective, majority voting will not necessarily produce the freedom-loss minimizing decision, since it does not incorporate the intensities that people have for their preferred collective decisions. Third, expansion of the membership of the coercive collective will lead to people subjecting themselves to coercive rules determined by the views of a broader group of people on issues other than those involving the various externalities. These costs will incent people in the original position to pursue alternatives to centralization as a method of addressing intercollective conflicts. Before discussing the primary method that people will use to address their interdependence, we will examine one other centralization cost.

Centralization may be an inefficient method of cooperation, even if people have the same worldview. Recall from the discussion in chapter 6 that Oliver Hart, Sanford Grossman, and John Moore showed that centralization has costs because of specific investments and incomplete contracts. In a recent paper, Philippe Aghion and his colleagues maintain that unexpected change increases the value of local information, leading more decentralized firms to outperform centralized companies.[284] Economists Ricardo Alonso, Wouter Dessien, and Niko Matouschek argue that decentralizing decisions to division managers can improve the overall operations of a corporation, even if coordination is important.[285] They assume that division managers have more information than management at headquarters and conclude that decentralization is better than centralized control if the division managers' incentives are aligned. However, their incentives do not need to be completely aligned, they just need to recognize their interdependence.

Their conclusions continue to be sound when people have different worldviews. The necessary ingredient for decentralized decision-making in the presence of spillovers, conflicts, and externalities is the recognition by the decision makers that there are benefits from some type of coordination and compromise. If people believe there are costs to not compromising, or benefits to compromising, then they can communicate and determine methods of reaching agreements on rules governing their behavior and actions. For the same reasons people form coercive collectives and voluntarily submit to collective rules, they can reach agreements that do not involve the formation or expansion of coercive entities.

Members of coercive collectives can find decentralized methods of reducing the costs of externalities. People in the original position recognize the benefits from collaboration and will use all the tools and methods at their disposal to increase their net returns from increasing coordination, given their differing worldviews. This will include forming and joining coercive collectives. It will also include having these coercive collectives enter mutual agreements. For example, economists Marco Battaglini and Bård Harstad argue that agreements can be structured to reduce issues associated with nonparticipation and free riding in environmental agreements.[286] They show the interdependence of contract duration, size of coalitions, and contract specification.

The credible equilibrium for a diverse population will be a combination of limited defense collectives, general defense collectives, limited and general nested collectives, local and transactional coercive collectives, noncoercive entities, and vast numbers of agreements between these entities. People exiting the original position do not need to solely rely on centralization to address conflicts. The incentives of members of nested collectives to modify their preferred rules to accommodate the preferences of nonmembers were discussed in chapter 13. Differences in laws between nested collectives will continue to exist, but the expectation of the benefits from cooperating with nonmembers will lead to some homogenization of laws and a reduction in extreme rules.

Repeated interaction between the members of local collectives will incent those collectives to reach mutual agreements on their various conflicts. Boroughs and other local entities will also address economies of scale through agreements, which can be adjudicated by some agreed-upon third-party coercive collective. As noted above, this occurs today. Many local communities enter bilateral and multilateral agreements on various services. The economist and Nobel laureate Elinor Ostrom and others conducted research on public-safety economies of scale in a variety of cities, including Chicago, St. Louis, Nashville, and Indianapolis.[287] In a later paper, she stated that none of this research revealed any instance where the decentralized provision of these services was inferior.[288]

Elinor Ostrom, who was married to the aforementioned Vincent Ostrom, spent much of her professional career examining the governance structure of "common-pool resources" such as waterways, lakes, fisheries, common grazing land, and forests. Her research led her to disagree with the commonly held opinion that people cannot design procedures that allow them to overcome the "tragedy of the commons," where they deplete a natural resource to their own disadvantage.[289] She argued that "organization" can occur in a decentralized environment.[290] It also led her to conclude that centralized entities such as the defense collective have not been historically effective at regulating natural resources. These conclusions and observations caused her to advocate for the adoption of decentralized approaches to collective problems. She preferred an approach that she called "polycentric," which is a governance structure involving agreements among various independent governmental entities.[291]

While some people will not agree with her conclusions or recommendations, many people in a diverse population will think there are better alternatives than centralized control. People who share her views will want to join defense collectives that allow for multiple methods of engendering cooperation, including the formation of multiple coercive and noncoercive entities, as well as agreements between these entities. The presence of diverse worldviews will lead to a credible equilibrium in which diverse defense collectives will incorporate many of Ostrom's polycentric concepts.

Not all domestic conflicts are local or even regional. There can be serious disagreements between the members of large nested collectives. There can even be domestic issues that affect everyone in the defense collective. However, there are alternatives to centralization. Regional and national domestic issues can be addressed through various bilateral and multilateral agreements. These could even be very broad agreements such as a common market among the nested collectives. An example of this latter type of agreement is the arrangement among the various countries in Europe to allow the "free" movement of various things, including people and products. These types of agreements and arrangements will allow the members of the nested collectives to address their differences without submitting to the majority preferences of everyone in the defense collective. However, there can be defense-collective rules on some domestic issues. Two of these were previously discussed. There can be others. However, the credible equilibrium outcome for a diverse membership will not be one where the defense collective is authorized to broadly affect domestic decisions and overrule nested collective laws.

The terms of the negotiated agreements between the nested collectives will be affected by numerous factors, including the level of interaction between the members of the nested collectives. The higher the level of cooperation and trade, the easier it will be for them to find common ground. The negotiated agreements, like all voluntary agreements, will incorporate the preferences of the members of the nested collectives, and, importantly, the intensities of those preferences. The terms of the negotiated agreements will be affected by those intensities. Defense-collective mandated decisions, decided by majority voting, do not incorporate intensities and may not even incorporate the preferences of the members of some of the nested collectives, if they are in the minority. Given the benefits of being members of the same defense collective, each of the affected parties will be willing to reach a greater compromise than they would if they were in different defense collectives. Furthermore, enhanced cooperation and trade following the formation of the defense collective will incentivize each of the large nested collectives to reach ongoing agreements to resolve their differences.

Decentralization is not preferred by everyone in the original position, but it is the credible equilibrium outcome unanimously accepted by everyone who joins a diverse defense collective. It will prove helpful to refer to this decentralized structure of coercive collectives formed by diverse people exiting the original position as "collectivity." Collectivity is a compromise structure of government, chosen by diverse people as they exit the original position. It consists of a limited defense collective and a polycentric type of domestic governance structure, which includes nested collectives and agreements between these coercive collectives.

19

★

FEDERALISM

The word "federalism" has rarely been used in our discussion. This omission has been deliberate for three reasons: (i) universal agreement on the meaning of federalism does not exist, (ii) historical American Federalism is associated with states' rights and slavery, and (iii) the institutional design of collectivity, while decentralized, has distinctive characteristics that are not captured in the traditional definitions of federalism. It is a unique type of federalism. To better understand collectivity, it will prove instructive to compare it to four different federalist concepts.

FISCAL FEDERALISM

"Fiscal federalism" is associated with the economist Wallace Oates.[292] He defined a federal government as one in which decisions are made by different internal units based on the preferences of their respective citizens. His concept of federalism can incorporate a general defense collective that uses regional decision makers to assist with collective decisions, a limited defense collective whose members are also the members of large nested collectives, and a compound collective. The fiscal federalist concept is only concerned with the economic efficiency of a government. It presumes that everyone has different preferences for the actions of their government. However, each citizen is also assumed to have the same worldview.

This perspective leads Oates to conclude that it is more efficient if public services are decided at the local level as long as the actions of the local governments do not have an impact on other local governments. On the other hand, if there are significant policy spillovers or externalities, he argued that the federal or central government should have the exclusive authority to make decisions. These include decisions over monetary policy, government spending designed to increase aggregate demand, and social welfare.

His conclusions do not accurately capture the decisions that diverse people in the original position will make. Oates's federalist concept is constructed around the idea that everyone has the same goals, and all agree on the best methods of accomplishing those goals. In his formulation, the only reason for decentralized decisions is that citizens have different preferences for various goods and services. Full decentralization, from his perspective, is constrained by externalities between the different domestic governments. He presumed that everyone will agree that Pareto optimality (see chapter 3) is the underlying moral code for designing governmental institutions.

Collectivity, on the other hand, is based on differing worldviews. People do not agree on the goals for collective action or on the best methods of accomplishing common goals. The world is too complex for Bayesian learning to occur; people can and will continue to have different models of how the world works. These internal models will not converge to one unified view based on more information. These underlying facts cause broadly liberal and diverse people in the original position to design a governance structure in which domestic governments can make independent domestic political decisions even when policy spillovers are significant.

The fundamental role of the defense collective is to defend its members from external threats. It has large economies of scale, which incentivizes many diverse people to join. This is as true for people in the original position as it is for the world in which we live. Daniel Elazar, a political scientist, states that a "superpower" must have a population of at least "two hundred million."[293] As these diverse people pursue domestic goals, they will increase their net gains from coercive collective action by forming two or more domestic governments that can make independent decisions unconstrained by the potential majority view that the actions of these governments may negatively affect each other.

People in the original position, like those who agree with Oates, will recognize the benefits from both the gains from scale that result from being a member of a larger government and having some domestic decisions made at the local level. However, they will also view centralization as the most appropriate method of handling domestic problems that broadly affect their citizens; they will have the worldview that the central government is best situated to handle issues such as air pollution and policies designed to equalize incomes. As such, they will prefer being members of a general defense collective where that collective has significant domestic authorities.

However, not every broadly liberal person will share his opinions on the benefits of centralization. If people with Oates's views insist that the defense collective has expansive domestic authorities, the group of people who will want to join them in collective defense will be significantly reduced. This will in turn cause people who share his opinions to join smaller, less efficient general defense collectives. A better alternative for them is to join a larger, more narrow defense collective and conduct their desired domestic policies in a large nested collective with people who share their views on the benefits of government intervention.

There will still be spillovers to other parts of the defense collective, but the costs of internalizing these externalities are too high in a world where people have different views on the efficacy of government spending. Spillovers occurred even in Oates's federalist government, since he did not propose only one world government. The economic policies of national governments will affect the citizens of other governments. People in the original position will use the new technology of coercive collectives to improve their lives by forming a variety of coercive and noncoercive entities. They will utilize agreements between these coercive collectives and other polycentric structures to address the remaining conflicts. However, externalities and spillovers cannot be completely addressed or eliminated in the complex world in which we live.

Oates's concept of federalism is too simplistic to capture the varied world that people in the original position will consider as they contemplate giving up their independence in anarchy. People who share the views of Friedrich Hayek and Robert Nozick will not prefer to join a defense collective that uses government spending to attempt to stabilize the economy. They are not alone; many people believe that the government-spending multiplier is less than one. That is, they think that increases in government spending reduces, instead of increases, economic welfare.[294] Similarly, a broad-based national program to reduce and attempt to eliminate economic inequality is not a social program consistent with everyone's views. For example, people who share Hayek's and Nozick's views do not place any positive value on pursuing these types of domestic goals. On the other hand, there are many people, including at least one of the reviewed authors, who would support these types of national programs. The overall net gains from collective action will be higher if people with both viewpoints join the same defense collective that has narrow domestic objectives and simultaneously join various-sized nested collectives to pursue domestic-related collective goals.

The existence of differing nested collectives will inevitably lead to policy spillovers as they pursue different rules and laws. The members of the affected nested collectives can address these conflicts through agreement and compromise. Of course, they may fail to reach a compromise, and any compromise reached could have been done in an inefficient manner. Nonetheless, as previously discussed, the more that nested collectives are connected, the more they are incentivized to reach agreements to address their conflicts.

TRADITIONAL FEDERALISM

William Riker's views on federalism will serve as the basis for the discussion of "traditional federalism."[295] He was a political scientist and federalist expert. He considered a government to be federalist if it had multilevels and if each level could make one or more independent decisions. His expansive concept of federalism would include collectivity, but it would also include many other governmental structures.

Riker's classification is so general that it does not capture the essence of why people in the original position will choose to form various coercive collectives, including a narrowly focused defense collective. The configuration of government affects the decisions a government will make. People with diverse worldviews in the original position will compromise and form a structure of government that appropriately balances the gains from being part of a large government against the costs of having to make joint decisions with people who have different worldviews. They will not form just any type of government that conforms to Riker's notion of federalism.

For example, per Riker's definition, the compound collective discussed in the prior chapter is a federalist government if the nested collectives that make up the compound government can make one independent decision. As discussed, diverse people in the original position will not compromise and agree to join a compound collective given the delegated power of the defense collective over domestic policies. The unique credible equilibrium structure of government for diverse people is a narrowly focused defense collective in which people preserve the authority to form various independent coercive collectives that have the combined authority to make almost all domestic decisions.

Many experts on governmental structure have the opinion that there is no logical method of dividing the responsibilities of different governments in a federalist government. For example, the economists Mikhail Filippov, Peter Ordeshook, and Olga Shvetsova reach this conclusion.[296] Their view seems to be that the limits of the defense collective are almost completely dependent on people's preferences. However, for diverse people exiting the original position, there is a logical limit to the scope of the defense collective. Failure to place severe limits on the central government's domestic authorities will allow people with differing worldviews to use the central government to overrule the decisions of the domestically focused nested collectives. The only credible equilibrium structure of government for diverse people who join the same defense collective is collectivity. There can be some domestic decisions that involve the defense collective, but these will be extremely limited in number.

An important component of the traditional federalist concept is that federalism is a union of different governments. It consists of smaller general governments coming together to form a larger general government, though the smaller governments retain some level of independence. Riker and others conceive of federalism as a bargaining solution between smaller governments and a newly formed central government. This is how many governments have been formed throughout history, and it serves to capture many aspects of the historical design of federalist governments. This perspective has led many scholars to view a federalist type of government as the best method for people to capture the gains from scale, while addressing diversity within the population. For example, the French philosopher Baron de Montesquieu famously preferred a "confederate republic," which to him was "a convention by which several petty states agree to become members of a larger one," because "[i]f a republic be small, it is destroyed by a foreign force; if it be large, it is ruined by an internal imperfection."[297] However, neither Montesquieu's nor Riker's perspective captures the dynamics of people in the original position. The bargain is not between different governments but between the diverse people in the original position; the bargainers are not monolithic governments but individuals seeking to more effectively cooperate with other individuals who happen to have different worldviews.

People in the original position will not first form small general governments, which then form a single central government. The big bang caused by the introduction of coercive collectives incents diverse people to form a series of governmental entities. They will form many central governments, not just one. Some of these central governments will be general collectives with broad powers. People who form these broad-based general defense collectives will have strong, nondiverse views on the value of integrating national defense with the other collective goals that people want to pursue. People who have these preferences but hold them less intensively, and people with more diverse viewpoints, will form a central government with narrow scope. They will simultaneously form coercive nested collectives that provide the framework for the introduction of new coercive collectives, agreements between these various entities, and noncoercive organizations.

Another aspect of the traditional federalist concept is the focus on constitutional design and the stability of the federation. Riker and others view federalism as inherently unstable, leading either to dissolution or to centralization under a powerful central government. These outcomes are another distinction between collectivity and traditional federalism. Diverse people in the original position will want to protect themselves from both risks and will seek to negotiate a constitution for the defense collective that reduces the risk of instability. They will place severe limits on the delegated powers of the defense collective. This reduces the possibility that the defense collective will become a general defense collective. It also reduces the danger that the minority will want to overthrow the defense collective or dissolve the defense collective. The ability for the minority of members of the defense collective to live under laws that better conform to their worldview will reduce social conflict. The inability of the majority to overrule the preferences of the minority on domestic collective decisions will reduce social unrest. The fewer decisions the defense collective must make, everything else being the same, the less likely it is that members will violently disagree with its decisions. A stable defense collective will not have the authority to interfere with the ability of its members to also be members of the nested collectives of their choice. It is a critical restriction in allowing people who place value on their worldview to have the highest chance to live the lives they prefer.

Given its importance to their overall well-being, members of the defense collective will want to ensure its survival. Irrespective of their worldviews, a diverse group of people who join in collective defense will want to agree to rules that provide the defense collective with sufficient authority and power to survive both external and internal threats. However, given their differing opinions on how this is best done, they will still need to reach a compromise decision. This could easily lead to a rule that provides the defense collective extensive authority, even over many domestic decisions, in the case of emergencies and war.

However, once the threat is past, its domestic authorities will again be severely restricted.

Based on the observed propensity for central governments to assume increasingly more power over the other governments under their protection, there have been some who have advocated other methods of limiting its power besides restricting its scope. For example, John Calhoun, an influential US senator from antebellum South Carolina, believed the states did not give up any rights in forming the United States, and that they had the independent ability to determine the limit of their powers. Diverse and broadly liberal people in the original position will not enact laws that concur with Calhoun's opinions. The constitution forming the defense collective will not give the authority to a member or a nested collective to ignore the laws passed by the defense collective within its delegated authority. Doing so will give those members and entities minority power over the defense collective and reduce the defense collective's ability to protect its members from both internal and external threats. The nonsupremacy of the defense collective, within its delegated sphere of responsibility, will cause decision-making to be more inefficient and increase the instability of the defense collective.

The economist James Buchanan wanted to limit the federal government's authority by allowing people to be able to secede from the federation.[298] He felt that this type of constitutional rule would place a limit on the central government's ability to pass laws that hurt the minority. However, secession, the ability of a group of members to take land that is under the jurisdictional control of the defense collective, is unlikely to be a rule that diverse people in the original position will include in the central government constitution. This right severely restricts the defense collective's ability to provide an adequate defense for the overall membership and decreases the stability of the defense collective. The possibility that a group of members can unilaterally remove land will require the defense collective to develop expensive redundancies around external defense to provide for the possibility that a group of members will exit and reduce security for the remaining members. In addition, it can allow some members unilaterally to put their selfish interests ahead of the collective interests, including the collective interest of joint defense in a time of war or emergency. This can potentially be exploited by enemies of the defense collective. The right of secession reduces many of the gains from collective defense. Controversial decisions around collective defense and other collective goals within the delegated scope of the defense collective will be harder to make, since they can cause some dissenting groups of members to exit joint defense. The costs of secession are so high for the remaining members that it effectively gives a veto to a minority of the membership over many defense-collective decisions. These costs will almost certainly cause a diverse membership to reject the right of secession. Instead, people will reduce the scope of the central government. This is the least costly and most effective method to allow people to live by the minority rule they prefer on domestic issues.

The instability concerns raised by traditional federalism are a function of the specific institutional design of traditional federalist governments. Extending the scope of responsibility of the defense collective much beyond external defense will lead to stability issues because of the incentive diverse members have to use the defense collective's decision mechanisms to achieve their worldview. Broad domestic responsibilities for the central government will either cause it to become a general government or cause people with minority worldviews to attempt to weaken it. A weak central government will be less likely to protect its citizens from both external and internal threats. Needing to ask groups of members to assist it in defending the overall membership from threats, allowing groups of members to ignore its decisions, or granting groups of members the right to secede will increase the probability that the defense collective will be unsuccessful at protecting its members from threats. These restrictions effectively turn the central government into an alliance of groups of members or of smaller governments. Defense alliances are less able to defend their members. As such, people in the original position will seek to design their defense collective to be a permanent bond for collective defense.

However, the negative aspects of alliances are not as relevant for domestic or nested coercive collectives. Many of the historical concepts of federalism do not address external defense. They are focused on domestic issues. For example, the anarchistic socialist Pierre-Joseph

Proudhon, who lived in the first part of the nineteenth century, viewed federalism as a nonpermanent union between different domestic governmental units and groups of people.[299] The exit of a nested collective from an alliance with other nested collectives may reduce the effectiveness of the union for the remaining members, but all the members of the nested collectives are still under the protection of the defense collective.

It is possible that many members of a diverse defense collective may want to participate in a large common market in which there are no tariffs and there is free movement of people. They can form a large nested collective to accomplish this, or they can join smaller nested collectives with differing laws and have these nested collectives establish a common-market alliance. The common-market union can have a broad range of characteristics. It can be a permanent agreement among the domestic governments with penalties for noncompliance enforced by a third party chosen by the members of the alliance. It can be for a limited term that requires periodic renegotiation. Alternatively, it can be a long-term agreement that allows new nested collectives to join and existing nested collectives to exit. Entry and exit can potentially be allowed with or without cause and with or without penalties.

Political scientist Peter Kurrild-Klitgaard's arguments for "opting-out" as a method of addressing conflicts seem to be applicable to these types of domestic alliances.[300] The specific agreement for the domestic alliance will depend on the worldviews of the parties as they change from time to time, the original alliance agreement, and the collective decision-making apparatus utilized by the nested collectives. The important point is that people exiting the original position have more degrees of freedom in designing the constitutions for nested collectives than they have for designing the constitution of the overall defense collective.

AMERICAN FEDERALISM

The third type of federalist concept is "American Federalism," conceived by the negotiators of the Constitution. Using Riker's definition, like collectivity, it is a specific type of federalist structure. It is a complex form of federalism and has changed over time, which has led to many different labels, including dual federalism, cooperative federalism, and coercive federalism. We will only focus on three of its characteristics. The first is the direct relationship that the central government has with its citizens. The second concerns the expansive powers of the central government in the presence of overlapping jurisdictions. The third characteristic is that the central government was formed by state governments that were effectively general coercive collectives that did not use either unanimous or majority voting to ratify any of their initial state constitutions or the US Constitution.

AMERICAN FEDERALISM: INDIVIDUALS

The first distinguishing feature of American Federalism is an advance in federal design, first developed by the founders of the United States. Prior to the US Constitution, the central government in a federalist structure was conceived as a compact between various subgovernments, and it operated through them to attempt to accomplish its goals. The consensus design of the Constitution is radically different. As Alexander Hamilton, in the *Federalist Papers*, argued:

> *The great and radical vice in the construction of the existing Confederation is in the principle of LEGISLATION for STATES or GOVERNMENTS, in their CORPORATE or COLLECTIVE CAPACITIES, and as contradistinguished from the INDIVIDUALS of which they consist. Though this principle does not run through all the powers delegated to the Union, yet it pervades and governs those on which the efficacy of the rest depends. Except as to the rule of apportionment, the United States has an indefinite discretion to make requisitions for men and money; but they have no authority to raise either, by regulations extending to the individual citizens of America.*[301]

He went on to state that

*if we still will adhere to the design of a national government,
or, which is the same thing, of a superintending power, under
the direction of a common council, we must resolve to incorporate into our plan those ingredients which may be considered
as forming the characteristic difference between a league and a
government; we must extend the authority of the Union to the
persons of the citizens—the only proper objects of government.*[302]

Under American Federalism, the central government directly
interacts with its citizens. It has the delegated power to enforce its
rules directly on its citizens without having to consult with any other
governments. This increases its overall efficiency and causes its citizens to view themselves as being members of a unified government.
American Federalism is a blend of a national government and traditional federalist principles. This aspect of American Federalism is the
same as collectivity. People in the original position form the defense
collective to accomplish specific goals. They do not first form nested
governments and use the agreed collective-decision rules for these
collectives to form the defense collective. In collectivity, people are
members of the defense collective and other coercive collectives. They
do not have to operate through one to determine the decisions of the
other. However, of the three characteristics of American Federalism,
the direct interaction of the central government with its individual citizens is the only characteristic diverse people in the original position
will compromise on and adopt as part of collectivity.

AMERICAN FEDERALISM: EXTENSIVE CENTRALIZED POWER

The second characteristic of American Federalism is the existence of
overlapping authorities and broad level of responsibilities for the central government. This is the current view of the Constitution by the
US Supreme Court. However, at the time the Constitution was being
debated, many people viewed that founding document as delegating
few authorities to the central government. For example, Madison
stated:

The powers delegated by the proposed Constitution to the federal government are few and defined. Those which are to remain in the State governments are numerous and indefinite. The former will be exercised principally on external objects, as war, peace, negotiation, and foreign commerce; with which last the power of taxation will, for the most part, be connected. . . . The regulation of commerce, it is true, is a new power; but that seems to be an addition which few oppose, and from which no apprehensions are entertained.[303]

Madison's interpretation of the power and authority of the central government under the Constitution was materially different than the actual authority the central government has legally exercised over the past 250 years. For example, in 2015, only 27 percent of the $3.9 trillion central government's net cost was spent on defense, homeland security, department of state, and veteran affairs. Total taxes raised via custom and excise taxes were only 4 percent of the $3.3 trillion revenues of the federal government.[304]

How could Madison have been so wrong? One explanation, of course, is that he was not being completely truthful in the *Federalist Papers* and that, like Hamilton, wanted a strong national government that had extensive powers. The better explanation would seem to be that, like many other people who ratified the Constitution, he underestimated the interaction of a few clauses in the Constitution, as Congress and successive Supreme Courts interpreted them. These clauses do not detail specific powers for Congress. For example, they do not directly state that Congress shall have the power and authority to:

1. build dams;
2. impose a national minimum wage;
3. regulate working conditions;
4. institute general insurance programs such as Social Security, Medicare, and universal health;
5. prohibit shipment of goods and people across state lines for any reason, including those involving immorality;

6. regulate all interstate activity, including new technology that involves citizens in more than one state such as railroads, phones, telegraph, and airlines;
7. regulate and control the prices of any goods or services;
8. impose laws and rules to regulate environmental pollution;
9. regulate marketing and manufacturing of food and drugs;
10. protect consumers;
11. operate businesses such as railroads;
12. prevent such practices as loan sharking;
13. license and operate a national bank;
14. condition the sharing of taxes with state and local governments on their adherence to central government policies; and
15. impose federally issued bills of exchange as the only legal tender.

Instead, the clauses under consideration are general statements. The four key clauses are: (i) commerce, (ii) tax and welfare, (iii) necessary and proper, and (iv) supremacy. The commerce clause provides Congress the power "to regulate Commerce with foreign Nations, and among the several States, and with the Indian tribes." The tax-and-welfare clause states: "The Congress shall have Power To lay and collect Taxes, Duties, Imposts and Excises, to pay the Debts and provide for the common Defence and general Welfare of the United States." The necessary-and-proper clause states that Congress has the authority "to make all Laws which shall be necessary and proper for carrying into Execution the foregoing Powers, and all the other Powers vested by the Constitution in the government of the United States." Finally, the supremacy clause states: "This Constitution and the Laws of the United States which shall be made in Pursuance thereof . . . shall be the supreme Law of the Land; and the Judges in every State shall be bound thereby, any Thing in the Constitution or Laws of any State to the Contrary notwithstanding."[305]

In the debate leading up to the adoption of the Constitution, many people feared that a mixture of some of these clauses could lead to virtually unlimited power by the central government. For example, Robert Yates, who was to become chief justice of New York's highest court, is thought to have written under the pseudonym Brutus, who stated:

> *The legislative power is competent to lay taxes, duties, imposts and excises; there is no limitation to this power . . . the legislature have authority to contract debts at their discretion; they are the sole judges of what is necessary, to provide for the common defense, and they only are to determine what is for the general welfare. This power, therefore, is neither more nor less than a power to lay and collect taxes, imposts and excises at their pleasure; not only the power to lay taxes unlimited as to the amount they may require, but it is perfect and absolute to raise them in any mode they please . . . the authority to lay and collect taxes is the most important of any power that can be granted; it connects with it almost all other powers, or at least will in process of time draw all others after it.[306]*

Hamilton, as part of the *Federalist Papers*, argued that these clauses in conjunction with the other parts of the Constitution would not lead to a vast central government, even though he favored a significant expansion of its authorities.

> *The administration of private justice between the citizens of the same State; the supervision of agriculture, and of the other concerns of a similar nature, all those things, in short, which are proper to be provided for by local legislation, can never be desirable cares of a general jurisdiction. It is therefore improbable, that there should exist a disposition in the federal councils, to usurp the powers with which they are connected; because the attempt to exercise those powers would be troublesome as it would be nugatory . . . It will always be far more easy for the State governments to encroach the national authorities than for the national government to encroach upon the State authorities.[307]*

The reason why these clauses, under certain interpretations, will lead to an extensive central government and why Brutus has been historically proved more prescient than Hamilton (at least as he expressed his views in the *Federalist Papers*) is twofold. One is the incentive, which was discussed in the prior chapter, for the majority to use the decision-making authority of the central government to affect their worldviews on a nationwide scale even though they could, if they so desired, limit them to statewide rules and laws. Second is the significant interconnectedness of almost all things that involve economics. The primary goal of a coercive collective and government, in general, is to increase cooperation and to increase people's interconnectedness. Over time, we would expect that the goal will be at least partially accomplished, and cooperation and trade will increase. Things that may have once been viewed as completely local will subsequently be considered as having regional, national, and global consequences. Madison, when he was president, captured the essence of this concept when he stated:

> *In the great system of political economy, having for its general object, the national welfare, every thing is related immediately or remotely to every other thing; and consequently, a power over one thing; and consequently, a power over any one thing, if not limited by some obvious and precise affinity, may amount to a power over every other. Ends & means may shift their character at the will, and according to the ingenuity of the Legislative body.*[308]

Or shift their character by the ingenuity of the Supreme Court.

In understanding the reach and interaction of these clauses, it will be helpful to understand the historical rationale for their inclusion and how their interpretation by both Congress and the courts have changed over time. As such, we will discuss each of the clauses except for the supremacy clause, which is noncontroversial in the absence of the other clauses.

Commerce Clause

Calvin Johnson, a law professor at the University of Texas, reviewed the discussion that took place at the various constitutional conventions on the commerce clause and grouped the rationale of the various proponents of the clause under four general categories.[309] He identified the most popular reason for its inclusion to be concern over taxing conflicts between the states. At the time, regulation of commerce seemed to be a euphemism for control over import and export taxes on nondomestic goods. This was the rationale that Madison, the sponsor of the clause, viewed as leading to its inclusion in the Constitution. In 1829, Madison explained the reason for the clause, writing that

> *it is very certain that it grew out of the abuse of the power by the importing States, in taxing the non-importing; and was intended as a negative & preventive provision agst. injustice among the States themselves; rather than as a power to be used for the positive purposes of the General Govt.*[310]

If Madison was correct, it is not clear why the commerce clause was needed, since, as Johnson mentions, the new Constitution provided Congress broad taxing authority and prohibited the states from taxing imports or exports.

The reason for the inclusion of the commerce clause that was least mentioned in Johnson's survey was concern over taxation of domestic imports and exports by the states. That this was a concern at all is curious since, as Johnson notes, the Articles of Confederation had a nondiscrimination clause for free people, which prohibited the imposition of a tax on out-of-state citizens. Specifically, the fourth article stated nonresidents "shall be entitled to all privileges and immunities of free citizens in the several states . . . and shall enjoy therein all the privileges of trade and commerce, subject to the same duties, impositions and restrictions as the inhabitants thereof respectively."[311] The Articles of Confederation's protection of "all the privileges of trade, and commerce" was not included in the ratified Constitution, although the interpretation by the Supreme Court that there is a "dormant" commerce clause effectively prevents the states from discriminating.

The other two reasons for the commerce clause that Johnson identified were also, in his opinion, "mercantilist" in that they either involved the desire by some for retaliatory taxes against other countries or the granting to ships owned by United States citizens the sole ability to carry goods produced in the states. From a mercantilist's perspective, the clause would give the central government the power to use taxes for these purposes, as well as other similar goals.

The commerce clause was one method of accomplishing these objectives. However, all or a subset of the states had other options to accomplish these types of objectives. They could have removed the restriction in both the Articles of Confederation and the Constitution that prohibited agreements among the states without the explicit approval of Congress. The states could have formed a common market that was overseen by elected representatives who were different than the members of Congress. Some states may have favored using import and export taxes to accomplish nonrevenue-related goals, and included this power as part of the common-market agreement or had it as another agreement among some or all the states. This reserved power of the states may have been viewed as being in direct conflict with the taxing power of the central government, since most taxes at the time were collected through import and export taxes. However, the existing constitutional provision on state import and export taxes would have eliminated this conflict.[312]

A common-market agreement among the states could have had flexible terms with a medium maturity or it could have been a permanent agreement. It could have included various penalties for noncompliance and made its terms subject to the jurisdiction of a third-party arbiter, including the central government. If the states had pursued a common market instead of adopting the commerce clause, the United States would be a much different country today. That is, of course, not what happened. The Constitution that was adopted included the commerce clause. But what powers did that clause provide to the central government? No one knows. However, "the judicial Power of the United States, shall be vested in one supreme Court."[313] The majority view of this body, as it changes from time to time, is the accepted law of the land.

In 1824, the Supreme Court, led by Chief Justice John Marshall, interpreted the commerce clause.[314] He stated, "Commerce, undoubtedly, is traffic, but it is something more; it is intercourse. It describes the commercial intercourse between nations, and parts of nations, in all its branches, and is regulated by prescribing rules for carrying on that intercourse."[315] He went on to elaborate:

> *To what commerce does this power extend? . . . these words comprehend every species of commercial intercourse between the United States and foreign nations . . . The subject to which the power is next applied is to commerce "among the several States." The word "among" means intermingled with . . . Commerce among the States cannot stop at the external boundary line of each State, but may be introduced into the interior.[316]*

The court's interpretation allowed the central government to regulate all interstate commerce as it changed over time, including transportation of goods and people. It included the power to regulate various industries, including trucking, railways, airlines, electric power, pipelines, radio, telephones, and stock exchanges.

In 1913, the Supreme Court upheld the Mann Act, which prohibited the interstate transportation of women for prostitution based on its interpretation of the commerce clause. Justice Joseph McKenna for the court stated that

> *we are one people, and the powers reserved to the states and those conferred on the nation are adapted to be exercised, whether independently or concurrently, to promote the general welfare, material and moral . . . if the facility of interstate transportation can be taken away from the demoralization of lotteries, the debasement of obscene literature, the contagion of diseased cattle or persons, the impurity of food and drugs, the like facility can be taken away from the systematic enticement to and the enslavement in prostitution and debauchery of women.[317]*

The broad interpretation of the commerce clause allowed the majority view of the central government on morals, in at least some instances, to supplant the views of the citizens of the states.

In a series of twentieth-century rulings, based on its understanding of the commerce clause, the Supreme Court validated a variety of central government laws, including regulation of food and drugs,[318] the right to form unions,[319] rules concerning minimum wages,[320] regulations concerning working conditions,[321] and regulation of milk prices.[322] Their reasoning can be summed up in the opinion of one of the cases that

> *the commerce power is not confined in its exercise to the regulation of commerce among the states. It extends to those activities intrastate which so affect interstate commerce, or the exertion of the power of Congress over it, as to make regulation of them appropriate means to the attainment of a legitimate end, the effective execution of the granted power to regulate interstate commerce . . . no form of state activity can constitutionally thwart the regulatory power granted by the commerce clause to Congress. Hence, the reach of that power extends to those intrastate activities which in a substantial way interfere or obstruct the exercise of the granted power.*[323]

These various rulings provided the legal basis for Congress to pass laws designed to increase farmers' incomes.

One of the beneficiaries from these central government programs was Roscoe Filburn, a fifth-generation farmer born in 1902. He had a small farm outside Dayton, Ohio, that he had inherited from his parents in the 1930s. Like many farmers, he raised dairy cattle and poultry and locally sold milk, eggs, and chickens. He also used some of his acreage to plant winter wheat to feed his animals, mill flour to make bread, and to harvest seeds for future plantings.

The price of agricultural commodities, including livestock, increased significantly during the First World War, leading to higher income for farmers. However, due to rising interest rates, recession, decreased exports, and technological change, prices fell following the war, causing farm incomes to fall and the value of farms to plummet. The federal government attempted to raise farmers' incomes by passing a series of tariffs that increased taxes on imported goods. Unfortunately, foreign governments also increased their import taxes, and US exports continued to fall. In the 1930s, Congress responded by passing a series of agricultural bills designed to increase farmers' incomes. The acts allowed the central government to take a variety of actions, including nonrecourse loans made to farmers to increase their indexed "real" incomes to those that existed prior to 1920, loans to foreign governments so they would purchase US agricultural products, direct purchases, destruction of "excess" production, incentivized reductions in planted acreage, licensing requirements for sellers of agricultural products, and marketing orders. These programs led to higher domestic prices for agricultural products and livestock. They increased the incomes of those involved in the agricultural business, including farmers, food distributors, food processors, and farm-equipment manufacturers and dealers. This also resulted in increased prices for domestic consumers, a significant number of defaulted loans to the US government, and a large surplus of government-owned food products. The surplus led to the development of a nationwide school-lunch program and to welfare programs like food stamps. It also led to the massive destruction of unsold inventory, including the killing of millions of small pigs.

Even though Filburn benefitted from these government programs, he and a few other farmers sued the government in 1941 because they had been fined for excess production of wheat. They thought they had been treated unjustly because the fine for overproduction had been increased between the time they planted their wheat in the fall and the time they harvested it in the summer. Claude Wickard, the secretary of agriculture, never publicly mentioned that the fine for overproduction was going to be increased. A component of their argument was that the federal government did not have the power to regulate their planting of wheat, since they were directly consuming almost all their production and were not engaged in wheat "commerce." In a unanimous decision, the Supreme Court disagreed. Justice Robert Jackson, writing for the court, stated, "But even if [Filburn's] activities be local, and though it may not be regarded as commerce, it may still, whatever its nature, be reached by Congress if it exerts a substantial economic effect on interstate commerce."[324]

Jackson continued:

> *It is well established by decisions of this Court that the power to regulate commerce includes the power to regulate the prices at which commodities in that commerce are dealt in and practices affecting such prices . . . One of the primary purposes of the Act in question was to increase the market price of wheat . . . But if we assume that it is never marketed, it supplies a need of the man who grew it which would otherwise be reflected by purchases in the open market. Home-grown wheat in this sense competes with wheat in commerce . . . This record leaves us no doubt that Congress may properly have considered that wheat consumed on the farm when grown, if wholly outside the scheme of regulation, would have a substantial effect in defeating and obstructing its purpose to stimulate trade therein at increased prices.*[325]

Agriculture, locally grown and consumed, even personally grown and consumed, is viewed within the purview of the "limited" central government. Based on Hamilton's earlier quotes, he would be happy but surprised at the expansiveness wrought by the commerce clause. As interpreted by successive Supreme Court decisions, the commerce clause provides for a broad general central government with respect to virtually all economic activity. Given the interconnectedness of trade and human cooperation, it could someday lead the courts to rule that the commerce clause also applies to noneconomic activity, since all human activity has some economic consequences.

The commerce clause is not a clause that diverse people in the original position will include in the constitution for the central government. It could be a clause in one or more of the domestic or nested collectives. But diverse people in the original position will reject it as a delegated central government power because it can be interpreted as providing the central government broad domestic powers to overrule the decisions of the nested collectives.

The expansive nature of the commerce clause, under its current interpretation, will effectively make a defense collective into a general defense collective, reducing or eliminating the benefits some members receive by being a member of nested and local collectives. While people who have a worldview like John Rawls may favor a policy like the commerce clause, people who have worldviews like that of Hayek or Nozick will not. Diverse people in the original position will allow domestic governments to make independent commerce decisions because that compromise decision increases net gains. Even though there can be problems and issues involving commerce that involve all or nearly all the members of the defense collective, the members of the defense collective will have diverse views on the best method to address them. Universal agreement does not exist on these issues. By incorporating a provision such as the commerce clause into the constitution for the defense collective, every member of that collective is subject to majority decision on the issues involving commerce. They have better options. A more flexible approach will be for the members to narrow the purview of the defense collective and encourage the various other coercive collectives in which they are members to reach agreements to address collective issues involving commerce.

Welfare Clause

The Supreme Court's current interpretation of the tax-and-welfare clause in the Constitution is similarly expansive. For example, in 1987, the Supreme Court upheld the federal government's authority to impose a national minimum drinking age by withholding some highway funding from the states. As Chief Justice William Rehnquist stated in the opinion for the court:

> *The Constitution empowers Congress "to pay the Debts and provide for the common Defence and general Welfare of the United States" . . . Incident to this power, Congress may attach conditions on the receipt of federal funds . . . The breadth of this power*

*was made clear in United States v. Butler . . . where the Court
. . . determined that the "power of Congress to authorize expenditure of public moneys for public purposes is not limited by
the direct grants of legislative power found in the Constitution."
Thus, objectives not thought to be within Article I's "enumerated
legislative fields," . . . may nevertheless be attained through the
use of the spending power and the conditional grant of federal
funds.*[326]

He continued:

*The spending power is of course not unlimited . . . The first of these
limitations is derived from the language from the Constitution
itself: the exercise of spending power must be in pursuit of
"the general welfare" . . . In considering whether a particular
expenditure is intended to serve general public purposes, courts
should defer substantially to the judgment of Congress.*[327]

As Justice Rehnquist stated, there are limits to the powers granted
by this clause. That said, as currently interpreted, the few restrictions
on its use do little to limit the scope of the federal government. Justice
Sandra Day O'Connor stated in her dissenting opinion in the case:

*If the spending power is to be limited only by Congress' notion of
the general welfare, the reality, given the vast financial resources
of the Federal Government, is that the Spending Clause gives
"power to the Congress to tear down the barriers, to invade the
states' jurisdiction, and to become parliament of the whole people, subject to no restrictions save such as are self-imposed."*[328]

The broad interpretation of the welfare clause by both Congress
and the Supreme Court has led to significant expansion of the central
government's authority and influence over the lives of its citizens. The
programs that are dependent on this understanding include such varied public initiatives as unemployment compensation, Social Security,
Medicare, land-grant colleges, disaster relief, funding for the arts,

maximum speed limits, regulation of public billboards, and increases in women's college sports programs. While the welfare clause is currently perceived to be an additional power of the central government, many people who voted for the Constitution thought it was intended to limit, restrict, or reduce central government authority.

In 1791, Congress passed a bill to authorize the creation of the first bank of the United States, over the objections of Madison. The president, George Washington, asked his attorney general, Edmund Randolph, for his opinion on the constitutionality of the bill. Even though Randolph had introduced the original Virginia plan for the Constitution that called for a strong national government and was a staunch supporter of Virginia ratifying the Constitution, he advised Washington that the bank was unconstitutional. Washington then asked his secretary of state, Thomas Jefferson, for his opinion. Jefferson also thought the bank was unconstitutional. He viewed it as violating the commerce clause and the necessary-and-proper clause, as well as the tax-and-welfare clause. In his written opinion to Washington, he stated:

> *They are not to lay taxes ad libitum for any purpose they please; but only to pay the debts or provide for the welfare of the Union. In like manner, they are not to do anything they please to provide for the general welfare, but only to lay taxes for that purpose. To consider the latter phrase . . . as giving a distinct and independent power to do any act they please, which might be for the good of the Union, would render all the preceding and subsequent enumerations of power completely useless . . . Certainly no such universal power was meant to be given them. It was intended to lace them up straitly within the enumerated powers.*[329]

Similarly, in 1817, Jefferson in a letter to his former treasury secretary Albert Gallatin stated, "Our tenet ever was . . . that Congress had not unlimited powers to provide for the general welfare, but were restrained to those specifically enumerated; and that, as it was never meant that they should provide for that welfare but by the exercise of the enumerated powers."[330]

Jefferson was not alone in his views on the restrictive nature of the welfare clause. In 1791, Madison, as a member of the House of Representatives from Virginia, argued that the bank bill was unconstitutional. Part of his reasoning concerned the welfare clause. He stated:

> *No argument could be drawn from the terms "common defence, and general welfare." The power as to these general purposes, was limited to acts laying taxes for them; and the general purposes themselves were limited and explained by the particular enumeration subjoined. To understand these terms in any sense, that would justify the power in question, would give to Congress an unlimited power; would render nugatory the enumeration of particular powers; would supercede all the powers reserved to the state governments. These terms are copied from the articles of confederation.*[331]

Later, in 1799, in a report to the Virginia legislature, he stated that

> *it will scarcely be said . . . they were ever understood to be either a general grant of power, or to authorize the requisition or application of money, by the old Congress, to the common defence and general welfare, except in cases afterwards enumerated, which explained and limited their meaning; and if such was the limited meaning attached to these phrases in the very instrument revised and remodeled by the present constitution, it can never be supposed that when copied into this constitution, a different meaning ought to be attached to them.*[332]

Washington considered vetoing the bank bill but asked his treasury secretary, Hamilton, the chief proponent in his administration of a nationally owned bank, his opinion on its constitutionality. Hamilton disagreed with his fellow cabinet members and viewed the bank as constitutional, relying primarily on the central government's ability to raise debt, the commerce clause, and the necessary-and-proper clause. Washington sided with his treasury secretary and did not veto the bank bill. Interestingly, Hamilton did not use the welfare clause in his justification for the bank. However, he did use it to justify another proposal he made to Congress to use central government resources to subsidize certain private manufacturing exporters.

In his report on manufacturers, Hamilton stated:

The terms "general Welfare" were doubtless intended to signify more than was expressed or imported in those which preceded; otherwise, numerous exigencies incident to the affairs of a nation would have been left without a provision . . . It is, therefore, of necessity, left to the discretion of the National Legislature to pronounce upon the objects which concern the general welfare . . . The only qualification of the generality of the phrase in question, which seems to be admissible, is this: That the object to which an appropriation of money is to be made general and not local; its operation extending in fact, or by possibility, throughout the Union, and not being confined to a particular spot.[333]

Supreme Court Justice Joseph Story used this statement by Hamilton verbatim in his 1833 book on the Constitution.[334] In the preface, he stated that his book was primarily based on the *Federalist Papers* and on "the extraordinary Judgments of Mr. Chief Justice Marshall upon constitutional law."[335] In his review of the welfare clause, Justice Story concluded that Hamilton's interpretation of the clause was correct based on three reasons: (i) "language of the clause"; (ii) it is "expedient, if not indispensable, for the due operations of the national government"; and (iii) "from the early, constant and decided maintenance of it by the government and its functionaries, as well as by many of our ablest statesmen from the very commencement of the Constitution."[336] Why should we care what an associate judge of the Supreme Court, who was eight years old at the time the Constitution was ratified, wrote in a book published in 1833? Interestingly and somewhat surprisingly, it is the basis of the Supreme Court opinion on the meaning of the welfare clause that is still relied upon today.

In 1936, for the first time, the Supreme Court ruled on the general welfare clause. Justice Owen Roberts gave the opinion of the court:

> *Since the foundation of the Nation, sharp differences have persisted as to the true interpretation of the phrase. Madison asserted it amounted to no more than a reference to the other powers enumerated in the subsequent clause of the same section; that, as the United States is a government of limited and enumerated powers, the grant of power to tax and spend for the general welfare must be confined to the enumerated legislative fields committed to the Congress . . . Hamilton, on the other hand, maintained the clause confers a power separate and distinct from these later enumerated, is not restricted in meaning by the grant of them, and Congress consequently has a substantive power to tax and to appropriate, limited only by the requirement that it shall be exercised to provide for the general welfare of the United States . . . Mr. Justice Story in his Commentaries, espouses the Hamiltonian position . . . Study of all these leads us to conclude that the reading advocated by Mr. Justice Story is the correct one.*[337]

As with the commerce clause, diverse people in the original position will not agree to form a diverse defense collective whose actions are governed by a constitution that has a provision as broad as the current interpretation of the welfare clause. A defense collective with a nearly unlimited authority to raise taxes, and which is authorized to use those taxes for the "general welfare," is essentially a general defense collective. A diverse group of people will have varying views on how best to improve the general welfare. Some, like those who share some combination of the views expressed by Rawls and John Harsanyi may think that broad "national" approaches are the best. Even then, they may disagree as to the best national approach. Unfortunately, the use of majority voting to determine the general welfare will not determine the best solution, nor will it determine the freedom-maximizing solution; it will only determine the solution that is most popular. People who share the worldviews of Hayek and Nozick will not want to join a defense collective in which they are subject to the majority view on the general welfare. They will not join a defense collective that has the authority to use its broad taxing powers to achieve the majority view regarding the general welfare. They and others will only join a defense collective whose authority over the general welfare is limited to narrow goals and means. While it is difficult to manage and run a government subject to a specific contract, a narrow and specific contract is the only method of limiting the scope and reach of the defense collective. Almost any ambiguity in the face of societal interconnectedness and majority voting will lead to a general defense collective.

Necessary-and-Proper Clause

The third important clause and the final one that will be reviewed is the necessary-and-proper clause. It states that Congress shall have the authority to make all laws that are necessary and proper to carry into execution the foregoing powers. It is currently interpreted as allowing Congress to pass all laws that have some effect on their delegated powers. It is viewed as giving Congress the means to attempt to accomplish their more general delegated powers and objectives. The meaning of the clause was specifically addressed by the Supreme Court in its unanimous 1819 opinion on the constitutionality of the second national bank act. Chief Justice Marshall in his opinion stated, "We find that it frequently imports no more than that one thing is convenient, or useful, or essential to another. To employ the means necessary to an end is generally understood as employing any means calculated to produce the end."[338]

Justice Marshall, as he did with the prior clause that we have reviewed, agreed with Hamilton's view of the necessary-and-proper clause. In Hamilton's 1791 opinion to Washington on the constitutionality of the first national bank bill, he stated that

> *necessary often means no more than needful, requisite, incidental, useful or conducive to . . . The whole turn of the clause containing it indicates, that it was the intent of the Convention,*

by that clause, to give a liberal latitude to the exercise of the specified powers.[339]

He continued:

The degree in which a measure is necessary, can never be a test of the legal right to adopt it; that must be a matter of opinion, and can only be a test of expediency. The relation between the measure and the end; between the nature of the mean employed toward the execution of a power, and the object of that power must be the criterion of constitutionality, not the more or less necessity or utility.[340]

While diverse people, exiting the original position, will not delegate the powers currently construed by the commerce and welfare clauses, they will agree to a condition like the necessary-and-proper clause. However, they will use their best efforts to construct the words of the clause so that almost no one could interpret it the way Justice Marshall viewed the necessary-and-proper clause. As discussed previously, people cannot fully enumerate every possible future decision the defense collective will make. They need to give the elected leadership of the defense collective the authority to pass laws to accomplish the objectives they assigned to the defense collective. As such, they must trust their elected representatives to make the appropriate decisions concerning the means, tactics, and strategies to accomplish the goals of the collective. In Justice Story's view, the clause was not necessary but was included to reduce "doubt" that the central government had the necessary ancillary powers to bring about the delegated powers.[341]

While Justice Story may be correct as to why it was included in the Constitution, his rationale is not the reason it will be included in the constitution forming and governing a diverse defense collective. In fact, many people forming a defense collective will be concerned that his, Justice Marshall's, and Hamilton's interpretations will be used by the majority to expand the delegated powers of the defense collective. Many people exiting the original position will be concerned with the critical question of how to give requisite authority to an entity that has limited delegated powers when those authorities involve coercive power and no other entity has the authority to overrule the entity's interpretation of its powers.

This concern will lead to a proviso similar to the necessary-and-proper clause both to give the government ancillary authority to exercise its delegated authority and to place a limit on the nature of those ancillary laws. Many people will be concerned that the majority will use the ancillary powers to pass laws and rules designed to accomplish nondelegated goals even though these laws may have some effect on delegated goals. To prevent this usurpation of power, they will compromise and limit the defense collective's laws to ones that are "requisite and appropriate." They will not limit them to ones that are "indispensably necessary," since they will want Congress to use its best judgment as to the means of accomplishing a goal without being limited to those means that are "absolutely necessary." However, they will include language in the constitution that is difficult to interpret as providing the central government with an ability to expand its domestic scope. This language will limit these ancillary laws to laws and rules that are means to a delegated end and not ends themselves, even if they have some effect on some delegated end. Interestingly, Robert Natelson[342] seems to argue that this was the original meaning of the clause and part of the central government's "agency" function. [343]

The constitution for a diverse defense collective will provide for a limit on the powers and authorities it grants to its elected officials and to the scope of the defense collective. A component of this limit will include a method for overruling the laws and rules established by these officials and their delegates if they exceed their power and authority. A subcomponent of this limit will be a restriction that all laws and rules must be designed to satisfy a delegated power or goal. Compliance with this restriction will be assigned to the judgment of an independent third party. This is not how Justice Story, Hamilton, and Justice Marshall viewed the necessary-and-proper clause. They viewed the word "necessary" to mean "*needful, requisite, incidental, useful*, or *conducive to*."[344] However, for most people there is a significant difference between "needful" and "useful" and between "requisite" and "incidental." Diverse people in the original position who agree to join a limited defense collective will not compromise and agree to a clause that reads, "Congress can make all laws which shall be incidental or useful for carrying into execution the foregoing powers"—at least as these words are used today. They will be concerned that this clause will authorize their future legislatures to pass laws that are goals themselves or affect goals beyond those that have been delegated to them. This wording will allow the passage of any law that has some incidental impact on a delegated power. They will reject this wording and compromise on a clause that restricts these ancillary laws to those that are *requisite and appropriate, not incidental or simply useful*, to accomplish a delegated power.

The people forming a diverse defense collective will empower a third party such as a court to determine if their representatives are exceeding their authority. They will authorize the court to make a judgment that the ancillary law is designed to accomplish a delegated goal. They will expect the court to reject a law as unconstitutional if it is just *incidental* to that delegated goal. They will not expect the court to determine if the law or rule works or accomplishes its designated goal. However, the court will have the authority to question whether the law is a goal of the legislation and only has some incidental, useful, or tangential relationship to a delegated power. Similarly, the court will be given the authority to reject a rule or law as unconstitutional if it is intended as a means to accomplish a goal or a power not delegated to the defense collective even if it can positively affect a designated power of the defense collective. Determining intent is an important component of limiting the defense collective to its delegated responsibilities.

The court or third party will be expected to reject a law if it is "too" broad to accomplish a delegated goal or if they judge that the defense collective strayed "too" far into the area of nondelegated goals. As part of their authority, the court can examine the work papers relating to the rationale and the justification for the ancillary law, including internal debates from various parts of the defense-collective administration. This is, of course, not the role that either Justice Marshall or Hamilton thought was appropriate for the Supreme Court, or any court for that matter. Not surprisingly, Justice Story also did not think that Congress's judgments and decisions with respect to this clause were subject to judicial overview if these ancillary laws had some effect on a delegated power. He stated:

> *If the legislature possesses a right of choice as the means, who can limit that choice? Who is appointed an umpire, or arbiter in cases, where a discretion is confided to a government? The very idea of such a controlling authority in the exercise of its powers is a virtual denial of the supremacy of the government in regard to its powers. It repeals the supremacy of the national government, proclaimed in the constitution.*[345]

Justice Story's concept of the delegated powers of a limited government are substantially at odds with the compromise that will be reached between people with differing worldviews who are in the original position. There is a significant difference between a limited collective and a general collective or between a limited government and a general government, especially as it relates to this clause. People in the original position who agree to form a diverse defense collective will limit its powers. A key component to limiting its power and scope is the authority and ability of a third party to question any law as to whether it is: (i) designed to accomplish a delegated goal, (ii) too broad to accomplish a delegated goal, or (iii) expanding the collective's goals. The third party will not be expected to question the overall effectiveness or necessity of the law. But the authority and ability to question the motivation for the law and its overall scope is critical to preventing a limited coercive collective from becoming a general coercive collective.

A constitution for a general collective that does not restrict the goals of that collective will not give this type of authority to a court or a third party. At the time of the ratification of the Constitution, all the states were general governments and their various constitutions did not incorporate a necessary-and-proper clause. The federal government was originally designed to be limited and obviously did have such a clause. This distinction did not seem to matter to Justice Story, Justice Marshall, or Hamilton. However, Randolph, in his opinion to Washington on the constitutionality of the first national bank, made such a distinction. As Hamilton stated, "The attorney general admits the rule, but takes a distinction between a State and the Federal Constitution. The latter, he thinks, ought to be construed with greater strictness, because there is more danger of error in defining partial rather than General powers."[346] Hamilton rejected this view and thought the central government required more latitude, since it was concerned with national issues. People who form and join a diverse defense collective will reject Hamilton's opinions on the expansive needs of the central government.

While the central government of the United States was purportedly designed to be a limited government, its current powers are extensive and extend much beyond those powers possessed by the states that are viewed as general governments. Diverse people who agree to exit anarchy for the benefits of both collective defense and other collective actions will not bestow any of their collectives with the full suite of powers currently viewed as delegated to the federal government of the United States. Its powers are simply too broad to incorporate the different worldviews of people in the original position. Its powers will allow the majority to impose their worldviews on the minority on issues and subjects far afield from concerns involving collective defense. Given the expansiveness of such concepts as money, commerce, revenue, welfare, taxes, and "necessary," it is quite easy, as we have seen, for members of Congress and the Supreme Court to effectively turn a limited defense collective into a general government.

AMERICAN FEDERALISM: STATES

The third and final characteristic of American Federalism is the structure of state governments. Nested collectives under collectivity are significantly different than states at the time of ratification of the Constitution. The states were all general governments. Suffrage was limited and representation was skewed. Furthermore, towns, districts, and counties were just instrumentalities of the states.

Legislative Scope of the State Governments

The thirteen states that joined together to form the United States were originally English colonies or provinces. Their original governance structure under English rule was like those of the private entities discussed in chapters 6 and 15. Their charters differed, but all were negotiated documents between the English crown and the founders or proprietors of the organizations. Over time, most provinces converted into royal colonies with some amount of local governance. But ultimate authority over the rules of the colonies resided in England. Their local governance structure, immediately prior to the American Revolution, was not the result of any type of voting among the general population. Instead, it was a product of their original charters, the views of the English government, and the views of local politicians.

At the beginning of the American Revolution, a subset of the citizens of each of the colonies seized coercive power from England and effectively converted each of the colonies into states.[347] In two of the states, the colonial legislatures assumed control and decided to govern the state under their unamended colonial charters. Self-appointed revolutionary committees of citizens took control of the other provinces. Some of these committees adopted new state constitutions. Others called for state constitutional conventions. The delegates to these state constitutional conventions became the new legislature in some of these states.

While the state charters and constitutions varied, with some placing restrictions on the laws and actions of the state, none of them placed limits on the scope of state activities. None of them reserved any powers to their citizens. And none of these governing documents allowed their citizens to form new coercive entities outside the power of the state. As such, each of the original states, as well as all the states today, were general governments. Their scope, prior to the ratification of the US Constitution, was unlimited. Even today, the only instrument that limits the scope of their activities is the Constitution.

The expansiveness of the powers of the state governments, at the time of the American Revolution, is readily understandable. The English government was and is a general government. When the subset of citizens seized control, a power vacuum developed that was filled by the ruling committees and legislatures. Each state effectively became mini Englands, minus the concept of monarchy, by vesting themselves with a combination of English power and their delegated local authorities. For example, the Rhode Island legislature that had been elected subject to the rules of the 1663 Rhode Island Royal Charter by King Charles II declared independence from England in May 1776. The legislature, by legislative decree, adopted the royal charter as the state's fundamental governing document and assumed control over the state government. The charter had established Rhode Island as a corporate entity and body politic that was essentially owned by the residents of the colony and subject to the laws of England, as they were modified from time to time. The charter charged the general assembly with "managing and dispatching of the affairs" of the company and "to make, ordeyne, constitute or repeal, such lawes statutes, orders and ordinances . . . shall seeme meete for the goode nad welfare of the sayd Company . . . bee not contrary and repugnant unto, butt, as neare as may bee, agreeable to the lawes of this our realme of England, considering the nature and constitutions of the place and people there."[348] The general assembly also had responsibility for establishing courts, appointing judges, and enforcing its law through fines and imprisonment. The Rhode Island charter did not in any way limit the scope of the activities of the general assembly and it endowed the general assembly with the monopoly over coercive power in the colony.

The coercive power of the Rhode Island general assembly was expansive but not unconstrained. For example, their laws and actions had to comport with English law. Like many people at the time, Elisha R. Potter Sr., who was the speaker of the assembly for many years, thought the assembly's powers should be more constrained. In 1818, he stated:

> *I am not afraid of exercising the powers of this house: I am not afraid to declare my views of the general assembly. The powers of this house are unlimited: they being without a written constitution, are omnipotent: they have as much right to govern the affairs of this state and the citizens, as the Supreme Ruler of the Universe has to manage his own affairs.*[349]

However, even Potter never proposed that Rhode Island should limit the scope of its authorized activities. The English government had certain limits on its actions but did not have any limit on the scope of its activities.

Rhode Island's coercive powers are just one example of the extent that the states were general governments. In late 1775, New Hampshire's and South Carolina's revolutionary committees solicited the Second Continental Congress's advice on the establishment of a state government. Congress responded that each should "call a full and free representation of the people, and that the representatives, if they think it necessary, establish such a form of government, as, in their judgment, will best produce the happiness of the people and most effectually secure peace and good order."[350] The New Hampshire committee sent notices to the towns in the province; most of them subsequently elected delegates to a province-wide convention. In January 1776, the delegates adopted a temporary constitution, and the delegates became the new government of the province. The constitution essentially vested all coercive power for the province in the popularly elected assembly.

This constitution was highly controversial for a variety of reasons, including the fact that the citizens of New Hampshire never directly voted for it. Three years later, another constitutional convention was elected by the majority of authorized voters. The constitution that was produced was rejected by the inhabitants of the state in town meetings. In 1781, another convention was elected, and it drafted another constitution, based on the recently adopted constitution of neighboring Massachusetts. Its ratification required a two-thirds vote by those residents who voted. It was also rejected. The convention stayed in session, and finally in 1783 a constitution was drafted and approved in 1784 by the *majority* of voters.

The new constitution had an extensive bill of rights and provided the ability for local governments and religious societies to elect their own teachers. It divided the coercive power of the state into three divisions: legislative, executive, and judicial. The legislative power was divided into two chambers, the senate and the house. "The senate and house . . . shall be stiled THE GENERAL COURT OF NEW

HAMPSHIRE . . . full power and authority are hereby given and granted to the said general-court, from time to time, to make, ordain and establish, all manner of wholesome and reasonable orders, laws, statutes, ordinances, directives and instructions . . . as they may judge for the benefit and welfare of this State."[351] Nothing in the constitution limited the scope of legislation, including the regulation and formation of local governments. While the general court was subject to the bill of rights and other restrictions in the state constitution, they were the sole judge of rules that improved the welfare of the citizens of New Hampshire as well as the only determinant of the reasonableness of these laws. As such, the legislature passed a wide range of bills that determined who could vote in local elections, awarded exclusive rights for individuals to operate ferry boats, approved lotteries, established new towns, provided for troops, maintained lighthouses, naturalized citizens, regulated commerce with other states and nations, and regulated commodities, including flaxseed, potash, "pearlash," beef, and pork. The legislature encouraged importation of drugs and wood in dyeing of cloth and passed laws protecting fish and deer.[352] Clearly, the New Hampshire government, like the government of Rhode Island, was a general government with few restrictions on its legislative power and no limit on the scope of its power.

The South Carolina revolutionary committee that asked the Continental Congress's advice in 1775 on the formation of a government had its start at the end of 1773 in a number of meetings in Charleston. A gathering in early 1774 established a "committee" to organize future meetings. A series of meetings were called, including three in July 1774 of representatives from the entire state. On July seventh they elected the delegates to the first Continental Congress, and on the eighth appointed a general committee of ninety-nine men to govern the meetings.[353] To expand their representation of the residents of the state, this committee announced that a "General Provincial Committee" was going to be formed, consisting of 184 delegates. Even though it was designed to make state governance more democratic, only forty-six of its members were from the backcountry that had the largest number of free people.[354] The General Provincial Committee responded to the Continental Congress's suggestions on the formation of a government by drafting a constitution and approving it without either a separate convention or submitting it to the people. Following the approval of the constitution, the General Provincial Committee became the General Assembly of South Carolina.

The first constitution of South Carolina vested all coercive power in the general assembly. There were no limits to the scope of its legislative authority and almost no restrictions on its power. Two years later, the general assembly drafted a new constitution and again approved it without submitting it to a popular vote. It divided the general assembly into a senate and house of representatives, both of which were to be elected by eligible voters of the towns and parishes. The new constitution provided for a limited number of rights for the freemen but did establish liberty of the press. It allowed for a change of the constitution by majority vote of the general assembly, and it continued to have apportioned representation dominated by the minority of white men in the lowlands. Another constitution was adopted in 1790, again without being submitted to the inhabitants of the state. Each of these constitutions vested complete coercive power over the region of South Carolina and its residents in the general assembly with few constraints on its power. And as with the other states, there were no curbs on the scope of its legislative authority.

The expansive powers that these original constitutions and charters granted to the states are an important element distinguishing collectivity from American Federalism. Each state was essentially a relatively small general defense collective. Even though each state had a diverse population in which people had differing worldviews, none had any limitations on the scope of their activities. While some people in the governmental structure of collectivity will opt to be members of general domestic collectives, the members of the defense collective will not agree to make it a general defense collective. Nor will everyone be members of general nested collectives. The credible equilibrium between diverse people will result in at least some people joining limited nested collectives.

A key feature of American Federalism is the centralization of authority within each state. Interestingly, this massive power the states possessed is a major reason for the increase in federal authority. The broad scope and the unrepresentative nature of these governments led many people to prefer an expansive federal government. In fact, the residents of many states thought their best option was to solicit federal government support to rectify the perceived injustices of the actions of the state governments. Members of the federal congress and the president, disagreeing with the policies of many of the states, broadly interpreted their power, and with Supreme Court concurrence, extended federal government influence over many general state activities.

Some of these original constitutions, including the federal constitution, stated they represented the will of the people coming together to form a union. However, none of them were approved by all the people, none were approved by a supermajority of the people, and none were approved by a majority of the people. All were written by a small group of white men and approved by a minority of the population. The state constitutions did establish a representative form of government. However, representatives were to be chosen by *some* of the residents of designated geographic areas under state control.

Voting Rights

While the qualification to vote differed by state, no state in the late eighteenth century allowed the entire adult population to vote. John Adams, the second president of the United States and the drafter of the Massachusetts constitution, held an opinion common at the time of the American Revolution, that suffrage should be limited. In a letter to a friend he wrote:

> *Such is the Frailty of the human Heart, that very few Men who have no Property, have any judgment on their own. They talk and vote as they are directed by Some Man of Property, who has attached their Minds to his Interest . . . [they are] to all Intents and Purposes as much dependent upon others, who will please to feed, cloath, and employ them, as Women are upon their Husbands, or Children on their Parents.* [355]

In the same letter, Adams stated, "There will be no End of it. New Claims will arise, women will demand a Vote . . . and every Man who has not a Farthing, will demand an equal Voice with any other in all Acts of State."[356]

Collectivity incorporates a much different conception of the importance of the individual, since negotiation and bargaining between diverse groups of people causes each person's worldview to be considered in the rules that govern the coercive collective. If everyone knows each person's worldview and can fully prespecify every decision, then collectivity will result in laws that minimize aggregate freedom losses. Without these abilities, diverse people in the original position who join in common defense will approximate collectivity by negotiating constitutions that form a limited defense collective, limited nested collectives, general nested collectives, and a polycentric agreement structure between the nested collectives. Representatives of these coercive collectives will be chosen through nonunanimous voting of all the members of each of the coercive collectives. The founding constitutions will be chosen by unanimous decision. This is the credible equilibrium result, not because some people have the moral view that each person's vote should count or because they think people should have equal political rights, but because each person adds some value to the collective effort. Each person uses their relevance to other people to negotiate equal political rights. Even if people with less wealth have higher discount rates and are more anxious to exit anarchy, their ability to bargain with a broad range of people will negate the inherent advantages of wealth and income.

Not everyone at the time of the American Revolution shared Adams's view on voting. Many states expanded male suffrage to include all male taxpayers, and most initially allowed freemen to vote irrespective of the color of their skin. Nonetheless, suffrage was significantly less than will result from collectivity. For example, in late-eighteenth-century Rhode Island, the legislature limited voters to freemen over the age of twenty-one who took an oath and who owned land worth at least forty (British) pounds. Restricting voting in this way followed from the view, shared by Adams, that property owners have a broader interest in the welfare of a political entity than tenant farmers, laborers, indentured servants, slaves, women (except property-owning widows), and people under twenty-one. Over time, under these voting rules, Rhode Island increasingly became less democratic as the population increased and people migrated to the cities.

New Hampshire was one of the most democratic states at the time of the American Revolution, allowing for broad male suffrage and apportionment that varied with population. Its constitution allowed all males over twenty-one, who paid a poll tax, to vote for both branches of the legislature. It apportioned the House of Representatives by the relative population of the towns and parishes. However, it limited members of the legislature by age, residency, and property.

South Carolina, on the other hand, was one of the least democratic states. It had a massive slave population. Adult white males, the only people who could vote in South Carolina, were less than 14 percent of the population at the time of the ratification of the US Constitution.[357] Donald Ratcliffe estimates that only 80 percent of adult white males were authorized to vote due to requirements that voters either own land or pay a minimum amount of taxes.[358] Furthermore, at least until 1808, South Carolina apportioned the legislature by a combination of both population and wealth. The low country, in and around Charleston, accounted for the bulk of the wealth and a minority of the white population. This allowed adult white males living in this part of the state to elect over half of the representatives to the state congress.[359] This seems to imply that less than 5 percent of the adult population of South Carolina had the power to elect the representatives who controlled the extensive coercive power of the state government at the time of ratification of the US Constitution.[360]

This situation cannot occur in collectivity. A diverse group of people exiting the original position will not agree to these types of voting restrictions. Nor will they agree to representation based on property, income, or wealth. People exiting anarchy will not agree to be slaves. People leaving the original position will not consent to live in captivity. They will not join a nested collective that allows someone like them to be a slave. People will form and join public-safety nested collectives that are focused on protecting them from their fellow members as well as from members of other nested collectives. This will include being protected from enslavement.

Municipalities and Counties

The final element of American Federalism that separates it from collectivity is the treatment of governmental entities other than states. Under collectivity, some people exiting the original position will join nested collectives that possess the general powers associated with American states. However, others will join coercive entities that have similar goals such as public safety and prevention of fraud but whose powers are limited and narrow. As members of these entities, they will retain the right to form other coercive entities that have an independent existence and are not subject to the authority of other nested collectives. These coercive entities will have their own constitutions, which instill their members with rights and responsibilities. Some of these entities will be small and local, like a community or a town. Others may be large regional organizations. Still others may have coercive powers without any geographic characteristic. Surprisingly, none of the constitutions of the original states provided these rights to their citizens. Each state had the ability to eliminate all existing governmental entities such as towns, cities, districts, or counties. Even though these local entities were an instrumental political force in the formation of state governments, the state constitutions did not ensure the independent existence of subgovernments. For example, Rhode Island, New Hampshire, and South Carolina were not restricted from eliminating towns, modifying the boundaries of local governments, or combining existing towns and counties into new governmental entities.

Following the ratification of the US Constitution, many people thought the management of their local affairs was an inherent right embodied in each of the state's constitutions. Thomas Cooley, a nineteenth-century chief justice of the Michigan Supreme Court, wrote that

> *the management of purely local affairs belongs to the people concerned, not only because of being their own affairs, but*

because they will best understand, and be most competent to manage them. The continued and permanent existence of local government is, therefore, assumed in all the state constitutions, and is a matter of constitutional right, even when not in terms expressly provided for.[361]

However, as discussed in chapter 17, the US Supreme Court disagreed with Cooley and ruled that political subdivisions of a state are only instrumentalities of the state and do not have an independent existence.

For example, in the early part of the twentieth century, Pennsylvania decided to combine the town of Allegheny into the city of Pittsburgh over the objections of the majority of its residents. The US Supreme Court ruled that the state had that right. Justice William Moody for a unanimous court stated:

Municipal corporations are political subdivisions of the state, created as convenient agencies for exercising such of the government powers of the state as may be entrusted to them . . . Neither their charters, nor any law conferring governmental powers . . . constitutes a contract with the state within the meaning of the federal Constitution. The state, therefore, at its pleasure, may modify or withdraw all such powers . . . repeal the charter and destroy the corporation. All this may be done, conditionally or unconditionally, with or without the consent of the citizens, or even against their protest.[362]

This implies that citizens of Pennsylvania have more governmental protection of their contractual rights in a private partnership or a private corporation than they do in the town in which they live. While many people in the original position will join coercive entities with extensive powers such as Pennsylvania, the credible equilibrium between diverse people will provide the ability for others to live in a state with limited powers where they have the right and authority to join other independent coercive collectives such as towns, cities, municipalities, counties, and regional governments.

The authority that state governments have over their local governments is typically called the Dillon Rule, after John Dillon, a nineteenth-century judge.[363] He advocated this type of power because he thought local governments were potentially more corrupt than state governments. He believed that a state's ability to control the local entity would improve the lives of their residents, since the state could overcome entrenched local interests. His concerns were real. Many local governments were corrupt. Centralization is, of course, one way of addressing this problem. He and others view larger government units as more capable of withstanding corruption since it is theoretically more difficult for third parties to influence a state government than a local government. This view of the benefits of centralization was also used by Madison to justify the ratification of the US Constitution. In the *Federalist Papers*, he stated:

> *Extend the sphere, and you take in a greater variety of parties and interests; you make it less probable that a majority of the whole will have a common motive to invade the rights of other citizens; or if such a common motive exists, it will be more difficult for all who feel it to discover their own strength, and to act in unison with each other. Besides other impediments, it may be remarked, that where there is a consciousness of unjust or dishonorable purposes, communication is always checked by distrust, in proportion to the number whose concurrence is necessary.[364]*

While centralization is a method of addressing local corruption and the problem Madison labels as "faction," it is not the only method, and it is not the tool that all people with diverse views will want to utilize. The problem with centralization is that the "true" worldview is unknowable and cannot be determined by majority vote. The Dillon Rule allows state governments to overrule the wishes of local voters. For many people, the cure of centralization is worse than the disease of corruption. Many people in the United States had this view and wanted more local control over their collective affairs than given by the original state constitutions. As such, many states modified their constitutions to allow for some measure of local control by becoming a "home rule" state. However, even these home-rule states still allow their legislatures to trump the decisions of the local communities. No existing state constitution allows the freedom and flexibility of home rule or nested collective rule that is available with collectivity.

Many people exiting the original position will hold the view that potential corruption of local governments can be significantly reduced through the same method they utilize to control larger governmental units: limits on their authority, unanimously accepted constitutions, and voting. This decentralized approach was not the organizational structure utilized by local government units in the United States at the time of ratification of the US Constitution. Their governing documents were even less democratic than the state constitutions. The charters of the original towns and local communities were not independently established by their citizens. Instead, they were approved by either the colonial legislatures or the state legislatures. Some of these charters allowed for control by a small percentage of the population. They did not necessarily establish democratic governance structures.

For example, Philadelphia, the capital of the United States at the time of the Declaration of Independence, had a charter from William Penn in 1701 that established it as a corporation. The charter was like the "constitution of an English town such as prevailed from the middle ages" in that it was "a close self-elected corporate body, existing, as it were, independently of the community in which it was constituted, and possessing certain powers to govern the inhabitants."[365] It concentrated these powers in the hands of twenty-two men who kept their membership for life. They annually elected the mayor and had the delegated power to choose the replacement for any member who died, resigned, or was removed for misconduct. They had complete coercive control over the city, including jurisdiction over crimes, subject to the laws and rules of the colony or the state. They passed laws governing roads, the police, the water supply, the indigent, firing guns, chimneys, dogs, horses, wages, gambling, cursing, and fraud, not all of which were understood or widely disseminated.[366] However, they did not have the power to tax, subsisting on fines, rents, fees, lotteries, and taxes authorized by the legislature to pay for municipal activities.

In 1777, the colonial assembly removed the powers of the twenty-two men who controlled the city; their prior authorities were effectively divided between the Supreme Executive Council that was responsible for state government, justices of the peace, and local commissioners.[367] Not until 1789 did the state establish a new city charter, which allowed the residents of the city to vote for the members of the municipal government. Even then, the citizens of the city had no direct input into the structure of the city government, except through periodic voting. In fact, a municipal charter was not put to popular vote until 1951. The citizens of Philadelphia were quite dependent on the state for overseeing the management of the city. People exiting the original position and opting for a decentralized governance structure will not choose this method of controlling the management of their local communities. Collectivity will result in the complete control of some local communities by their citizens. Some people will give their local communities more autonomy and independence than any town, city, or municipality had at the time of the ratification of the US Constitution.

COMPETITIVE FEDERALISM

The final federalist concept is "competitive federalism," which holds that a government composed of many independent levels of government is more efficient at solving and addressing collective goals than a unitary government. People who advocate competitive federalism view these independent levels of government as competing for citizens and resources, which leads the smaller governments to better align their policies and services to those held by their citizens. While many people advocate federalism for these reasons, the writings of economists Gordon Tullock, Alessandra Casella, Bruno Frey, and Reiner Eichenberger will be considered as representative of the entire concept of competitive federalism.[368]

Tullock conceived of federalism as a central government and a series of subsidiary governments, where the subsidiary governments can arise spontaneously to satisfy the preferences of potential citizens and residents.[369] An example he used is the formation of gated communities and their associated governance structure. He thought that competition will lead to government being more responsive to their citizens' desires and more successful in developing policies and procedures. Tullock labeled his view of competitive federalism as "sociological federalism."[370] He argued that a smaller government is best able to meet its citizens' needs, given the diversity of people's wants. However, he thought that this force can be offset by the gains from a larger population. The optimal magnitude of each government, for him, is then determined by these opposing forces. In addition, like Oates, he thought there is a broader role for the central government due to spillover effects from the interaction of these smaller governments. For example, he thought that income should be centrally redistributed and that the central government should guarantee free trade.

Tullock's concept of sociological federalism has aspects of collectivity, since it presumes that people will be governed by the coercive entity of their choice. However, it reflects his worldview and not the diverse worldviews of people in the original position. Not everyone has the same domestic social goals or the same intensity for their preferences. Some people will want equality to be a goal; other people who have views similar to Nozick and Hayek will not think there is any value to pursuing income or wealth equality. In fact, they are likely to view the goal of income equality as either unethical or counterproductive. On the other hand, people who share Rawls's views will value a large government whose main function is helping those members who are worse off than others. Everyone will not agree that income should be centrally redistributed or that free trade should exist throughout the defense collective. As such, diverse people exiting anarchy will not compromise and agree to sociological federalism.

Although Tullock assumed each person has different preferences, he also seemed to implicitly assume they have the same worldview. This led him to advocate that each government should expand until its common marginal net benefits are zero. This is not the derived equilibrium result from diverse people in the original position. Under the simplifying assumptions of perfect voice and perfect entry, each coercive collective expands until the marginal productivity gains are equal to the marginal person's freedom losses. In a more realistic environment, people in the original position will try to approximate these results through constitutions, the constitutional process, periodic voting, entry, exit, and ongoing contracting. Importantly, people's marginal costs from participating in government are not the same. In the limit, each person will receive the same gross gains from the defense collective. However, each person can have and probably will have different psychic losses from compromising and accepting governmental laws and rules.

Casella, Frey, and Eichenberger (hereafter CFE), like Tullock, appear to be proponents of federalism, albeit a type of federalism that has few historical precedents.[371] Frey and Eichenberger propose a federal constitutional clause that provides individuals and smaller governmental units with the right to form new governmental units that have coercive power and the ability to tax their citizens. In the title of their book they label these new voluntary governments as *Functional, Overlapping, and Competing Jurisdictions* or "FOCJ." They seem to view traditional governments, as well as politicians, as having conflicts with the citizens they are serving. They argue that competing FOCJ will more align the interests of their citizens with governmental policies and services. They appear to think that voting is insufficient to appropriately control political forces. CFE argue that the ability for individuals and local governments to form and join governments specialized by function and potentially overlapping will lead to enhanced competition for governmental services. Frey and Eichenberger suggest that almost all the emergent FOCJ will have a single goal and not have any geographic requirements.[372]

There are many parallels between Tullock's sociological federalism, FOCJ, and limited nested collectives. Limited nested collectives naturally arise out of bargaining by diverse people in the original position and will continue to morph in response to people's changing views and changes in circumstances after people exit the original position. Unlike the defense collective whose value is dependent on continued stability, limited nested collectives need not be designed to last forever, and new limited nested collectives can arise as conditions change and in response to people's preferences. A significant number of people in a diverse defense collective will want the advantages offered by competing limited nested collectives. They will favor competition among local governments and will want the ability to be members of specialized functional governments. However, not everyone will hold this view. Many people with worldviews that significantly differ from those advocating competitive federalism will think that the benefits of decentralized limited nested collectives are not sufficient to cover the costs. For example, people who share Rawls's views will not be in favor of FOCJ or naturally occurring limited nested collectives, since these entities will interfere with and potentially thwart centrally controlled policies around maximizing the welfare of the least-well-off members of the nested collective.

Collectivity incorporates aspects of competitive federalism but allows for the existence of general governments for those people who want to be "free" from its individualistic tendencies. It is also not reliant on rules designed to ensure a competitive environment. Diverse people exiting the original position will form specialized defense collectives or central governments with limited functionality. These diverse people will also form two or more nested collectives that focus on public safety. In a sufficiently diverse defense collective, one of these public-safety nested collectives will be a general government and at least one will be a limited government with a membership that overlaps other nested collectives. The limited public-safety nested collective shares some of the characteristics of FOCJ, and its members can be individuals or local collectives. It can also be geographically focused. However, given the diversity of worldviews of those in the defense collective, many people will not want to be members of FOCJ. Their first choice would be to join a general government and potentially a unitary one, but they will compromise and agree to be a member of a limited defense collective, since that allows them to also be part of a general government for all collective goals except those concerning external defense.

Bargaining between diverse people in anarchy will result in a credible equilibrium where broadly liberal people will join a limited defense collective that shares many aspects with FOCJ. The limited defense collective is functional and at least initially competes for members, as people in the original position maximize their net gains by associating with others with similar worldviews. However, it differs in how it overlaps with other jurisdictions. Importantly, it also differs from FOCJ, since its members do not receive their right to join it from another coercive institution. Its members' rights and obligations are solely a function of its initial constitution and original membership. A limited defense collective will have overlapping jurisdictions with nested collectives, but not with other defense collectives. As such, CFE's concept of FOCJ seems to be more applicable to limited nested collectives. Even here, the right to join a government that has the characteristics of FOCJ is not a right under the limited defense collective's constitution, but a right reserved by members of certain nested collectives.

People in the original position will compromise and unanimously agree that members of a central government can either be members of general or limited nested collectives. They will also agree that members of certain general nested collectives cannot simultaneously be members of one or more limited nested collectives. This is the credible equilibrium compromise because not everyone exiting anarchy will want to be governed by a limited government. Not everyone will agree that a limited or functional government competing with other limited governments is the optimal method of reducing the conflicts between managers and members of a collective. Many people exiting the original position will not want to be members of a competitive federalist governance system because they may be concerned that it will lead to "political balkanization."

They may want to live in and be members of a coercive collective that has centralized policies around issues such as the environment. Some people will prefer that local governments do not have an independent existence so that issues such as whether to allow hydraulic fracking are decided centrally, instead of being determined by a local government. Similarly, many people will want centralized rules concerning food standards because they think food distributors will determine that it is too expensive to meet the various regulations of different governments. As such, they will be concerned that distributors will supply food to everyone in the defense collective based on the rules of the most conservative nested collective. They will be concerned that one nested collective, potentially even a small one, can effectively determine the type of food available to people in other jurisdictions. For example, some people were concerned that Vermont's decision to require GMO (genetically modified organism) labeling on food would lead to labeling in states that do not require it and result in higher costs for everyone. Some people will prefer a more centralized approach where these issues can be debated, and where these types of externalities can be internalized.

People with views similar to Rawls, who believe that FOCJ will make issues such as redistribution more complicated, will prohibit the formation of voluntary governments within their domestic government. Frey and Eichenberger seem to respond to this by allowing the FOCJ's decisions to be overridden by the central government on issues such as redistribution. This additional provision addresses some of the concerns of people who share Rawls's views, but it is unlikely to convince everyone who views equality as a worthy goal, since many people will still view FOCJ as making it more difficult to manage equality. Furthermore, people who have views like Hayek and Nozick will not want to be subject to a coercive collective that enforces minimum levels of equality. In the credible equilibrium compromise of collectivity, people will not be required to make these trade-offs.

Frey and Eichenberger argue that FOCJ will expand to minimize spillovers, but this is not true of nested collectives. Nested collectives expand until no one will receive any incremental net gain from joining. This expansion obviously reduces spillovers and externalities, since it leads to some very large nested collectives. But it does not minimize them. The net benefits from internalization and the size of a nested collective are reduced by the disparity in people's worldviews. Therefore, conflicts between the members of different collectives will continue to exist and will not be minimized by the formation of different nested collectives. However, as was argued above, without merging, the different coercive nested collectives can bargain and negotiate with one another and thereby reduce their conflicts. They can consent to have their agreements and contracts subjected to laws that are binding; only the defense collectives are "sovereign" in this sense.

Frey and Eichenberger argue that the ability to form FOCJ should be guaranteed by the central government's constitution. They also seem to believe that the freedoms that are an integral part of the European Union, such as the unrestricted movement of people, services, and goods, are critical and must be rights guaranteed by that constitution. They appear to do so even though they acknowledge the broad regulatory impact resulting from the enforcement of these freedoms by the European Union. They also seem to argue the central government should establish a regulatory infrastructure around FOCJ to ensure competition.[373] Like Tullock, they appear to be advocating a specific worldview, not a compromise that people exiting the original position will make.[374] Diverse people exiting anarchy will not compromise and approve a constitution for the defense collective that has these rights. Some will have the opinion that these domestic rights and responsibilities are not the ones they want, and many others will be concerned with the real possibility that they can be used to convert the limited central government into an extensive one.

In the review of American Federalism, we examined the effect that broad clauses such as commerce and welfare can have on the power of the central government. Mandates such as free trade and free mobility of goods and services can have similar effects on the regulatory power of the central government, since externalities and spillovers exist. Nonetheless, a number of political philosophers, in addition to Tullock, who favor limited government have supported these types of federal powers. For example, Richard Epstein, a noted libertarian, seems to think the federal government needs this delegated domestic power because he is concerned that domestic governments will not be able to cooperate in the absence of centralized control.[375] The fact that some state governments have historically tried to be economically discriminatory and have not reached agreements with each other does not imply that powers such as the commerce clause are necessary. In the United States, the states have been legally hampered in their ability to enter interstate compacts because of the broadness of the interpretations of the Constitution and the limitations in the Constitution on agreements between the states. Domestic governments will recognize their interdependence, and in the absence of these restrictions, will at least attempt to enter bilateral and multilateral agreements, potentially including the formation of a common market. Since domestic governments can find ways to cooperate without central direction, diverse people in the original position will narrow the scope of the federal government and rely on the self-interests of the domestic governments to enter agreements to address their conflicts and lack of scale.

They will do so because the domestic power of the central government to protect the freedom of the market will provide the legal authority for people who desire an even more extensive central government to broadly interpret the power. Barry Weingast, who seems to think federalism is important and who also appears to favor a central government power like the commerce clause, acknowledges that the preferences of the majority of people in the United States changed following the Great Depression and that this led to "a reinterpretation" of the Constitution.[376] The narrow interpretation of the commerce clause that both he and Epstein appear to prefer cannot be guaranteed in an environment of diverse worldviews. The potentially broad power of these types of central governmental authorities can easily lead to extensive centralized regulations concerning social policies, competition, and trade. These constitutional clauses provide both the managers of the defense collective and the judges on the defense collective's courts the ability to interpret these rights and powers according to their personal worldviews. Diverse members of the defense collective will use these federal authorities to impose their majority preferences on the minority. Instilling these types of rights in the defense collective's constitution effectively makes it a general government. This will cause diverse and broadly liberal people in the original position to severely limit the domestic scope of the central government.

Broadly liberal people in the original position will also not compromise and accept what Robert Inman and Daniel Rubinfield label as "democratic federalism," which they seem to argue is a "compromise" between people who have the diversity of opinions of the five authors.[377] It is a central government with broad scope that uses representatives elected by members of local governments to make decisions. This is not the equilibrium agreement between broadly liberal and diverse people, since it will allow the majority view of the members (or their representatives) of the defense collective to supplant the views of the members of the nested collectives. Instead, the credible equilibrium between diverse people will strictly constrain the domestic responsi-bilities and scope of the central government. Its constitutional remit will not include such issues as equality or even the free movement of people, goods, or services. These rights and obligations will be reserved by the individual members of the defense collective and included in the constitutions of those nested collectives whose members desire them. In addition, the domestic governments will have the delegated power to enter agreements with other domestic governments.

PART SIX

THE JUST GOVERNMENT

20

JUSTICE AS CHOICE

THE PURE VEIL AND COLLECTIVITY

In chapters 2 and 3, various procedures were discussed that were designed to produce a consensus among people with differing political philosophies. These included Adam Smith's sympathetic and impartial spectator, voting, use of a jury, public deliberation, and "justice as impartiality." None of these produced a consensus that will be accepted by diverse people. However, as we demonstrated, bargaining in the original position will amalgamate their views, even though people with differing political opinions can, and most likely will, continue to believe that their worldviews are the most accurate representation of reality. Bargaining led to the conclusion that broadly liberal and diverse people exiting the original position will agree to a specific form of government. Each of them will determine it is in their best interest and consistent with their perception of how the world works to live under coercive rules determined by a government organized under the institutional structure of collectivity.

We also examined the veil-of-ignorance procedural device favored by John Rawls and John Harsanyi. Even though it was designed to remove people's biases and produce fair and just decisions, Harsanyi and Rawls disagreed on the compact reached by people behind the veil. However, by making the veil more opaque and obscuring each person's worldview, even their own, a consensus is achievable. An agreed structure of government can be derived by asking imaginary people behind the veil to design a framework for social decision-making that will satisfy each of them once they remove the veil and their endowments and worldview are revealed to them. The obvious question is: What will they determine behind this "pure veil"? Will they agree that justice as fairness or utilitarianism is the best political structure for the society that contains all of them?

No. Instead, people who have diverse and broadly liberal worldviews will agree to live in a society that has the governance structure of collectivity. Why is this the result of the deliberations behind the pure veil? Because people behind the veil are all assumed to be logical, and any other structure will make some of them worse off once they remove the veil. To see this, let's place five imagined people behind the pure veil who have worldviews consistent with the views of the five authors and examine their options in designing a common government.

One theoretical outcome is that behind the pure veil, they will decide to form a single unitary government whose policies conform to one of the five's worldviews. They all know that at least one of them will be satisfied with this result. However, four of them will not be pleased. Depending on which worldview they choose and which worldview they discover is theirs, they could be exceedingly dissatisfied with their choice. Will any of them pick Rawls's philosophy or the worldview embraced by Robert Nozick? The gains are potentially great if they happen to have either Nozick's or Rawls's. However, the risks are high. By picking a specific government organized under a specific worldview, each of them has only a 20 percent chance of living in a coercive environment consistent with their actual worldview and an 80 percent chance of being unsatisfied after removing the veil. Given these risks, which one will they choose?

This is a classic case of decision-making under uncertainty. Logical people will place themselves in the position of each of the other people, and rank the various worldviews according to how they view the philosophies of the other people. For example, each of them will put themselves in the place of the person who has Rawls's views and rank each of the competing philosophies from this perspective. The person who shares Rawls's views will obviously prefer Rawls's worldview to those of the others, and it is likely that they will prefer Amartya Sen's views to Harsanyi's, Harsanyi's to Friedrich Hayek's, and Hayek's to Nozick's worldview. Each of the people behind the veil will conduct this thought experiment as if they are each of the philosophers. From chapter 3, we imagined the following preferences were held by each of them:

	N-1 (four points)	N-2 (three points)	N-3 (two points)	N-4 (one point)	N-5 (zero points)
RAWLS	*Rawls*	*Sen*	*Harsanyi*	*Hayek*	*Nozick*
SEN	*Sen*	*Rawls*	*Harsanyi*	*Hayek*	*Nozick*
HARSANYI	*Harsanyi*	*Sen*	*Rawls*	*Hayek*	*Nozick*
HAYEK	*Hayek*	*Nozick*	*Sen*	*Harsanyi*	*Rawls*
NOZICK	*Nozick*	*Hayek*	*Harsanyi*	*Sen*	*Rawls*

While the person may be able to logically deduce each author's preferences, it is much less likely that they can consistently determine the "intensity" each author has for these rankings. That is, how much more did Rawls prefer Harsanyi's views to Hayek's views relative to his preference for Nozick's?

A further complication exists when comparing the intensity across authors. For example, each of the people behind the veil will need to assess the intensity of Sen's imagined relative preference for Hayek's views over Nozick's views, compared with the intensity of Rawls's relative preference for Hayek's views over Nozick's worldviews. Given this uncertainty, each of them is likely to use some form of estimation. They may use a simple linear device of giving more weight to the author's own view and a progressively lower weight to the author's less favored worldviews. Since they do not know which of these worldviews is their actual worldview until they remove the veil, they will logically assume it is equally likely they are one of the people behind the veil. This will lead them to choose the author's worldview that has the highest weighted average score.

This process is essentially the Bayesian procedure advocated by Harsanyi. Each person chooses the highest weighted average worldview of the group of authors, since no one has information as to which of the worldviews they will prefer when they remove the veil. While each of them can chose different weights, given their level of information, it would not be surprising if each of them chooses the same linear weights. If each of them chooses weights of four for the most preferred, three for the second most preferred, and zero for the least preferred, the result is equivalent to the Borda Count voting procedure that was discussed in chapter 3.

Given the imagined preferences of each of the authors, this voting procedure resulted in Sen's worldview as being the winning one. This result is obviously dependent on: (i) the accurate assessment of each person's preferences, (ii) the number of differing views, and (iii) the relative similarity of the worldviews. Nonetheless, any group of logical people placed behind a veil, which does not allow anyone to identify the worldview that belongs to any person, including themselves, and that decides as a group to have laws that conform to only one of the author's worldviews, will not chose an extreme worldview. Each of them will choose the worldview that has the highest weighted average of the potential worldviews.

Furthermore, unlike real-world voting, the veil eliminates each individual's incentive to vote strategically. Nonawareness of their own worldview will cause each of them to use their actual assessment of everyone else's actual worldview preferences in their voting or negotiations with other people behind the veil. This will produce the highest expected value worldview. They will still only have a one-in-five chance of being able to live in a society with coercive rules that conform to the worldview they actually prefer; however, given the circumstances, it allows them to be subject to laws that have the highest expected value. Given the imagined preferences of the group of authors, the pure-veil procedural device does not result in the group choosing either utilitarianism advocated by Harsanyi or the difference principle popularized by Rawls, even though both utilized the veil procedure or the equal probability method as a key component of justifying their worldview.

A relevant question one or more of the people behind the veil may ask is why all of them must live under common rules. Why do they have to be subject to the same governmental policies? Given their differences of opinion on how the world works and the relevant impact of governmental rules and policies, each of them may be better off if they could live in a society subject to coercive rules that conformed to their preferred worldview. However, there is a cost to having five different governments. Stated differently, there are gains from all of them being in the same collective. To assess whether it is beneficial to each of them to live under a common set of laws once they remove the veil, each must value the relevant trade-offs between one unified government compared to multiple governments. Each of the people behind the pure veil will attempt to effectively become a sympathetic, unbiased observer of the social arrangement that will be preferred by each of them once the veil is removed.

They will do so by comparing the gains each person receives from being in a collective situation with each combination of people to the value each person places on accepting compromise decisions from these various combinations. They will want to place each person in the social situation where they have the highest net gain. The compromise worldview in each combination of authors is unlikely to be a weighted average of their worldviews. Instead, it will be a negotiated worldview that combines elements of the relevant authors' views. The specific compromise worldview chosen will be the one that produces the highest expected gains for the people behind the veil. Unlike each of the author's pure worldviews, the compromise worldview need not be logically consistent.

Every person behind the pure veil will examine the difference between: (i) the perceived value each person places on the compromise worldview of each combination of people, and (ii) the perceived value each person places on their pure worldview. This is equivalent to each person's freedom losses from each combination of people. Every person behind the veil will want to place all five people in the position that has the highest perceived value to that person, weighing the trade-offs between a social situation that includes more people with the attendant higher freedom losses from accommodating a larger group of diverse people.

Behind the pure veil, they will essentially reason through a five-person bargaining situation from each of their perspective. Each person will choose the compromise worldview that minimizes aggregate freedom losses given each combination of worldviews. Of course, the accurate assessments of the freedom-maximizing decisions require that each of the people behind the veil has an in-depth understanding of the worldview of all five people behind the veil.

Given each of the author's writings it seems likely that each of them: (i) places a high value on collective action, (ii) believes his worldview is the most accurate model of the real world, and (iii) thinks that the other authors' models of the world are inherently flawed. These common perceptions will probably lead the people behind the veil to place each of the authors in a common government with a compromise worldview not at the extremes of any of the pure worldviews of the authors. That is, they will view the gains from collective action involving all five people as sufficiently large to cover the aggregate freedom losses from the freedom-maximizing decisions.

However, as we have discussed throughout the last few chapters, the people behind the veil have more degrees of freedom when designing a method to pursue collective action assisted by coercively enforced rules than just a unitary government whose rules and laws are determined by a compromise worldview. They are not compelled to cause each of them to live under one compromise worldview, even though they all seem to place significant value on at least some type of collective action. They can adjust the structure of government so that it accommodates different worldviews on domestic issues. By eliminating the constraint of a unitary government, the people behind the pure veil can significantly increase the net gains for some of the people, while not significantly reducing the value for those people who place importance on a centrally administered government.

For example, Rawls placed significant emphasis on a centrally administered domestic government guided by the difference principle. He seemed absolutely convinced this is the fairest and most just method of pursuing collective action for people who have morals similar to those of the five authors. Anything short of this, in his view, effectively discriminates against the less fortunate members of a common society. The others seem to think he is wrong, but not all for the same reasons. He, of course, seemed to believe they are wrong. Determining which if any of them is correct is impossible. However, the governmental function of external defense is only tangentially related to Rawls's broader concern with distributive justice and to the other authors' views on nondefense-related social goals. By allowing people with the views of these five authors to live under common rules for external defense and differing rules with respect to distributive justice, the expected net gains from collective action for each of the people behind the veil is increased. The authors' worldviews seem to be sufficiently compatible that they can coexist under the same common government, especially one that has a limited central government and choice in domestic nested collectives. In fact, as discussed earlier, Rawls's justice as fairness only applies to a domestic government that does not have defensive responsibilities. As such, justice as fairness is applicable to a general nested collective, not to a central government. The imagined people behind the veil will choose the functions and powers for the central government that are the lowest common denominator (least) number of allocated powers the authors think should be attributable to government. Limiting the functionality of the central government increases the expected value of a common society for people behind the veil because it is equally probable that they have any one of the five authors' worldviews and only a one-in-five chance that they have Rawls's worldview.

The pure veil effectively converts each of the potentially biased individuals—biased because each of them is likely convinced that their worldview is the most accurate conception of reality—into unbiased sympathetic observers who want what is best for the group. Behind the pure veil, each of them will agree to centralized rules for external defense and differentiated rules for most domestic decisions. The inability to fully specify the constitution will lead each of them to support the existence of multiple domestic governments and place severe limits on the scope of the federal government. The governing principle of collectivity allows each person to make the least accommodation in their worldview to achieve collective action. The logical and unbiased theoretical people behind the veil will choose this type of coercive arrangement because any other structure of government will reduce the expected value of the situation, given their lack of knowledge of the *true* implications of collective policies and procedures.

JUSTICE AS CHOICE

The bargaining analysis in the prior chapters of a diverse group of people exiting anarchy produced an objective structure of government. Irrespective of one's worldview, if it fits in the category of being broadly liberal, everyone will agree to the same structure of government. Collectivity, a limited defense collective coupled with both general and limited nested collectives, is the logical method that results from the bargain reached by broadly liberal people with diverse worldviews as they exit the original position. As shown in the prior section, the pure-veil procedure will also produce this structure of government for people with these types of worldviews. Even though people will agree on very few social actions, using either the procedure of bargaining from the original position or the pure veil, they will all agree that collectivity is the best approach to coercive collective effort. It is not the optimal structure for a nondiverse group of people, but it is the governmental structure that will be chosen by pluralistic people bargaining in the various original positions and by diverse people who are behind the pure veil.

But is collectivity a just structure of government? Is it fair to its members? Fairness and justness are normative or relative concepts completely dependent on each person's worldview. For people to conclude that collectivity is just, they either must agree that collectivity, as a form of government, produces just social actions—actions consistent with their personal sense of justness—or alternatively, they must conclude that collectivity is consistent with a form of government derived through a fair or just process.

Collectivity can be just if everyone in a society who uses it as their governing structure thinks the laws produced by it are inherently just. For example, some people agree with Rawls's conclusions that the least-well-off members of society *should* receive preferential treatment from those people who are relatively more advantaged. Some agree with Sen's conclusions that people with less capabilities *should* receive societal help from those who have more opportunity so that every person has a higher chance of living the life that has more value to them. Some also agree with Harsanyi that people who are near death *should* receive less of society's scarce resources to artificially keep them alive. People with these views think these rules and outcomes are just. These views on just outcomes are often held not because people agree with the process in which the conclusions were derived, but because the societal actions are consistent with their personal worldviews.

Not everyone will think each of the laws produced by each of the governments that compose collectivity are inherently just. The laws produced by collectivity will not be completely consistent with each person's worldviews. The central government's decisions are compromises that theoretically reflect each person's preferences, but need not result in laws many people think are inherently just. The domestic governments will produce laws that differ from one another. Even if people think the laws in their domestic government are just, they will not think differing laws in neighboring domestic governments are inherently just.

Furthermore, none of the five authors argues for collectivity as the governing framework for society. Given its structure, some of the governments that are components of collectivity will likely produce laws that each of them will agree with. But many of these domestic governments will also produce laws inconsistent with the authors' worldviews. People who share their views will not think all the rules produced by collectivity are inherently just. Therefore, if collectivity is a just form of government, it must be because it is derived through a just process.

The relevant question, then, is whether people think either the bargaining process or the pure-veil process are *just* procedures. Let's examine the veil procedure first. Who would disagree that it's a just procedure? No one behind the veil has an advantage. People behind the veil are completely unbiased about everything that makes them an individual, including endowments and worldview. They are all impartial. As Nozick notes, impartiality and unbiasedness are traditional characteristics of just processes.[378]

Of course, from some people's worldview, that is exactly the problem with the pure-veil process. Some may be so convinced their worldview is the correct one that they will not accept the pure-veil process as just. Given circumstances, they may compromise, but they do not accept the legitimacy of worldviews that differ from their own. For example, if one of the people behind the pure veil believes that God has communicated with them, either directly or through writings, and those communications require a noncollectivity form of government, then they will not view the pure-veil process as just. People in this position and with this worldview will be convinced their view is the correct one. They will believe that other worldviews not in complete conformity with their own are categorically wrong. Obviously, if everyone thinks this person has the correct worldview, then they will convert to that same worldview. If they all agree, the veil will not be necessary. They are all behind the pure veil as a procedure to derive a consensus structure of government because they a priori do not agree on social policies.

To accept the pure-veil procedure as fair, people must acknowledge the original assumptions that were made about the knowledge level of the people behind the veil. They must accept the concept that each of the people behind the pure veil has a different worldview and that no one's worldview, including their own, is the *accurate* model of reality. They can still think they have the best of the available worldviews, but they must agree they cannot definitively prove the accuracy of their worldview to those who have differing views. They must also believe it is not immoral or unacceptable for other people to hold worldviews that differ from their own. If they admit that other people can legitimately have different views, beliefs, and morals, and if they concur with the stream of logic that was employed to reason through the options available to people behind the pure veil, then and only then will they agree the pure-veil procedure is just. If it is, then the results from the procedure are also just, and collectivity is a just form of government for people with different worldviews and different views of justice and fairness.

On the other hand, if one or more of the people behind the veil sincerely believes their views and beliefs are the only accurate worldview, then they will not accept the procedure as just and will not view collectivity as just. If everyone is convinced that they, and they alone, have the correct worldview, then no one will accept the pure-veil procedure as just. In which case, since collectivity is the logically determined structure of government by people behind the pure veil, there are no just structures of government between people with diverse worldviews that can be derived by the pure-veil procedure. The only just structure of government for people who will not accept the possibility that other people have a legitimate difference in views is to form or join a government with people with similar beliefs. An important corollary to this line of reasoning is that collectivity is the only just government between people with substantially different worldviews that can be derived by the pure-veil process. Collectivity is the only just government among people with diverse and broadly liberal worldviews. Stated somewhat differently, if a country is pluralistic and has a government that does not resemble collectivity, then it is not a completely just form of government as determined by an unbiased process such as the pure-veil procedure.

The pure-veil process is an example of the type of "procedural justice" advocated by Rawls and discussed in chapter 2. It is defined as a procedure: (i) that uses a just methodology, (ii) that is used to determine political decisions, and (iii) in which no additional criteria are imposed on its determinations. Both Rawls and Harsanyi thought their processes were just. We previously questioned why they didn't produce the same political structure for society. An even more important query from our perspective is, why didn't they derive collectivity? It seems clear: each of them failed to remove all the biases from their procedures and analysis.

In establishing a veil-type procedure, great care must be taken to ensure that all sources of asymmetry and variations between people are removed. Unfortunately, each person's worldview is intricately intertwined with how they perceive the world and with the social actions they think are moral and just. For a veil or equal probability procedure to be just across people with different conceptions of just social actions, it must eliminate each person's ideology without removing their ability to reason. It must distance each person from their worldview so they can reason in an unbiased fashion about the structure of society for a pluralistic group of people. The pure-veil procedure does exactly that. Unfortunately, neither Rawls's veil nor Harsanyi's equal probability thought experiment sufficiently obscured people's worldviews. As such, neither of their procedures is a just process across people with different worldviews. This does not imply that Rawls's and Harsanyi's worldviews and moral philosophies are any less correct than anyone else's. It simply implies that their version of the veil procedure cannot be used to produce a just form of government across a population that does not share their views of the world.

The only just form of government for people who have the varied worldviews of the five theorists is collectivity, since the just process of the pure-veil procedure derived it. This is true even though the domestic outcomes from applying this derived form of justice will differ in the various nested collectives, since their policies and laws are based on differing ideologies.

It is not mere happenstance that people behind the pure veil derived the same structure of government as people exiting anarchy unanimously agreed to form. As discussed above, the procedural device of the pure veil effectively requires each of the people behind the veil to reason through a bargaining process like the negotiation between diverse people in the original position. The critical question is whether this bargaining process, the one that has been used throughout this book, is a just one.

Not all contractual negotiations are just. It is entirely possible for a contract negotiated by one or more people to be viewed as unfair from the perspective of the worldviews of the five authors. The key requirements for the contractual process to be viewed as fair for the diverse people with these worldviews seems to be: (i) everyone is logical and no one makes bargaining mistakes; (ii) everyone has the same level of information and no one is the victim of fraud; (iii) an unbiased bargaining procedure is used; (iv) no one has superior bargaining ability or skill that affects the bargaining outcome; (v) no one is "forced" to agree to the bargaining contract; and (vi) everyone who is a party to the contract agrees to all of its terms.

The bargaining analysis that has been used to derive collectivity assumes that everyone has the same bargaining model and will not make any bargaining mistakes. Some researchers attribute people's inability to understand the complicated nature of reality to limits on people's reasoning. Herbert Simon, a Nobel Prize–winning economist, thought the best method of modeling this type of situation is to assume that people have "bounded rationality."[379] He and others, including Reinhard Selten, the mathematician mentioned in the discussion on bargaining in chapter 7, thought that people do not make decisions by performing complex optimization calculations.[380] Instead, they argued that people use various heuristics to make decisions in complex situations. Neither Simon nor Selten viewed people as illogical; they just believed that people are incapable of doing the complex analyses required in many decision-making situations. In general, both Simon and Selten were correct. However, the analysis in this book is concerned with the structure of government between people who have imperfect models of the world because of the complicated character of political decisions, but who *do not make logical mistakes* in bargaining over their desired form of government. People are assumed to be capable of correctly reasoning through the optimal bargaining response even though they cannot perfectly sort through the complexities of the world. From a justice perspective, this is an important distinction. We are seeking a just structure of government for imperfect people.

Everyone in the original position is also assumed to have the same level of information. Differences in people's worldviews are assumed to be the result of the complicated nature of reality and are not due to differences in people's levels and types of information. As was discussed in chapter 3, people can agree to disagree on political decisions because everyone cannot prove that those with a different worldview are definitively wrong. Equal information does not cause people's worldviews to converge with reality or to the *true* representation of the world. People disagree on moral, philosophical, and religious issues even though knowledge and information increase over time. Scientific and economic progress do not cause people's underlying views of the world to completely converge. Equal information is an important characteristic of the original position. Bargaining is conducted in an open and transparent process where everyone has the same level of information concerning all aspects of the bargaining process, including the agreements and potential agreements of the other people in the original position. No one is defrauded. No one is fooled.

Additionally, no one in the original position is forced to use a bargaining procedure that is biased. The Binmore variation of Rubinstein's bargaining protocol is used to remove any first-mover advantage in bilateral bargaining, and the various paths of forming the collective are averaged in multi-person bargaining. Each person reasons through their bargaining options and agrees on everyone's optimal decisions without taking time to actually bargain. People are assumed to have differing discount rates, but as was shown in chapter 11, this does not give people with lower discount rates a bargaining advantage in a government composed of a large number of people. Simplifying the analysis by assuming that everyone has the same discount rate and the same incentive to exit anarchy will not change the conclusion that people with differing worldviews will choose collectivity as the equilibrium structure of government.

While anarchy is a poor environment, given its lack of collective action and inherent violence, no one is coerced to agree to a specific type of coercive collective. People are not forced to exit anarchy and accept specific constitutional contract terms. Anarchy and the various original positions are assumed to be stable. People in anarchy are modeled as using some part of their scarce resources to defend themselves, but each is left with sufficient resources to continue to exist. Remaining in anarchy is a real choice. A person will only decide to exit anarchy if the social terms they are offered are acceptable. The status quo is assumed not to be changed by the existence of collective defense. While some may not have survived anarchy, the survivors are viewed as unbiased representatives of humanity. People are biased by their worldviews and potentially biased by their endowments, but the original position does not discriminate among worldviews. People with widely varied worldviews are assumed to survive in the original position. Collectivity and the various constitutions that underlie each of the collectives are viewed as a cost-reducing institutional structure and not as survival mechanisms. As such, people are incentivized to join collectives with others who share their goals and whose worldviews are sufficiently compatible. The costs of anarchy are presumed to be high but not infinite. Each person can logically decide to remain in the original position or to take the good and the bad by joining one or more coercive collectives.

However, what if the assumption about stability of the status quo is modified? The diversity of worldviews will still lead to the formation of diverse democratic defense and nested collectives. This conclusion is a result of the following logic.

Sufficient diversity in worldviews will include people whose views are not broadly liberal. By definition, these people will use collective force to impose their views onto others. If there are a sufficient number of these people who also have a similar worldview, they are likely to form a general defense collective. The simultaneous existence of democratic defense collectives, aggressive general defense collectives, and people who decide to remain in anarchy is potentially unstable given the productivity benefits of collective defense (and offense). It is entirely possible that anarchical defense cannot survive in a world with aggressive collective offense. Collective defense is a dominant technology. People who remain in anarchy may not have the resources to adequately defend themselves from a defense collective bent on their destruction, and at a minimum may have to devote more resources to their defense.

The introduction of the technology of coercive collectives potentially destabilizes the anarchical equilibrium. It is a positive externality for those who decide to join in collective defense, but it could be a negative externality for those who wish to remain in anarchy. This phenomenon is similar to the impact of other types of technological change discussed by Princeton University economist Avinash Dixit.[381] Given its dominance, coercive collective formation could be preferred by only a few people and yet lead to everyone joining a coercive collective.

Stated somewhat differently, the introduction of coercive collectives may not be a Pareto improvement for everyone. Even though it leads to significant improvements in human society given its ability to encourage cooperation, some people will prefer anarchy due to the freedom losses caused by accepting collective decisions they do not prefer. The inherent productivity superiority of coercive collective action will potentially eliminate the original status quo as an alternative. As such, some people will determine it is in their best interest to join some type of coercive collective, even though they have extensive freedom losses and would have preferred that collective defense had never been discovered. Since anarchy is no longer an option, they are induced to join the coercive collectives that minimize their net losses.

Importantly, the potential negative externalities generated by the introduction of coercive collectives does not change the structure of those collectives. A population with diverse worldviews will still form different defense collectives. These large defense collectives composed of people with diverse and broadly liberal worldviews will still be democratic. The members of these diverse defense collectives will also continue to form various other types of coercive collectives and other entities to improve cooperation. The possibility that the status quo of anarchy has been destabilized does not change any of the conclusions concerning the overall structure of coercive collective formation. Similarly, the possibility that the formation of coercive collectives can cause people to undertake costly moves does not modify the overall structure of those collectives. The structure and existence of coercive collectives in a world of varied worldviews is invariant with respect to both worldviews and to potential negative externalities. Therefore, the same structure of government is obtained by bargaining, irrespective of whether some people in the original position are unaffected by the existence of collective defense, incentivized to join in collective defense, or induced to join in collective action. Under these circumstances, to view collectivity as unjust, one must view the introduction of government as unjust. That said, the assumption used throughout the book is that people can remain in anarchy, which implies that no one is forced to join in coercive collective action.

Finally, the bargaining process allows everyone to participate in the determination of the equilibrium structure of government. The members of each of the collectives unanimously make the choice to become members. Any member that determines it is in their best interest to join a coercive collective is allowed to join. Each of the constitutions that are the base governing documents for each of the collectives is unanimously agreed to by every one of its members.

This leads to the conclusion that the bargaining process that resulted in collectivity as the preferred governmental structure is just for those whose views are broadly liberal. This process either treats each of the people in the bargaining situation symmetrically and equally, or any remaining inequality has no impact on the bargaining outcome. Each of the bargainers is logical and did not make any errors in reasoning through the bargaining analysis. The bargainers all have the same level of information and no one is the victim of any type of fraud. Each of the bargainers freely and voluntarily agrees to the constitution or social contract that is the fundamental agreement in each of the coercive collectives. Even though each of the bargainers has a different worldview, the pluralistic people who decide to join in common defense all agree to collectivity as the appropriate umbrella political structure to enable them to address their various social goals.

For these reasons, collectivity is not only a just form of government; it is the only just form of government for a broadly liberal and pluralistic group of people. Collectivity is essentially "justice as choice," since it allows a choice in domestic political structure, enabling people to have a higher probability of being subject to domestic laws consistent with their worldviews.

JUSTICE AS CHOICE AND THE FIVE AUTHORS

Even though collectivity is the only just government for broadly liberal and pluralistic people, people do not have to act justly. Those who wish to *act* justly will support collectivity, as will people in the original position and people behind the pure veil who accept the fact that people can legitimately have differing worldviews. But what about people who want to pursue their own worldview in the real world? Are there other reasons to support collectivity? Yes, people who want everyone to follow their worldview can support it. It requires the smallest amount of compromise between pluralistic people. This is the reason it is the compromise structure of government that people behind the veil and in the original position, who want societal rules to comport with their worldview, will agree to. Collectivity allows diverse people the most freedom to pursue their own hypothesis of the good, as determined by their own worldview. Yet none of the five authors proposed collectivity. Each of them likely thought their worldview was a just template for government. Based on the authors' published works, what are the likely views of *justice as choice* by those whose views are similar to the worldviews of the five authors?

Maybe somewhat surprisingly, there are not significant conflicts between Rawls's justice as fairness and justice as choice. Under collectivity, people who have worldviews like Rawls can pursue justice as fairness in their domestic government, if there are enough people with this view. The ability for others to pursue different policies in other nested collectives should not cause significant freedom losses for people who share Rawls's views, since, as stated previously, justice as fairness only applies to a *domestic* government. In deriving what he viewed as the just structure of government, Rawls focused on a closed multigenerational *domestic* society. He analyzed intergovernmental relationships in his later book, *Law of Peoples*. Even though he also employed the concept of the original position in his analysis of the political structure between governments, he did not advocate one über world government. He argued that differing societies and differing groups of people can "justly" pursue domestic political structures that are not justice as fairness if they are not outlaw societies bent on aggression against other people or do not persecute their own citizens. None of these positions conflicts with collectivity and justice as choice.

Rawls thought that domestic governments will not give up sufficient control to form a larger federated government, although he did think confederations, alliances, treaties, and general agreements between governments are likely. He argued for toleration between different societies, even between liberal and nonliberal people. His views fit within the concept of collectivity. His preferred society can be viewed as a general nested collective among other nested collectives (both general and limited), whose members are also members of a larger central limited purpose defense collective.

Rawls viewed the world as too diverse to have justice as fairness apply to all societies. He also argued that justice as fairness or any other political ideology should not be forced onto other "decent" people. He did not even think money should be used by one society to encourage more liberal policies within another decent society. Therefore, people who share Rawls's worldview can accept the just existence of other nested collectives that pursue different worldviews. They will prefer that everyone accepts justice as fairness, but they should not deny "decent" people the opportunity to pursue their own worldview. Since the other authors all have "decent" worldviews, people who share Rawls's worldview and don't want to act justly can still accept collectivity as an inherently just structure of government.

People who possess views that are similar to Sen's worldview can probably also accept collectivity, even if it was not produced by a just process. As was discussed earlier, he does not seem to think we can use a procedure such as the pure veil or bargaining to determine societal rules. He appears to think the best approach for determining just social policies is through public reasoning and public discussion of the various alternatives. While people who have worldviews similar to his worldview will likely favor the increased probability offered by justice as choice of having one or more nested collectives include social policies that focus on people's broadly defined freedoms, they will unlikely think it is inherently just for another nested collective to have unemployment exacerbated by what they perceive to be that collective's poor policies. They will unlikely think it is inherently fair for people to be born in a nested collective that does not have universal health care. They will probably want these nested collectives to change their policies and will want to use public reasoning as a method of accomplishing this.

But since they share Sen's views, they will also probably recognize the diversity of people's goals and abilities, the complex nature of reality, and the fact that people can logically disagree and arrive at "conflicting judgments."[382] If public reasoning quickly led to a convergence of worldviews and a consensus answer to social goals and methods of accomplishing these goals, then collectivity will not be necessary. On the other hand, if convergence of worldviews never occurs or occurs over an extended period, then public reasoning will not result in a quick consensus. The question before them and us is: What should the structure of government be in an environment where people have diverse worldviews? It is going to be a long wait for public reason to cause their worldviews to converge. Social decisions and social actions need to take place in the interim. A structure of government is needed while we wait for convergence. Collectivity or justice as choice seems to be the only answer without forcing people to live by a single compromise worldview.

Collectivity allows people who value being part of a large, safe government and who have strongly held liberal political views the highest chance to live under laws that most comport to their worldview. Achieving a consensus among like-minded people is obviously quicker and simpler than achieving agreement among people with differing views. Collectivity provides a formal structure that allows people with similar worldviews to govern themselves, while allowing them to achieve the efficiencies of being protected by a larger, more stable central government. In conjunction with public reason, it should result in the greatest number of people being quickly subject to the coercive rules consistent with the most popularly conceived effective approach to social goals and social methods. It also allows people with strong minority opinions on domestic issues to follow rules closer to those they prefer.

Sen seems to have specific, well-reasoned views as to the most appropriate governmental policies. Unfortunately, no matter how well he argues for his point of view, people are likely to still disagree with his solutions to societal issues. What are the choices for people who share his views? They will continue to advocate for their preferred social rules. But they cannot rely on democratic governments to adopt his policies, since they do not think majority voting always produces the correct or best answer to social policies. They do not have the power to force people to agree with his views or to follow his policies. Even if they have the power to coerce people to follow his formulae for improving people's lives, it is unlikely they will feel morally justified in using that power. Under these conditions, they can agree that collectivity is the best available and only a priori just approach to government for pluralistic people.

However, they will not think each government that is part of collectivity produces the optimal social policies. Therefore, they can accept it but will probably want it to be only a temporary solution. Living under the rules of one or more of its governments, they will want sympathetic people to use public reasoning to convince everyone to adopt Sen's preferred social policies. If they are successful and everyone agrees, then a more unified structure is optimal. Viewing this book as part of the public dialogue, their acceptance of its conclusions is consistent with the robustness of Sen's concept of public reason. In a very real sense, collectivity operationalizes the type of "deliberative democracy" that many advocate when people reasonably disagree.[383]

Turning to Harsanyi's worldview, people who think his political philosophy is the most accurate representation of reality can also a priori accept collectivity. He thought the use of the heuristic of imaginative empathy—of placing yourself in everyone's position in addressing solutions to societal conflicts—is the best method for social decision-making. This led him to advocate rule-based utilitarianism.

He recognized that many people do not view utilitarianism as the appropriate moral code, though he still believed it produces laws and rules that address social conflicts better than other methods of resolving interpersonal conflicts. But what if people who determine the laws are not utilitarians? What if the majority of people in a democratic government, including their elected representatives, follow other political philosophies such as justice as fairness? People who share his views will obviously think the majority is wrong and the legislature will make the wrong choices. But what are their alternatives, besides expressing disagreement? Harsanyi did not think majority rule, in and of itself, always produces the best social policies. Under these circumstances, people who share Harsanyi's views and do not want to act justly by accepting the fact that they may be wrong can still agree collectivity is the best structure for society. Justice as choice allows a large group of people who feel strongly that they want to live in a society that determines its rules based on utilitarianism to have the highest probability of that philosophy, at least in determining their domestic laws and social procedures.

But what if people who share Harsanyi's views are in the majority? Can they still accept collectivity, if they want their worldview to be the guide for social policy and do not otherwise want to act justly? Maybe, because Harsanyi believed people can have differing views on social policies due to the complexity of social problems. While he acknowledged that people can disagree on complex social issues, he did not derive collectivity as the moral structure of government because he did not formally include differing worldviews into his modeling. His basic assumptions caused him to reduce his analysis of societal decision-making to a consensus view of one person. A more robust analysis, incorporating people with differing worldviews, would have led him to derive justice as choice for the umbrella structure of government with at least one of the general nested collectives following rule-preference utilitarianism. Therefore, if utilitarians accept the fact that people's worldviews can differ for logically valid reasons, they can accept collectivity.

Can people who share Hayek's worldview support justice as choice as the appropriate umbrella structure of government, even if they cannot accept the fact that he may be wrong? Potentially so, since they will value the ability collectivity provides for people to live in a domestic society whose policies follow Hayek's worldview. However, like those who share the other authors' views, they will still want to convince people who disagree with them that they are wrong.

Hayek's writings favor a more traditional type of competitive federalism instead of collectivity. He preferred a broad federal government whose activities are curtailed by a strong constitution. As discussed in chapter 2, he thought the constitution should provide for extensive personal liberties but not for social or economic rights. Hayek had the opinion that just laws can be "discovered" by structuring congress in a way that makes it more responsive to people's views. He may be correct if everyone has his worldview.

But people who have the varied worldviews of the other four theorists will not all agree that Hayek's political philosophy is optimal and that social and economic rights are unimportant. As such, people have not been willing to adopt his proposed constitution. Even if it was adopted, given the authority it bestows on the central government, it could easily lead to policies contrary to Hayek's views.

The best alternative for a large group of people who cannot accept the fact that his worldview may be wrong is still to accept justice as choice. At a minimum, this allows them to live under the dominion of a domestic government that follows his views. This domestic government can have a constitution that follows Hayek's principles and be controlled by a congressional structure that is divided the way he advocates. Collectivity will enhance the probability that they will discover what they perceive to be inherently just domestic laws. This government is likely to provide public goods, but it will not have a monopoly over the provision of these goods and services. It is also likely to allow smaller independent domestic governments to form. Under collectivity, its laws will be outside the scope of the central government, even if the majority of members of the national legislature prefer different domestic policies.

While Hayek did not propose justice as choice, it is compatible with his broad philosophical views. He argued that knowledge and information are diffused, that people learn from observing other people's successes and failures, and that knowledge is created by experimentation. Dispersed knowledge causes disagreements, because people are unable to correctly recognize true knowledge from mere opinion. Collectivity expands freedom even broader than the policies Hayek advocated because it allows people the highest chance of having their differing worldviews matter.

Hayek's philosophy is one in which governmental policies allow for the largest *individual* freedom and the least interference from government, irrespective of their worldviews. This is not because he thought *individual* freedom is a desirable end, but because he thought it will lead to maximal change and in turn to the highest societal income and wealth creation. However, change does not have uniform effects. It causes or allows people to lose their jobs and communities to change their character, and fosters severe inequality of incomes, wealth, and opportunities. Many people find these consequences of his policies unacceptable and want government programs to ameliorate some of the negative consequences of change allowed by liberal economic theory. People can accept his views on dispersed information without accepting his conclusions that governmental policies different from his preferred laws will make things worse. Hayek could not definitively prove his point of view, and his detractors cannot prove theirs. They each have different worldviews. Collectivity allows people who both agree and disagree with Hayek to differentially address the costs of economic progress.

Hayek did not propose collectivity because he did not consistently apply his concepts to politics. He did not believe that pure logic or reasoning can lead to economic progress; he did not think people responsible for a centralized government can reason through the appropriate methods of providing the goods and services that will lead to increases in economic welfare. He thought increases in societal income require people to have sufficient freedom to pursue their own ideas. However, when it comes to the structure of government and to the best governmental policies, he thought his logically reasoned views should be applied to the broad aspects of a structure for the determination of just laws. He did not recognize that he and the other authors he disagreed with are essentially philosophical entrepreneurs with differing perceived knowledge. Consistently applying his concepts will lead people who share his views to justice as choice. Logic can lead to the limited number of governing principles that comprise collectivity. But logic cannot lead to the extensive principles advocated by Hayek when people have differing worldviews. People who share Hayek's views and accept that others can logically have different worldviews can embrace collectivity because it provides the ultimate in freedom for people to use their perceived knowledge to undertake their personal and social goals. Justice as choice provides the highest chance for the discovery of just laws for people who have differing worldviews but value the safety of being citizens of a large government.

Finally, let's address collectivity from the perspective of people who share Nozick's views but believe it is impossible for him to be wrong. Justice as choice has elements of his views, but it allows for the existence of domestic governments much more extensive than he a priori thought would be just. Collectivity is not the night-watchman state. It consists of a central government with exceedingly limited scope, but it incorporates the possibility of extensive domestic governments. Collectivity provides a framework for the limited domestic government that focuses only on public safety, contract enforcement, and fraud that Nozick thought was just, to exist side by side with the broader centrally administered governments favored by Rawls and Harsanyi.

Will this type of umbrella structure of government be acceptable to people who think Nozick's worldview cannot possibly be wrong? Potentially so, if they are convinced that the domestic governments with scopes broader than the minimal government have a citizenship that embraces this governing ideology, and no one is the subject of some type of fraud or coercion.

Nozick argued that morals are designed to enhance cooperation and that people can legitimately have differing ethics. This led him to embrace libertarianism as the structure that allows people to live in the society that is most accommodative to differing moral beliefs. By expanding his notion of ethics to the broader concept of worldview, those who share his political philosophy can accept collectivity as the most ethical structure of government for people with the varied worldviews and ethical views of the five authors, since it allows for the highest level of coordination.

They can also agree to collectivity as the organizing principle for a society composed of broadly liberal people because it is derived from an "objective" procedure. In fact, using his terminology, collectivity is "strongly objective."[384] As such, people who share his views can conclude that justice as choice is a moral method of increasing cooperation for people with the worldviews of the five authors and is more ethical (for the group of authors) than libertarianism.

In addition, justice as choice is consistent with Nozick's competitive federalist structure of "meta-utopias" when people have differing worldviews. He thought that libertarianism would lead people to form smaller governments that allow them to live in a way they believe is best. However, his analysis does not correctly incorporate the existence and impact of differing worldviews. People's philosophies affect their views of how best to live their lives and how others should be treated by their government. This will lead people who share the opinions expressed by Rawls and Harsanyi to prefer broader and more centrally administered societies. Collectivity allows these broader domestic "meta-utopias" to develop side by side with narrower domestic governments. Justice as choice also addresses Nozick's questions over the responsibilities of the central government. Under collectivity it will have broad powers with respect to external defense and exceedingly limited powers concerning domestic issues. Therefore, people who share his views can accept collectivity even if they do not want to be just.

21

THE RIGHT TO BE WRONG

RIGHTS AND OBLIGATIONS

Rights seem to be at the core of each of the five authors' philosophical views. Rights are complex phenomena. Some rights correspond to government's responsibility to protect what Friedrich Hayek described as people's personal sphere where individuals can make their own decisions without interference from others, including the state. Some people label these types of rights as natural rights. Other rights are those potential actions that some view the government as owing to its citizens, because they are citizens or because they are human beings. These could be political rights such as participation in the social process. They could be economic rights, including a meaningful job or a living wage. They could be social rights such as nondiscrimination and respect from others. Rights are similar to the concept some people have of freedom. The philosopher Isaiah Berlin divided freedom into positive freedoms like economic rights and negative freedoms where government protects people's personal space.[385]

However, none of these rights are without cost. They impose some obligations on other people that they may not want. In fact, rights can be viewed as inverse obligations and obligations as negative rights. One person's right is another person's obligation not to interfere with those rights. Rights are relative phenomena—relative to other people as individuals or as members of a group. The important question is where people want to draw the line between their rights and their obligations or, alternatively, where people "should" draw the line.

People's views on rights and obligations are dependent on their worldviews, and given the complexity of the interaction of people in a social setting, people's opinions on these rights will rarely converge. Some phenomena such as inequality, the pace of technological change, economic volatility, and climate change are so complex that opinions differ on whether they are legitimate issues for government to address. Chapter 12 examined the issue of murder and noted that even though it is a universally acknowledged societal problem, people have varied opinions on how best to address it. These differing opinions lead to conflicting views about people's rights and obligations. In determining people's rights, many questions must be asked and answered. What is murder? When is self-defense murder? Should people be able to stand their ground? Should victims and families have rights? How should murder be punished? Is the death penalty ever acceptable? Should torture ever be condoned? Is abortion murder? Is euthanasia murder? What are the "best" methods of preventing murder? How do we adopt new methods and rules for preventing murder? How do we determine if people are guilty of murder? Should people be able to own guns and knives? The list is almost endless. Should people be able to produce pornography? Should people be able to view pornography? Should prostitution be legal? Should homosexuality be legal? Should people have the ability to manufacture and consume alcohol? What are the best methods of reducing fraud? Should fraud be a crime against society? Should governmental regulations exist to prevent fraud, and if so, what specific type of regulations? Should regulations exist to control the quality of goods? What are the best methods to increase product safety?

In a democracy, temporary majorities will determine the answers to some of these questions and thereby determine people's resulting rights and obligations; answers to other questions will be determined or at least significantly influenced by constitutional provisions designed to protect the minority from the changing views of the majority. For example, consider the "right" to own a gun. For some, the right to own a gun is part of their personal sphere. In their opinion, they should have the right to decide if they should own a gun whether the gun is for self-defense, hunting, or just to possess. Others view the right to own a gun as a potential threat to their welfare and a reduction in their right to be protected from gun violence. They view sanctioned possession of guns by private individuals as a reduction in their right to be protected by the state. The differing views on the right of citizens to possess guns are not just a difference of opinion on whether legal gun ownership causes more violent crime or whether it deters crime. People with differing worldviews will not agree on the answers; they are unlikely to even agree on the facts. Even if they did, they would still disagree on the remedy. If it could definitively be proven that guns do not lead to more violent crime, would people who view gun ownership as wrong really change their view? And vice versa? Yale Law School professor Dan Kahan argues that people may not utilize data to modify their opinions when the data conflicts with their worldview.[386]

In establishing a government, people must set up a process to make decisions even when everyone disagrees. Each government must address societal conflicts and, in the process, determine rights and obligations. Collectivity is the governmental structure that allows broadly liberal and diverse people to best address these differing views.

Chapter 6 discussed the types of conflicts that exist in any multi-person entity composed of diverse individuals. Every government, commonwealth, coercive collective, partnership, limited liability company, and corporation is confronted with potential conflicts between the entity and its members, owners, or citizens. Each of these entities is also confronted with the potential conflicts that exist between their members because of their association with the entity. These conflicts were divided into three broad groupings, one of which was the relative allocation of the benefits provided by the entity. This is the conflict that John Rawls focused on in his theory of justice as fairness. Rawls was concerned with "distributive justice" and thought governmental rules should revolve around addressing this conflict. His view was that each member of society has an obligation to assist the least-well-off group of people to enable them to increase their share of primary goods. He thought the least-well-off group of people had a "right" to this assistance from the rest of society.

Like Rawls, many people are firmly of the belief that collaboration cannot exist without government, and all the benefits from people's joint efforts are due to government and thus are the appropriate subject of a social compact. Others may think people can be productive and cooperate to at least some extent in the absence of government. Government to them may be critical, but it is only a tool or method of improving cooperation and not the sole cause of all the benefits from collaborative effort. Nozick thought government is essential, but he did not think it is the cause of all human progress. He had the opinion that taxation for the purpose of modifying the distribution of income and wealth is unjustifiable and unethical. Other people, including people who share Hayek's views, also focus on the value that potential gains and losses and differential levels of income and wealth have on discovering and utilizing knowledge. Whose views are correct?

As we have previously discussed, that question cannot be answered. The world is simply too complex. There are few truths that relate to societal issues. Therefore, a right to receive an equal share of the social product or a right to receive a larger share because you do not have the advantages or the capabilities of other people are not universally accepted rights. Similarly, a requirement to support people who are poor or provide aid to people who are socially less capable is not a universally acknowledged social obligation. By forming independent domestic governments, people with differing conceptions of how best to address the conflicts that relate to the gains from collaboration can assign the rights and the obligations to members of their nested collective they view as most appropriate.

As was stated above, distribution conflicts are important, but they are not the only conflicts that exist in a coercive collective, or any collective, for that matter. Depending on one's worldview, these types of distribution conflicts may not even be the most important or critical social conflicts to address. For example, the second category of conflicts, the rights and obligations that members of a collective have with respect to the collective itself, have historically been viewed as more critical conflicts that need to be addressed by a constitution.

RIGHTS AND CONFLICTS WITH THE GOVERNMENT

People have varying opinions as to those circumstances when the majority or the majority's representatives should be prohibited from imposing their decisions onto individual behavior. There is a definite conflict between an individual citizen's "right" to act and society's "right" to determine the best methods of protecting society from behavior that is viewed (by some citizens) as unacceptable. The constitutional question is whether there are some potential governmental processes or laws broadly viewed as unjust so that the government should be restricted from their use. The dual question is whether there are personal rights broadly viewed as so critical that the majority view should be restricted. The original, unamended US Constitution contained only a few rights; this relative paucity was a major source of controversy in many of the state ratification committees. Of course, as discussed in part five, the constitution for a federal government that has limited domestic scope would be expected to contain few enumerated rights.

These original rights in the Constitution included the right of protection from illegal detention by the state (writ of habeas corpus), the right to a trial (no bills of attainder), and no retroactive laws (no ex post facto laws).[387] Not surprisingly, given the diversity of worldviews of US citizens, even these few rights have proven to be contentious.

The writ of habeas corpus gives a prisoner the right to have a court review the rationale for the prisoner's incarceration. Even though the right to the use of the "Great Writ" under normal conditions is widely viewed as an important individual right, many have believed the government should have the ability to suspend people's right to use the writ. For that reason, the Constitution allows the government to suspend a prisoner's right to the writ when public safety is at risk from rebellion or invasion. The government has controversially utilized this right from time to time. For example, President Abraham Lincoln and, later, Congress prevented many citizens of the Union states from using the writ during the US Civil War, including people arrested for protesting the draft.[388] More recently, the federal government attempted to prohibit foreign detainees held at the US naval base at Guantanamo

Bay, Cuba, from using the writ. The Supreme Court, in a five-to-four ruling, decided the federal government had overstepped its authority under the Constitution and that prisoners in a territory controlled by the United States had access to the writ.[389] Justice Antonin Scalia, in his dissent, argued that this decision could be extremely limiting to the government, since the government was only allowed under the Constitution to suspend the writ for rebellion or invasion, effectively giving more rights to noncitizens than possessed by citizens. People with differing worldviews obviously have varying opinions on both the rights prisoners in Guantanamo have and "should have." However, unlike the issue of distributional rights, disagreements over enemy-combatant rights cannot be reduced through the use of nested collectives, since these rights relate to issues under the domain of the central government. These rights must be decided through a combination of the constitution and political process applicable to the central government.

The US Constitution's restriction on ex post facto laws follows from the widely held view that laws should apply only to people's future actions and not to past conduct. The relevant question is whether the majority should be restricted from interfering in any way with actions that were legal at the time they were conducted. In the United States, the historical controversy concerning ex post facto laws[390] is whether the prohibition applies to all laws or only to criminal laws.[391] Many people, including at least one of the aforementioned authors, Hayek, thought all laws should be certain and generally applicable to everyone. If the government can impose a law that modifies the legal consequences of past actions, then that type of law is obviously not certain and may not be generally applicable. For example, if the government has the authority to pass retroactive laws, then it can use its knowledge of people's past actions to develop new legislation that targets specific individuals or makes specific types of past actions illegal. For people who share Hayek's worldview, this twenty-twenty-hindsight legislation increases uncertainty, makes people more conservative in their actions and investments, and reduces expected societal income.

While the Constitution prohibits ex post facto laws, this has been interpreted by the Supreme Court as only prohibiting retroactive criminal laws and not applying to civil or contract law. As such, the government is currently allowed to pass legislation that imposes penalties for violations of civil statutes for actions that were previously conducted if it is not designed to punish. The current interpretation also allows the government to enact laws that alter contracts, as long as those laws do not violate other clauses in the Constitution such as the prohibition of taking property without compensation or the due-process clause. Many think people should have the "right" to be protected from retroactive criminal laws but that the personal "right" to be protected from retroactive civil legislation fails to overcome the broader need for the government to have the "right" to pass civil laws that could make people's prior actions illegal. Other people disagree. Like distributional rights, ex post facto laws primarily relate to domestic laws, which implies that nested collectives can address differing views on the right to be protected from them.

As was mentioned earlier, many of the state ratifying conventions criticized the Constitution for not including a more extensive set of rights. This led many of the states' ratifications to include instructions to their representatives of the US Congress to attempt to modify the Constitution by adding certain rights. The eventual results were the first ten amendments to the Constitution, which are colloquially known as the Bill of Rights. The group of rights in the Bill of Rights that relate to conflicts between the federal government and its citizens include: free exercise of religion, right to bear arms, no required quartering of soldiers, protection against unreasonable searches, no warrants without probable cause, restriction against double jeopardy, right to remain silent, due process of law, just compensation for taking private property, speedy and public trials by an impartial jury, public assistance for defense counsel, right to a jury trial for civil disputes, no excessive bail or fines, and no unusual or cruel punishments. Following the passage of the Fourteenth Amendment, the US Supreme Court and other federal and state courts have interpreted these rights as applying to the state and local governments. Almost all of these rights have raised historical issues and have been the subject of significant public debate and numerous court cases.

For example, many of these personal rights have built-in conflicts with people's concerns over public safety. This is especially true for the Fourth Amendment right to privacy, which prohibits unreasonable searches and requires warrants to be issued only if there is probable cause. This right provides a zone of individual privacy, but in so doing it obviously somewhat restricts the government's ability to obtain evidence, prosecute crimes, and prevent new crimes. It reduces the efficiency of law enforcement to protect the community. Some people think this inefficiency is necessary and justified to protect people's innate privacy; others believe criminals can unjustifiably use this privacy right to evade arrest and prosecution. The existence of the right makes it more complicated for the government to prevent both domestic and international terrorism. Some people believe the Fourth Amendment should be broadly interpreted to protect people's individual freedom; other people think the right should be narrowly construed to protect people's safety. The differing views of Supreme Court justices have likely affected their interpretation of the amendment, specifically on how they define reasonableness and the need for warrants. The court has allowed searches based on subpoenas, which typically require the lower standard of "relevance" rather than a warrant issued by a judge based on probable cause. They have also allowed the government to have access to people's electronic records held by a third party, without first obtaining a warrant. The National Security Agency, which, among other tasks, attempts to prevent terrorism, has relied on this interpretation to extensively collect information on citizen's phone calls, including the numbers they called and the length of the calls (metadata). Not surprisingly, their efforts have been controversial.

RIGHTS AND COLLECTIVE-DECISION CONFLICTS

The last type of conflict is the difference of opinion members of an entity may have with respect to the goals and objectives of the entity, as well as the difference of opinion they may have with respect to the method and processes of accomplishing the entity's determined goals.

Unfortunately, entities, even governmental entities, are faced with decision congestion. They must make decisions, but people with differing worldviews and economic interests have varying opinions as to the most appropriate decision the entity should make to accomplish its goals as well as different views as to its goals. Historically, the existence of this type of conflict has led to democracy and the demand by people to participate in the political process of determining societal rules. The basic right associated with this type of conflict is the right to vote. The Bill of Rights has others, including freedom of speech, freedom of the press, right to peacefully assemble, and the right to petition for grievances. Like the other rights in the Constitution, these rights have been the source of controversy. For example, as discussed in part five, universal suffrage is a relatively recent right. A critical question is whether these rights, which address people's differing views, are sufficient for a diverse group of people to address the conflict caused by decision congestion. Is there a right missing?

To answer this question, let's review the analysis of the hypothetical world of the original position. In the original position, decision congestion among a diverse population leads to freedom losses, as people reason that it is in their considered best interest to compromise with people who have worldviews within a certain range of their own worldview. In a large population, the credible equilibrium between diverse people results in a compromise where everyone receives the same gross gain, different levels of freedom losses, and different net gains from collective defense. It results in people joining different defense collectives and forming nested collectives to address domestic differences of opinion. It also leads to each of these coercive collectives adopting the decisions that minimize the freedom losses of its members—not the freedom loss of each member, but of the overall membership. The decision process of minimizing freedom losses is not a result of people's moral convictions. It is used because it allows those in the original position to maximize their net gains, given the productivity gains from collective action and people's differing worldviews. In so doing, it does not discover the truth; it does not produce the most moral decision; it may not determine a decision that any person preferred; and it certainly does not produce complete freedom for a diverse group of people. However, it is the best method for a diverse group of people in the original position to reach a consensus on a set of coercive rules.

The analysis in the prior chapter showed this decision process is a "just" procedure. This procedure revealed certain logical conclusions about how a diverse group of people "should" logically govern themselves. Interestingly, the procedure also uncovered a few, and only a few, "rights" that a diverse group of "just" people will unanimously agree each member of society will possess. One of these rights is to be an equal part of the political process, the process of determining the coercive rules for society. Equal participation is not a result of moral conviction. It is simply the result of the just bargaining situation between unequal but diverse people in the original position.

The overall process will lead to differential rules and laws in different defense and nested collectives. However, the negotiated ability to be an integral part of the decision process is universal and can be viewed as a fundamental right of every member in every collective. This right can lead nondiverse people with certain worldviews to subject themselves to a nondemocratic process in which laws are determined by one person or by someone's interpretation of God's laws. However, for a broadly liberal and diverse group of people, the process will lead to the organizational structure of collectivity. The fundamental right to be involved in the political process is more than just having one's worldview be equally considered in determining the consensus worldview. It includes the important right to be able to form and join independent domestic governments in which each member's worldview is a component of determining the means and methods of accomplishing the goals of the nested collective.

The right to elect the president and members of the federal congress is not sufficient for those in the original position to maximize their net gains and achieve the most they can from compromising with people with differing worldviews. They will negotiate for the additional right to form and join nested collectives not controlled or influenced by the policies and laws of the central government. To achieve the most from collaboration in a world characterized by differing worldviews, people in the original position will bargain for the right to form and join a wide variety of domestic coercive collectives or independent domestic governments.

This negotiated right is not in everyone's a priori interest, even though each person who joins a diverse collective from the original position will compromise and agree that people will have this right. For people who prefer a large domestic government organized around the unifying principle of justice as fairness, and for people who favor fiscal federalism, the unilateral right to form nested collectives is inefficient. Centralization for some or all collective activities, from their perspective, is a better method for structuring society, since these independent domestic governments are not isolated. The actions of these domestic governments and the actions of their members will affect the members of other domestic governments. Policy spillovers and externalities will exist and conflicts will remain. As such, some people will think the right to form domestic governments is not needed and is wrong. However, broadly liberal and diverse people in the original position, even people with worldviews similar to Rawls or Oates, will agree to join a central government that allows people to form various independent domestic governments because that is the cost of increasing the membership of the central government in a world of diverse points of view. These domestic governments need not be the small competitive governments advocated by Gordon Tullock, which were discussed in chapter 19. Large, all-encompassing domestic governments preferred by Rawls can exist side by side with the specialized competitive domestic governments preferred by Tullock. This is a critical degree of freedom as people exit anarchy. However, it is an even more important right in the "real" world where people do not have complete information about everyone's worldviews and must use voting to make societal decisions.

In chapter 16, we argued that decisions based on voting will not necessarily produce the freedom-maximizing decision because voting does not use people's intensities for their preferences. Intensities can lead more people to vote and to be more vocal about their preferences.[392] But voting, even in the presence of the other rights such as free speech and free association, will not always produce the decisions that minimize people's freedom losses. As was discussed, majority voting may not even

produce a consistent decision. While many people view universal suffrage and majority voting as important control rights, especially for their
psychological benefit, they are fairly weak rights with respect to resolving the conflict between people with differing worldviews who are members of the same central government faced with decision congestion.

The right to associate with other people in independent domestic governments significantly expands people's ability to reduce the
conflicts associated with differing points of view about appropriate governments policies. The differing policies within each of these
domestic governments will be viewed as wrong from the perspective
of the members of the other domestic governments. The right of association in independent domestic governments is effectively the "right
to be wrong."[393] It is the right to have a choice in different coercively
enforced domestic rules, even if the majority of people think some of
these domestic rules are based on wrong premises and are immoral.
The right to be wrong is the right to have a unique, broadly liberal
worldview and live under domestic laws more in conformity with this
worldview than would be determined in a unitary government.

Many people will view the existence of independent domestic
governments of varying sizes and scope as inefficient, but they are
only inefficient if everyone has the same worldview. If people have
differing worldviews and do not have complete information as to the
worldviews of others, the existence of multiple independent domestic governments leads to the increasing effectiveness of decisions. The
interaction of the domestic governments and the interaction of their
citizens with the citizens of other domestic governments will lead to
conflicts and the resultant desire for them to resolve these conflicts
through negotiation and compromise. If people have the same worldview, these conflicts can be better resolved through centralization.
If everyone knows the truth, then they can have consistent governmental policies that incorporate this truth. However, the existence of
multiple worldviews within the membership of the same central government, and the inability to determine the truth, implies that these
domestic conflicts are better reconciled through agreements that are
not all encompassing, have time limits, and are limited in scope. The
impact of the lack of public information on everyone's worldview, and

the inability to observe people's true intensities for rival political deci-sions, enhances the importance of some decentralization, since the process of negotiation between the domestic governments and their members involves more information than just people's preferences. It includes people's intensities for their preferences and is therefore a more efficient mechanism for producing coercive domestic decisions than just relying on majority voting by members of the central govern-ment. This does not imply that negotiation between the domestic gov-ernments is free or perfectly efficient. In fact, these governments may not reach an agreement. Negotiations in real life have inherent costs. However, constitutions, limited contracts between domestic govern-ments, and majority voting within the central government and within the domestic governments are more likely to result in decisions that enhance societal gross gains from collaboration than decisions pro-duced by majority voting in an all-powerful central government. The right to be wrong is more likely to result in people on average being more satisfied with interacting with other people, even though some people will rather have more centralized rules.

The right to be wrong in conjunction with the right of universal suffrage can be viewed as "fundamental rights," since they effectively determine the process the state will use to make decisions and grant people additional rights and obligations. Like other rights, they are controversial. But unlike most other rights, they are *universal reasoned* rights that *should* exist in every diverse government. The right to be wrong is essentially the right to have a differing worldview and the right to live under domestic rules with people who have a relatively similar worldview. Like other rights, it also is an obligation—an obliga-tion to allow other people to attempt to live the lives that provide them the highest value by living under coercive domestic laws that can vary from the majority view. It is an obligation to respect others' world-views. It is an obligation on the part of each person to acknowledge the fact that their views may not be right, and that other people's opinions and views may not be wrong. The right to be wrong is an obligation to allow citizens of differing domestic governments to act on what people think are wrong opinions and beliefs. As political philosopher John Locke stated, "For where is the man that has incontestable evidence of the truth that he holds, or of the falsehood of all he condemns; or can say that he has examined to the bottom of his own, or other men's opinions?"[394]

The right to be wrong is the result of a just process. As such, each constitution for a central government that has a pluralistic citizenry will severely limit the central government's domestic scope, and everyone will have the opportunity to be citizens of either general or limited domestic governments. Under a just constitution for a central government, people will have the right to be wrong in their choice of domestic societal rules. This right is likely to be implicit within the constitution of the central government, since all explicit rights are subject to some group's interpretation (e.g., the Supreme Court) of the constitution. The implicit right to be wrong can be achieved by limiting the scope of the central government and reserving all powers not delegated to the central government for the people who can then choose whether to be a citizen of a centrally managed domestic government or a series of decentralized domestic governments.

The fact that the right to be wrong is a just right for citizens of a pluralistic society implies that each person who wants to be a just member of that society must favor the inclusion of the right as part of the set of rights guaranteed by the government. They can compromise on many other rights, since people have differing worldviews. But a just person will not compromise on the right for people to be governed by differing independent domestic governments—even when they view the policies of some of these governments to be wrong.

RIGHT TO BE WRONG AND THE US CONSTITUTION

The US Constitution does not explicitly include the right to be wrong, nor is it a right the US Supreme Court has interpreted to be a right under the Constitution. How is this possible? If the right to be wrong is one of the fundamental rights for a pluralistic society, how can it not be a right under the Constitution? There are only two possibilities. Either the right is not in the Constitution and the Constitution is missing a right that would be produced by a just procedure among diverse and broadly liberal people, or the right is an implicit right under the Constitution, but one that has historically not been acknowledged.

The original un-amended Constitution was a remarkable document that had many redeeming qualities; however, as discussed above, it lacked a series of rights that many people thought were important, which over time has led to a number of amendments. That the original Constitution could be unjust from some people's perspectives is not surprising, since it appears that a just process neither produced it nor determined its terms. Rawls argued that there does not exist a real-world process to determine a just political contract. Procedural justice, for Rawls, is only possible through a reasoned process such as the original position. He is probably correct, but unfortunately, as was shown, his procedure did not eliminate all biases. The process that produced the un-amended Constitution seems to be procedurally unjust for many reasons. These include the facts that: (i) a minority of the population chose the delegates to the Constitutional Convention and the state ratifying conventions, (ii) the delegates made decisions through majority voting, and (iii) the population had differing levels of information. However, following its ratification, it was amended. Many of those amendments restricted the actions of the federal government by providing certain rights for people subject to the Constitution. Could some combination of these rights imply that people in the United States have the constitutional right to be wrong?

The amended Constitution directly recognizes the possibility that people have rights that are not enumerated. The Ninth Amendment states: "The enumeration in the Constitution, of certain rights, shall not be construed to deny or disparage others retained by the people." Similarly, the Tenth Amendment reserves powers not delegated to the United States to either the states "or to the people."[395] But how are these unenumerated rights to be identified? Over time, the Supreme Court has used the due-process clauses to identify some of these rights. The due-process clause of the Fifth Amendment prohibits the central government from depriving "any person of life, liberty, or property, without due process of law." The Fourteenth Amendment places the same restriction on the states. Due process "of law" has been interpreted by the Supreme Court to refer to "substantive due process" where the majority view must give way to the "fundamental" rights retained by the people rather than referring to a failure by the government to follow a specific legal process.

In a recent case where the Supreme Court held that individuals have an unenumerated right (in this instance, same-sex marriage) that was not historically acknowledged, Justice Anthony Kennedy, writing for the majority of the court in *Obergefell v. Hodges*, stated:

> *In addition these liberties extend to certain personal choices central to individual dignity and autonomy, including intimate choices that define personal identity and beliefs . . . The identification and protection of fundamental rights is an enduring part of the judicial duty to interpret the Constitution. That responsibility . . . requires courts to exercise reasoned judgment in identifying interests of the person so fundamental that the State must accord them its respect . . . History and tradition guide and discipline this inquiry but do not set its outer boundaries . . . That method respects our history and learns from it without allowing the past alone to rule the present . . . The nature of injustice is that we may not always see it in our own times. The generations that wrote and ratified the Bill of Rights and the Fourteenth Amendment did not presume to know the extent of freedom in all of its dimensions, and so they entrusted to future generations a charter protecting the right of all persons to enjoy liberty as we learn its meaning. When new insight reveals discord between the Constitution's central protections and a received legal stricture, a claim to liberty must be addressed.*[396]

He continued by writing that

> *rights come not from ancient sources alone. They rise, too, from a better informed understanding of how constitutional imperatives define a liberty that remains urgent in our own era . . . Indeed, in interpreting the Equal Protection Clause, the Court has recognized that new insights and societal understandings can reveal unjustified inequality within our most fundamental*

institutions that once passed unnoticed and unchallenged . . .
Of course, the Constitution contemplates that democracy is the
appropriate process for change, so long as that process does not
abridge fundamental rights . . . The idea of the Constitution
"was to withdraw certain subjects from the vicissitudes of polit-
ical controversy, to place them beyond the reach of majorities
and officials and to establish them as legal principles to be
applied by the courts" . . . This is why "fundamental rights may
not be submitted to a vote; they depend on the outcome of no
elections."[397]

The line of thinking that led the Supreme Court to come to the
reasoned judgment that people under the Constitution have the fundamental right of privacy and other rights with respect to marriage,
family relationships, procreation, contraception, and child rearing
could also lead them to judge that people have the fundamental right
to differences in opinion as to the domestic laws they want to govern themselves. They could reason that people's liberty is materially
reduced by not having the right to form and be citizens of independent
domestic governments—independent from the policies of the central
government, as well as independent of the policies and laws of the
states. They could reason and agree with the analysis throughout this
book that justice requires that people must have the choice to associate
with other people in domestic governments both limited and extensive. Majority voting, freedom of speech, and freedom of the press are
not sufficient rights for pluralistic people to govern themselves. People
with differing worldviews require the right to be free from almost all
the domestic rules established by the majority of people in the United
States; people need to be accorded the power to govern themselves
under the limited powers of the central government, as long as they
are citizens of some domestic government that accords them the delegated power to determine the laws to appropriately govern themselves.

The unenumerated rights determined by substantive due process
are some of the most highly contentious issues that have been historically addressed by the Supreme Court. Chief Justice Roberts, in his
dissenting opinion in *Obergefell*, stated:

The Constitution . . . "is made for people of fundamentally differing views" . . . Our precedents have required that implied fundamental rights be "objectively, deeply rooted in this Nation's history and tradition," and "implicit in the concept of ordered liberty, such that neither liberty nor justice would exist if they were sacrificed" . . . The only way to ensure restraint in this delicate enterprise is "continual insistence upon respect for the teachings of history, solid recognition of the basic values that underlie our society, and wise appreciation of the great roles [of] the doctrines of federalism and separation of powers."[398]

The right to be wrong is derived by an objective process for broadly liberal people with differing worldviews. It is inextricably related to the historical debate on federalism; but, as we discussed, it depends on a broader type of federalism than is currently interpreted to be the federalist structure that exists under the US Constitution. Collectivity envisions a central government with extensive authority over external threats but with limited powers over domestic issues; it also incorporates various independent domestic governments more varied than the states of the union. Federalism that is incorporated in collectivity is really nothing more than a diverse form of "home rule." Could the Supreme Court have historically misinterpreted people's right to home rule under the Constitution? It is certainly possible.

In Justice Samuel Alito's dissenting opinion in the same case, he states, "The system of federalism established by our Constitution provides a way for people with different beliefs to live together in a single nation."[399] Justice Alito is correct, but the current interpretation of federalism by the Supreme Court does not allow people to sufficiently live under the laws that most accord with their worldviews, causing discord within society. The will of the majority has trumped people's ability to have laws determined by others with relatively similar worldviews. Laws and rules are important to many people; for these people to live the lives they most value, they need to have more influence over domestic laws and policies than can be achieved by voting and public discussion at the level of the central government. Home rule is the most fundamental of rights for people of differing views. This is not a new concept.

> *The preservation of this "Home Rule" by the States is not a cry of jealous Commonwealths seeking their own aggrandizement at the expense of sister States. It is a fundamental necessity if we are to remain a truly united country . . . . We are safe from the danger of any such departure from the principles on which this country was founded just so long as the individual home rule of the States is scrupulously preserved.*[400]

Franklin Roosevelt gave this speech when he was governor of New York. This may be surprising because as president, Roosevelt was associated with a broad and expansive central government. His speech shows that people's worldviews can change over time or at least with circumstances. But it also highlights, along with the dissenting opinions of Justices Roberts and Alito, the historical importance and significance of federalism and home rule.

The question for the justices of the Supreme Court, if they ever were asked to make a reasoned judgment as to people's fundamental right to be wrong, is whether people's liberty of home rule has been deprived by both the United States and the state governments. The justices could come to the reasoned view that people have a fundamental right to be wrong because it accords with the nation's history, it is logical, and it is consistent with the values embedded in the Constitution. In Justice Roberts's dissenting opinion in *Obergefell*, he also argues that

> *a Justice's commission does not confer any special moral, philosophical, or social insight . . . There is indeed a process due the people on issues of this sort—the democratic process. Respecting that understanding requires the Court to be guided by law, not any particular school of social thought.*[401]

While this may be a sound assessment of judgments regarding the rights related to marriage, it would not be a valid criticism of a decision validating the right to be wrong, since that right is not dependent on one particular worldview. It is one of the few social rights that can be logically deduced given pluralistic schools of thought. The democratic process in and of itself is incapable of determining this right because this right determines the "just" democratic process. That is why it is not only a fundamental right, but *the* fundamental right for a pluralistic liberal people.

A judgment of this type would, of course, surprise many people, but maybe they should not be surprised, since as Roosevelt also stated, "The United States Constitution has proved itself the most marvelously elastic compilation of rules of government ever written."[402] However, a determination that people in the United States have the constitutional right to the federalist political process of collectivity will overturn many historical precedents. This right will require that the court narrowly interpret both the powers of the federal government and the states. Given the significance of the change, it will also require the court to design a process to ease the transition to the newly "found" right to be wrong. One such process could be the formation of districts or regional governments composed of multiple states. The existing Constitution could be "pushed down" to these districts as their founding governance document. Each of the districts could then either leave the Constitution as is or follow the process of amending the constitution contained within the Constitution. The end result would be choice in domestic governments, under the protection of a limited central government. Given the diversity of views within the United States and the autonomy and delegated power to the citizens of each of the districts, some of these regions would more than likely be broad and powerful centrally managed domestic governments. Others would be limited domestic governments in which people would have the right to form various types and sizes of other independent domestic governments. Those districts that chose the former would need to amend their constitutions to eliminate people's authority to form independent governments within the district. These districts that did so would resemble the type of federalist structure currently interpreted by the Supreme Court to apply to the federal government. Other districts could be more like the type of government preferred by Nozick.

FINAL THOUGHTS

The conclusion to this theoretical inquiry into the political process that would arise from a group of broadly liberal people in the original position with varying worldviews is that they will unanimously choose justice as a unifying principle for their agreed structure of government. Those who decide to exit anarchy will recognize that they need to voluntarily subject themselves to coercive rules to increase cooperation. Each will accept everyone's right to have a different ideology and to live under domestic laws that most conform to their worldview, constrained only by the number of people who share their views and by other living conditions they value.

This does not imply they will not try to convince people with differing views they are wrong. People will continue to think they are right and people with differing social philosophies are wrong. But each of them is incentivized to compromise with people who have differing views because of the perceived benefits of coercive collective action. These citizens of large federal governments will agree to allow everyone to be citizens of independent domestic governments—because it is in their own best interest. This is the logical result of people in an original position who attempt to maximize their net gains from coercive collective action by using a just bargaining process. In a sufficiently large population of broadly liberal and diverse people, the desire to live under rules most in accord with one's worldview will cause each of them to compromise but to suffer differentially from that compromise.

Not everyone in the original position will have worldviews that can be categorized as broadly liberal, and not all broadly liberal people will have views on external defense that are compatible. This will lead to an equilibrium of differing governments that focus on external defense. Some of these will be unitary, populated by people with similar views—views potentially guided by religious beliefs. Others will have citizens with diverse views, which, given incomplete constitutional contracts, will lead to the federalist structure of collectivity. This type of government consists of a central government that has narrow powers—powers focused on external defense. It has a series of domestic governments: some large, some small that are focused on allowing people to establish their preferred domestic rules to engender cooperation. Each of these governments, both central and domestic, will have a central governing structure determined by a constitution. All will make their decisions through a process that involves many factors, including their constitution, periodic voting, elected officials, judges, and public debate. Federal and domestic governments will also enter into agreements with other governments concerning additional ways to cooperate, to resolve conflicts, and to address externalities. The process of reaching these agreements is necessarily costly, since it is a method of societal decision-making that incorporates people's preferences and intensities for their preferred decisions.

Collectivity is the only just structure of government for a broadly liberal and pluralistic people, but does it satisfy some type of utopian ideal? H. G. Wells, author of *The Time Machine*, wrote one of the seminal modern books on utopia, and toward the end of the book he asks:

> *Why should not all these peoples agree to teach some common language, French, for example, in their common schools, or to teach each other's languages reciprocally? Why should they not aim at a common literature, and bring their various common laws, their marriage laws, and so on, into uniformity? Why should they not work for a uniform minimum of labour conditions through all their communities? Why, then, should they not—except in the interests of a few rascal plutocrats—trade freely and exchange their citizenship freely throughout their common boundaries? . . . What is there to prevent a parallel movement of all the civilised Powers in the world towards a common ideal and assimilation? Stupidity—nothing but stupidity, a stupid brute jealousy, aimless and unjustifiable. The coarser conceptions of aggregation are at hand, the hostile, jealous patriotisms, the blare of trumpets and the pride of fools; they serve the daily need though they lead towards disaster.*[403]

Wells's view of utopia cannot be reconciled with a world where people have differing worldviews. His views encapsulate the classic concept held by many people that utopia is grand, perfect, but unattainable because people are stupid or greedy or powerful or uneducated. His concepts follow in a long tradition of the thinking of the smartest people who have ever lived,[404] who thought they had perfect insight into how the social world works and that utopia could be achieved by society following their preferred schemes and processes.[405] For example, the political philosopher Karl Marx, in his *Critique of the Gotha Programme*, argued that communism would ultimately result in an allocation of value from those who can to those who "need."[406]

While many of Wells's and Marx's preferred policies have been incorporated into the laws of various countries, their broad concepts will not be the structure people in the original position will choose. Nor do their policies produce a just structure of government for people with diverse worldviews. People will choose to be citizens of a vast government (or at least protected by one) because external defense has massive economies of scale that cannot be achieved without centralization. However, coercive collective action relative to domestic decisions can be disaggregated, even though many of these actions also have significant economies of scale. Many people will willingly suffer the relative inefficiency of being members of a smaller domestic government for the gain in freedom from living under laws and coercive procedures closer to the ones they prefer and value. In a just society, people will allow them this freedom even though some would prefer everyone to be subject to common domestic rules.

People have differing views not because they are stupid or selfish, although they may have these attributes. Their views differ because the social world is too complicated for people to reason through all the interconnections to determine the truth. It appears too complex for the five authors to come to agreement on their preferred social policies, even though it seems clear that their advocated policies and approaches to societal problems are not due to stupidity, selfishness, education, or prejudice. These differing views, together with incomplete constitutions, will lead broadly liberal people who want to act justly to accept collectivity as their preferred structure of government.

Is this utopia? Not under the traditional definition. People exiting the original position and forming coercive collectives have addressed the fundamental conflicts involved with increasing their level of cooperation. Their bargaining has shown how a just government can be structured for broadly liberal people with differing worldviews. The result is a kaleidoscope of governments, some general, some limited, organized in a polycentric fashion. While this complex web of cooperation allows diverse people to be subject to laws more compatible to their worldviews than is possible under existing governments, it is not utopia. Utopia requires everyone to have the same worldview. It also requires that worldview to be the accurate representation of the implications of all social interaction. In a world where the truth concerning social interaction cannot be known, people can use public discussion to narrow the range of disagreement, but utopia cannot exist. The best that can be achieved is for people to be on a path to utopia. This path consists of people living under rules they view as the most accurate approximation of the truth. Collectivity allows people with the broadly liberal and diverse worldviews of the five authors to jointly cooperate in defense while simultaneously living under domestic rules that best fit their worldviews. Collectivity provides everyone the right to be wrong, and it is the only just structure of government for a broadly liberal people with diverse worldviews. People will still disagree with many laws and governmental procedures. But the laws produced by collectivity are produced by a just process, and they are the best that nonperfect people, who have irreconcilable politics, can achieve.

NOTES

★

PART ONE: DIFFERING WORLDVIEWS

I: INTRODUCTION

1   Romina McGuinness, "French back burkini ban: Only six per cent against beach rule, survey finds," *Express* (UK), August 26, 2016, http://www.express .co.uk/news/world/704223/French-burkini-ban-six-per-cent-against-beach -rule. The French polling group Ifop found that 64 percent of the people they asked in August 2016 approved of the burkini ban.

2   Inti Landauro and William Horobin, "'Burkini' Goes Against French Values, Says French Prime Minister," *Wall Street Journal*, August 17, 2016, https:// www.wsj.com/articles/burkini-goes-against-french-values-says-french -prime-minister-1471444201.

3   *The Sydney Morning Herald*, "France's top court suspends 'illegal' burkini ban that 'breaches fundamental freedoms,'" August 27, 2016, http://www .smh.com.au/world/frances-top-court-suspends-illegal-burkini-ban-that -breaches-fundamental-freedoms-20160826-gr2gke.html.

4   David Hume, *Idea of a Perfect Commonwealth* (Indianapolis: Liberty Fund, 2016), http://oll.libertyfund.org/titles/boll-70-david-hume-idea-of-a -perfect-commonwealth-1777.

5   Walter Block and Thomas J. DiLorenzo, "Is Voluntary Government Possi- ble? A Critique of Constitutional Economics," *Journal of Institutional and Theoretical Economics* 156, no. 4 (2000): 567–582. Block and DiLorenzo argue that "voluntary government" cannot happen. While a voluntary gov- ernment has never historically existed, it is theoretically conceivable and is a useful concept for deriving a just structure of government when people have differing worldviews.

6   Ronald Dworkin, *Taking Rights Seriously* (Cambridge, MA: Harvard University Press, 1978); and Ronald Dworkin, *Justice for Hedgehogs* (Cambridge, MA: Harvard University Press, 2011).

7   Dworkin, *Justice for Hedgehogs* (2011), 356.

2: COMPETING POLITICAL PHILOSOPHIES

8   John Rawls, *A Theory of Justice* (Cambridge, MA: The Belknap Press of Harvard University Press, 1971); John Rawls, *Political Liberalism* (New York: Columbia University Press, 1993); and John Rawls, *The Law of Peoples with "The Idea of Public Reason Revisited"* (Cambridge, MA: Harvard University Press, 2002). The review of his political philosophy is primarily based on *A Theory of Justice*, but his later works are utilized.

9   Rawls, *A Theory of Justice* (1971), 140.

10   Rawls, *Political Liberalism* (1993), 14.

11   Rawls, *A Theory of Justice* (1971), 15.

12   Rawls, *The Law of Peoples with "The Idea of Public Reason Revisited"* (2002).

13   Immanuel Kant, *Perpetual Peace*, translated by W. Hastie (Philadelphia: Slought Foundation, 1891).

14   Rawls, *The Law of Peoples with "The Idea of Public Reason Revisited"* (2002), 79.

15   Amartya Sen, *The Idea of Justice* (Cambridge: Harvard University Press, 2009); and Amartya Sen, *Development as Freedom* (New York: Anchor Books, 2000. Most of the discussion of Sen's views are based on my interpretation of his writings in these two books.

16   Adam Smith, *The Theory of Moral Sentiments* (Indianapolis: Library of Economics and Liberty, 1982), book 1, section 1, chapter 5, paragraph 43.

17   Sen, *The Idea of Justice* (2009), 17.

18   Sen, *Development as Freedom* (2000), 17.

19   Sen, *The Idea of Justice* (2009), 251.

20   Jonathan Derbyshire, "*Prospect* Interviews Amartya Sen," *Prospect*, July 18, 2013, https://www.prospectmagazine.co.uk/magazine/prospect-interviews -amartya-sen-the-full-transcript-jonathan-derbyshire.

21   John C. Harsanyi, "Cardinal Welfare, Individualistic Ethics, and Interpersonal Comparisons of Utility," *Journal of Political Economy* 63 (1955): 309–321; John C. Harsanyi, "Can the Maximin Principle Serve as a Basis for Morality? A Critique of John Rawls' Theory," *American Political Science Review* 69 (1975): 594–606; John C. Harsanyi, "Nonlinear Social Welfare Functions," *Theory and Decisions* 6 (1975): 311–332; John C. Harsanyi, "Morality and the Theory of Rational Behavior," in *Utilitarianism and*

Beyond, edited by Amartya Sen and Bernard Williams (Cambridge: Cambridge University Press, 1982); and John C. Harsanyi, "Does Reason Tell Us What Moral Code to Follow and, Indeed, to Follow Any Moral Code at All?" *Ethics* 96, no. 1 (1985): 42–55. The review of Harsanyi's worldview is primarily based on these papers.

22 Harsanyi, "Morality and the Theory of Rational Behavior" (1982), 56.

23 Ibid., 45.

24 Friedrich A. Hayek, *The Constitution of Liberty* (Chicago: University of Chicago Press, 1960); Friedrich A. Hayek, *Law, Legislation and Liberty, Volume 1: Rules and Order* (Chicago: University of Chicago Press, 1973); Friedrich A. Hayek, *Law, Legislation and Liberty, Volume 2: The Mirage of Social Justice* (Chicago: University of Chicago Press, 1976); and Friedrich A. Hayek, *Law, Legislation and Liberty, Volume 3: The Political Order of a Free People* (Chicago: University of Chicago Press, 1979). The discussion of Hayek's political philosophy is based primarily on these works.

25 Hayek, *The Constitution of Liberty* (1960), 207.

26 David Ricardo, *The Works and Correspondence of David Ricardo: On the Principles of Political Economy and Taxation*, vol. 1, edited by Pierro Sraffa, with the collaboration of M. H. Dobb (Indianapolis: Liberty Fund, 2004); and Adam Smith, *An Inquiry into The Nature and Causes of The Wealth of Nations*, edited by Edwin Cannan, with an introduction by Max Lerner (New York: The Modern Library, 1937). David Ricardo (1772–1823) was a political economist who developed the important concept of "comparative advantage." It states that countries can efficiently trade even if one of them is absolutely more efficient at producing goods than all of the others. As long as people are *relatively* more efficient, then trade or collective action is in everyone's interest. This idea and the concept of the benefits of the division of labor, attributed to Adam Smith (1723–1790), are the basic reasons why collective action is so important.

27 Hayek, *The Constitution of Liberty* (1960), 82.

28 Robert Nozick, *Anarchy, State, and Utopia* (New York: Basic Books, 1974).

29 "Professor Robert Nozick," *Telegraph* (UK), January 28, 2002, http://www .telegraph.co.uk/news/obituaries/1382871/Professor-Robert-Nozick.html.

30 Nozick, *Anarchy, State, and Utopia* (1974), 169.

31 Ibid., 312.

3: AMALGAMATING DISPARATE WORLDVIEWS

32 Owenism is a type of socialism popularized by Robert Owen in the nineteenth century. He thought that people's environment was an essential

element in the development of their character. As such, he advocated that communities be established for the poor.

33   John Stuart Mill, *Utilitarianism*, 1863 edition (Kitchner: Batouche Books, 2001), 54.

34   Amartya Sen, *Development as Freedom* (New York: Anchor Books, 2000), 255–261.

35   Joseph A. Schumpeter, *Capitalism, Socialism and Democracy* (New York: Harper & Row, 1975), 83.

36   Immanuel Kant, *Critique of Judgment: Including the First Introduction,* translated and introduction by Werner S. Pluhar, with a forward by Mary J. Gregor (Indianapolis: Hackett Publishing Co., 1987), 111. *Weltanschauung* is translated as "intuition of the world."

37   Douglass C. North, *Transaction Costs, Institutions, and Economic Performance* (San Francisco: International Center for Economic Growth, 1992), 8. Other examples are John H. Holland, Keith J. Holyoak, Richard E. Nisbett, and Paul R. Thagard, *Induction: Process of Inference, Learning, and Discovery* (Cambridge: MIT Press, 1986), 354; and Anthony Downs, *An Economic Theory of Democracy* (New York: Harper, 1957), 96.

38   John Rawls, *Political Liberalism* (New York: Columbia University Press, 1993), 13.

39   Krishna K. Ladha, "The Condorcet Jury Theorem, Free Speech, and Correlated Votes," *American Journal of Political Science* 36, no. 3 (1992): 617–634; and Krishna K. Ladha, "Condorcet's Jury Theorem in Light of De Finett's Theorem: Majority-Rule Voting with Correlated Votes," *Social Choice and Welfare* 10, no. 1 (1993): 69–85.

40   Leonard J. Savage, *The Foundations of Statistics*, 2nd revised edition (New York: Dover Publications, 1972) provides an in-depth discussion of Bayesian decision-making.

41   John Harsanyi, "Games with Incomplete Information Played by 'Bayesian Players' Part I," *Management Science* 14, no. 3 (1967): 159–182; John Harsanyi, "Games with Incomplete Information Played by 'Bayesian Players' Part II," *Management Science* 14, no. 5 (1968): 320–334; and John Harsanyi, "Games with Incomplete Information Played by 'Bayesian Players' Part III," *Management Science,* 14 (1968): 486–502.

42   Stephan Lewandowsky, Ullrich K. H. Ecker, Colleen M. Seifert, Norbert Schwarz, and John Cook, "Misinformation and Its Correction: Continued Influence and Successful Debiasing," *Psychological Science in the Public Interest* 13, no. 3 (2012): 106–131.

43   Robert J. Aumann, "Agreeing to Disagree," *The Annals of Statistics* 4, no. 6 (1976): 1236–1239; and Robert J. Aumann, "Correlated Equilibrium as an Expression of Bayesian Rationality," *Econometrica* 55, no. 1 (1987): 1–8.

44   John D. Geanakoplos and Heraklis M. Polemarchakis, "We Can't Disagree Forever," *Journal of Economic Theory* 28, no. 1 (1982): 192–200.

45   Aanund Hylland and Richard Zeckhauser, "The Impossibility of Bayesian Group Decision Making with Separate Aggregation of Beliefs and Values," *Econometrica* 47, no. 6 (1979): 1321–1336.

46   Brian Barry, *A Treatise on Social Justice: Justice as Impartiality*, vol. 2 (Oxford: Clarendon Press, 1995).

47   See T. M. Scanlon, "Contractualism and Utilitarianism," in *Utilitarianism and Beyond*, edited by Amartya Sen and Bernard Williams (Cambridge: Cambridge University Press, 1982): 103–129, for a discussion of his view on contractualism.

48   Stephen Morris, "The Common Prior Assumption in Economic Theory," *Economics and Philosophy* 11 (1995): 227–253. Morris provides a discussion of the traditional assumption in economic analysis that people have common models of how the world works. This assumption makes any analysis more tractable, since in its absence the structure of people's model differences must somehow be established or assumed. However, the bargaining analysis that will be used in the forthcoming discussion presumes that people have differing models of the world that lead to differing judgments on social goals and governmental policies. But they are also assumed to have a "common" model with respect to determining the optimal bargaining outcome.

PART TWO: ANARCHY AND INTERPERSONAL CONFLICTS

4: INDIVIDUALS AND BARGAINING

49   John C. Harsanyi, *Essays on Ethics, Social Behavior, and Scientific Explanation* (Boston: D. Reidel Publishing Co., 1980); John C. Harsanyi, "Morality and the Theory of Rational Behavior," in *Utilitarianism and Beyond*, edited by Amartya Sen and Brian Williams (Cambridge: Cambridge University Press, 1982); and John C. Harsanyi, *Rational Behavior and Bargaining Equilibrium in Games and Social Situations* (Cambridge: Cambridge University Press, 1989). These are examples of Harsanyi's work in which he does not explicitly use bargaining.

50   James M. Buchanan and Gordon Tullock, *The Calculus of Consent: Logical Foundations of Constitutional Democracy* (Ann Arbor: University of Michigan Press, 1971), 62.

51   David P. Gauthier, *Morals by Agreement* (Oxford: Clarendon Press, 1986).

52 Ehud Kalai and Meir Smorodinsky, "Other Solutions to Nash's Bargaining Problem," *Econometrica* 43, no. 3 (1975): 513–518.

53 Ken Binmore, *Game Theory and the Social Contract, Volume 1: Playing Fair* (Cambridge, MA: The MIT Press, 1994), 82; and Michele Marie Uzan-Milofsky, *David Gauthier's Contractarian Moral Theory*, (Ann Arbor, MI: Proquest LLC, 2014), PhD thesis.

54 Binmore, *Game Theory and the Social Contract, Volume 1: Playing Fair* (1994); Ken Binmore, *Game Theory and the Social Contract, Volume 2: Just Playing* (Cambridge, MA: The MIT Press, 1998); and Ken Binmore, *Natural Justice* (Oxford: Oxford University Press, 2005).

55 Binmore, *Game Theory and the Social Contract, Volume 1: Playing Fair* (1994), 80.

56 Ibid., 78.

57 Joseph Heath, "Methodological Individualism," *Stanford Encyclopedia of Philosophy*, January 21, 2015, https://plato.stanford.edu/entries /methodological-individualism/ has a discussion of the term.

58 Amartya Sen, *The Idea of Justice* (Cambridge, MA: The Belknap Press of the Harvard University Press, 2009), 245.

59 Joshua Miller, "Billionaires Buffett and Gates: Tax Us More!" ABC News, November 28, 2010, http://abcnews.go.com/ThisWeek/billionaires-buffett -gates-tax-us/story?id=12259003 provides an example.

5: THE WIDE, WIDE WORLD OF PHILOSOPHICAL ANARCHY

60 Rajiv Sethi, "Nash Equilibrium," *International Encyclopedia of the Social Sciences*, 2nd edition (Detroit: Macmillan, 2007): 540–542, http://www .columbia.edu/~rs328/NashEquilibrium.pdf. Sethi provides a discussion of the Nash equilibrium, named after John Nash. Nash was a mathematician who won the Nobel Prize in economics for his contributions to game theory.

61 John Locke, *Two Treatises of Government*, edited by T. Hollis (London: A. Millar et. al, 1764), http://oll.libertyfund.org/titles/locke-the-two -treatises-of-civil-government-hollis-ed.

62 The early philosophers such as Thomas Hobbes, David Hume, John Locke, etc., called it the "state of nature." Today it usually goes under the rubric "anarchy." When many people hear the word "anarchy," they typically either think of chaos or the failure of government. Both concepts are consistent, since the abrupt elimination of any type of government, even a corrupt one, is typically followed by violence and disorder. However, it is less clear that this has to be the theoretical situation before the formation of government (i.e., in the original position).

63 Thomas Hobbes, *Leviathan* reprinted from the edition of 1651 with an Essay by the late W. G. Pogson Smith (Oxford: Clarendon Press, 1909).

64 Ibid., book 1, chapter 13, 96.

65 Ibid., 96–97.

66 Carl von Clausewitz, *On War*, edited by A. Rapoport (London: Penguin Books, 1982), 123.

67 Winston C. Bush and Lawrence S. Mayer, "Some Implications of Anarchy for the Distribution of Property," *Journal of Economic Theory* 8 (1974): 401–412.

68 Michael Taylor, *The Possibility of Cooperation* (Cambridge: Cambridge University Press, 1987).

69 Michelle R. Garfinkel and Stergios Skaperdas, "Economics of Conflict: An Overview," April 2006, http://www.socsci.uci.edu/~sskaperd /GarfinkelskaperdasHB0306.pdf.

70 Stergios Skaperdas, "Cooperation, Conflict and Power in the Absence of Property Rights," *The American Economic Review* 82, no. 4 (1992): 720–739.

71 Garfinkel and Skaperdas, "Economics of Conflict: An Overview" (2006).

72 Jack Hirshleifer, *The Dark Side of the Force: Economic Foundations of Conflict Theory* (Cambridge: Cambridge University Press, 2001).

73 The paradox of power does not exist in every situation. For example, if fighting is extremely effective, the person with higher initial resources will invest relatively more in arming and increase his or her probability of winning. Nonetheless, in some situations, the stronger and better-endowed side need not win.

74 Thomas C. Schelling, *Arms and Influence* (New Haven: Yale University Press, 2008).

75 Mancur Olson, *The Logic of Collective Action* (Cambridge, MA: Harvard University Press, 1971).

76 Ibid., 2.

77 Garfinkel and Skaperdas, "Economics of Conflict: An Overview" (2006).

78 Daron Acemoglu and James A. Robinson, "A Theory of Political Transitions," *The American Economic Review* 91, no. 4 (2001): 938–963; and Robert Powell, "War as a Commitment Problem," *International Organization* 60, no. 1 (2006): 169–203.

79 Jean-Jacques Rousseau, *The Major Political Writings of Jean-Jacques Rousseau: The Two Discourses & The Social Contract*, translated and edited by John T. Scott (Chicago: University of Chicago Press, 2012), 93. See also Brian Skyrms, *The Stag Hunt and the Evolution of Social Structure* (Cambridge: Cambridge University Press, 2004).

80   See John C. Harsanyi, *Rational Behavior and Bargaining Equilibrium in Games and Social Situations* (Cambridge: Cambridge University Press, 1989).

81   Robert Axelrod, "An Evolutionary Approach to Norms," *The American Political Science Review* 80, no. 4 (1986): 1095–1111.

82   Peter T. Leeson, "The Law of Lawlessness," *Journal of Legal Studies* 38 (2009): 471–503.

83   Steven D. Levitt and Sudhir Alladi Venkatesh, "An Economic Analysis of a Drug-Selling Gang's Finances," *The Quarterly Journal of Economics* 115, no. 3 (2000): 755–789.

84   Ibid., 758.

85   Edward P. Stringham, "The Extralegal Development of Securities Trading in Seventeenth Century Amsterdam," *Quarterly Review of Economics and Finance* 43 (2003): 321–344.

86   Ibid., 332.

87   Oliver E. Williamson, *Markets and Hierarchies: Analysis and Antitrust Implications* (New York Free Press, 1975), 9.

88   George Akerlof, "The Market for 'Lemons': Quality Uncertainty and the Market Mechanism," *The Quarterly Journal of Economics* 84, no. 3 (1970), 488–500. Akerlof, in his famous article on "lemons," provides a discussion of the impact from being unable to distinguish a good car from a bad car (lemon). Good cars will not be produced.

89   Benjamin Klein and Keith B. Leffler, "The Role of Market Forces in Assuring Contractual Performance," *Journal of Political Economy* 89, no. 4 (1981): 615–641. Economists Klein and Leffler analyzed an analogous situation. For them, the only effective way to prevent cheating is to persuade sellers to stay in the market, since every time a seller leaves the industry they are incentivized to first cheat the buyer. They suggest that the market (buyers as a group) will be willing to offer sellers prices higher than would be produced in a competitive market to induce them not to cheat. Under these circumstances, sellers are earning excess profits that should incentivize them to stay in the industry and not cheat the buyers, but it will also lead to a desire for others to enter the industry. Klein and Leffler argue that this competition will lead to "firm-specific" investments. Successful sellers are then competitively required to make these investments that only have direct value to them. The presence of these sunk costs implies that the seller is worth more as an ongoing concern.

90   Stringham, "The Extralegal Development of Securities Trading in Seventeenth Century Amsterdam," (2003), 336.

91   Robert M. Townsend, "Optimal Multiperiod Contracts and the Gain from Enduring Relationships under Private Information," *Journal of Political*

Economy 90, no. 6 (1982): 1166–1186. The potential need for investment in sunk investments has been recognized by a wide variety of people. Townsend's paper is an example.

92   Murray N. Rothbard, *For a New Liberty: The Libertarian Manifesto* (New York: Collier, 1978).

93   David Friedman, *The Machinery of Capital: A Guide to Radical Capitalism*, 2nd edition (Open Court Publishing Company, 1989), http://www .daviddfriedman.com/The_Machinery_of_Freedom_.pdf.

6: CONFLICTS WITHIN ORGANIZATIONS

94   Michael C. Jensen and William H. Meckling, "Theory of the Firm: Managerial Behavior, Agency Costs and Ownership Structure," *Journal of Financial Economics* 3, no. 4 (1976): 305–360.

95   Dennis H. Robertson, *The Control of Industry* (Selwyn: J. Nisbit, 1923), 85.

96   Armen Alchian and Harold Demsetz, "Production, Information Costs, and Economic Organization," *The American Economic Review* 62, no. 5 (1972): 777–795.

97   Sanford J. Grossman and Oliver D. Hart, "The Costs and Benefits of Ownership: A Theory of Vertical and Lateral Integration," *Journal of Political Economy* 94, no. 4 (1986): 691–719; and Oliver Hart and John Moore, "Property Rights and the Nature of the Firm," *Journal of Political Economy* 98, no. 6 (1990): 1119–1158.

98   Aristotle, *The Nicomachean Ethics of Aristotle*, translated by F. H. Peters, M. A., 5th edition (London: Kegan Paul, Trench, Truedbner & Co., 1893), book III, part IV.

99   Edgar Stanton Maclay, *A History of American Privateers* (New York: D. Appleton and Company, 1924).

100   Peter T. Leeson, *The Invisible Hook: The Hidden Economics of Pirates* (Princeton: Princeton University Press, 2009); and Peter T. Leeson, "Anarrgh-chy: The Law and Economics of Pirate Organization," *Journal of Political Economy* 115, no. 6 (2007): 1049–1094.

101   John Esquemeling, *The Buccaneers of America: A True Account of the Most Remarkable Assaults Committed of Late Years upon the Coast of the West Indies by the Buccaneers of Jamaica and Tortuga, both English and French*, introductory essay by Andrew Lang, edited by William Swan Stallybrass, translated by Alonso De Bonne-Maison (London: George Routledge & Sons Ltd., 1684), 60.

102   Captain Charles Johnson, *A General History of the Pyrates: From Their First Rise and Settlement in the Island of Providence, to the Present Time. With the*

remarkable Actions and Adventures of the two Female Pyrates Mary Read and Anne Bonny, 2nd edition, with considerable additons (T. Warner, 1724): 209, http://www.gutenberg.org/files/40580/40580-h/40580-h.htm. Probably written under a pseudonym.

103 Ibid., 230.

104 Ibid., 232.

PART THREE: THEORY OF VOLUNTARY GOVERNMENT

7: BARGAINING: A PRIMER

105 Ingolf Stahl, *Bargaining Theory* (Stockholm: Stockholm School of Economics, 1972).

106 Ariel Rubinstein, "Perfect Equilibrium in a Bargaining Model," *Econometrica* 50, no. 1 (1982): 97–109.

107 Reinhard Selten, "Multistage Game Models and Delay Supergames," *Economic Sciences* (December 9, 1994): 200–229, http://www.nobelprize.org/nobel_prizes/economic-sciences/laureates/1994/selten-lecture.pdf.

108 Avner Shaked and John Sutton, "Involuntary Unemployment as a Perfect Equilibrium in a Bargaining Model," *Econometrica* 52, no. 6 (1984): 1351–1364.

109 Frank P. Ramsey, "A Mathematical Theory of Savings," *The Economic Journal* 38, no. 152 (1928): 543–559.

110 Amartya Sen, "On Optimizing the Rate of Savings," *Economic Journal* 71 (1961): 479–496.

111 Ken Binmore, *Game Theory and the Social Contract: Just Playing* (Cambridge, MA: The MIT Press, 1998), 122 fn.

112 Ken Binmore, "Perfect Equilibria in Bargaining Models, 1982," in *The Economics of Bargaining* (Oxford: Basil Blackwell, 1987).

113 In comparing the two methods, it is important to adjust the compounding rates to reflect each person's instantaneous discount rate.

114 Let φ_i be the ith person's discount factor, which incorporates his or her time discount rate. The average difference in present values is weighted by:

$$\frac{1}{1-\varphi_1\varphi_2}$$

115 In the traditional formulation of Rubinstein's model, where the first person has a bargaining advantage, the first person bargains for x_1^* which is equal to:

$$x_1^* = \frac{1-\varphi_2}{1-\varphi_1\varphi_2}$$

In the limit, as the length of each bargaining period approaches zero, this reduces to:

$$x_1^* = \frac{r_2}{r_1 + r_2}$$

where r_i is the ith person's instantaneous discount rate that underlies his or her discount factor:

$$\varphi_i$$

116 The person with the lowest discount rate (the person who has a 10 percent instantaneous discount rate) bargains for $20/(10+20) = 0.6666$. The person with the highest discount bargains for $10/(10+20) = 0.3333$.

8: COLLECTIVE DEFENSE

117 Let d_i represent the positive quantity of defense for individual i. Also let this person's marginal value from an incremental unit of defense be MU_i which is assumed to continually decrease as the quantity of defense increases. In addition, let A_i represent each person's constant positive linear value for all other goods. C represents their common constant marginal costs of defense. That is, each incremental unit of defense has the same cost, represented by C. Under these assumptions, each person in anarchy will choose the d_i where:

$$C = \frac{MU_i}{A_i}$$

This is their optimal quantity of defense, d_i^*.

118 The marginal cost of anarchical defense is the same for each person and equal to C. This implies that each person's total cost of equilibrium anarchical defense is:

$$TC_i = C \bullet d_i^* + FC_i$$

where d_i^* is the optimal quantity of anarchical defense by person i and FC_i is their fixed cost of anarchical defense. The total cost of collective defense is:

$$\sum_{i=1}^{N} TC_i - N \cdot K$$

119 If there are N people in anarchy who all agree to join in collective defense, then the optimal quantity of collective defense occurs where:

$$\sum_{i=1}^{N} C = N \cdot C = \sum_{i=1}^{N} \frac{MU_i}{A_i}$$

120 See Paul A. Samuelson, "The Pure Theory of Public Expenditure," *The Review of Economics and Statistics* 36, no. 4 (1954): 387–389.

121 Recall that we are still assuming that people have perfect information about their own values as well as perfect information about every other person's values.

122 Bernard Bailyn, *The Ideological Origins of the American Revolution*, enlarged edition (Cambridge, MA: Belknap Press, 1992), 62; and J. Trenchard and M. Walter, *An Argument Showing, that a Standing Army is inconsistent with A Free Government, and absolutely destructive to the Constitution of the English Monarchy* (London, 1697). Bernard Bailyn, in his classic discussion of the American Revolution, argues that the fear of standing armies was "derived" from earlier English writers like John Trenchard.

123 James Madison, "Avalon Project - Madison Debates - June 29," avalon.law .yale.edu/18th_century/debates_629.asp.

124 Patrick Henry, "Article 1, Section 8, Clause 16: Document 10, Patrick Henry, Virginia Ratifying Convention (June 5, 1788)," in *The Founders' Constitution*, vol. 3 (Chicago: University of Chicago Press, 1987), http://press-pubs .uchicago.edu/founders/print_documents/a1_8_16s10.html.

125 James Madison, "Article 1, Section 8, Clause 12: Document 27, Debate in Virginia Ratifying Convention (June 14, 1788)," in *The Founders' Constitution*, vol. 3 (Chicago: University of Chicago Press, 1987), http://press-pubs .uchicago.edu/founders/documents/a1_8_12s27.html.

126 James Wilson, "Article 1, Section 8, Clause 12: Document 13, James Wilson, Pennsylvania Ratifying Convention (December 11, 1787)," in *The Founders' Constitution*, vol. 3 (Chicago: University of Chicago Press, 1987), http:// press-pubs.uchicago.edu/founders/print_documents/a1_8_12s13.html.

127 Marion Mills Miller, *Great Debates in American History: From the Debates in the British Parliament on the Colonial Stamp Act (1764–1765) to the Debates in Congress at the Close of the Taft Administration (1912–1913)*, vol. 9 (New York, Current Literature Publishing Company, 1913), 194–196.

128 Ibid. Lee was previously the governor of Virginia and known as "Light-Horse Harry." He was related to John Randolph.

129 *The All-Volunteer Military: Issues and Performance* (The Congress of the United States - Congressional Budget Office, July 2007), 3. Not all of the draftees served "in country."

130 Robert J. Samuelson, "Faculty Will Consider Second Draft Proposal," *The Harvard Crimson* (January 6, 1967), http://www.thecrimson.com/article /1967/1/6/faculty-will-consider-second-draft-proposal/.

131 James Tobin, "On Limiting the Domain of Inequality," *Journal of Law & Economics* 13, no. 2 (1970): article 2, 270.

132 Article 5 of the North Atlantic Treaty Organization, http://www.nato.int /cps/en/natohq/official_texts_17120.htm, is an example.

133 Amartya Sen, *The Argumentative Indian: Writings on Indian History, Culture and Identity* (London and New York: Allen Lane, 2005), chapter 12: India and the Bomb.

134 John Rawls, *The Law of Peoples with "The Idea of Public Reason Revisited"* (Cambridge: Harvard University Press, 2002), 9.

135 These are traditionally called Von Neumann-Morgenstern utility functions.

136 John von Neumann and Oskar Morgenstern, *Theory of Games and Economic Behavior* (Princeton: Princeton University Press, 1953). Von Neumann and Morgenstern used cardinal utility, labeling it "transferable utility."

137 Erik Lindahl, "Just Taxation—A Positive Solution," in *Classics in the Theory of Public Finance*, edited by Richard A. Musgrave and Alan T. Peacock (New York: Palgrave Macmillan, 1958), 168–176.

138 Each person is assumed to contribute the same amount of efficiency to collective defense by reducing the total fixed costs of collective defense by K per incremental person.

139 Each person's total cost of anarchical defense is equal to:

$$TC_i = C \bullet d_i^* + FC_i$$

The total fixed cost of collective defense for two people is equal to:

$$FC_1 + FC_2 - K$$

9: TWO-PERSON COLLECTIVE DEFENSE

140 Sarah agrees to receive her freedom losses of 10 plus a percentage of the net gains of 60 equal to Sam's instantaneous discount rate of 10 divided by the sum of their instantaneous discount rates of 30.

141 John Tierney, "The Big City; Two-Bedroom Quandary," *The New York Times Magazine*, June 14, 1998, http://www.nytimes.com/1998/06/14/magazine /the-big-city-two-bedroom-quandary.html; and Julian Sanchez, "Robert Nozick's Final Interview," Libertarianism.org, July 26, 2001, https://www .libertarianism.org/publications/essays/robert-nozicks-final-interview.

142 John Stuart Mill, *Utilitarianism*, 1863 edition (Kitchner: Batouche Books, 2001), 10.

143 In the simple two-person defense collective, we are abstracting from the issues related to actual enforcement of their agreement.

10: THREE-PERSON COLLECTIVE DEFENSE: COMPETING POLITICS

144 Suchan Chae and Jeong-Ae Yang, "The Unique Perfect Equilibrium of an N-person Bargaining Game," *Economics Letters* 28, no. 3 (1988): 221–223; Martin J. Osborne and Ariel Rubinstein, *Bargaining and Markets* (San Diego: Academic Press, 1990); Suchan Chae and Jeong-Ae Yang, "An N-person Pure Bargaining Game," *Journal of Economic Theory* 62, no. 1 (1994): 86–102; Vijay Krishna and Roberto Serrano, "Multilateral Bargaining," *Review of Economic Studies* 63, no. 1 (1996): 61–80; Vincent J. Vannetelbosch, "Rationalizability and Equilibrium in N-person Sequential Bargaining," *Economic Theory* 14, no. 2 (1999): 353–371; Chen-Ying Huang, "Multilateral Bargaining: Conditional and Unconditional Offers," *Economic Theory* 20, no. 2 (2002): 401–412; and Sang-Chul Suh and Quan Wen, "A Multi-Agent Bilateral Bargaining Model with Endogenous Protocol," *Economic Theory* 40, no. 2 (2009): 203–226; Jean-Jacques Herings and Arkadi Predtetchinski, "Sequential Share Bargaining," *International Journal of Game Theory* 41, no 2 (2012): 301–323. These are examples of academic research in this area.

145 For example, let F_i^D be person i's freedom losses from three-person collective defense. And let F_i^{ij} be person i's freedom losses from two-person collective defense involving person j. The net gains from adding person z to the coalition between i and j is given by:

$$K - (\sum_{l=1}^{3} F_l^D) + F_i^{ij} + F_j^{ij}$$

where l represents $i, j,$ and z. If the freedom-maximizing decisions in adding person z to the two-person coalition of i and j does not result in a change from the freedom-maximizing decisions between i and j. That is:

$$F_i^D = F_i^{ij}$$

and

$$F_j^D = F_j^{ij},$$

then the net gains of adding person z reduces to:

$$K - F_z^D.$$

146 Margaret's (person z) partial equilibrium allocation along this partial credible equilibrium path is given by:

$$\frac{1}{2}(K - (\sum_{l=1}^{3} F_l^D) + F_i^{ij} + F_j^{ij}) + F_z^D.$$

147 Cali's (person i) partial equilibrium allocation from adding Margaret is given by:

$$\frac{1}{2}(K - F_i^{ij} - F_j^{ij}) + \frac{1}{4}(K - (\sum_{l=1}^{3} F_l^D) + F_i^{ij} + F_j^{ij}) + F_i^D.$$

148 As stated previously, technically there are six different paths that can be reduced to three because of the symmetry of two-person bargaining under the assumption that the length of each bargaining period in the limit approaches zero. This simplification will not hold for populations beyond three.

149 Lloyd S. Shapley, "Utility Comparison and the Theory of Games," Rand Corporation (1967), https://www.rand.org/pubs/papers/P3582.html.

150 Faruk Gul, "Bargaining Foundation of Shapley Value," *Econometrica* 57, no. 1 (1989): 81–95; Eyal Winter, "The Demand Commitment Bargaining and Snowballing Cooperation," *Economic Theory* 4, no. 2 (1994): 255–273; Sergiu Hart and Andreu Mas-Colell, "Bargaining and Value," *Econometrica* 64, no. 2 (1996): 357–380; and Ani Dasgupta and Stephen Chiu, "On Implementation via Demand Commitment Games," *International Journal of Game Theory* 27 (1999): 161–190. These works are some of the research on multiple-person noncooperative bargaining situations in which equilibrium allocations are equal to the Shapley Value.

151 Under the assumption that each two-person coalition has positive net gains and none of the allocations along any of the paths has needed to be capped at K, the credible equilibrium allocation to person i in bargaining with persons j and z, and where l refers to person i, j, and z, is given by:

$$\frac{1}{3}\left(2K - \sum_{l=1}^{3} F_l^D - \frac{1}{4}\left(F_i^{ij} + F_j^{ij} + F_i^{iz} + F_z^{iz}\right) + \frac{1}{2}\left(F_j^{jz} + F_z^{jz}\right)\right) + F_i^D.$$

11: DEMOCRATIC DEFENSE COLLECTIVE

152 Net gains for the N-person defense collective are:

$$(N-1) \bullet K - \sum_{i=1}^{N} F_i^D$$

where person i's freedom losses from the freedom-loss minimizing decisions are given by:

$$F_i^D .$$

153 In the limit, no one's equilibrium allocation of gross gains is affected by relative or absolute freedom losses in any of the partial credible equilibrium paths. Therefore, in the limit, each person's gross gains are equal to:

$$K .$$

Their net gains are:

$$K - F_i^D .$$

154 Albert O. Hirschman, *Exit, Voice, and Loyalty: Responses to Decline in Firms, Organizations, and States* (Cambridge: Harvard University Press, 1970).

155 Consumer surplus is the excess value a person receives from paying a given price of a good versus the maximum price he or she would pay for each quantity of the good.

12: DOMESTIC COLLECTIVE GOALS AND METHODS

156 *State of Ohio v. Thomas*, 673 N.E. 2d 1339-1343 (1997 Ohio).

157 Teresa Thomas - The National Registry of Exonerations - University of Michigan Law School," https://www.law.umich.edu/special/exoneration /.../casedetail.aspx?

158 *State of Ohio v. Thomas* (1997).

159 Ibid.

160 Ibid.

161 "Guns," Gallup Poll, 2016, http://www.gallup.com/poll/1645/guns.aspx.

162 Ibid.

163 *State v. Ronald Quarles*, 85-87-C. A. (1986).

164 Ibid.

165 "2015 Crime in the United States," Federal Bureau of Investigation, n.d., https://ucr.fbi.gov/crime-in-the-u.s/2015/crime-in-the-u.s.-2015/tables /table-1.

166 "2010 Crime in the United States," Federal Bureau of Investigation, n.d., https://ucr.fbi.gov/crime-in-the-u.s/2010/crime-in-the-u.s.-2010 /tables/10tbl01.xls.

167 "International Homicides (per 100,000 people)," The World Bank (2017).

168 Bruce L. Benson, *The Enterprise of Law: Justice Without the State* (San Francisco: Pacific Research Institute, 1990).

169 Mirjan R. Damaška, *The Faces of Justice and State Authority: A Comparative Approach to the Legal Process* (New Haven: Yale University Press, 1986), introduction.

170 Edward L. Glaeser and Andrei Shleifer, "Legal Origins," *The Quarterly Journal of Economics* 117, no. 4 (2002): 1193–1229.

171 Rafael La Porta, Florencio Lopez-de-Silanes, and Andrei Shleifer, "The Economic Consequences of Legal Origins," *Journal of Economic Literature* 46, no. 2 (2008): 285–332, 326.

172 Bryce Lyon, *A Constitutional and Legal History of Medieval England* (New York: Harper, 1960).

173 "Death Penalty," Gallup Historical Trends, 2016, http://www.gallup.com /poll/1606/death-penalty.aspx.

174 Pope John Paul II, "Evangelium Vitae," Libreria Editrice Vaticana (1995), http://w2.vatican.va/content/john-paul-ii/en/encyclicals/documents/hf _jp-ii_enc_25031995_evangelium-vitae.html.

175 Cesare Bonesana di Beccaria, "An Essay on Crimes and Punishments (1764)" (Indianapolis: Liberty Fund, n.d.), http://oll.libertyfund.org /titles/2193.

176 Gary S. Becker, "Crime and Punishment: An Economic Approach," *The Journal of Political Economy* 76, no. 2 (1968): 169–217.

177 See Richard A. Posner, "An Economic Theory of the Criminal Law," *Columbia Law Review* 85, no. 6 (1985): 1193–1231; and Richard A. Posner, "Law and Economics Is Moral," *Valparaiso University Law Review* 24, (1990): 163–173.

178 "EU Guidelines on the Death Penalty," Council of the European Union, n.d., www.consilium.europa.eu/uedocs/cmsUpload/10015.en08.pdf; and "Belarus: First Death Sentence in 2017," Worldwide Movement for Human Rights, March 21, 2017, https://www.fidh.org/en/region/europe-central-asia /belarus/belarus-first-death-sentence-in-2017.

179 "Death Penalty," Gallup Poll, 2016, www.gallup.com/poll/1606/death-penalty .aspx.

180   Art Swift, "Americans: 'Eye for an Eye' Top Reason for Death Penalty," Gallup Poll, October 23, 2014, http://www.gallup.com/poll/178799/americans-eye-eye-top-reason-death-penalty.aspx.

181   *McGautha v. California*, 402 U.S. 183 (1971).

182   Ibid.

183   Ibid.

184   Ibid.

185   *Furman v. Georgia*, 408 U.S. 238 (1972).

186   Ibid.

187   Ibid.

188   Ibid.

189   Ibid.

190   *Gregg v. Georgia*, 428 U.S. 153 (1976).

191   Ibid.

192   Ibid.

193   Kevin Robinson, "Florida Executes Kormondy for Rape, Murder," *Pensacola News Journal*, January 15, 2015, http://www.pnj.com/story/news/crime/2015/01/14/pensacola-man-executed-tomorrow-kormondy/21752779/; and Alexia Fernandez, "Rape Survivor's Journey Comes Full Circle With Execution of Attacker," *WUFT*, February 5, 2015, https://www.wuft.org/news/2015/02/05/rape-survivors-journey-comes-full-circle-with-execution-of-attacker/.

194   Dana Ford, "Oklahoma Executes Charles Warner," *CNN*, January 15, 2015, http://www.cnn.com/2015/01/15/us/oklahoma-execution-charles-frederick-warner/index.html.

195   *Hill v. State*, 263 GA 37, 427 S.E. 2d 770, 774 (1993)

196   State of Missouri vs. David Zink, https://missourideathrow.com/2009/02/zink-david/.

197   *Kennedy v. Louisiana* 554 U.S. 407 (2008).

198   Sarah Elks, "Drug Taken Before Pregnancy Confirmed," *The Australian*, October 13, 2010, http://www.theaustralian.com.au/news/nation/drug-taken-before-pregnancy-confirmed/news-story/22580a3b698434b999993440d5aa05c4.

199   Sarah Elks, "Couple Accused of Procuring Abortion Not Ready for Child, Court Hears," *The Weekend Australian*, October 12, 2010, http://www.theaustralian.com.au/news/nation/couple-accused-of-procuring-abortion-not-ready-for-child-court-hears/news-story/64326d9cf849ee9ab04d0631a651b888.

200 Cosima Marriner, "Abortion Couple Not Aware They Broke Law," *The Sydney Morning Herald*, September 19, 2009, http://www.smh.com.au /national/abortion-couple-not-aware-they-broke-law-20090918-fvcg.html.

201 Cosima Marriner, "Couple Face Jail After Drugs Used to Abort Pregnancy," *The Sydney Morning Herald*, September 4, 2009, http://www.smh.com.au /national/couple-face-jail-after-drugs-used-to-abort-pregnancy-20090903 -fa3j.html; and "Cairnes Woman Tegan Leach Pleads Not Guilty in Queensland's First Trial for a Home Abortion," *The Courier Mail*, October 12, 2010, http://www.couriermail.com.au/news/queensland/pro-choice -activists-protest-as-cairns-couple-face-trial-for-using-abortion-drug /news-story/fbe4cba7ef48db3df66aa69a580e87a3.

202 Wendy Carlisle, "Crown Kicks Own Goal in QLD Abortion Trial," *ABC News*, October 14, 2010, http://www.abc.net.au/news/2010-10-15/crown -kicks-own-goal-in-qld-abortion-trial/2298608.

203 Queensland Maternity and Neonatal Clinical Guidelines Program, "Thera-peutic Termination of Pregnancy," *Queensland Government* (April 2013), 6.

204 George Williams and Ngaire Watson, "Abortion Laws: Time to Reform?" *Precedent* no. 102 (January/February 2011): 38–41.

205 Ibid.

206 Ibid.

207 http://www.cherishlife.org.au/.

208 Sarah Elks, "Verdict Proves Abortion Laws No Longer Relevant, Say Pro-Choice Advocates," *The Weekend Australian*, October 14, 2010, http://www .theaustralian.com.au/news/nation/jury-out-in-landmark-abortion -trial/news-story/088df6f3d533f919f8703dfef05e660b.

209 "Abortion," Gallup Poll, 2017, www.gallup.com/poll/1576/abortion.aspx.

210 *Roe v. Wade*, 410 U.S. 113 (1973).

211 *Planned Parenthood of Southeastern Pa. v. Casey*, 505 U.S. 833 (1992).

212 Ibid.

213 Brief for Ronald Dworkin, Thomas Nagel, Robert Nozick, John Rawls, Thomas Scanlon, and Judith Jarvis Thomson as Amici Curiae in Support of Respondents: State of Washington v. Harold *Glucksberg*, Nos. 95-1858, 96–110 (December 10, 1996), https://cyber.harvard.edu/bridge/Philosophy /philbrf.htm.

214 J. L. Mackie, *Ethics: Inventing Right and Wrong* (Harmondsworth: Penguin Books, 1990).

215 Patrick Devlin, *The Enforcement of Morals* (London: Oxford University Press, 1965).

216 Ibid., 10.

217 Ronald Dworkin, *Taking Rights Seriously* (Cambridge: Harvard University Press, 1978); and H. L. A. Hart, *Law, Liberty, and Morality* (London: Oxford University Press, 1967).

218 Robert P. George, *Making Men Moral: Civil Liberties and Public Morality* (Oxford: Clarendon Press, 2001), 20.

219 Ibid., 45.

220 Saint Thomas Aquinas, *Summa Theologica*, question 96, article 2, 791.

221 John Stuart Mill, *On Liberty*, edited, with an introduction by Elizabeth Rapaport (Indianapolis: Hackett Publishing Company, Inc., 1978), 9.

222 Hart, *Law, Liberty, and Morality* (1967), 47.

223 Robert Nozick, *Invariances: The Structure of the Objective World* (Cambridge: Belknap Press of Harvard University Press, 2001), 282.

224 "FDA at a Glance: FDA-Regulated Products and Facilities," US Food & Drug Administration, April 2017, https://www.fda.gov/downloads /AboutFDA/Transparency/Basics/UCM553532.pdf.

225 "About FDA: What We Do," US Food & Drug Administration, April 4, 2017, https://www.fda.gov/aboutfda/whatwedo/.

226 *Mariann Hopkins v. Dow Corning Corporation*, 33 F.3d 1116 (U.S. Court of Appeals for the Ninth Circuit, August 26, 1994).

227 Ibid.

228 Jane Meredith Adams, "Victim of Silicone Breast Implants Wants Value Placed on Women's Lives," *Chicago Tribune*, February 9, 1992, http:// articles.chicagotribune.com/1992-02-09/news/9201120870_1_dow -corning-mariann-hopkins-silicone.

229 Ibid.

230 *Mariann Hopkins v. Dow Corning Corporation* (1994).

231 Zarina S. F. Lam and Dileep Hurry, "Dow Corning and the Silicone Implant Controversy" *Historical Working Papers*, 156 (1992): 3, http://scholar.smu .edu/business_workingpapers.

232 Gina Kolata, "A Case of Justice, or a Total Travesty? How the Battle Over Breast Implants Took Dow Corning to Chapter 11," *The New York Times*, June 13, 1995, http://www.nytimes.com/1995/06/13/business/case -justice-total-travesty-battle-over-breast-implants-took-dow-corning -chapter.html.

233 "Dow Corning Shuts Down Silicone Breast Implant Production Lines," UPI, January 14, 1992, http://www.upi.com/Archives/1992/01/14/Dow -Corning-shuts-down-silicone-breast-implant-productionlines /9633695365200/.

234 R. R. Cook and L. L. Perkins, "The Prevalence of Breast Implants Among Women in the United States," *Immunology of Silicones* (1996): 419–425.

235 Memorandum by the Medical Devices Agency (B 1) (April 4, 2001).

236 David Bernstein, "The Breast Implant Fiasco," *California Law Review* 87, no. 2 (1999).

237 Re: Breast Implant Litigation, 11F. Supp. 2nd 1217 (D. Colo. 1998).

238 Institute of Medicine, *Safety of Silicone Breast Implants*: "Conclusions and Research Recommendations" (Washington, DC: National Academies Press, 1999).

239 Milton Friedman and Rose Friedman, *Free to Choose: A Personal Statement* (San Diego: Harcourt Brace Jovanovich, 1990).

240 Jackie Farwell, "Judge Overturns Maine Law Allowing Prescription Drug Imports," *Bangor* [ME] *Daily News*, February 24, 2015, http://bangordailynews.com/2015/02/24/health/judge-overturns-maine-law-allowing-prescription-drug-imports/.

13: DOMESTIC GOVERNMENTS

241 The analysis, thus far, assumes that the gains from government and taxes are completely interchangeable and that every person is selfish with respect to both. To derive a broader tax policy in some of the nested collectives, the linkage of government gains and taxes could be eliminated. People could then be modeled as seeking to maximize the net gains from government, which are not fungible with taxes.

242 Guido Tabellini, "The Scope of Cooperation: Values and Incentives," *The Quarterly Journal of Economics* 123, no. 3 (2008): 905–950, 938.

PART FOUR: COLLECTIVE RULES, SERVICES, AND DECISIONS

14: COLLECTIVE RULES AND TYPES OF VOLUNTARY GOVERNMENTS

243 John Rawls, *The Law of Peoples with "The Idea of Public Reason Revisited"* (Cambridge: Harvard University Press, 2002), 90.

244 Underage Drinking . . . Actions Have Consequences, http://www.closterboro.com/closter/Departments/Police%20Department/Underage%20Drinking%20Advisory.pdf.

15: COLLECTIVE SERVICES AND NONCOERCIVE ORGANIZATIONS

245 The Philadelphia Contributionship was organized by Benjamin Franklin in 1752. Like any collective, including a coercive collective, the members of a mutual insurance company must agree to its rules. The provision of fire insurance has aspects of science, but it also involves a variety of judgments that must be made concerning insurable risks, investments, and the prices that should be charged for various types of risks. See Mutual Assurance Company (Green Tree) records, 1784–1995, Collection 2189, www2.hsp .org/collections/manuscripts/m/MutualAssurance2189[FINAL].html.

246 Jon H. Hanf and Maximilian Iselborn, "How to deal with quality problems of German wine cooperatives: A double principal-agent approach," Academy of Wine Business Research and Hochschle Geienheim University, June 2014, http://academyofwinebusiness.com/wp-content/uploads/2014/07 /BM05_Iselborn_Maximilian.pdf.

247 Ibid.

248 James M. Buchanan, "An Economic Theory of Clubs," *Economica* 32, no. 125 (1965): 1–14.

249 Mark V. Pauly, "Clubs, Commonality and the Core: An Integration of Game Theory and the Theory of Public Goods," *Economica,* 34 (1967): 314–324; Eitan Berglas, "On the Theory of Clubs," *Papers and Proceedings of the American Economic Association* 66 (1976): 116–121; Eitan Berglas and David Pines, "Clubs, Local Public Goods and Transportation Models A Synthesis," *Journal of Public Economics* 15 (1981): 141–162; Richard Cornes and Todd Sandler, *The Theory of Externalities, Public Goods and Club Goods* (Cambridge: Cambridge University Press, 1986); and Alessandra Casella, "On Markets and Clubs: Economic and Political Integration of Regions with Unequal Productivity," *American Economic Review Papers and Proceedings* (1992): 115–121. These papers are a subset of the available research.

250 Todd Sandler and John Tschirhart, "Club Theory: Thirty Years Later," *Public Choice* 93, no. 3/4 (1997): 335–355.

251 Kristian Behrens, Gilles Duranton, and Frédéric Robert-Nicoud, "Productive Cities: Sorting, Selection, and Agglomeration," *Journal of Political Economy* 122, no. 3 (2014): 507–553.

252 Oded Hochman, David Pines, and Jacques-François Thisse, "On the Optimal Structure of Local Governments," *The American Economic Review* 85, no. 5 (1995): 1224–1240.

253 Duncan Black and Vernon Henderson, "A Theory of Urban Growth" *Journal of Political Economy* 107, no. 2 (1999): 252–284.

16: MAJORITY VOTING AND FREEDOM-MAXIMIZING DECISIONS

254 The concept is so important that Harvard University economist Oliver Hart was the corecipient of the Nobel Prize in economics in 2016 for his contributions to the study of incomplete contracts. See "Oliver Hart - Facts," Nobelprize.org, https://www.nobelprize.org/nobel_prizes/economic .../hart-facts.html.

255 Kenneth J. Arrow, *Social Choice and Individual Values*, forward by Eric S. Maskin (New Haven, CT: Yale University Press, 2012).

256 Allan Gibbard, "Manipulation of Voting Schemes: A General Result," *Econometrica* 41 (1973): 587–601; and Mark Allen Satterthwaite, "Strategy-Proofness and Arrow's Conditions: Existence and Correspondence Theorems for Voting Procedures and Social Welfare Functions," *Journal of Economic Theory* 10, no. 2 (1975): 187–217.

257 Amartya Sen, "The Impossibility of a Paretian Liberal," *Journal of Political Economy* 78, no. 1 (1970): 152–157.

258 Amartya Sen, "The Possibility of Social Choice," *The American Economic Review* 89, no. 3 (1999): 364.

259 Kenneth O. May, "A Set of Independent Necessary and Sufficient Conditions for Simple Majority Decision," *Econometrica* 20, no. 4 (1952): 680–684.

260 David Mayers and Clifford W. Smith Jr., "Contractual Provisions, Organizational Structure, and Conflict Control in Insurance Markets," *The Journal of Business* 54, no. 3 (1981): 407–434.

261 J. David Cummins, Mary A. Weiss, and Hongmin Zi, "Organizational Form and Efficiency: The Coexistence of Stock and Mutual Property-Liability Insurers," *Management Science* 45, no. 9 (1999): 1254–1269.

262 Oliver Hart, Andrei Shleifer, and Robert W. Vishny, "The Proper Scope of Government: Theory and an Application to Prisons," *Quarterly Journal of Economics* 112, no. 4 (1997): 1127–1161.

263 James M. Buchanan, *The Limits of Liberty: Between Anarchy and Leviathan* (Chicago: University of Chicago Press, 1975); James M. Buchanan, *Liberty, Market and State: Political Economy in the 1980s* (Brighton: Harvester Wheatsheaf Books, 1986); Gordon Tullock, "Social Cost and Goverment Action," *The American Economic Review* 59, no. 2 (1969): 189–197; Gordon Tullock, *Wealth, Poverty, and Politics* (New York: Basil, Blackwell, 1988); Mancur Olson Jr., "The Principle of 'Fiscal Equivalence': The Division of Responsibilities among Different Levels of Government," *American Economic Review* 59, no. 2 (1969): 479–487; William A. Niskanen, "The Peculiar Economics of Bureaucracy," *The American Economic Review* 58, no. 2 (1968): 293–305; William H. Riker, *Federalism: Origin, Operation, Significance* (Boston: Little, Brown, 1964); and Anthony Downs, *An Economic Theory of Democracy* (New York: Harper, 1957).

264 Gene M. Grossman and Elhanan Helpman, "Protection for Sale," *The American Economic Review* 84, no. 4 (1994): 833–850; and Gene M. Grossman and Elhanan Helpman, "Electoral Competition and Special Interest Politics," *The Review of Economic Studies* 63, no. 2 (1996): 265–286.

265 Mancur Olson, *The Rise and Decline of Nations: Economic Growth, Stagflation, and Social Rigidities* (New Haven: Yale University Press, 1982).

17: TIME AND COLLECTIVE ACTION

266 Daron Acemoglu, George Egorov, and Konstantin Sonin, "Dynamics and Stability of Constitutions, Coalitions, and Clubs," *American Economic Review* 102, no. 4 (2012): 1446–1476.

267 Ludwig von Mises, *Human Action: A Treatise on Economics* (Auburn: Ludwig von Mises Institute, 1998) provides Mises's views.

268 Alan Ebenstein, *Friedrich Hayek: A Biography* (Houndmills, Basingstoke: Palgrave Macmillan, 2001).

269 Benjamin I. Page and Robert Y. Shapiro, *The Rational Public: Fifty Years of Trends in Americans' Policy Preferences* (Chicago: University of Chicago Press, 1992).

270 Robert Y. Shapiro and Yaeli Bloch-Elkon, "Political Polarization and the Rational Public" (May 2, 2006 Draft), http://themonkeycage.org/Shapiro %2520and%2520Bloch.pdf. Shapiro and Bloch-Elkon provide a review of some of the criticisms.

271 Gerald C. Wright, Robert S. Erikson, and John P. McIver, "Measuring State Partisanship and Ideology with Survey Data," *The Journal of Politics* 47, no. 2 (1985): 469–489.

272 Paul Brace, Kevin Arceneaux, Martin Johnson, and Stacy G. Ulbig, "Does State Political Ideology Change over Time," *Political Research Quarterly* 57, no. 4 (2004): 529–540.

273 Charles M. Tiebout, "A Pure Theory of Local Expenditures," *Journal of Political Economy* 64, no. 5 (1956): 416–424.

274 Paul W. Rhode and Koleman S. Strumpf, "Assessing the Importance of Tiebout Sorting: Local Heterogeneity from 1850 to 1990," *The American Economic Review* 93, no. 5 (2003): 1648–1677.

275 Ibid., 1649. To corroborate their time-series study they also use a cross-sectional analysis on communities in 1980 and 1990.

276 *Atkin v. Kansas*, 191 U.S. 207 (1903).

277 Chun-Chung Au and J. Vernon Henderson, "Are Chinese Cities Too Small?" *The Review of Economic Studies* 73, no. 3 (July 2006): 549–576.

278 M. Kent Jennings, Laura Stoker, and Jake Bowers, "Politics across Generations: Family Transmission Reexamined," *The Journal of Politics* 71, no. 3 (2009): 782–799.

279 Elias Dinas, "Why Does the Apple Fall Far from the Tree? How Early Political Socialization Prompts Parent-Child Dissimilarity," *British Journal of Political Science* 44, no. 4 (2014): 827–852.

PART FIVE: CONSTITUTION FOR THE BROADLY LIBERAL FEDERAL GOVERNMENT

18: CENTRALIZATION AND COMPOUND GOVERNMENT

280 Vincent Ostrom, *The Meaning of American Federalism: Constituting a Self-Governing Society* (San Francisco: ICS Press, 1994); and Vincent Ostrom, *The Political Theory of a Compound Republic: Designing the American Experiment*, 3rd edition, revised and enlarged (Lanham, MD: Lexington Books, 2008).

281 David Card and Alan B. Krueger, "Minimum Wages and Employment: A Case Study of the Fast-Food Industry in New Jersey and Pennsylvania," *The American Economic Review* 84, no. 4 (1994): 772–793.

282 David Neumark and William Wascher, "Minimum Wages and Employment: A Review of Evidence from the New Minimum Wage Research," National Bureau of Economic Research (November 2006), Working Paper No. 12663.

283 Jacques Crémer and Thomas R. Palfrey, "Federal Mandates by Popular Demand," *Journal of Political Economy* 108, no. 5 (2000): 905–927.

284 Philippe Aghion, Nick Bloom, Brian Lucking, Raffaella Sadun, and John Van Reenen, "Turbulence, Firm Decentralization and Growth in Bad Times," National Bureau of Economic Research (April 2017), Working Paper No. 23354.

285 Ricardo Alonso, Wouter Dessein, and Niko Matouschek, "When Does Coordination Require Centralization," *American Economic Review* 98, no. 1 (2008): 145–179.

286 Marco Battaglini and Bård Harstad, "Participation and Duration of Environmental Agreements," *Journal of Political Economy* 124, no. 1 (2016): 160–204.

287   Elinor Ostrom and Roger B. Parks, "Suburban Police Departments—Too Many and Too Small," in *The Urbanization of the Suburbs*, vol. 7, *Urban Affairs Annual Reviews*, edited by Louis H Masotti and Jeffrey K. Hadden (Beverly Hills: Sage Publications, 1973): 367–402; Bruce D. Rogers and C. McCurdy Lipsey, "Metropolitan Reform: Citizen Evaluations of Performance in Nashville-Davidson County, Tennessee," *Publius* 4, no. 4 (1974): 19–34; and Gordon P. Whitaker, Elinor Ostrom, and Roger B. Parks, "Using Citizen Surveys to Evaluate the Organization of Policing," presented to the National Conference on Criminal Justice Evaluation, February 1977, https://www.ncjrs.gov/pdffiles1/Digitization/45676NCJRS.pdf.

288   Elinor Ostrom, "Beyond Markets and States: Polycentric Governance of Complex Economic Systems," *The American Economic Review* 100, no. 3 (2010): 641–672.

289   Garrett Hardin, "The Tragedy of the Commons," *Science* 162 (December 1968): 1243–1248. The phrase "tragedy of the commons" is often associated with Hardin.

290   Elinor Ostrom, *Understanding Institutional Diversity* (Princeton: Princeton University Press, 2005), 237.

291   Paul Dragos Aligica, "Rethinking Governance Systems and Challenging Disciplinary Boundaries: Interview with Elinor Ostrom," in *Elinor Ostrom and the Bloomington School of Political Economy: Volume 1, Polycentricity in Public Administration and Political Science*, edited by Daniel H. Cole and Michael D. McGinnis (Lanham, MD: Lexington Books, 2015), 61.

19: FEDERALISM

292   Wallace E. Oates, "An Essay on Fiscal Federalism," *Journal of Economic Literature* 37, no. 3 (1999): 1120–1149; Wallace E. Oates, "Toward A Second-Generation Theory of Fiscal Federalism," *International Tax and Public Finance* 12, no. 4 (2005): 349–373; and Wallace E. Oates, *Fiscal Federalism* (Northampton: Edward Elgar Publishing, 2011).

293   Daniel J. Elazar, *Exploring Federalism* (Tuscaloosa: University of Alabama Press, 1987), 111.

294   Robert J. Barro and Charles J. Redlick, "Macroeconomic Effects from Government Purchases and Taxes," *Quarterly Journal of Economics* 126, no.1 (2011): 51–102.

295   William H. Riker, *Federalism: Origin, Operation, Significance* (Boston: Little, Brown and Co., 1964).

296   Mikhail Filippov, Peter Ordeshook, and Olga Shvetsova, *Designing Federalism: A Theory of Self-Sustainable Federal Institutions* (Cambridge: Cambridge University Press, 2004).

297 Charles-Louis de Secondat, Baron de Montesquieu, *The Complete Works of M. De Montesquieu*, 4 vols. (London: T. Evans, 1777), vol. 1, book IX, chapter 1, 165, September 10, 2017, http://oll.libertyfund.org/titles/1855.

298 James M. Buchanan, "Federalism as an Ideal Political Order and an Objective for Constitutional Reform," *Publius* 25, no. 2 (1995): 19–27. He also examined the potential benefits of secession in James M. Buchanan and Roger L. Faith, "Secession and the Limits of Taxation: Toward a Theory of Internal Exit," *The American Economic Review* 77, no. 5 (1987): 1023–1031.

299 Pierre-Joseph Proudhon, "The Principle of Federation," in *Theories of Federalism: A Reader*, edited by Dimitrios Karmis and Wayne Norman (New York: Palgrave, 2005).

300 Peter Kurrild-Klitgaard, "Opting-Out: The Constitutional Economies of Exit," *American Journal of Economics and Sociology* 61, no. 1 (2002): 123–158; and Peter Kurrild-Klitgaard, "Exit, Collective Action and Polycentric Political Systems," *Public Choice* 143, nos. 3–4 (2010): 339–352.

301 Alexander Hamilton, "Federalist No. 15: The Insufficiency of the Present Confederation to Preserve the Union," The Avalon Project, Yale Law School, 2008, http://avalon.law.yale.edu/18th_century/fed15.asp.

302 Ibid.

303 James Madison, "Federalist No. 45: The Alleged Danger from the Powers of the Union to the State Governments Considered," The Avalon Project, Yale Law School, 2008, http://avalon.law.yale.edu/18th_century/fed45.asp.

304 "Financial Report of the United States Government: Fiscal Year 2015," US Department of the Treasury (February 25, 2016).

305 *The Constitution of the United States of America, as Amended* (United States Government Printing Office, July 25, 2007). The first three Constitutional clauses can be found in Article I, Section 8; the fourth is in Article VI, Clause 2.

306 Brutus, "The Antifederalist Papers No. 17: Federalist Power Will Ultimately Subvert State Authority," ThisNation.com, http://www.thisnation.com /library/antifederalist/17.html.

307 Alexander Hamilton, "Federalist No. 17: The Same Subject Continued: The Insufficiency of the Present Confederation to Preserve the Union," The Avalon Project, Yale Law School, 2008, http://avalon.law.yale.edu/18th_century /fed17.asp.

308 "James Madison to Spencer Roane, 2 September 1819," National Archives, https://founders.archives.gov/documents/Madison/04-01-02-0455.

309 Calvin H. Johnson, "The Panda's Thumb: The Modest and Mercantilist Original Meaning of the Commerce Clause," *William & Mary Bill of Rights Journal* 13, no. 1 (2004): 1–56.

310 "James Madison to Joseph C. Cabell, 13 February 1829," National Archives, https://founders.archives.gov/documents/Madison/99-02-02-1698.

311 *Confederation and Perpetual Union Between The States of New Hampshire, Massachusetts Bay, Rhode Island, and Providence Plantations, Connecticut, New York, New Jersey, Pennsylvania, Delaware, Maryland, Virginia, North Carolina, South Carolina, and Georgia* (Williamsburg: Alexander Purdue, 1777), https://www.loc.gov/rr/program/bib/ourdocs/articles.html.

312 *The Constitution of the United States of America, as Amended* (United States Government Printing Office, July 25, 2007), Article I, Section 10.

313 Ibid., Article III, Section 1.

314 Earlier in his career, Justice John Marshall had been a delegate to the Virginia convention that debated ratifying the Constitution. He was a staunch supporter of a broad central government and was part of the majority vote when the Virginia delegates narrowly approved the US Constitution, 89 to 79.

315 *Gibbons v. Ogden*, 22 U.S. 1 (1824).

316 Ibid.

317 *Hoke v. United States*, 227 U.S. 308 (1913).

318 *Hipolite Egg Co. v. United States*, 220 U.S. 45 (1911).

319 *NLRB v. Jones & Laughlin Steel Corp.*, 301 U.S. 1 (1937).

320 *West Coast Hotel Co. v. Parrish*, 300 U.S. 379 (1937).

321 *United States v. Darby*, 312 U.S. 100 (1941).

322 *United States v. Wrightwood Dairy Co.*, 315 U.S. 110 (1942).

323 Ibid.

324 *Wickard v. Filburn*, 317 U.S. 111 (1942).

325 Ibid.

326 *South Dakota v. Dole*, 483 U.S. 203 (1987).

327 Ibid.

328 Ibid.

329 "Jefferson's Opinion on the Constitutionality of a National Bank: 1791," The Avalon Project, Yale Law School (2008), http://avalon.law.yale.edu/18th _century/bank-tj.asp.

330 "Document 25: Thomas Jefferson to Albert Gallatin, 16 June, 1817," *The Founders' Constitution*, vol. 2 (Chicago: University of Chicago Press, 1987), article 1, section 8, clause 1, press-pubs.uchicago.edu/founders/documents /a1_8_1s25.html.

331 "The Bank Bill, [2 February] 1791," *Founders Online*, National Archives, last modified June 29, 2017, http://founders.archives.gov/documents

/Madison/01-13-02-0282. [Original source: *The Papers of James Madison*, vol. 13, *20 January 1790–31 March 1791*, edited by Charles F. Hobson and Robert A. Rutland (Charlottesville: University Press of Virginia, 1981), pp. 372–382.]

332   "The Report of 1800, [7 January] 1800," *Founders Online*, National Archives, last modified June 29, 2017, http://founders.archives.gov/documents /Madison/01-17-02-0202. [Original source: *The Papers of James Madison*, vol. 17, *31 March 1797–3 March 1801 and supplement 22 January 1778–9 August 1795*, edited by David B. Mattern, J. C. A. Stagg, Jeanne K. Cross, and Susan Holbrook Perdue (Charlottesville: University Press of Virginia, 1981), pp. 303–351.]

333   *Alexander Hamilton's Famous Report of Manufactures, In His Report to Congress December 5, 1791, In His Capacity as Secretary of the Treasury* (Boston: Home Market Club, 1892), 55–56.

334   Joseph Story, *Commentaries on the Constitution of the United States: With a Preliminary Review of the Constitutional History of the Colonies and States Before the Adoption of the Constitution*, abridged edition (Boston: Hilliard, Gray and Company, 1833), 348–349.

335   Ibid., v.

336   Ibid., 347.

337   *United States v. Butler*, 297 U.S. 1 (1936).

338   *McCulloch v. Maryland*, 17 U.S. 316 (4 Wheat 316) (1819).

339   "Hamilton's Opinion as to the Constitutionality of the Bank: 1791," The Avalon Project, Yale Law School, 2008, avalon.law.yale.edu/18th_century /bank-ah.asp.

340   Ibid.

341   Story, *Commentaries on the Constitution of the United States: With a Preliminary Review of the Constitutional History of the Colonies and States Before the Adoption of the Constitution* (1883), 441.

342   Robert G. Natelson, "The Agency Law Origins of the Necessary and Proper Clause," *Case Western Law Review* 55, no. 2 (2004): 243–322, 247.

343   Gary Lawson and Patricia Granger, "The 'Proper' Scope of Federal Power: A Jurisdictional Interpretation of the Sweeping Clause," *Duke Law Journal* 43, no. 267 (1993): 268–336. Lawson and Granger argue that the word "proper" is the crucial part of the clause that limits the scope of the federal government.

344   Story, *Commentaries on the Constitution of the United States: With a Preliminary Review of the Constitutional History of the Colonies and States Before the Adoption of the Constitution* (1883), 438.

345   Ibid., 436.

346 "Hamilton's Opinion as to the Constitutionality of the Bank: 1791," The Avalon Project, Yale Law School, 2008, avalon.law.yale.edu/18th_century/bank-ah.asp.

347 Willi Paul Adams, *The First American Constitutions* (Lanham, MD: Rowman & Littlefield Publishers, 2001); and Marc W. Kruman, *State Constitution Making in Revolutionary America* (Chapel Hill: The University of North Carolina Press, 1997). These two works discuss state constitutions following the American Revolution.

348 "Charter of Rhode Island and Providence Plantations—July 15, 1663," The Avalon Project, Yale Law School, 2008, avalon.law.yale.edu/17th_century/ri04.asp.

349 H. Niles, editor, *Niles' Weekly Register: Containing Political, Historical, Geographical, Scientifical, Astronomical, Statistical, Economical, and Biographical Documents, Essays, and Facts; Together with Notices of the Arts and Manufactures, and a Record of the Events and Times*, vol. IV, New Series. (Baltimore: Franklin Press, 1819): 319.

350 W. F. Dodd, "The First State Constitutional Conventions, 1776–1783," *The American Political Science Review* 2, no. 4 (November 1908): 545–561, 546.

351 *Early State Papers of New Hampshire Including the Constitution of 1784, Journals of the Senate and House of Representatives, and Records of the President and Council from June 1784 to June 1787 with an Appendix*, vol. XX, compiled and edited by A. Stillman (Manchester: John C. Clarke, Public Printers, 1891), 15.

352 *Laws of New Hampshire: Including Public and Private Acts, Resolves, Votes, Etc., Volume Five, First Constitutional Period, 1784–1792*, edited by Henry Harrison Metcalf (Concord: Rumford Press, 1916); and *Laws of New Hampshire: Including Public and Private Acts, Resolves, Votes, Etc., Volume Eight, Second Constitutional Period, 1811–1820*, edited and published under the direction of the secretary of state (Concord: Evans Printing Co., 1920).

353 David Duncan Wallace, *A Chapter of South Carolina Constitutional History* (Nashville: Cumberland Presbyterian Publishing House, 1900).

354 David Duncan Wallace, *South Carolina: A Short History 1520–1948* (Columbia: University of South Carolina Press, 1951), 256.

355 "Document 10: John Adams to James Sullivan, 26 May 1776," *The Founders' Constitution*, vol. 1 (Chicago: University of Chicago Press, 1987), chapter 13: Representation, press-pubs.uchicago.edu/founders/documents/v1ch13s10.html.

356 Ibid.

357 Heads of Families at the First Census 1790, retrieved from US Census, https://www2.census.gov/prod2/decennial/documents/1790m-02.pdf.

358 Donald Ratcliffe, "The Right to Vote and the Rise of Democracy, 1787–1828," *Journal of the Early Republic* 33 (2013): 219–254.

359 Wallace, *South Carolina: A Short History 1520–1948* (1951), 341–344. He states that the low country had a white population of 28,644 out of a total white population of 140,178. He also states that the low country had 75 percent of state wealth.

360 An estimate of 5 percent is based on the assumptions that the proportion of adult white males under sixteen and white women were distributed uniformly between the low country and backcountry in 1790.

361 Thomas M. Cooley, *The General Principles of Constitutional Law in the United States of America*, 3rd edition, edited by Andrew C. McLaughlin (Boston: Little, Brown, and Company, 1898), 343.

362 *Hunter v. Pittsburgh*, 207 U.S. 161 (1907).

363 John F. Dillon, LL.D., *Commentaries on the Law of Municipal Corporations*, 3rd edition, revised and enlarged, Vol. I (Boston: Little, Brown, and Company, 1881).

364 James Madison, "Federalist Papers No. 10: The Same Subject Continued: The Union as a Safeguard Against Domestic Faction and Insurrection," The Avalon Project, Yale Law School, 2008, http://avalon.law.yale.edu/18th_century/fed10.asp.

365 Edward Allinson and Boies Penrose, "City Government of Philadelphia," *Johns Hopkins University Studies in Historical and Political Science*, Fifth Series I–II, edited by Herbert B. Adams (Baltimore: N. Murray, 1887), 15–16.

366 Ibid., 25–33.

367 John Russell Young, *Memorial History of the City of Philadelphia from Its First Settlement to the Year 1895, Vol I, Narrative and Critical History 1681–1895* (New York: New York History Company, 1895).

368 James Buchanan, "Federalism as an Ideal Political Order and an Objective for Constitutional Reform," *Publius* 25, no. 2 (1995): 19–27; Thomas R. Dye, *American Federalism: Competition Among Governments* (Lexington, MA: Lexington Books, 1990); and Yingyi Qian and Barry R. Weingast, "Federalism as a Commitment to Preserving Market Incentives," *The Journal of Economic Perspectives* 11, no. 4 (1997): 83–92. These are examples of other works concerning competitive federalism.

369 Gordon Tullock, *The New Federalist* (Vancouver: Fraser Institute, 1994).

370 Ibid.

371 Alessandra Casella and Bruno Frey, "Federalism and Clubs: Towards an Economic Theory of Overlapping Political Jurisdictions," *European Economic Review* 36, nos. 2–3 (1992): 639–646; Bruno S. Frey and Reiner

Eichenberger, *The New Democratic Federalism for Europe: Functional, Overlapping and Competing Jurisdictions* (Cheltenham: Edward Elgar, 1999); and Bruno S. Frey, "A Utopia? Government Without Territorial Monopoly," *Journal of Institutional and Theoretical Economics* 157, no. 1 (2001): 162–175.

372   Aviezer Tucker and Gian Piero de Bellis, editors, *Panarchy: Political Theories of Non-Territorial States* (New York: Routledge, 2016). Tucker and de Bellis's book presents a variety of articles describing and advocating "panarchy." Panarchy is similar to FOCJ. In particular, it is a system of nonterritorial, voluntary independent governments. Their book includes the article from 1860, by Paul-Emile de Puydt, in which he coins the term. While every domestic government does not have to have a monopoly over territory, the requirements of external defense, the existence of externalities, and differing worldviews imply that the complete elimination of all territorial governments are unlikely to be the equilibrium decision by the broadly liberal person as they exit the original position.

373   Bruno S. Frey and Reiner Eichenberger, *The New Democratic Federalism for Europe: Functional, Overlapping and Competing Jurisdictions* (1999), 73-74.

374   Ibid., 96. Frey and Eichenberger argue that their concepts are not due to their politics. While the idea of FOCJ is not based on a specific political opinion, their proposals for their preferred constitution seem to based on their worldview.

375   Richard A. Epstein, "Exit Rights Under Federalism," *Law and Contemporary Problems* 55, no. 1 (1992): 147–165; and Richard A. Epstein, *The Classical Liberal Constitution: The Uncertain Quest for Limited Government* (Cambridge, MA: Harvard University Press, 2014).

376   Barry R. Weingast, "The Economic Role of Political Institutions: Market-Preserving Federalism and Economic Development," *Journal of Law, Economics, & Organization* 11, no. 1 (1995): 1–31, 27.

377   Robert Inman and Daniel Rubinfeld, "Economics of Federalism," in *Oxford Handbook of Law and Economics*, vol. 3, edited by Francesco Parisi (Oxford: Oxford University Press, 2017): 84–105.

PART SIX: THE JUST GOVERNMENT

20: JUSTICE AS CHOICE

378   Robert Nozick, *Invariances: The Structure of the Objective World* (Cambridge, MA: The Belknap Press of the Harvard University Press, 2001).

379   Herbert A. Simon, *Models of Man: Social and Rational; Mathematical Essays on Rational Human Behavior in a Social Setting* (New York: Wiley, 1957).

380   Reinhard Selten, "Bounded Rationality," *Journal of Institutional and Theoretical Economics* 146, no. 4 (December 1990): 649–658.

381   Avinash Dixit, "Clubs with Entrapment," *The American Economic Review* 93, no. 5 (2003): 1824–1829.

382   Amartya Sen, *The Idea of Justice* (Cambridge: Harvard University Press, 2009), 394.

383   Jurgen Habermas, *Between Facts and Norms: Contribution to a Discourse Theory of Law and Democracy*, translated by William Rehg (Cambridge MA: The MIT Press, 1998), James Bohman, *Public Deliberation: Pluralism, Complexity, and Democracy* (Cambridge, MA: The MIT Press, 2000); and Jon Elster, editor, *Deliberative Democracy* (Cambridge: Cambridge University Press, 1998). These are three examples of a significant literature on deliberative democracy.

384   Nozick, *Invariances: The Structure of the Objective World* (2001), 236.

21: THE RIGHT TO BE WRONG

385   Isaiah Berlin, "Two Concepts of Liberty," in *Four Essays on Liberty* (Oxford: Oxford University Press, 1969).

386   Dan M. Kahan, "Cultural Cognition and Public Policy," Yale Law School Faculty Scholarship Series, Paper 103 (2006), http://digitalcommons.law .yale.edu/cgi/viewcontent.cgi?article=1102&context=fss_papers.

387   *The Constitution of the United States of America, as Amended* (United States Government Printing Office, July 25, 2007). These three rights are in Article I, Section 9.

388   *Ex parte Milligan*, 71 U.S. 2 (1866).

389   *Boumediene v. Bush*, 553 U.S. 723 (2008).

390   *Calder v. Bull* 3 U.S. 386 (1798) is the original Supreme Court case that ruled on the issue.

391   William W. Crosskey, "True Meaning of the Constitutional Prohibition of Ex-Post-Facto Laws," *University of Chicago Law Review* 14, no. 4 (1947): 539-566; and Steve Selinger, "The Case Against Civil Ex Post Facto Laws," *Cato Journal* 15, nos. 2–3 (1995–1996): 191–213 provide a discussion of the clause.

392   James Buchanan and Gordon Tullock, *The Calculus of Consent* (Ann Arbor: University of Michigan Press, 1971); Nicholas R. Miller, "Logrolling, Vote

Trading, and the Paradox of Voting: A Game-Theoretical Overview," *Public Choice* 30 (1977): 51–75; Alessandra Casella, Aniol Llorente-Saguer, and Thomas R. Palfrey, "Competitive Equilibrium in Markets for Votes," *Journal of Political Economy* 120, no. 4 (2012): 593–658; and "storable votes" in Alessandra Casella, *Storable Votes: Protecting the Minority Voice* (Oxford: Oxford University Press, 2012). These are some of the works that advocate various voting structures that consider people's intensities for their political preferences.

393　Jonah Goldberg, "Does America Still Believe in the Right to be Wrong?" *National Review*, September 27, 2017. While this book was being edited, Jonah Goldberg, a Fellow at the American Enterprise Institute, wrote an article about what he terms "the right to be wrong." He argues that a basic tenant of US culture is that people have the right to have different views, even if others are convinced they are wrong. In this book, the "right to be wrong" is much more than the *cultural* right to have a different view; it is the fundamental *legal* right to have different domestic laws even if some people think these laws are wrong. This right is not an unconditional right for a person to live under laws that are completely in accord with their worldview.

394　John Locke, *Locke's Essays. An Essay Concerning Human Understanding and a Treatise on The Conduct of the Understanding* (Philadelphia: Hayes & Zell, 1854), 432.

395　*The Constitution of the United States of America, as Amended* (United States Government Printing Office, July 25, 2007).

396　*Obergefell v. Hodges*, 576 U.S. (2015).

397　Ibid.

398　Ibid.

399　Ibid.

400　Franklin Delano Roosevelt, "Radio Address on States' Rights, March 2, 1930," in *Public Papers of the Presidents of the United States: Franklin D. Roosevelt 1937*, vol. 6, 570–572, http://www.fdrlibrary.marist.edu /_resources/images/msf/msf00371.

401　*Obergefell* (2015).

402　Roosevelt, "Radio Address on States' Rights, March 2, 1930," 570.

403　Herbert George Wells, *A Modern Utopia*, with illustrations by E. J. Sullivan (New York: Charles Scribner's Sons, 1905), 350–351.

404　The list of people includes Francis Bacon, François-Noël Babeuf, Marques de Condorcet, Charles Fourier, William Godwin, Immanuel Kant, Karl Marx, Robert Owen, Henri de Saint-Simon, and B. F. Skinner.

405 Frank E. Manuel and Fritzie P. Manual, *Utopian Thought in the Western World* (Cambridge MA: Harvard University Press, 1979) and George Kateb, *Utopia and Its Enemies* (New York: Schocken Books, 1972), are two works that discuss the various aspects of utopian opinion.

406 Karl Marx, *Critique of the Gotha Programme* (Peking: Foreign Languages Press, 1972), 17.

INDEX

ABOUT THE AUTHOR

— ★ —

Michael T. Hutchins was trained as an economist and has over thirty years of experience in finance. His expansive career has included roles in academia as an assistant professor of finance at Syracuse University; in investment banking as a managing director at Salomon Brothers responsible for structured finance and debt capital markets; in securities and trading at UBS as managing director and global head of fixed income, rates, and currencies; and in senior executive-level positions as president at Dillon Read Capital Management and as CEO of PrinceRidge Group. Hutchins is currently an executive vice president, head of the investments and capital markets division, and member of the senior operating committee at Freddie Mac. He is responsible for managing liquidity, financing, single family securitization, and derivative activities as well as managing Freddie Mac's portfolio of single-family securities and loan investments.

Hutchins earned his PhD in economics from the University of North Carolina, Chapel Hill, and his BA in economics and mathematics from Washington University. *Irreconcilable Politics: Our Rights Under a Just Government* is his first book.

Made in the USA
Columbia, SC
07 August 2021